Park Guide and Map

ENGLISH

MW0100884₃

A DINOLAND

FREE

	Restrooms		AED
	Accessible Restrooms		Gift Shop
	Telephone		Smoking Area
	Coin Lockers		Escalator
	Restaurant		Information Desk
	Café/Refreshments		

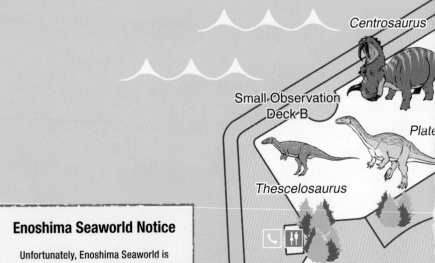

Centrosaurus

Small Observation Deck B

Plate

Thescelosaurus

Enoshima Seaworld Notice

Unfortunately, Enoshima Seaworld is not currently open, as there are no longer Ichthyosaurs at Enoshima Dinoland. Please see the "About Ichthyosaurs" section on our homepage for details.

Futabasaurus

Enoshim

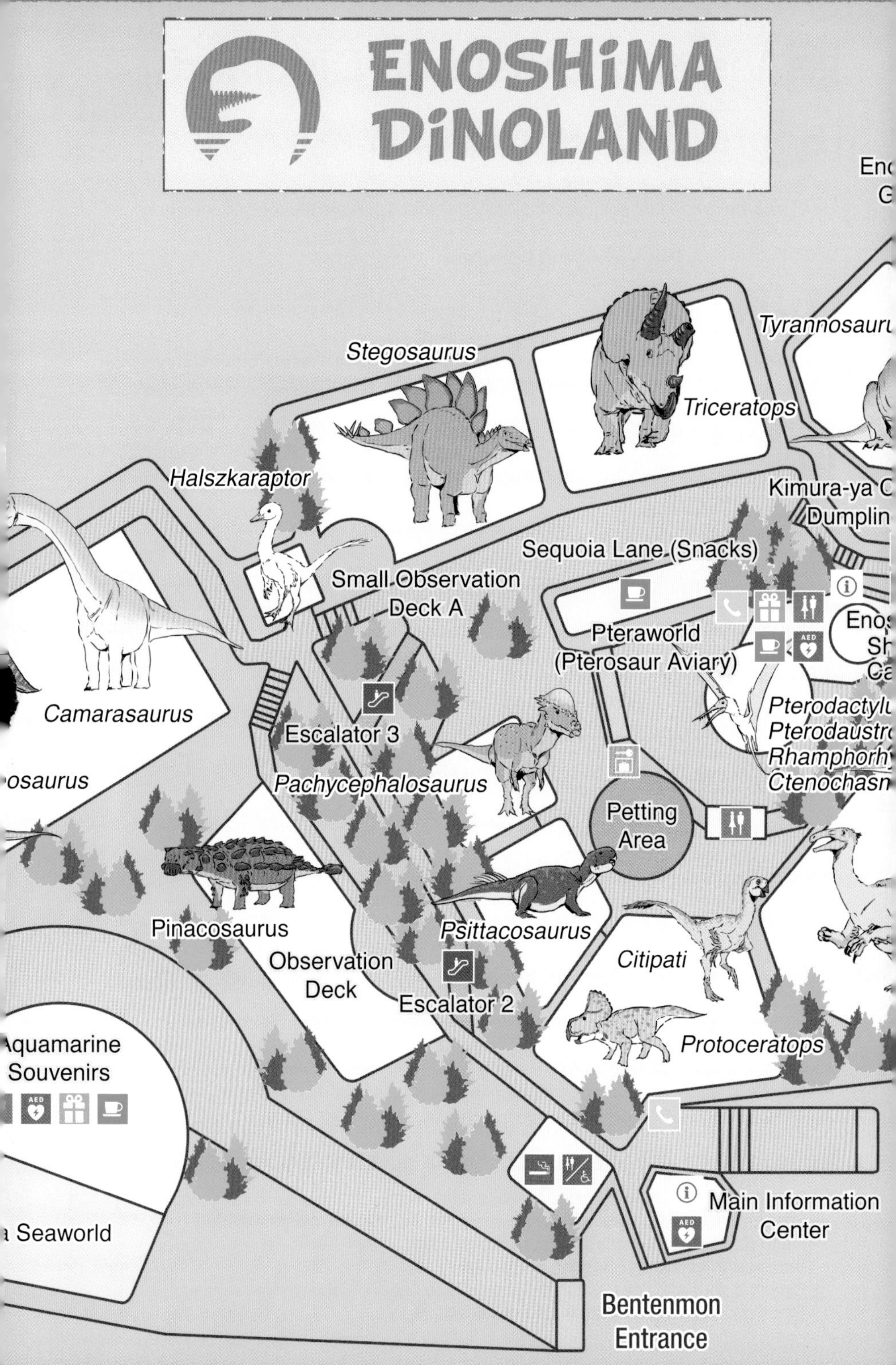
ENOSHIMA DINOLAND
Stegosaurus
Triceratops
Halszkaraptor
Small Observation Deck A
Sequoia Lane (Snacks)
Pteraworld (Pterosaur Aviary)
Camarasaurus
Escalator 3
Pachycephalosaurus
Petting Area
Pinacosaurus
Psittacosaurus
Observation Deck
Escalator 2
Citipati
Protoceratops
Souvenirs
Main Information Center
Bentenmon Entrance

Visiting Enoshima Dinoland

Hours | 9:00 AM to 5:00 PM

- Visitors are admitted until 4:00 PM.
- Please be aware that some exhibits may be closed or have reduced hours due to weather or dinosaur health.
- Park operating hours are subject to change.

Tickets

	Single Admission	Group Admission (Per person; groups of 15 or more)	Annual Pass
General Admission (College age and up)	2,000 Yen	1,800 Yen	8,000 Yen
Seniors (Age 65 and up)	1,500 Yen	1,350 Yen	6,000 Yen
Students (Middle and High School)	1,000 Yen	900 Yen	———
Children (Up to 6th grade)	600 Yen	540 Yen	———

- A valid school ID is necessary for Student admission.
- Disabled guests and up to one caretaker are admitted free with approved documentation.
- Annual passes are valid for a full year from the day of purchase.

Park Closed | Every Monday (except for national holidays)
Year-End holiday period (December 29 to January 1)

- In the event that a national holiday falls on a Monday, Enoshima Dinoland will be open that day and closed the following Tuesday instead.
- Please see our homepage or follow us on social media for the latest schedule updates.

Park Access | Twenty minutes' walk from Enoshima Station

- Park guests must enter through the main gate. The Bentenmon Entrance is not open to the public.
- We ask that guests who visit by car only use the Enoshima Dinoland parking lot. We strongly recommend the use of public transportation on holidays, as the parking lot can get crowded.

To ensure a safe, pleasant day for our guests *and* our dinosaurs…

- Pets are not permitted in Enoshima Dinoland.
- Service animals such as seeing-eye dogs and hearing dogs are permitted.
- Flash photography of our dinosaurs is prohibited.
- Please refrain from feeding the dinosaurs.
- Please dispose of any trash in the proper receptacle or take it home with you.
- Smoking is prohibited outside of designated areas.

About Enoshima Dinoland

Enoshima Dinoland was opened on May 1, 1990 and is the only privately owned and operated dinosaur park in Japan (as of 2022). Though we're also the smallest dino park in Japan, the island of Enoshima gives us the best of both worlds—a lush, natural setting only a stone's throw from the Tokyo metropolitan area. We hope you enjoy your visit to our little oasis for both people and dinosaurs!

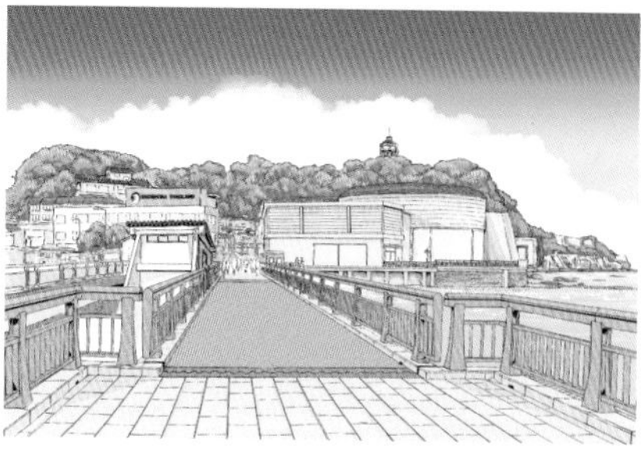

Gift Shop

Shimakaze

Here, you'll find a large selection of souvenirs and shareable snacks to commemorate your time with our dinosaurs. Take home a memory!

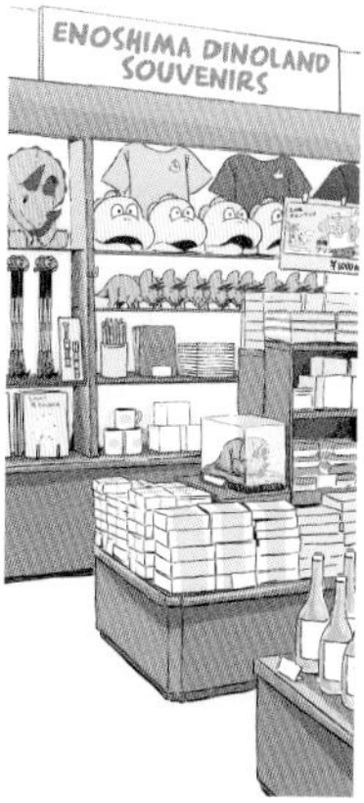
ENOSHIMA DINOLAND
SOUVENIRS

Refreshments

Sequoia Lane

Don't forget to visit Sequoia Lane, where a variety of dino-shaped snacks only available at Enoshima Dinoland await!

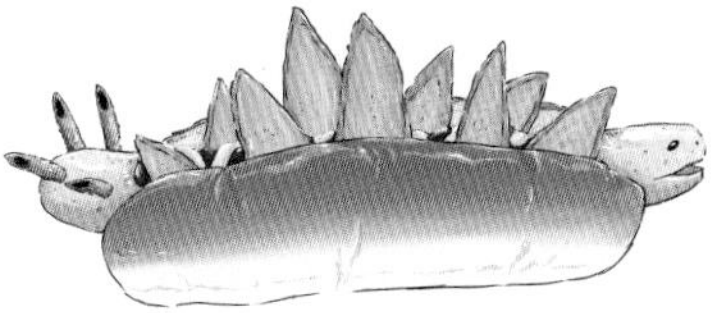

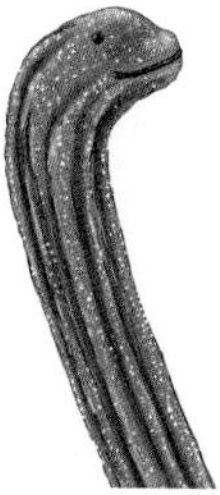

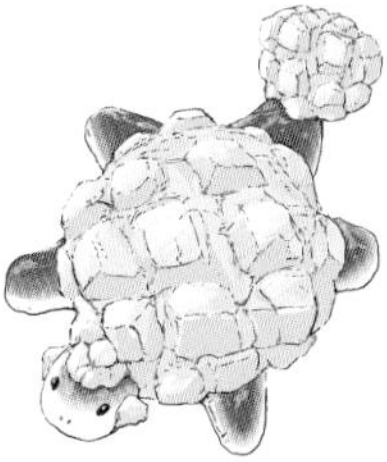

Keep up with us!

Official Homepages:

https://www.comicbunch.com/manga/bunch/dinosan/
https://sevenseasentertainment.com/series/dinosaur-sanctuary/

Official Twitter Account:

@DinosanOfficial

https://www.twitter.com/DinosanOfficial

Fujiko's Café

ree Horns (Souvenirs)

a

Spinosaurus

Troodon

Giganotosaurus

Dilophosaurus

a Sea Candle
aze Gift Shop
mmonite

us

Edmontosaurus

Deinocheirus

n Entrance

Petting Area

Open from April to the first week of November
Weekdays: 11:00 AM – 12:00 PM
Weekends and Holidays: 11:00 AM – 1:00 PM

- Groups of up to two are admitted for
  ten minutes at a time.
- Five groups are admitted at once.
- Please wash your hands and disinfect your
  shoes before entering.
- Reservations are necessary. Please see our
  homepage for details.

⚠ WATCH OUT FOR BLACK KITES!

These birds have been known to swoop in on guests to steal
their food. While injury is uncommon, they do have sharp claws.
Please take care to protect yourself and your belongings.

In most cases, Enoshima Dinoland is not liable for damages if
you are attacked by a black kite while in the park. If you are
hurt, please notify the nearest employee for treatment.

DINOSAUR SANCTUARY

3

STORY AND ART BY

ITARU KINOSHITA

RESEARCH CONSULTANT: SHIN-ICHI FUJIWARA

CHARACTERS

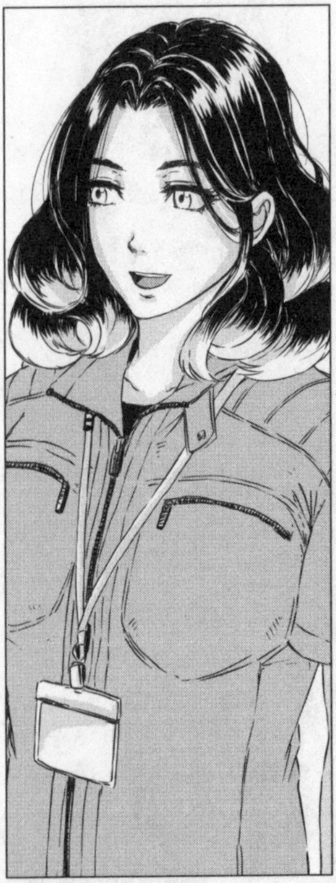

KIRISHIMA KARIN

Dinokeeper in charge of Enoshima Dinoland's ceratopsians. She's strong-willed and sisterly.

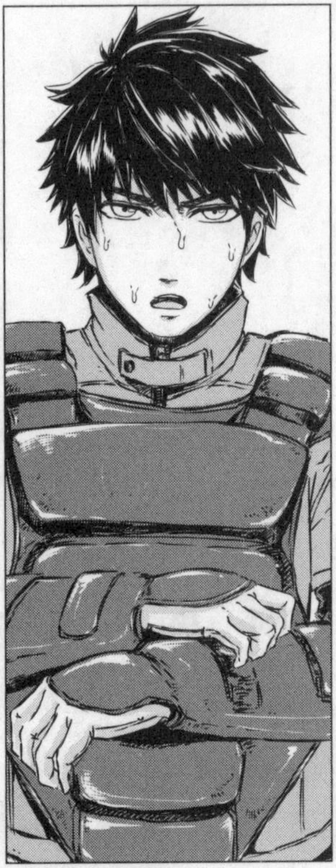

KAIDOU ARATA

Dinokeeper in charge of Enoshima Dinoland's theropods. He's strict on the job but has a caring side.

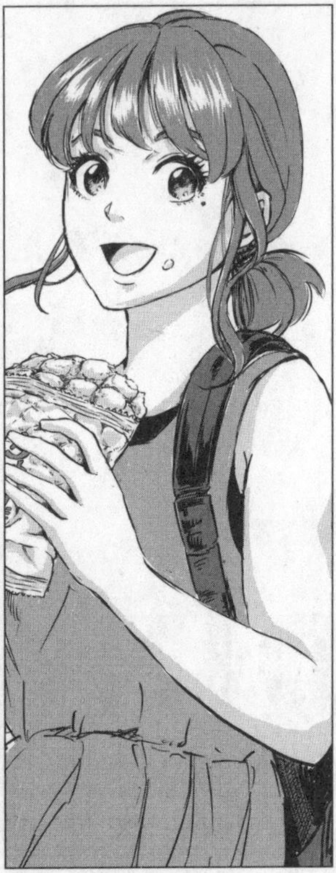

SUMA SUZUME

A rookie dinokeeper recently employed at Enoshima Dinoland. Primary interests: Dinosaurs and food.

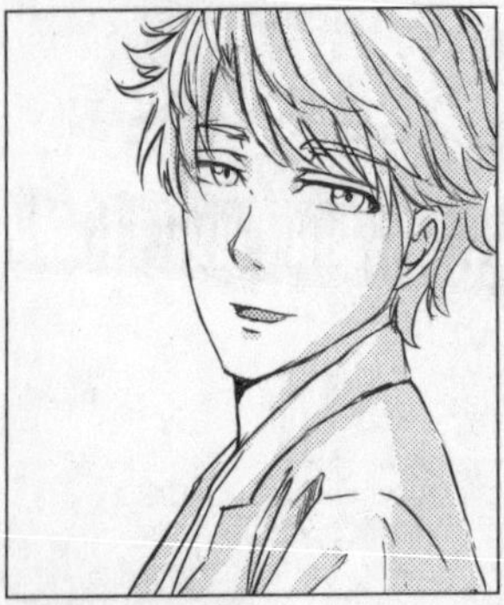

SHIRANUI REN

Dinosaur veterinarian. His cool, distant demeanor belies an earnest tenderness...towards dinosaurs, at least.

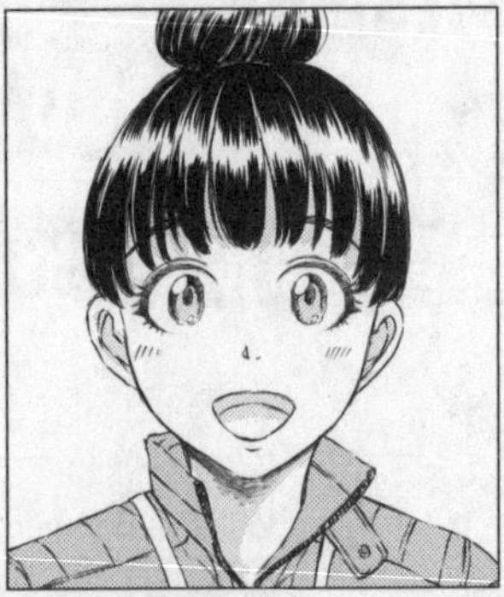

HOSHINO KURUMI

Dinokeeper in charge of Dinoland's sauropods, prosauropods, and dinosaur feed. She's from Fukuoka, just like Suzume.

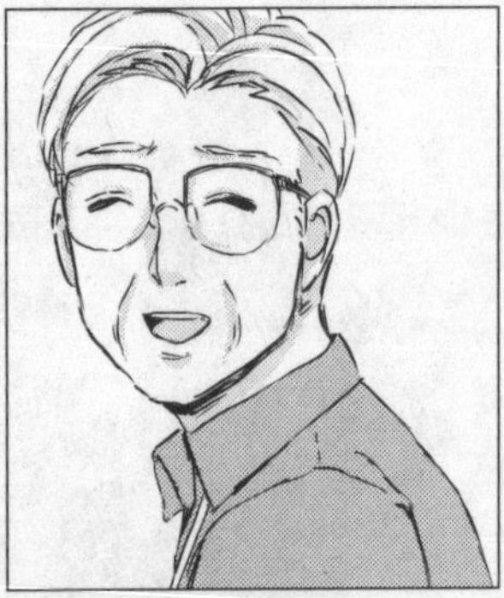

OGINO TAKATOSHI

Chief curator and manager of Enoshima Dinoland. Though mild-mannered, he's devoted to keeping the park running.

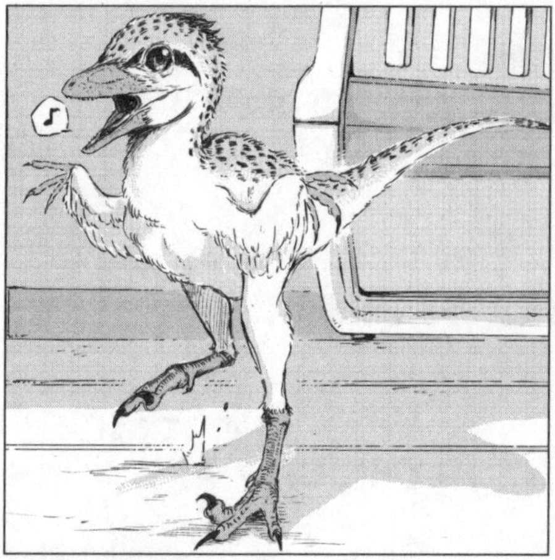

BENKEI (MALE)

A rambunctious young *Troodon.*

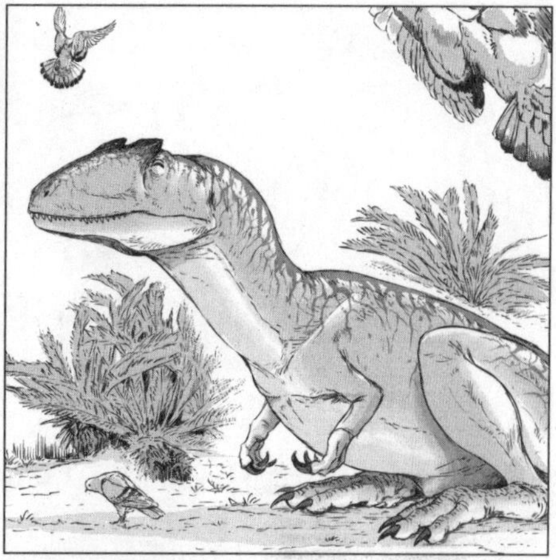

ICHIGO (FEMALE)

A nervous *Allosaurus.*

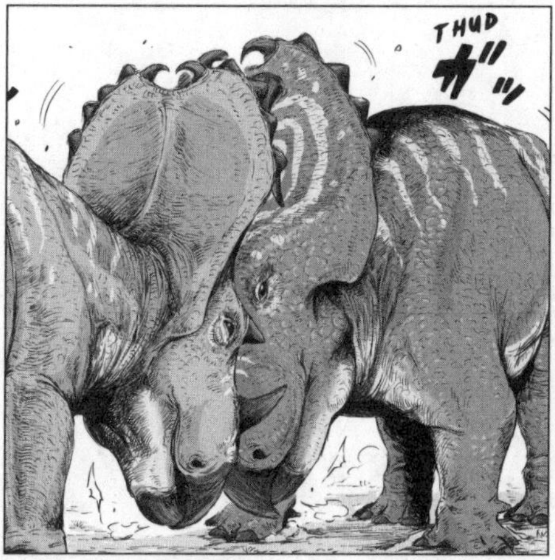
THUD

DAIKICHI (MALE) AND SHOUKICHI (MALE)

A pair of *Centrosauruses* who often fight over the same female.

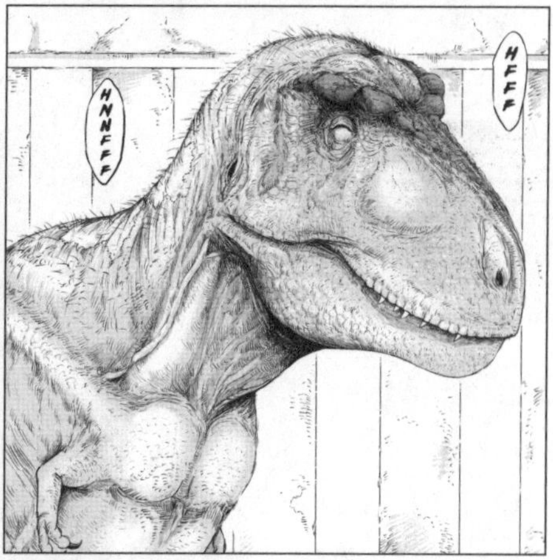
HFFF
HNNFFF

HANAKO (FEMALE)

An elderly *Tyrannosaurus.*

STORY

In 1946, a shocking discovery was made on a remote island: actual, surviving dinosaurs. Careful breeding and genetic manipulation led to the restoration of other truly extinct species, causing a worldwide dino boom. However, this newfound fascination cooled off after a disaster at Enoshima Dinoland—a disaster that Kaidou Arata witnessed firsthand.

From raising a baby *Troodon* to throwing a birthday party for a geriatric *T. rex*, Suzume's orientation period as a new dinokeeper has certainly kept her busy! But now her three-month trial run with the theropod department is over, and it's time for her to get to know the rest of the staff at Dinoland...

CONTENTS

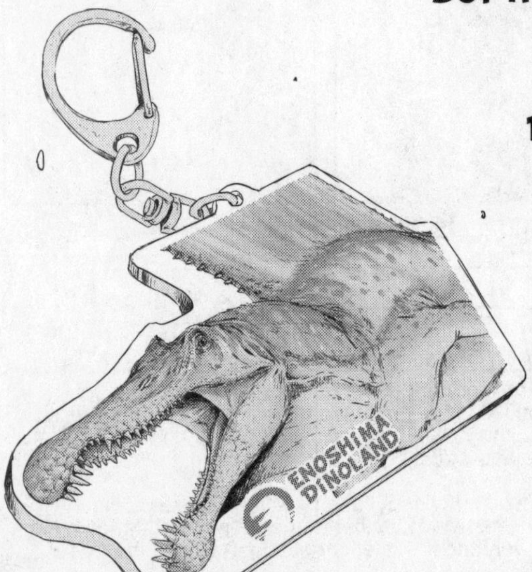

ENOSHIMA DINOLAND

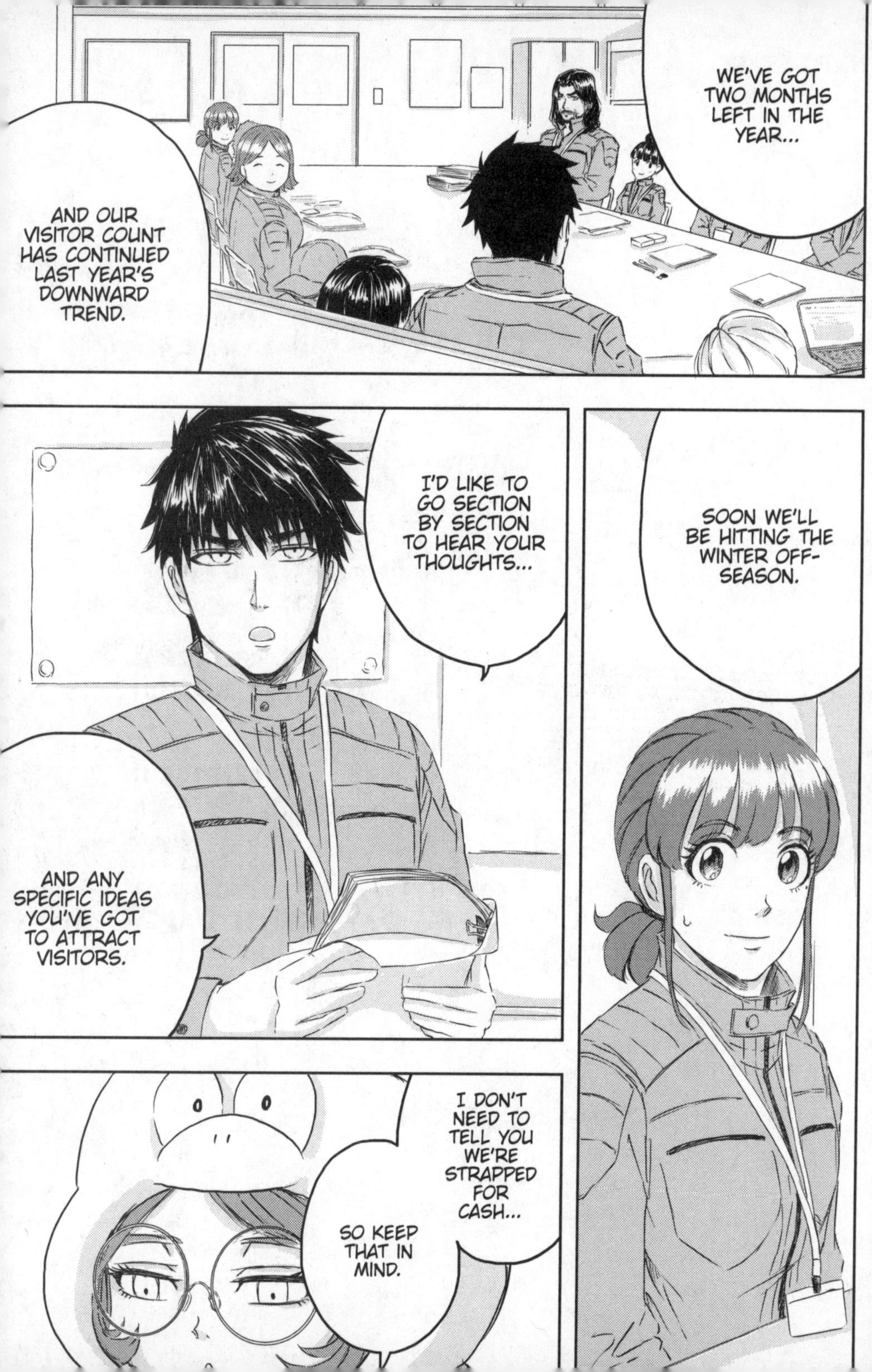
WE'VE GOT TWO MONTHS LEFT IN THE YEAR...
AND OUR VISITOR COUNT HAS CONTINUED LAST YEAR'S DOWNWARD TREND.
SOON WE'LL BE HITTING THE WINTER OFF-SEASON.
I'D LIKE TO GO SECTION BY SECTION TO HEAR YOUR THOUGHTS...
AND ANY SPECIFIC IDEAS YOU'VE GOT TO ATTRACT VISITORS.
I DON'T NEED TO TELL YOU WE'RE STRAPPED FOR CASH...
SO KEEP THAT IN MIND.

CHAPTER 12 A NEW ROLE

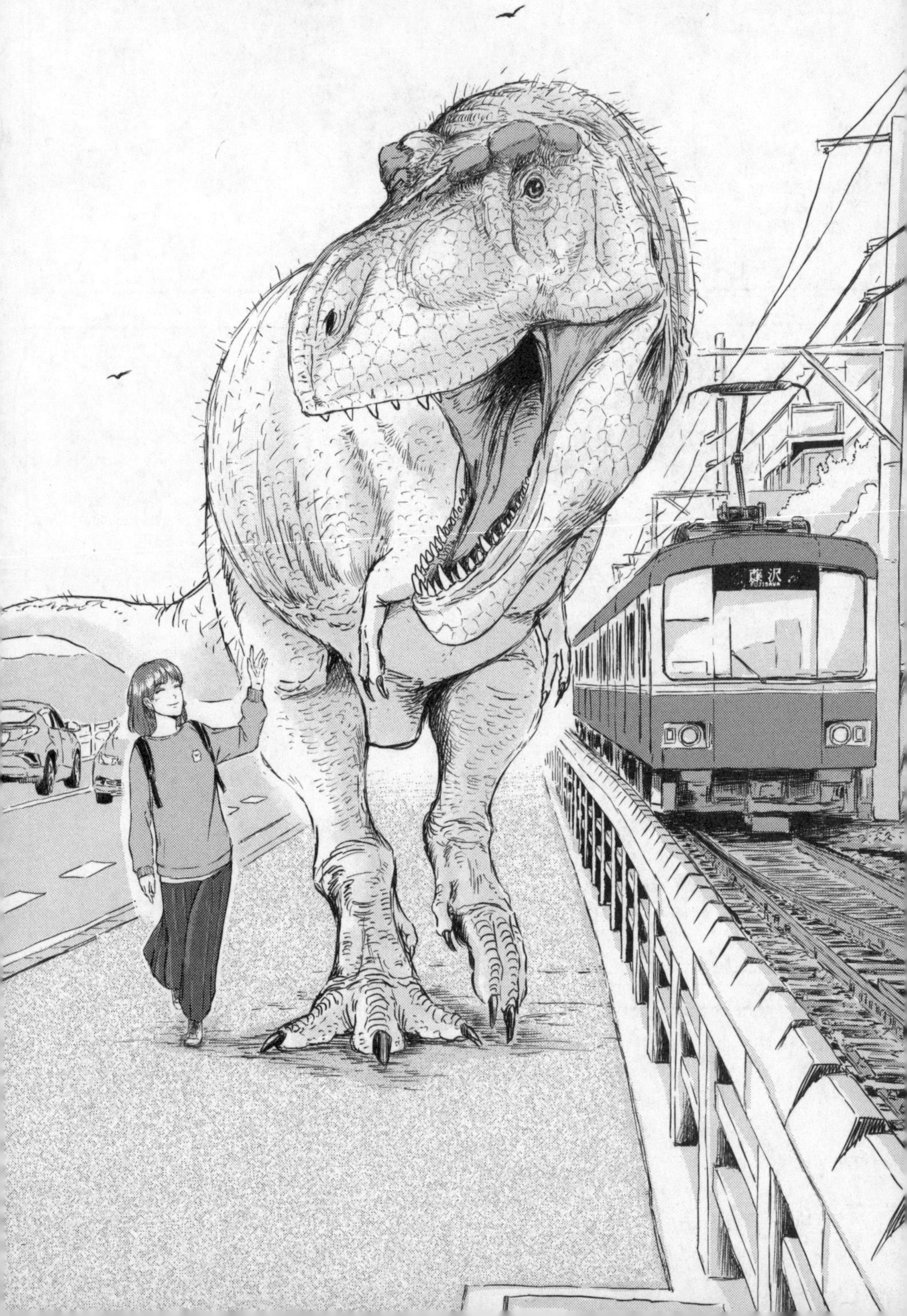
藤沢

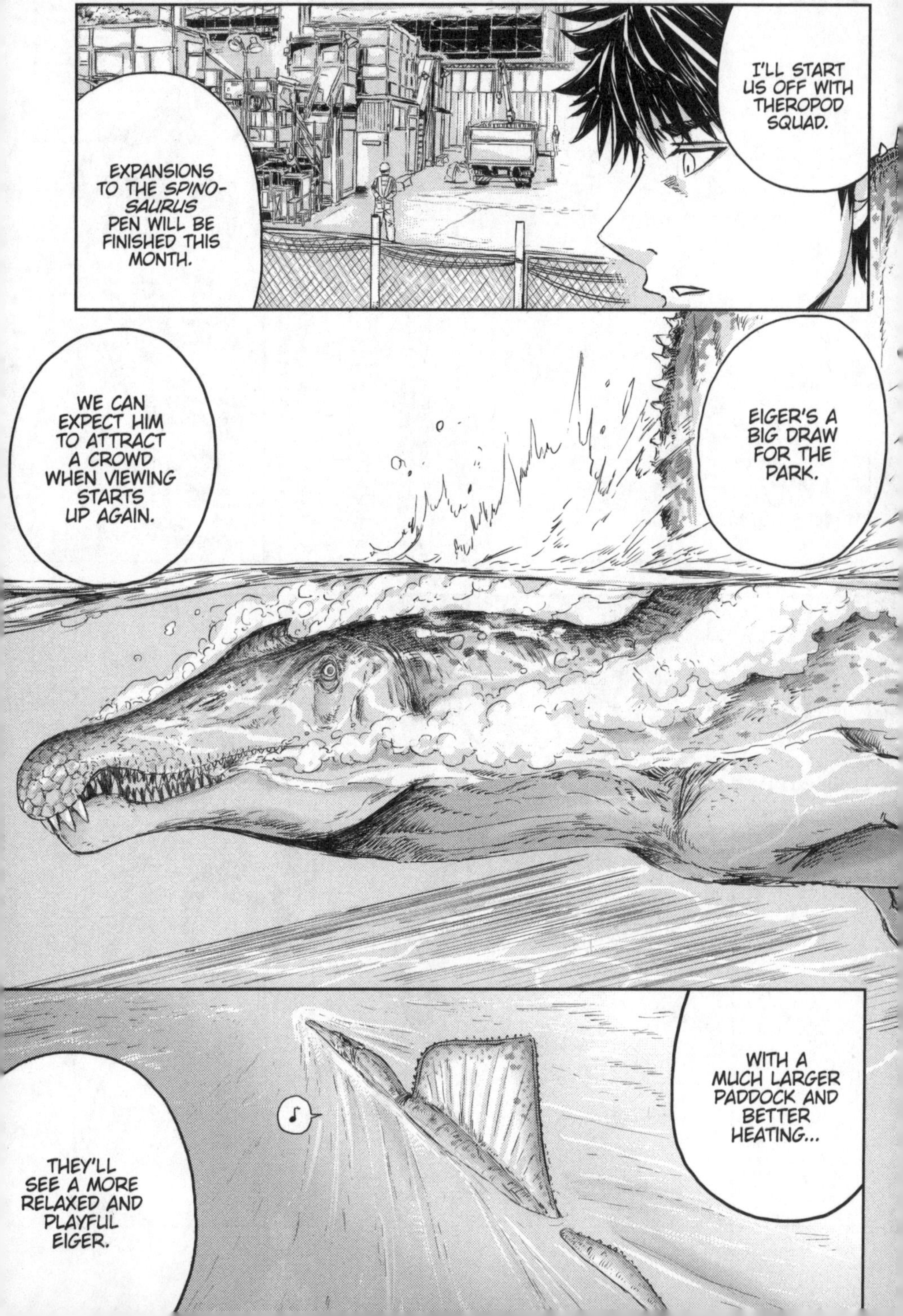
I'LL START US OFF WITH THEROPOD SQUAD.
EXPANSIONS TO THE *SPINOSAURUS* PEN WILL BE FINISHED THIS MONTH.
EIGER'S A BIG DRAW FOR THE PARK.
WE CAN EXPECT HIM TO ATTRACT A CROWD WHEN VIEWING STARTS UP AGAIN.
WITH A MUCH LARGER PADDOCK AND BETTER HEATING...
♪
THEY'LL SEE A MORE RELAXED AND PLAYFUL EIGER.

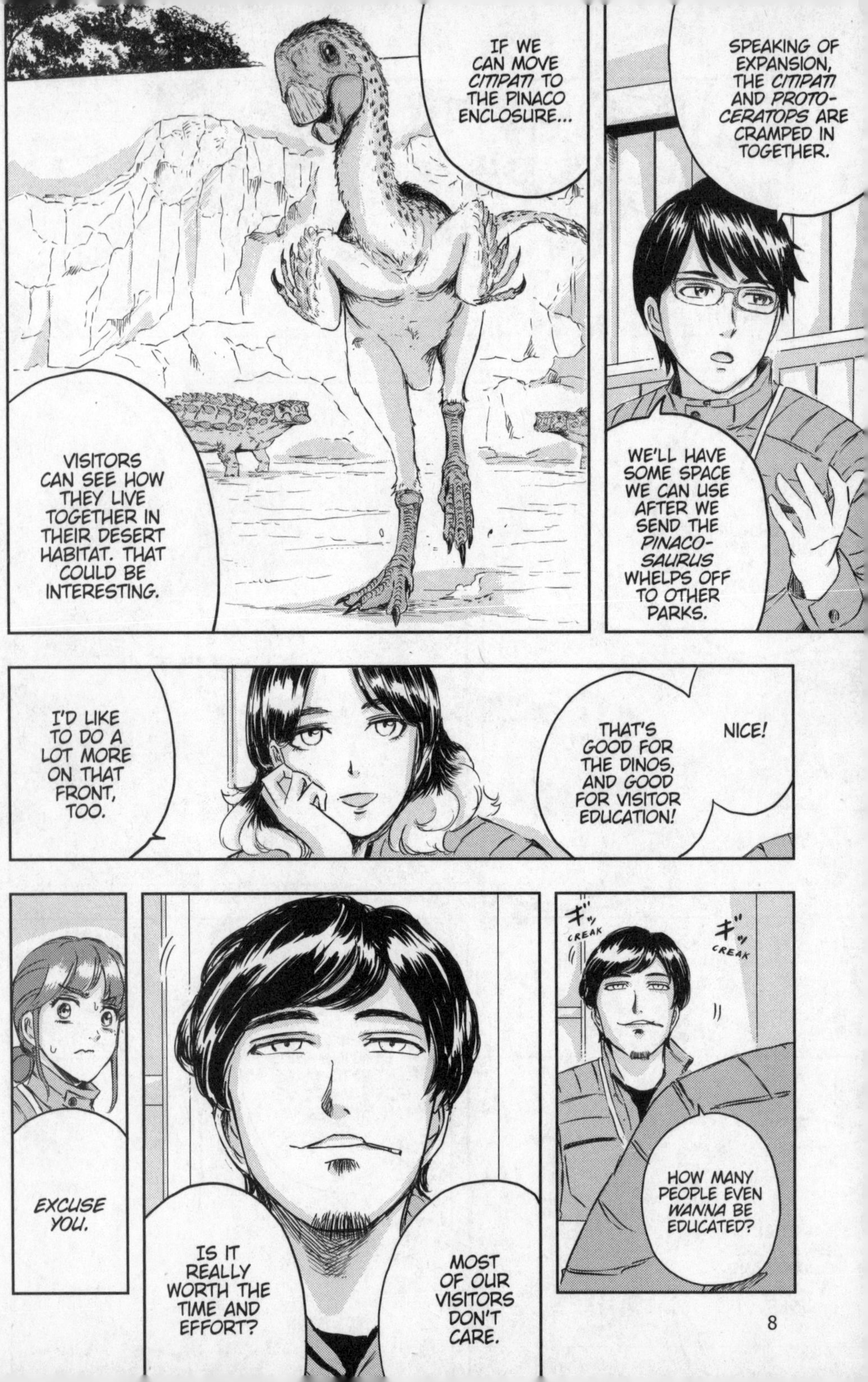
SPEAKING OF EXPANSION, THE *CITIPATI* AND *PROTOCERATOPS* ARE CRAMPED IN TOGETHER.
WE'LL HAVE SOME SPACE WE CAN USE AFTER WE SEND THE *PINACOSAURUS* WHELPS OFF TO OTHER PARKS.
IF WE CAN MOVE *CITIPATI* TO THE PINACO ENCLOSURE...
VISITORS CAN SEE HOW THEY LIVE TOGETHER IN THEIR DESERT HABITAT. THAT COULD BE INTERESTING.
NICE!
THAT'S GOOD FOR THE DINOS, AND GOOD FOR VISITOR EDUCATION!
I'D LIKE TO DO A LOT MORE ON THAT FRONT, TOO.
ギッ CREAK
ギッ CREAK
HOW MANY PEOPLE EVEN *WANNA* BE EDUCATED?
MOST OF OUR VISITORS DON'T CARE.
IS IT REALLY WORTH THE TIME AND EFFORT?
EXCUSE YOU.

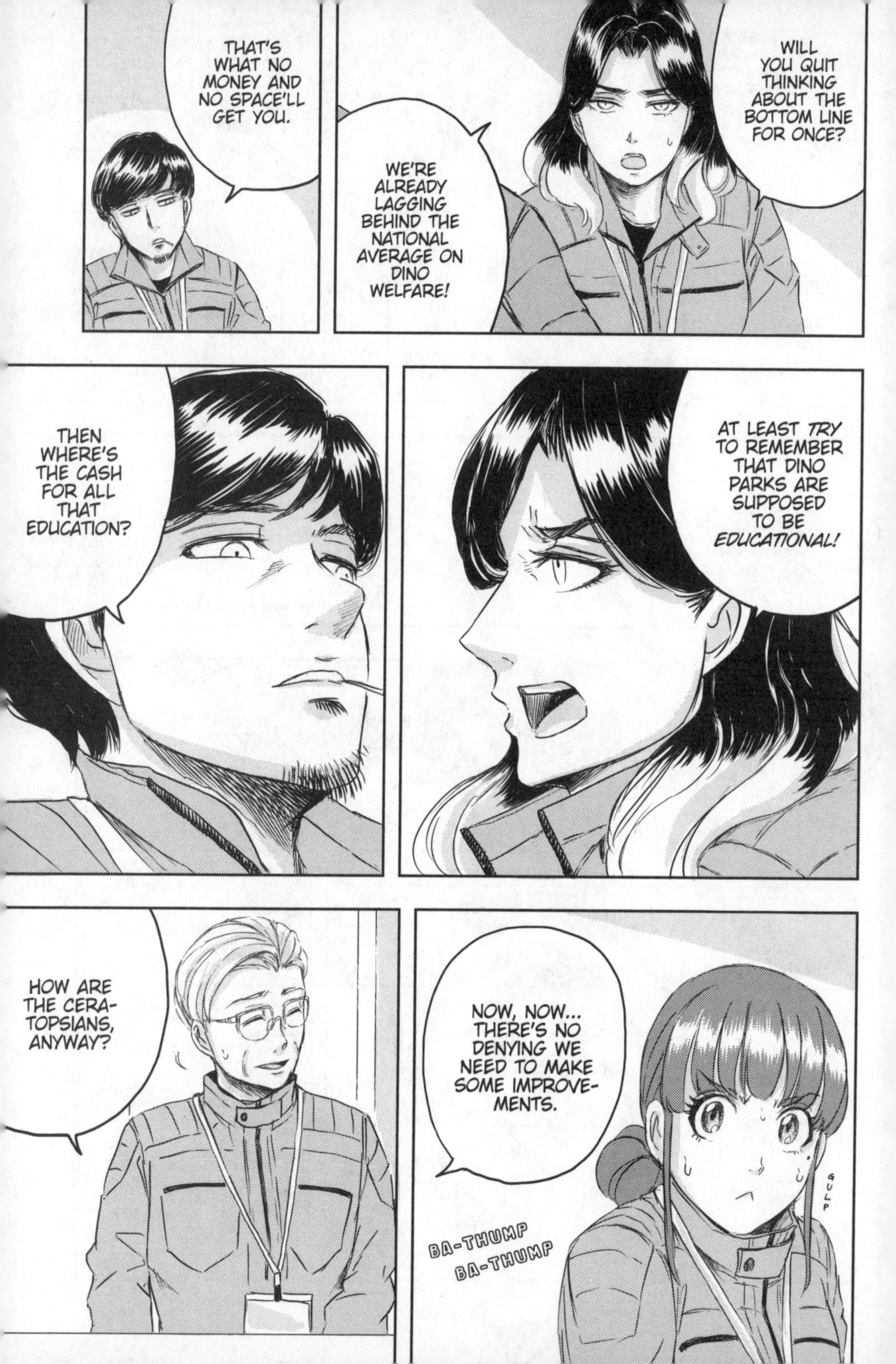
WILL YOU QUIT THINKING ABOUT THE BOTTOM LINE FOR ONCE?
WE'RE ALREADY LAGGING BEHIND THE NATIONAL AVERAGE ON DINO WELFARE!
THAT'S WHAT NO MONEY AND NO SPACE'LL GET YOU.
AT LEAST *TRY* TO REMEMBER THAT DINO PARKS ARE SUPPOSED TO BE *EDUCATIONAL!*
THEN WHERE'S THE CASH FOR ALL THAT EDUCATION?
GULP
NOW, NOW... THERE'S NO DENYING WE NEED TO MAKE SOME IMPROVE-MENTS.
BA-THUMP
BA-THUMP
HOW ARE THE CERA-TOPSIANS, ANYWAY?

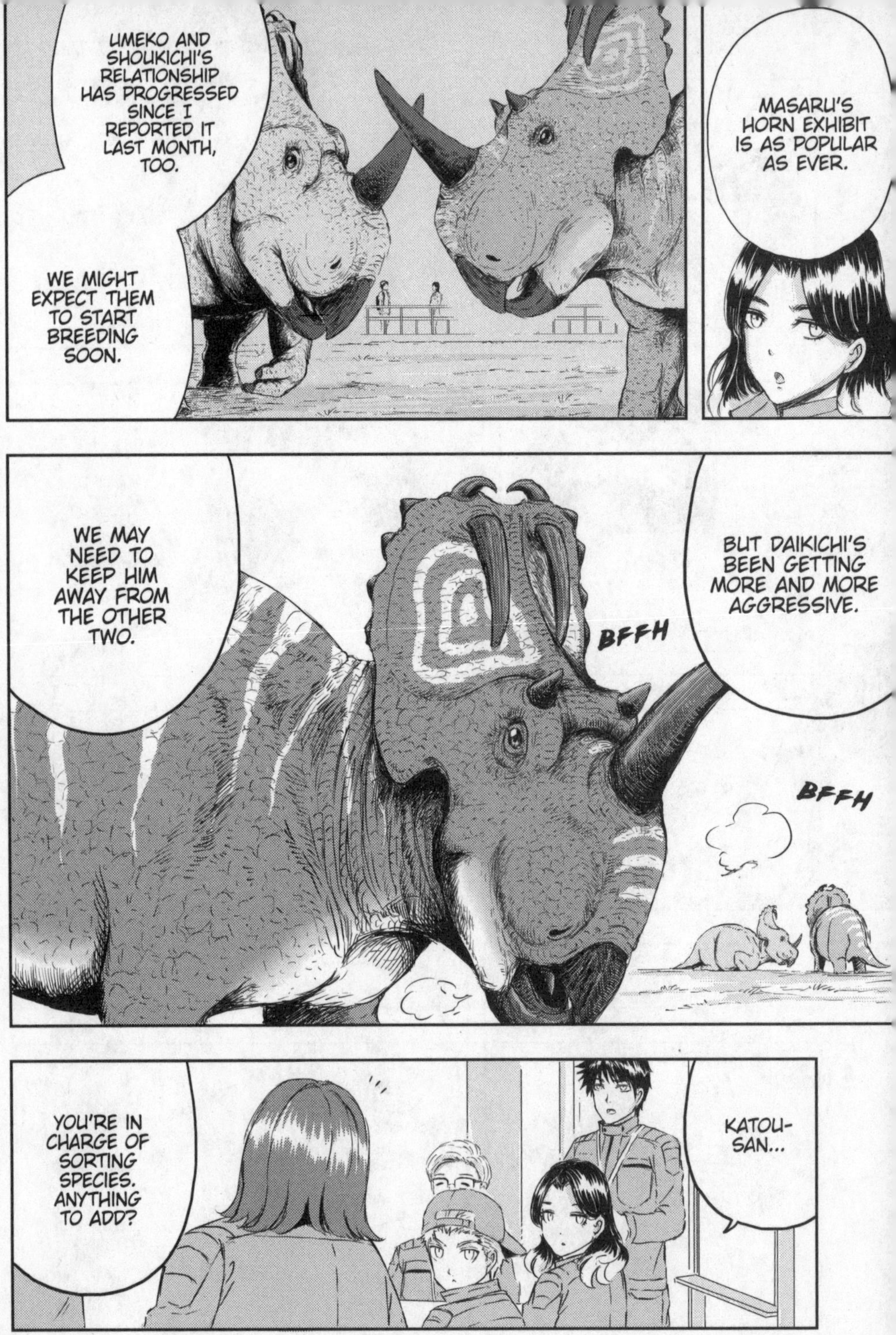
MASARU'S HORN EXHIBIT IS AS POPULAR AS EVER.
UMEKO AND SHOUKICHI'S RELATIONSHIP HAS PROGRESSED SINCE I REPORTED IT LAST MONTH, TOO.
WE MIGHT EXPECT THEM TO START BREEDING SOON.
BUT DAIKICHI'S BEEN GETTING MORE AND MORE AGGRESSIVE.
BFFH
BFFH
WE MAY NEED TO KEEP HIM AWAY FROM THE OTHER TWO.
KATOU-SAN...
YOU'RE IN CHARGE OF SORTING SPECIES. ANYTHING TO ADD?

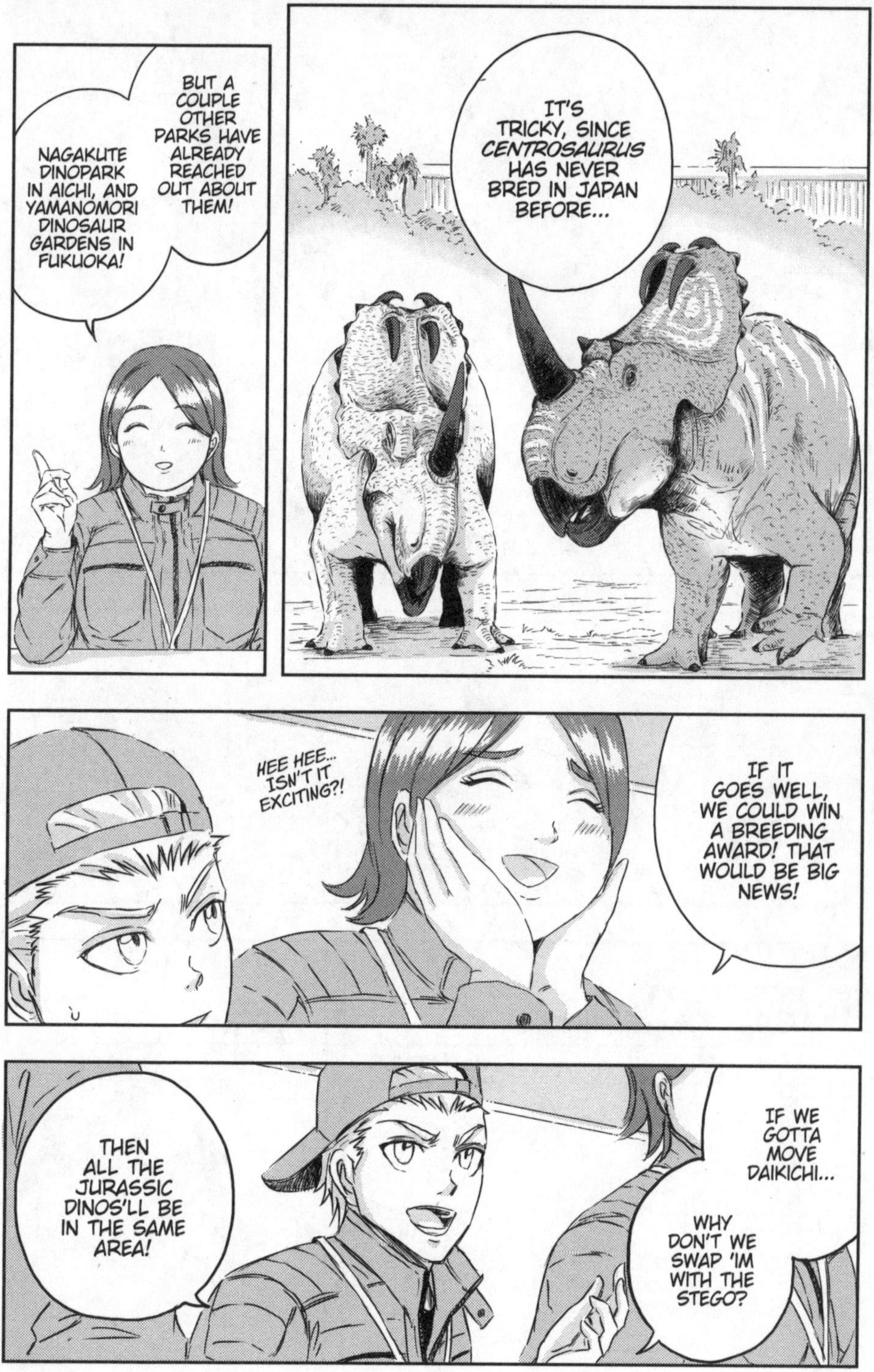
IT'S TRICKY, SINCE *CENTROSAURUS* HAS NEVER BRED IN JAPAN BEFORE...
BUT A COUPLE OTHER PARKS HAVE ALREADY REACHED OUT ABOUT THEM!
NAGAKUTE DINOPARK IN AICHI, AND YAMANOMORI DINOSAUR GARDENS IN FUKUOKA!
IF IT GOES WELL, WE COULD WIN A BREEDING AWARD! THAT WOULD BE BIG NEWS!
HEE HEE... ISN'T IT EXCITING?!
IF WE GOTTA MOVE DAIKICHI...
WHY DON'T WE SWAP 'IM WITH THE STEGO?
THEN ALL THE JURASSIC DINOS'LL BE IN THE SAME AREA!

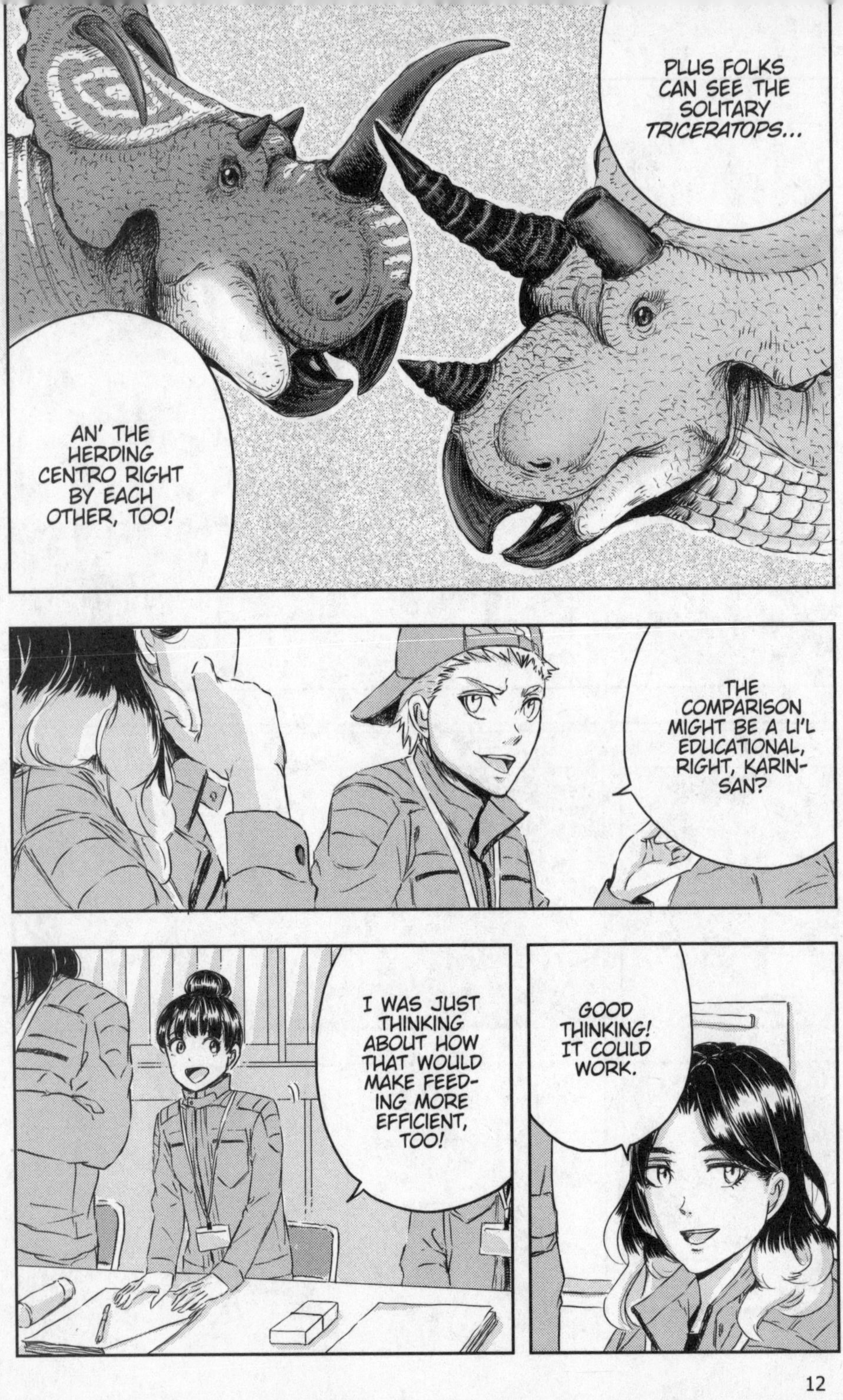
PLUS FOLKS CAN SEE THE SOLITARY *TRICERATOPS*...
AN' THE HERDING CENTRO RIGHT BY EACH OTHER, TOO!
THE COMPARISON MIGHT BE A LI'L EDUCATIONAL, RIGHT, KARIN-SAN?
GOOD THINKING! IT COULD WORK.
I WAS JUST THINKING ABOUT HOW THAT WOULD MAKE FEED-ING MORE EFFICIENT, TOO!

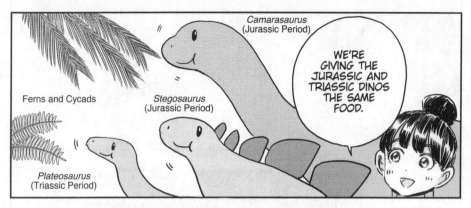

Camarasaurus (Jurassic Period)
WE'RE GIVING THE JURASSIC AND TRIASSIC DINOS THE SAME FOOD.
Ferns and Cycads
Stegosaurus (Jurassic Period)
Plateosaurus (Triassic Period)
IF DAIKICHI AND THE STEGO SWAP PLACES...
Stegosaurus
Triceratops
Camarasaurus
Centrosaurus
Plateosaurus
Thescelosaurus
IT'LL MAKE FEEDING TIME A LOT EASIER!
ASSUMING WE MOVE THESCELO TO BE WITH THE OTHER CRETACEOUS DINOS SOON!
WE'D NEED TO DO ALL THIS ON OFF-DAYS.
CAN WE MAKE ROOM FOR IT, BOSS?
I'D SAY SO! LET'S GO WITH THIS PLAN.
TCH.

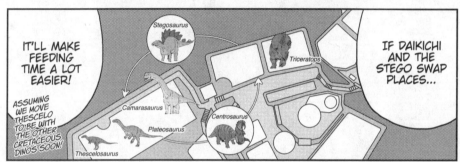

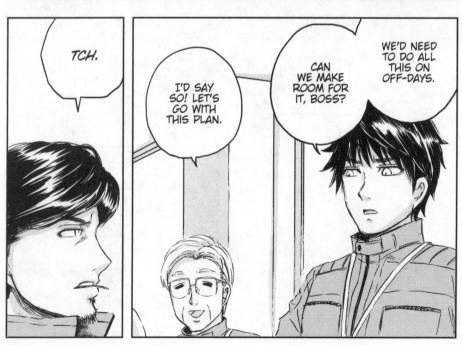

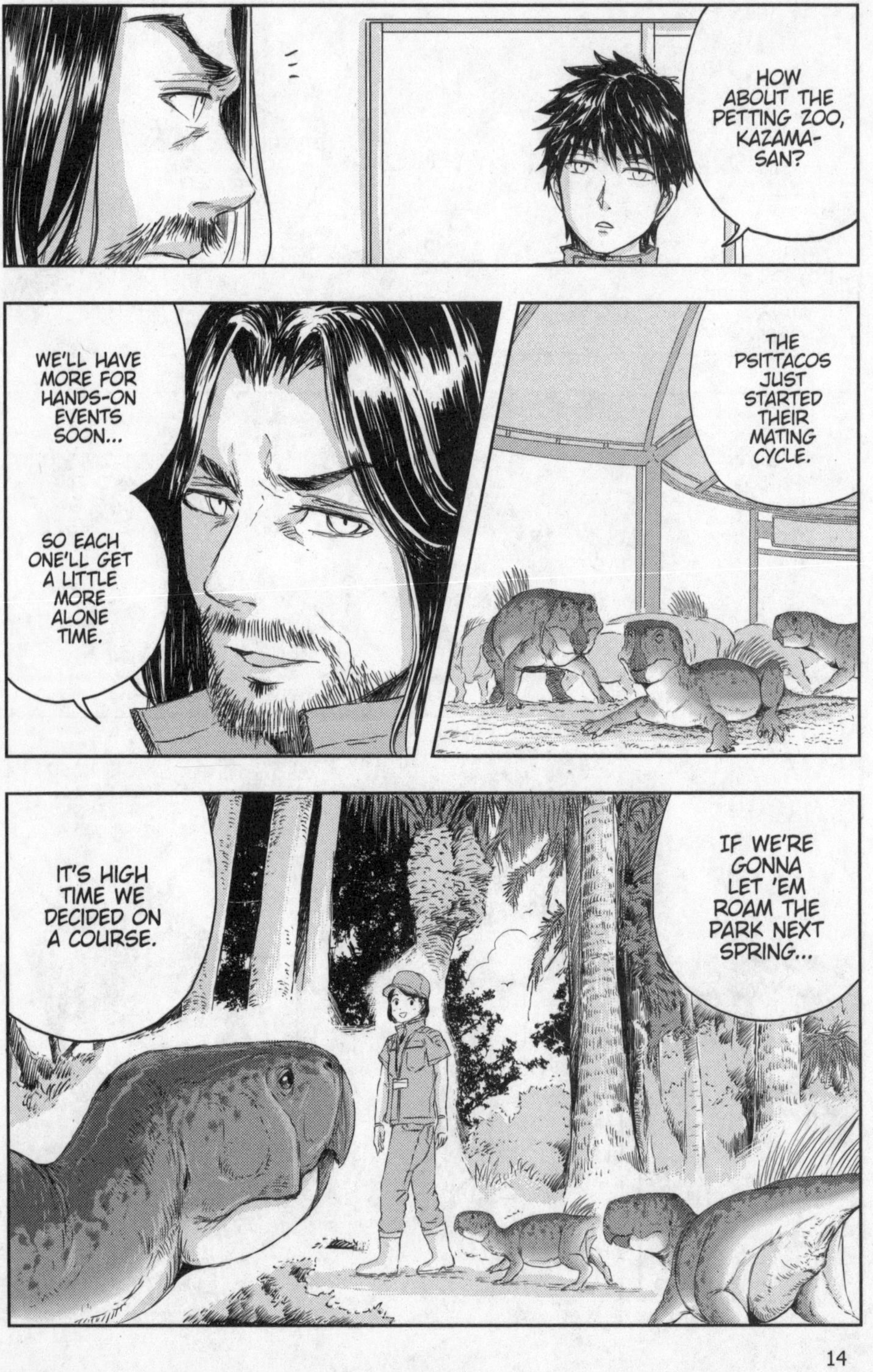
HOW ABOUT THE PETTING ZOO, KAZAMA-SAN?
THE PSITTACOS JUST STARTED THEIR MATING CYCLE.
WE'LL HAVE MORE FOR HANDS-ON EVENTS SOON...
SO EACH ONE'LL GET A LITTLE MORE ALONE TIME.
IF WE'RE GONNA LET 'EM ROAM THE PARK NEXT SPRING...
IT'S HIGH TIME WE DECIDED ON A COURSE.

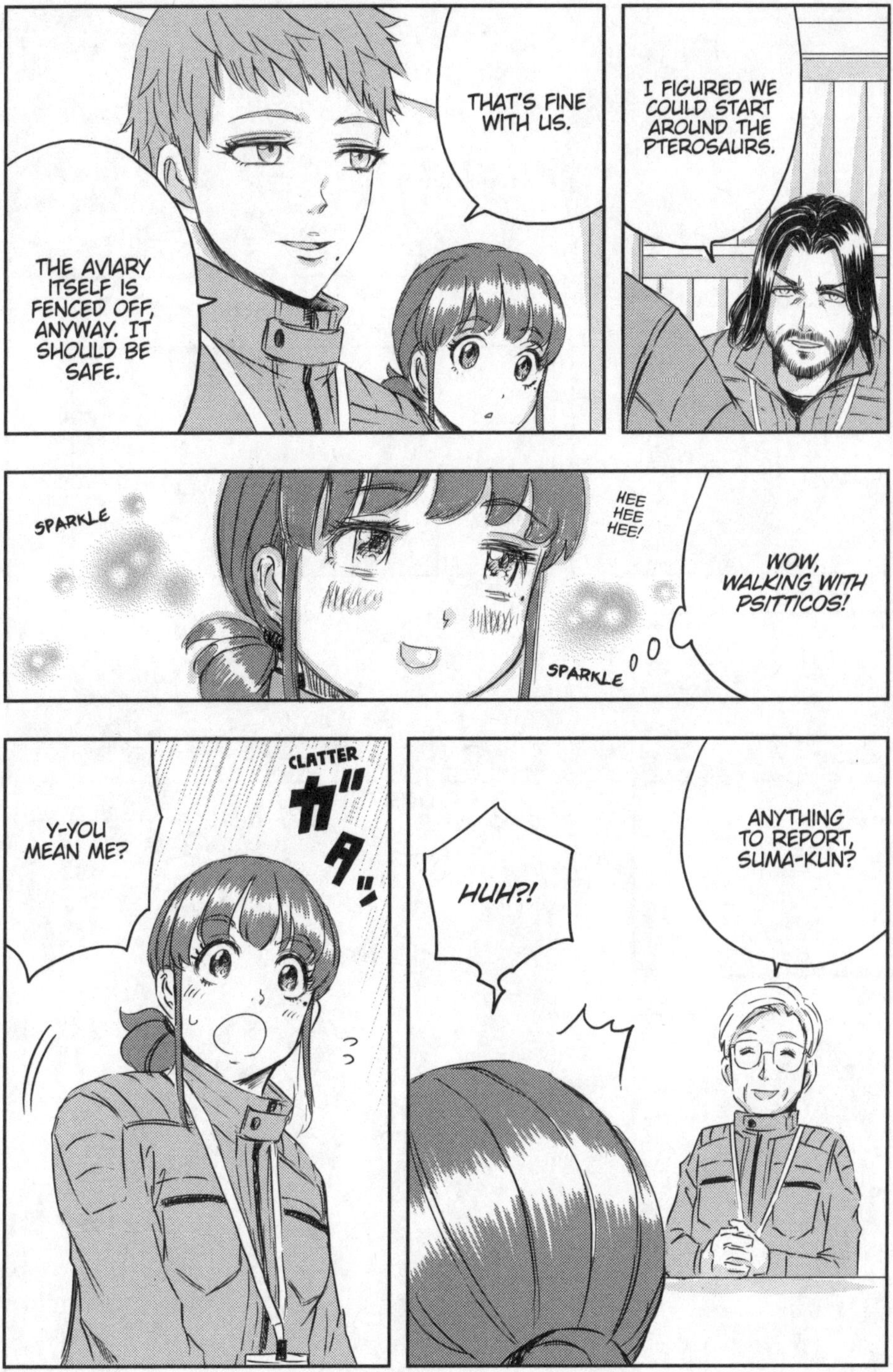
I FIGURED WE COULD START AROUND THE PTEROSAURS.
THAT'S FINE WITH US.
THE AVIARY ITSELF IS FENCED OFF, ANYWAY. IT SHOULD BE SAFE.
WOW, WALKING WITH PSITTICOS!
HEE HEE HEE!
SPARKLE
SPARKLE
ANYTHING TO REPORT, SUMA-KUN?
HUH?!
CLATTER
ガタッ
Y-YOU MEAN ME?

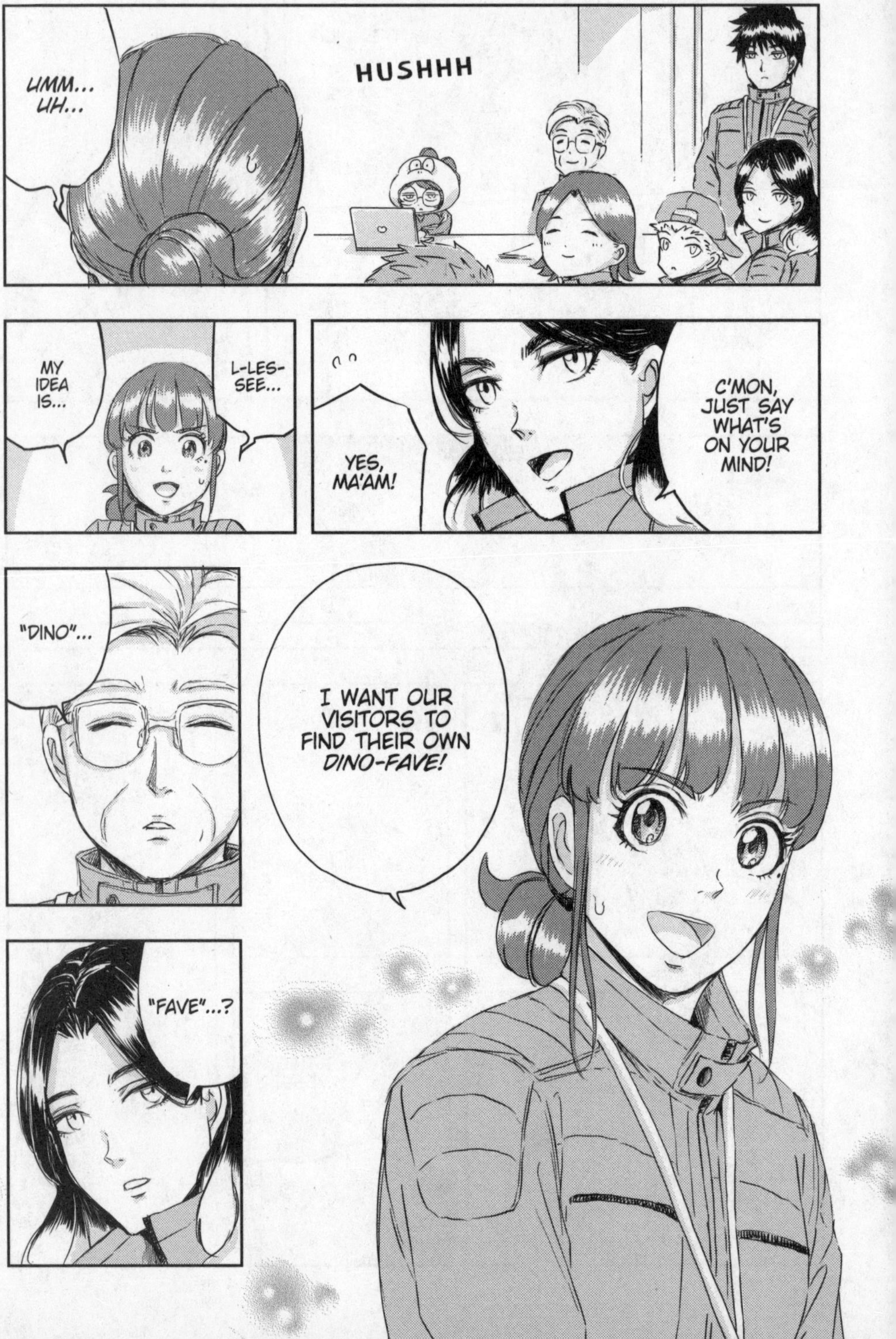
HUSHHH
UMM... UH...
C'MON, JUST SAY WHAT'S ON YOUR MIND!
YES, MA'AM!
L-LES-SEE...
MY IDEA IS...
I WANT OUR VISITORS TO FIND THEIR OWN *DINO-FAVE!*
"DINO"...
"FAVE"...?

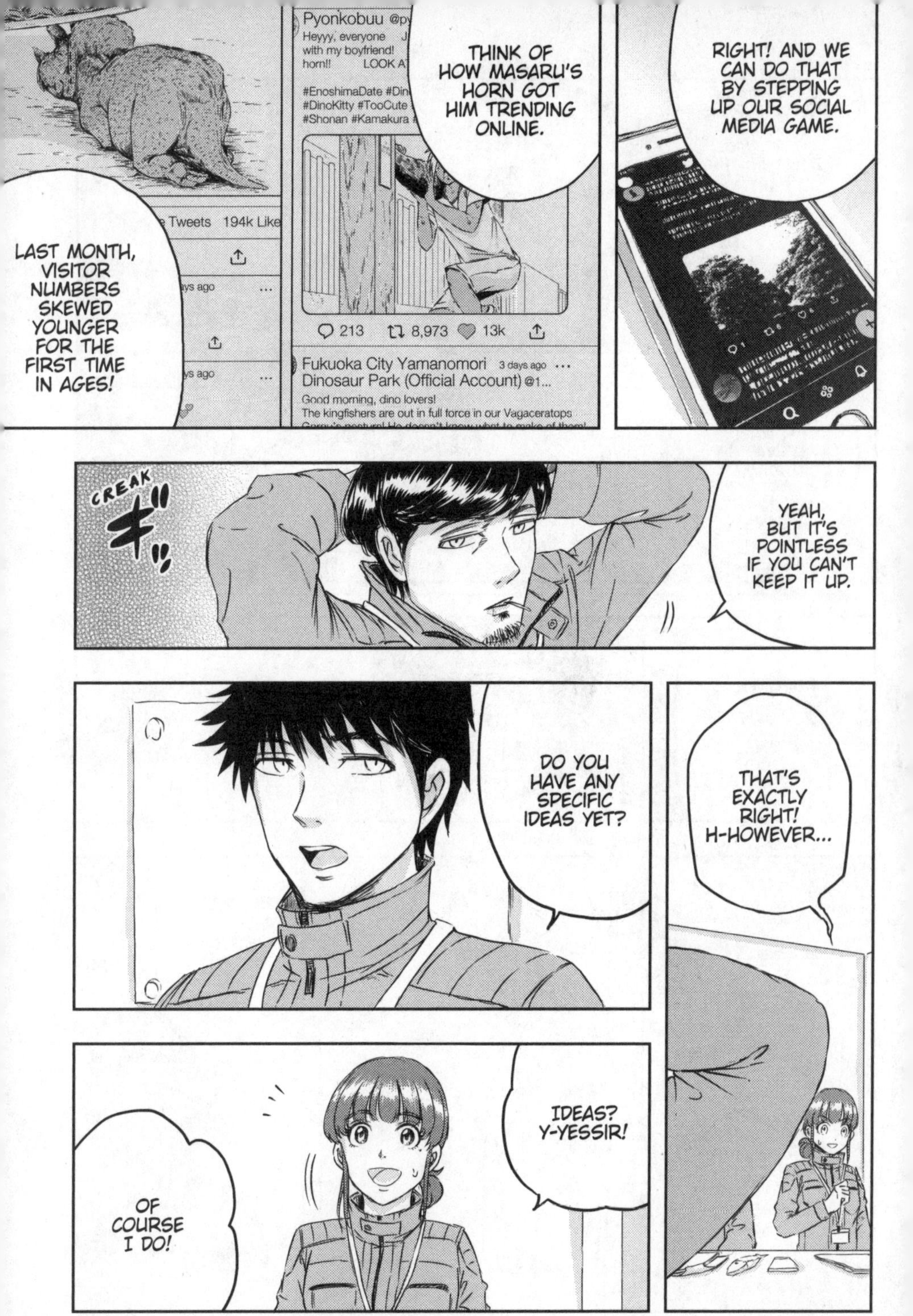
RIGHT! AND WE CAN DO THAT BY STEPPING UP OUR SOCIAL MEDIA GAME.
Pyonkobuu
Heyyy, everyone
with my boyfriend!
#EnoshimaDate
#DinoKitty #TooCute
#Shonan #Kamakura
213 8,973 13k
Fukuoka City Yamanomori Dinosaur Park (Official Account) 3 days ago
Good morning, dino lovers!
The kingfishers are out in full force in our Vagaceratops
THINK OF HOW MASARU'S HORN GOT HIM TRENDING ONLINE.
Tweets 194k Like
LAST MONTH, VISITOR NUMBERS SKEWED YOUNGER FOR THE FIRST TIME IN AGES!
YEAH, BUT IT'S POINTLESS IF YOU CAN'T KEEP IT UP.
CREAK
THAT'S EXACTLY RIGHT! H-HOWEVER...
DO YOU HAVE ANY SPECIFIC IDEAS YET?
IDEAS? Y-YESSIR!
OF COURSE I DO!

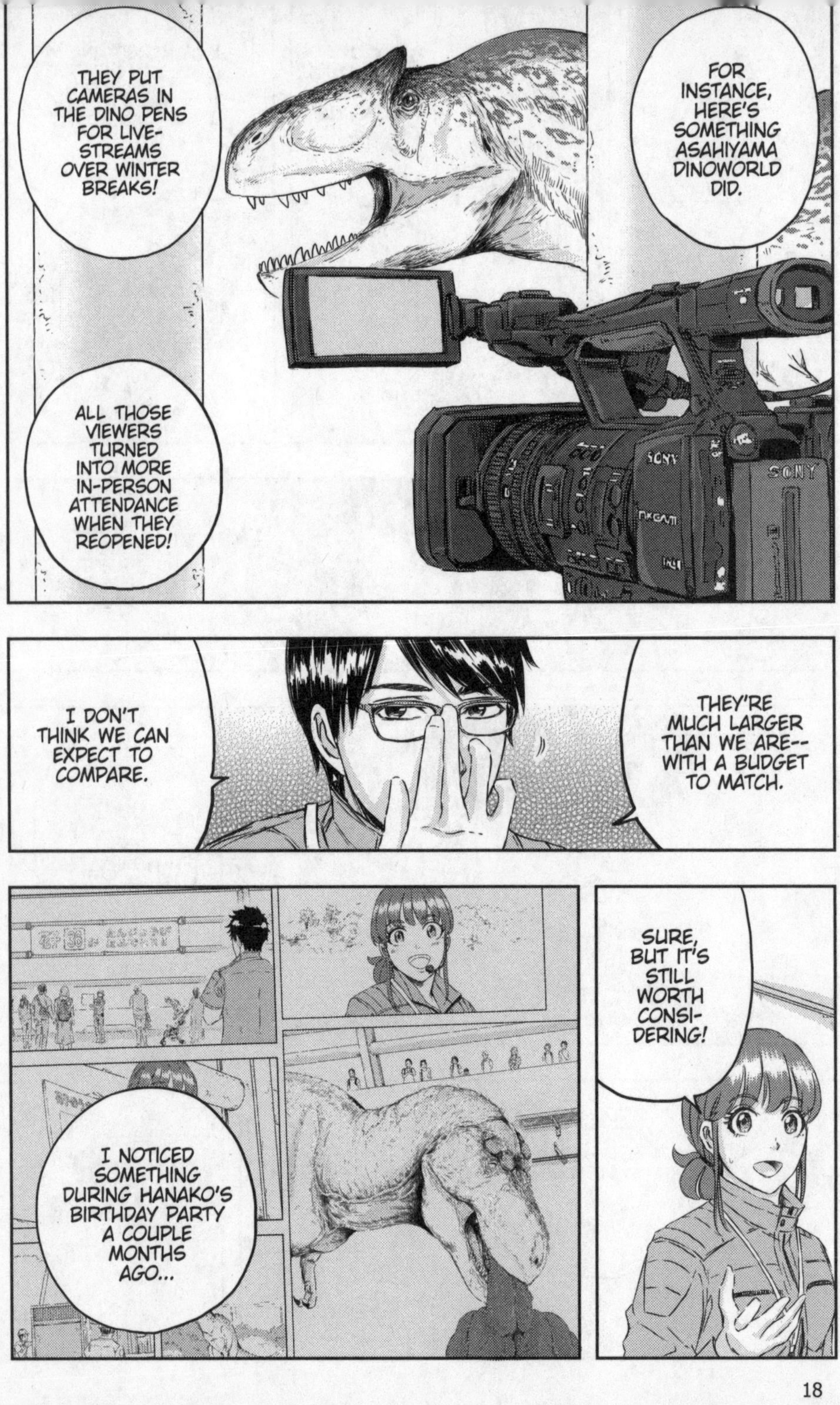
FOR INSTANCE, HERE'S SOMETHING ASAHIYAMA DINOWORLD DID.
THEY PUT CAMERAS IN THE DINO PENS FOR LIVE-STREAMS OVER WINTER BREAKS!
ALL THOSE VIEWERS TURNED INTO MORE IN-PERSON ATTENDANCE WHEN THEY REOPENED!
THEY'RE MUCH LARGER THAN WE ARE--WITH A BUDGET TO MATCH.
I DON'T THINK WE CAN EXPECT TO COMPARE.
SURE, BUT IT'S STILL WORTH CONSI-DERING!
I NOTICED SOMETHING DURING HANAKO'S BIRTHDAY PARTY A COUPLE MONTHS AGO...

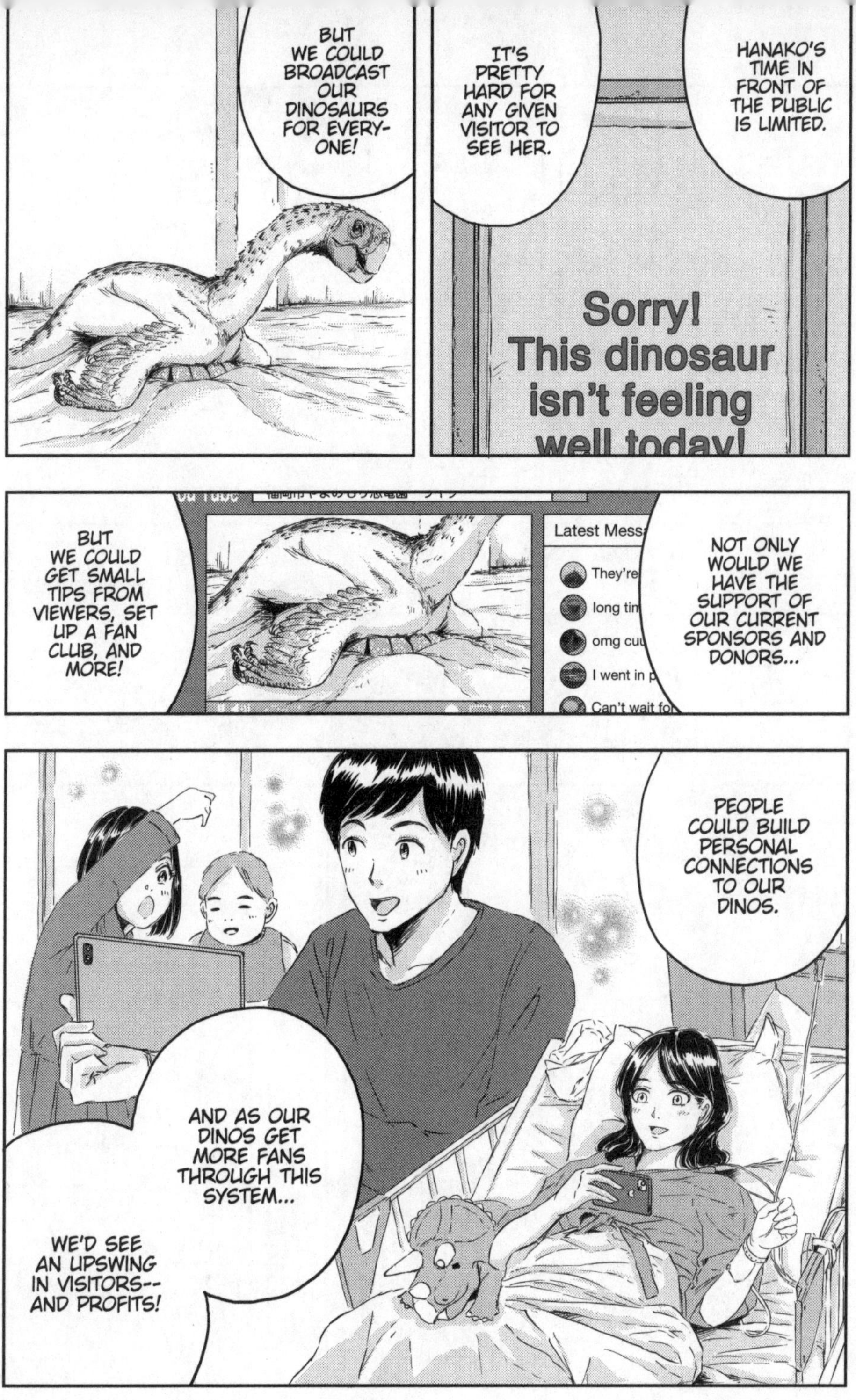
HANAKO'S TIME IN FRONT OF THE PUBLIC IS LIMITED.
IT'S PRETTY HARD FOR ANY GIVEN VISITOR TO SEE HER.
Sorry! This dinosaur isn't feeling well today!
BUT WE COULD BROADCAST OUR DINOSAURS FOR EVERY-ONE!
NOT ONLY WOULD WE HAVE THE SUPPORT OF OUR CURRENT SPONSORS AND DONORS...
BUT WE COULD GET SMALL TIPS FROM VIEWERS, SET UP A FAN CLUB, AND MORE!
PEOPLE COULD BUILD PERSONAL CONNECTIONS TO OUR DINOS.
AND AS OUR DINOS GET MORE FANS THROUGH THIS SYSTEM...
WE'D SEE AN UPSWING IN VISITORS--AND PROFITS!

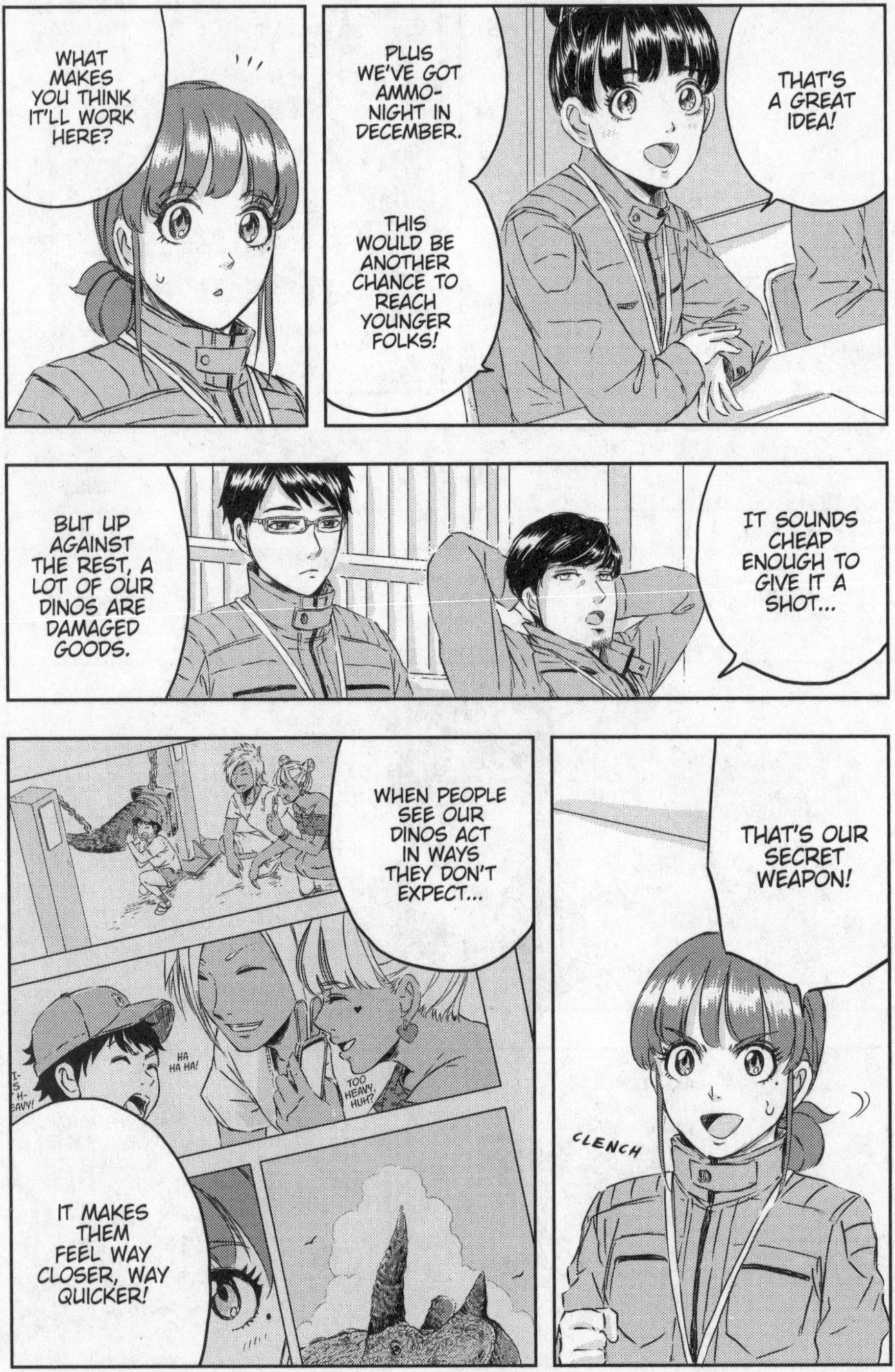
THAT'S A GREAT IDEA!
PLUS WE'VE GOT AMMO-NIGHT IN DECEMBER.
THIS WOULD BE ANOTHER CHANCE TO REACH YOUNGER FOLKS!
WHAT MAKES YOU THINK IT'LL WORK HERE?
IT SOUNDS CHEAP ENOUGH TO GIVE IT A SHOT...
BUT UP AGAINST THE REST, A LOT OF OUR DINOS ARE DAMAGED GOODS.
THAT'S OUR SECRET WEAPON!
CLENCH
WHEN PEOPLE SEE OUR DINOS ACT IN WAYS THEY DON'T EXPECT...
HA HA HA!
TOO HEAVY, HUH?
I-IS H-HEAVY!
IT MAKES THEM FEEL WAY CLOSER, WAY QUICKER!

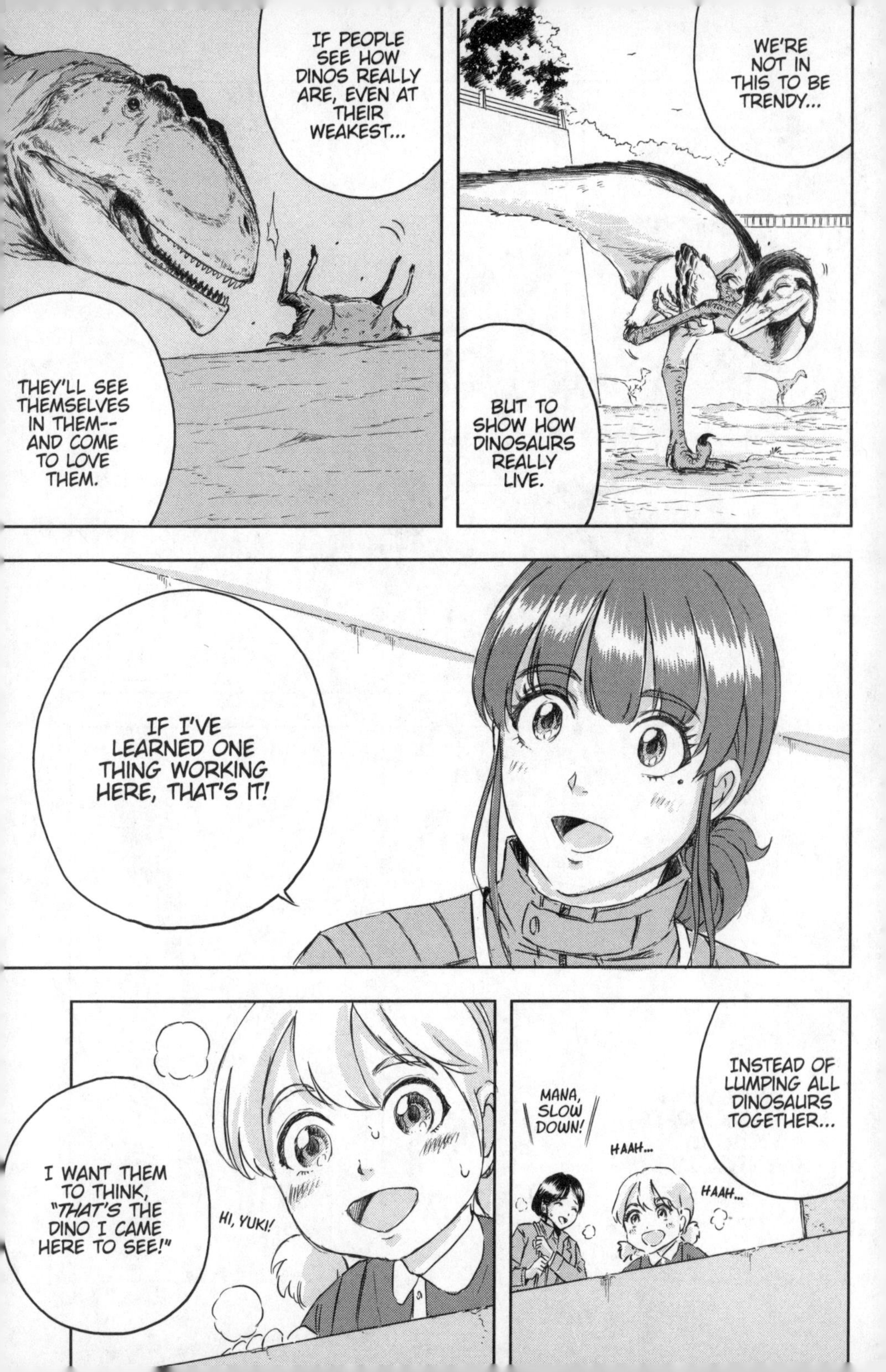
WE'RE NOT IN THIS TO BE TRENDY...
BUT TO SHOW HOW DINOSAURS REALLY LIVE.
IF PEOPLE SEE HOW DINOS REALLY ARE, EVEN AT THEIR WEAKEST...
THEY'LL SEE THEMSELVES IN THEM--AND COME TO LOVE THEM.
IF I'VE LEARNED ONE THING WORKING HERE, THAT'S IT!
INSTEAD OF LUMPING ALL DINOSAURS TOGETHER...
MANA, SLOW DOWN!
HAAH...
HAAH...
I WANT THEM TO THINK, "*THAT'S* THE DINO I CAME HERE TO SEE!"
HI, YUKI!

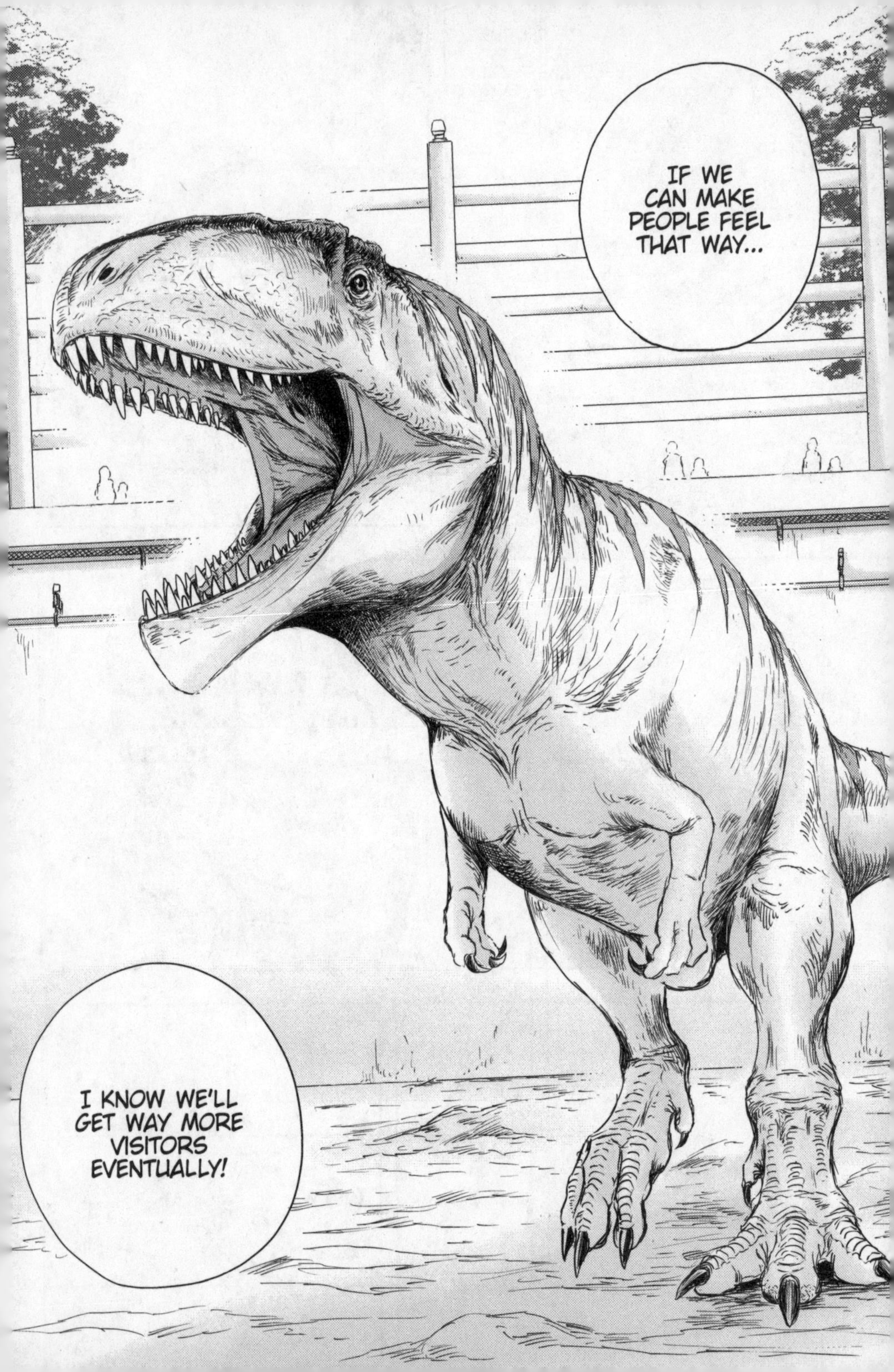
IF WE CAN MAKE PEOPLE FEEL THAT WAY...
I KNOW WE'LL GET WAY MORE VISITORS EVENTUALLY!

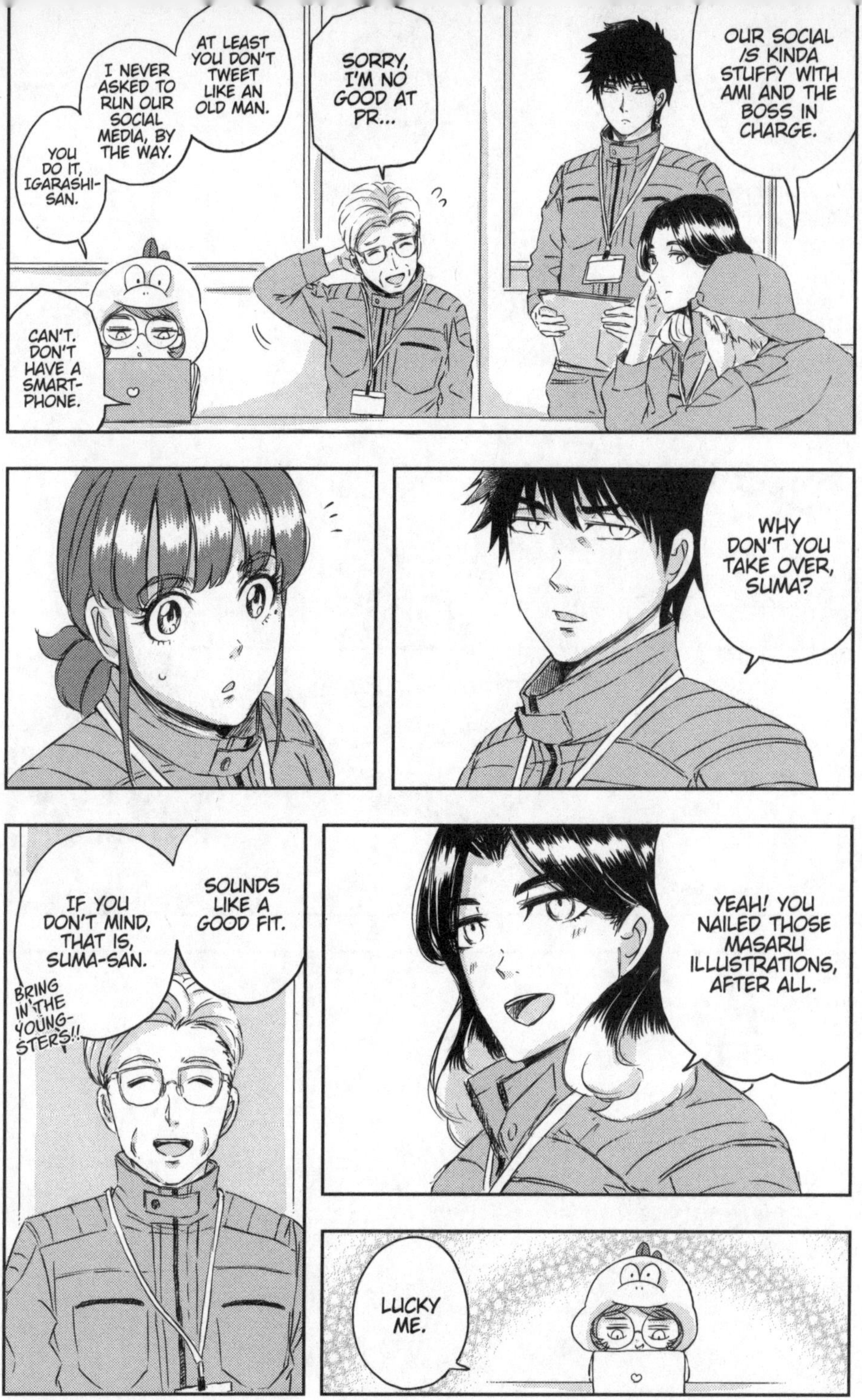
OUR SOCIAL IS KINDA STUFFY WITH AMI AND THE BOSS IN CHARGE.
SORRY, I'M NO GOOD AT PR...
AT LEAST YOU DON'T TWEET LIKE AN OLD MAN.
I NEVER ASKED TO RUN OUR SOCIAL MEDIA, BY THE WAY.
YOU DO IT, IGARASHI-SAN.
CAN'T. DON'T HAVE A SMARTPHONE.
WHY DON'T YOU TAKE OVER, SUMA?
YEAH! YOU NAILED THOSE MASARU ILLUSTRATIONS, AFTER ALL.
LUCKY ME.
SOUNDS LIKE A GOOD FIT.
IF YOU DON'T MIND, THAT IS, SUMA-SAN.
BRING IN THE YOUNGSTERS!!

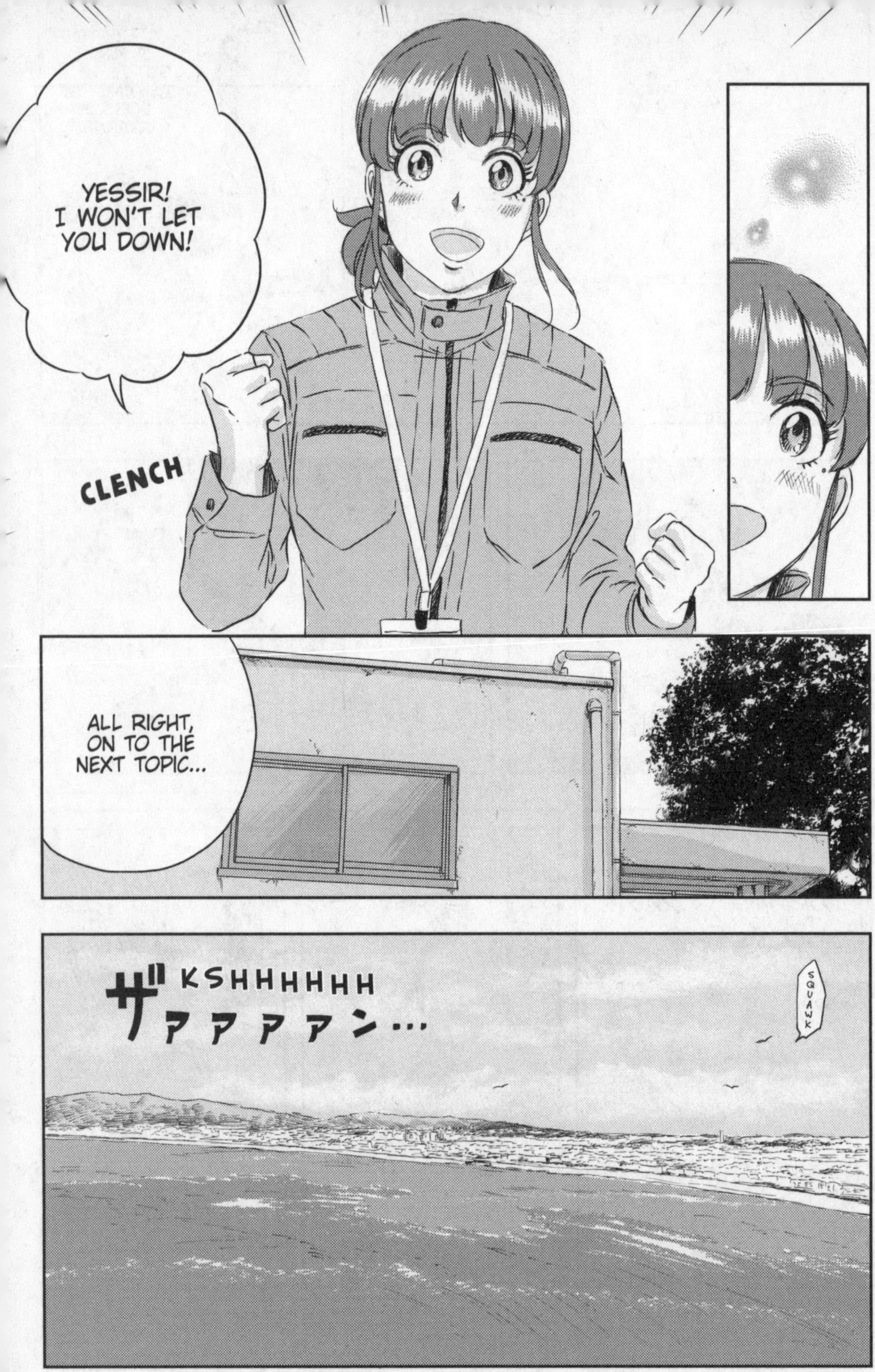
YESSIR! I WON'T LET YOU DOWN!
CLENCH
ALL RIGHT, ON TO THE NEXT TOPIC...
ザァァァァン…
KSHHHHHH
SQUAWK

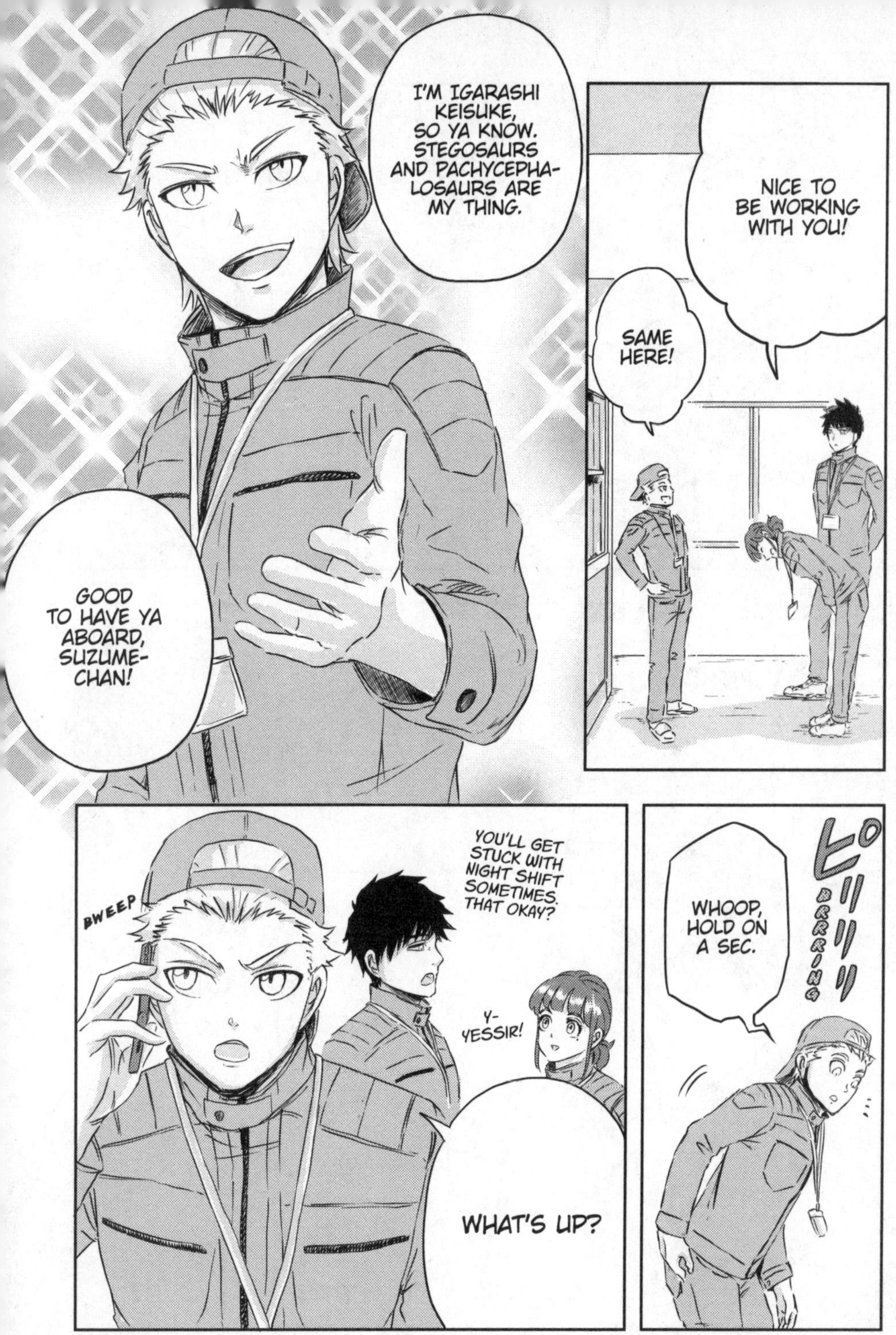
NICE TO BE WORKING WITH YOU!
SAME HERE!
I'M IGARASHI KEISUKE, SO YA KNOW. STEGOSAURS AND PACHYCEPHALOSAURS ARE MY THING.
GOOD TO HAVE YA ABOARD, SUZUME-CHAN!
ピリリリ
BRRRING
WHOOP, HOLD ON A SEC.
YOU'LL GET STUCK WITH NIGHT SHIFT SOMETIMES. THAT OKAY?
Y-YESSIR!
BWEEP
WHAT'S UP?

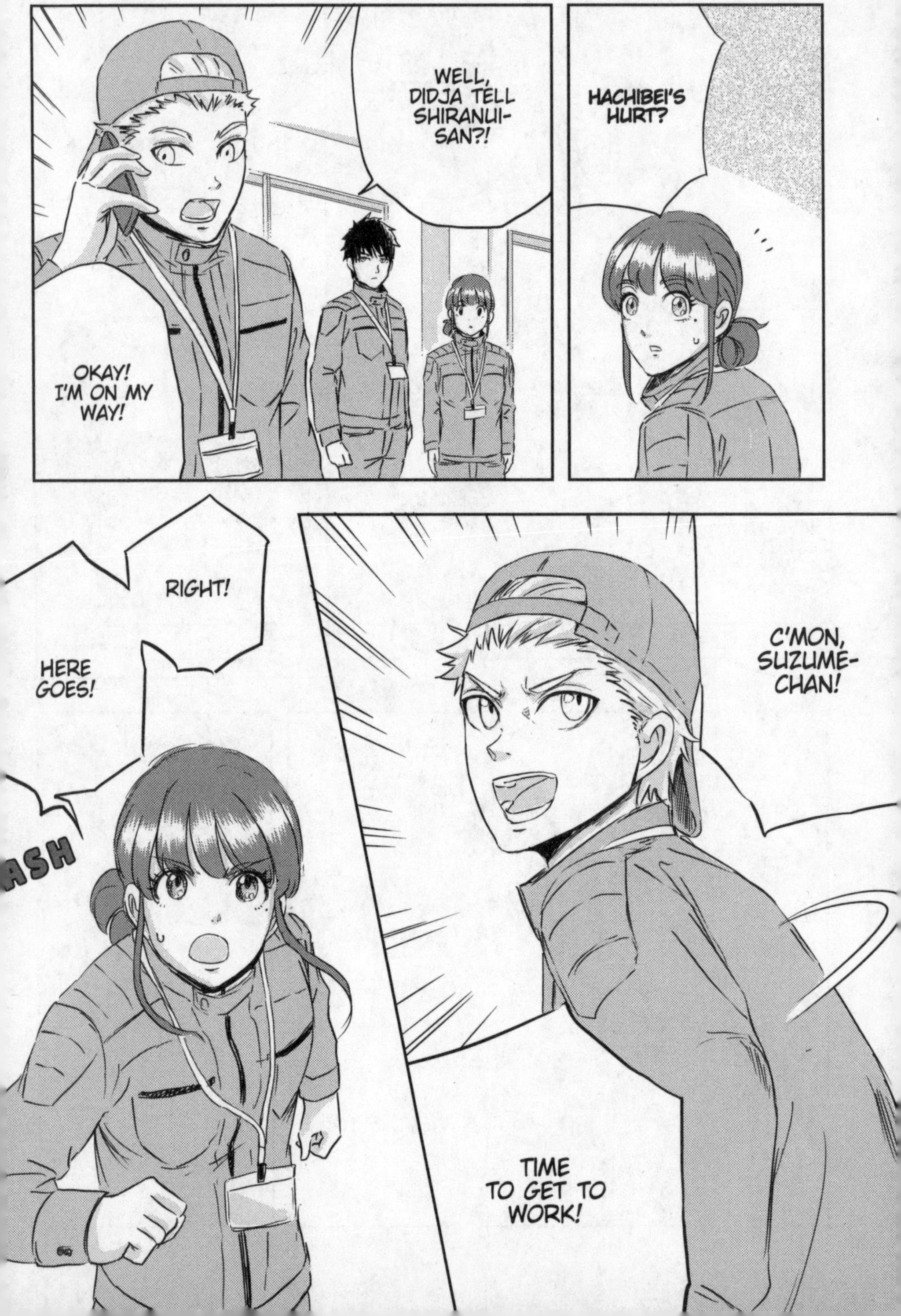
HACHIBEI'S HURT?
WELL, DIDJA TELL SHIRANUI-SAN?!
OKAY! I'M ON MY WAY!
C'MON, SUZUME-CHAN!
TIME TO GET TO WORK!
RIGHT!
HERE GOES!
ASH

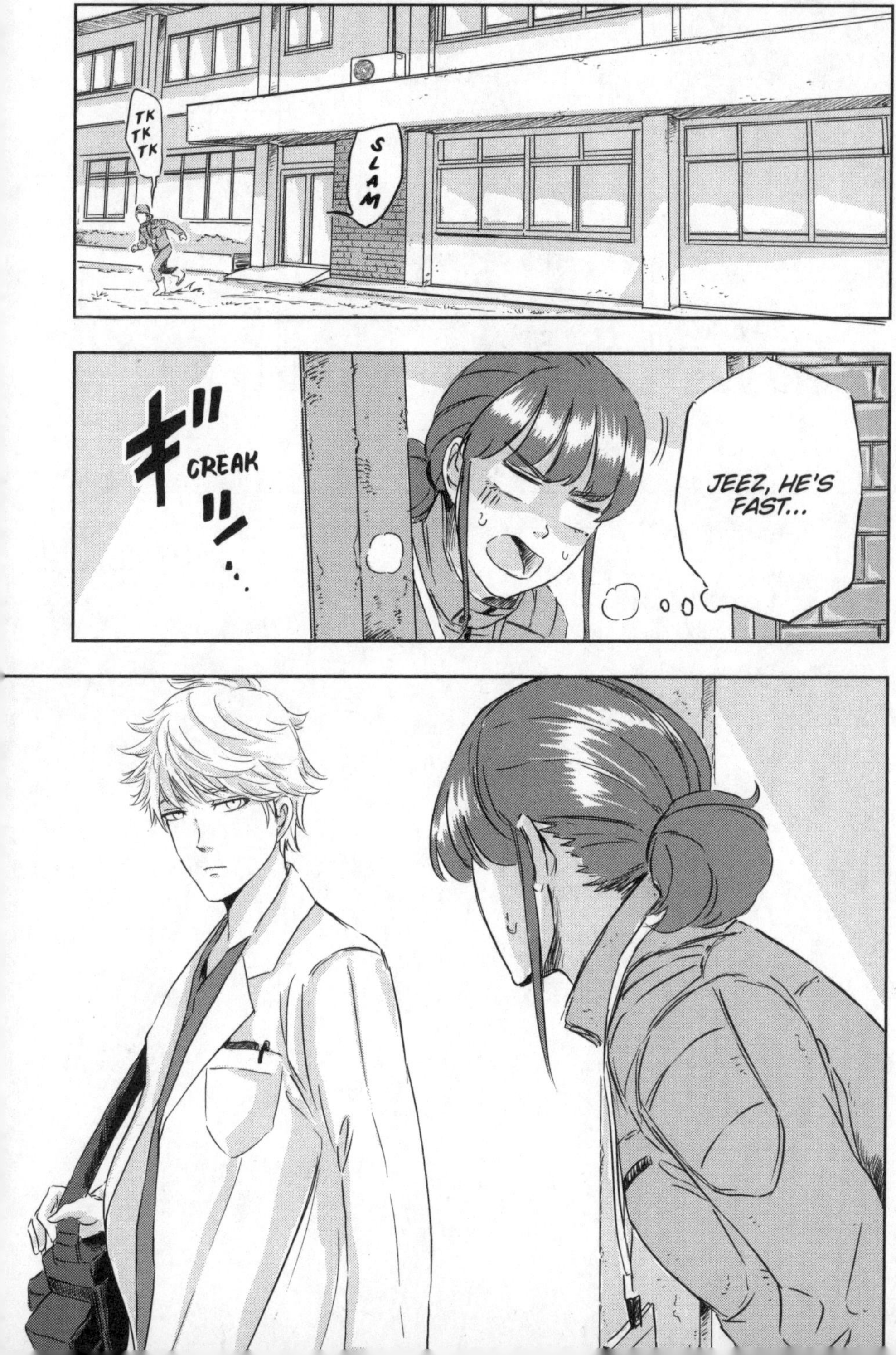
SLAM
TK TK TK
JEEZ, HE'S FAST...
CREAK

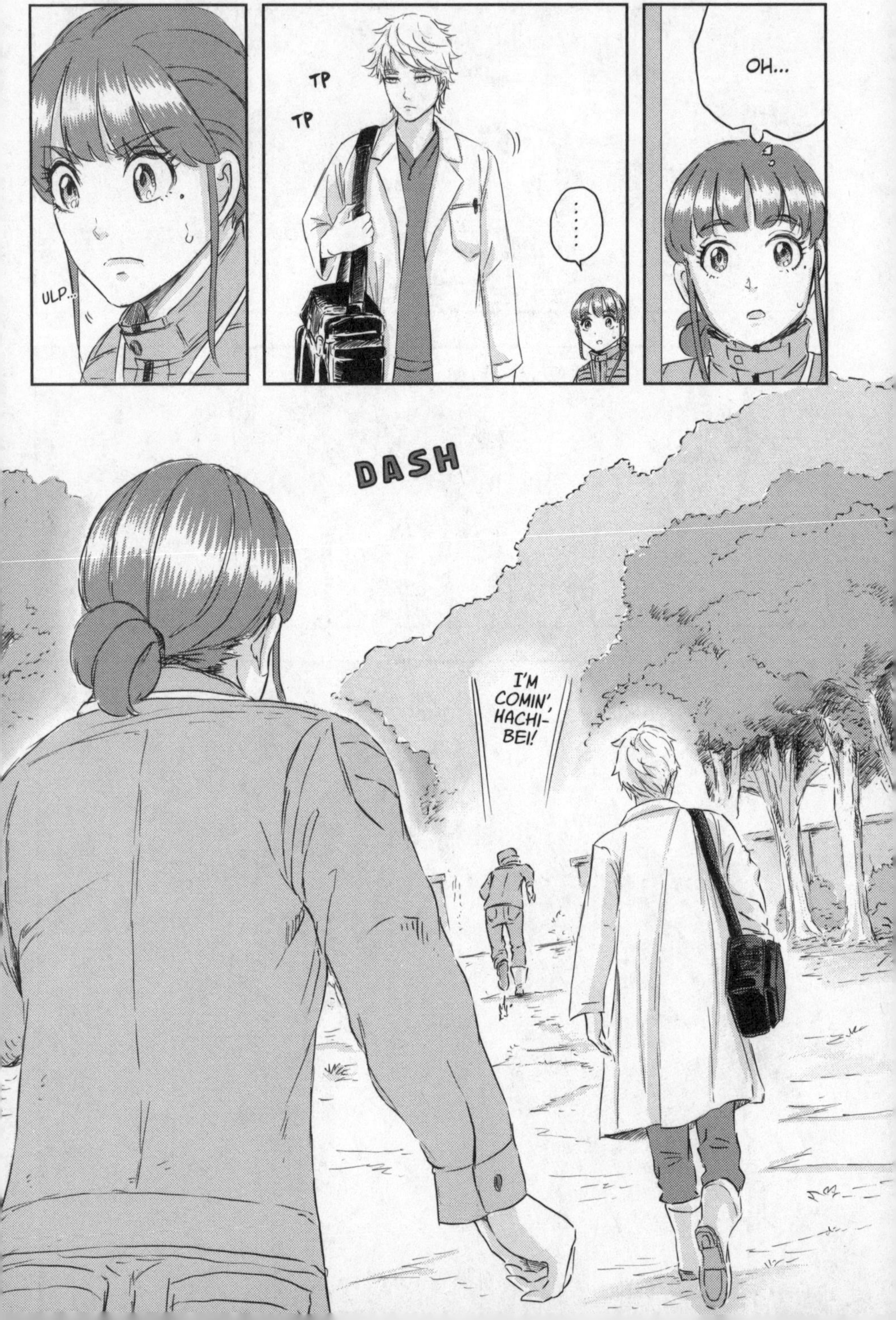
OH...
TP
TP
......
ULP...
DASH
I'M COMIN', HACHI-BEI!

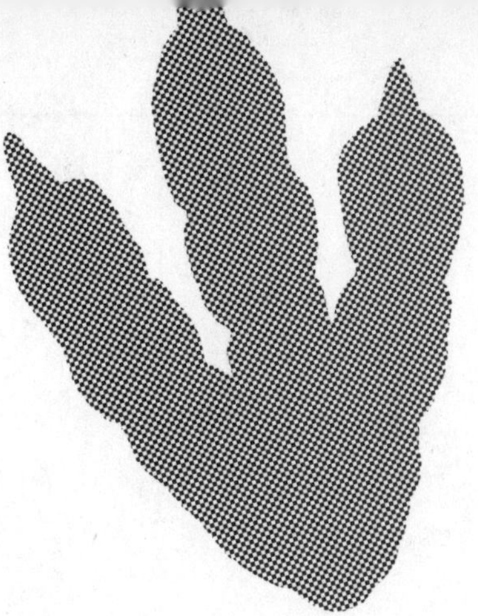
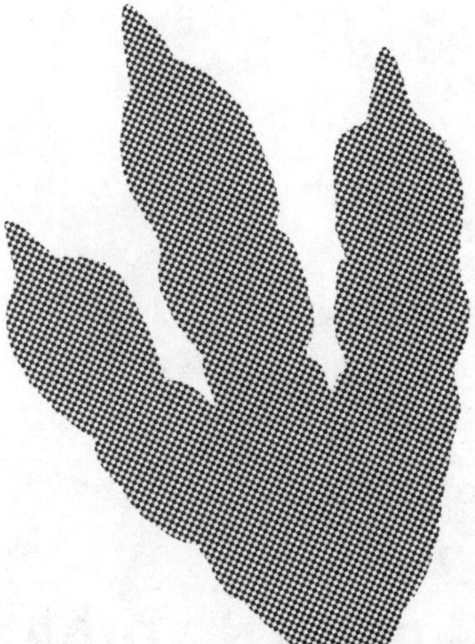

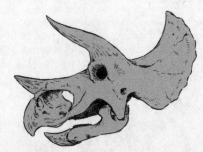

DINOSAUR SANCTUARY

Dr. Dino's Lab Log

FILE. 12 Space and Time—All in One Place

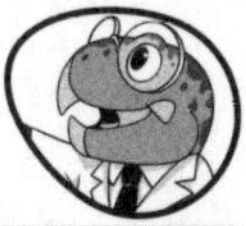

When you visit a zoo, you can see animals from all regions of the globe—from tropical rainforests to arid deserts, and from seas to swampy marshes—all gathered together in the same place. It's great for getting a sense of how widespread the animal kingdom is. Enoshima Dinoland takes it even further than a real-world zoo. The animals there come from different geologic periods, from the Late Triassic to the Late Cretaceous. It's sacred ground that covers wide swaths of both space and time. Each location *and* each period had its own climate and vegetation. Dinosaurs adapted to those conditions and coexisted by marking out their habitats and food in those ecosystems. Dinoland visitors can compare different types of dinosaur side by side—a rare opportunity that would surely make anyone more eager to learn about how they interacted with their environments and fellow animals.

The search for knowledge is a major motivator for us human beings, which means places like zoos and museums, where that search finds continuous satisfaction, make for fantastic entertainment. But if an exhibit is put together with only profit in mind, it won't satisfy that human curiosity for very long. The zoos and museums that truly inspire their visitors to constant observation—and thus continuous discovery—design their exhibits with charm and originality. This isn't easy! Caretakers, curators, and researchers have to put in an overwhelming amount of work that isn't immediately apparent from the exhibits themselves. Of course, there is a school of thought that prizes the visitor's experience as a sightseer, but I think it all comes into being thanks to the staff's behind-the-scenes efforts to show visitors the joy in the search for knowledge.

Shifting gears: How do we go about figuring out whether a particular extinct animal formed herds? One important basis for making that judgment lies in "bone beds." These are collections of hundreds or even thousands of bones from the same species—young and old, male and female—brought together by river flooding. The discovery of a bone bed would certainly suggest that species lived in large herds. There are also fully articulated fossil specimens of several animals arranged as if they were nesting together, which suggest that they lived in smaller groups. Lastly, if there are fossilized footprints from the same species all headed in the same direction, that's a strong indicator that they traveled in herds, too.

So what about the dinosaurs of the family Ceratopsidae? Did they form herds or not? The answer might depend on their specific species. There are several bone beds that contain the remains of thousands of specimens of *Centrosaurus* and *Pachyrhinosaurus,* suggesting that they lived in very large herds. On the other hand, though hundreds of *Triceratops* fossils have been discovered, they've nearly all been lone wolves. (Well, lone *Triceratopses.*) At the very least, there's no evidence that adult *Triceratops* formed groups—though an example has been reported of a few younger *Triceratops* being found in the same location, which was big news in the paleontology community.

Anyway, lions and tigers are closely related, but lions live in prides, while tigers are solitary. Whether the animals in question are extinct or not, you can't take for granted that all members of similar species will behave like each other. Fascinating, isn't it?

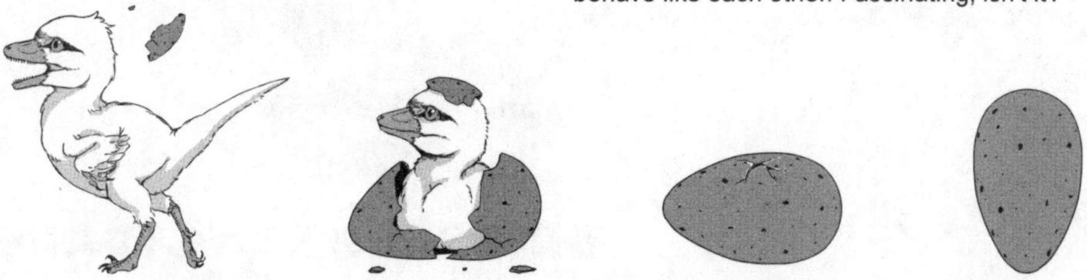

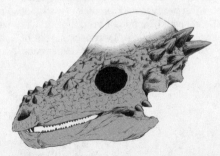

DINOSAUR SANCTUARY

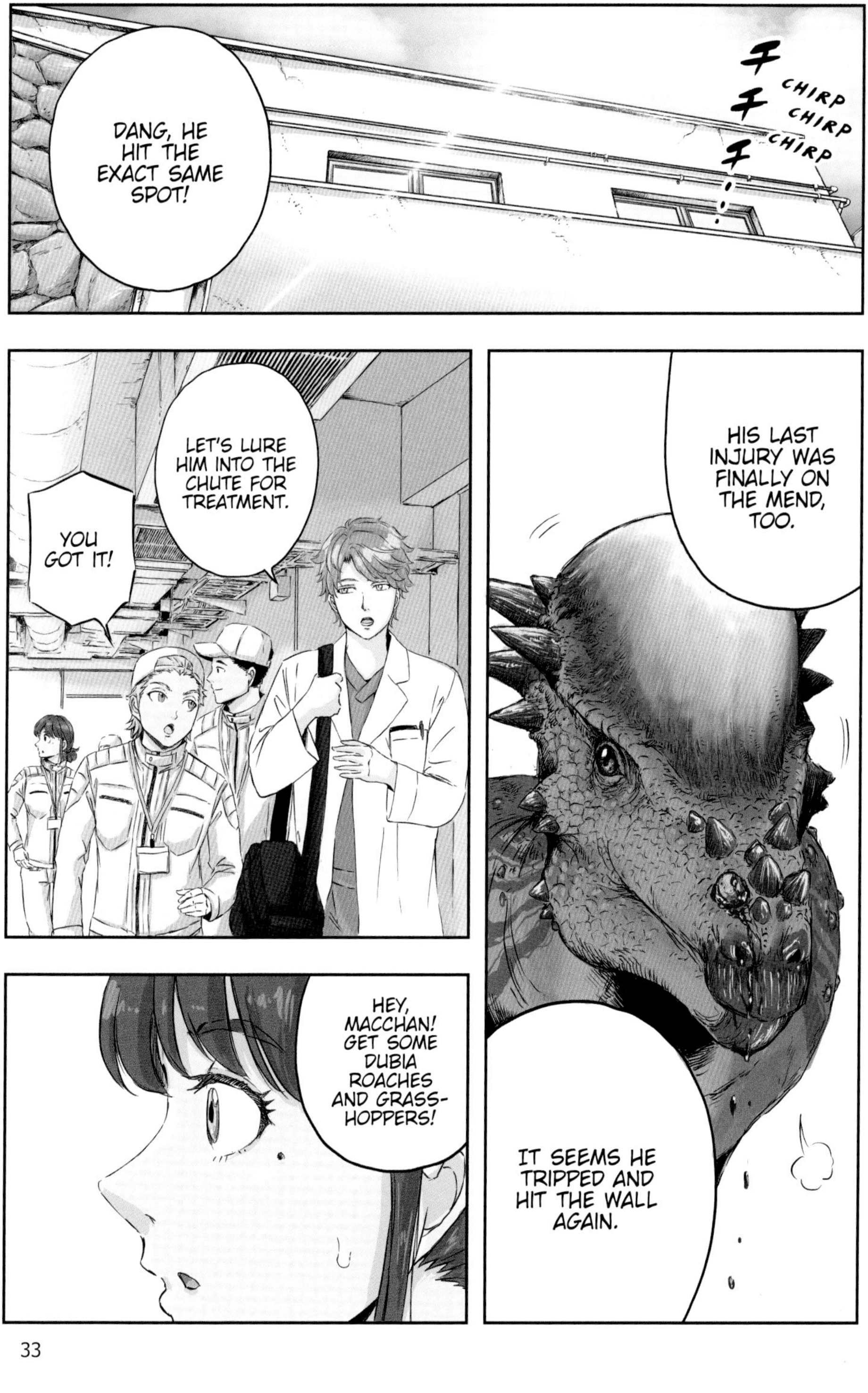
チ CHIRP
チ CHIRP
チ CHIRP
DANG, HE HIT THE EXACT SAME SPOT!
HIS LAST INJURY WAS FINALLY ON THE MEND, TOO.
IT SEEMS HE TRIPPED AND HIT THE WALL AGAIN.
LET'S LURE HIM INTO THE CHUTE FOR TREATMENT.
YOU GOT IT!
HEY, MACCHAN! GET SOME DUBIA ROACHES AND GRASS-HOPPERS!

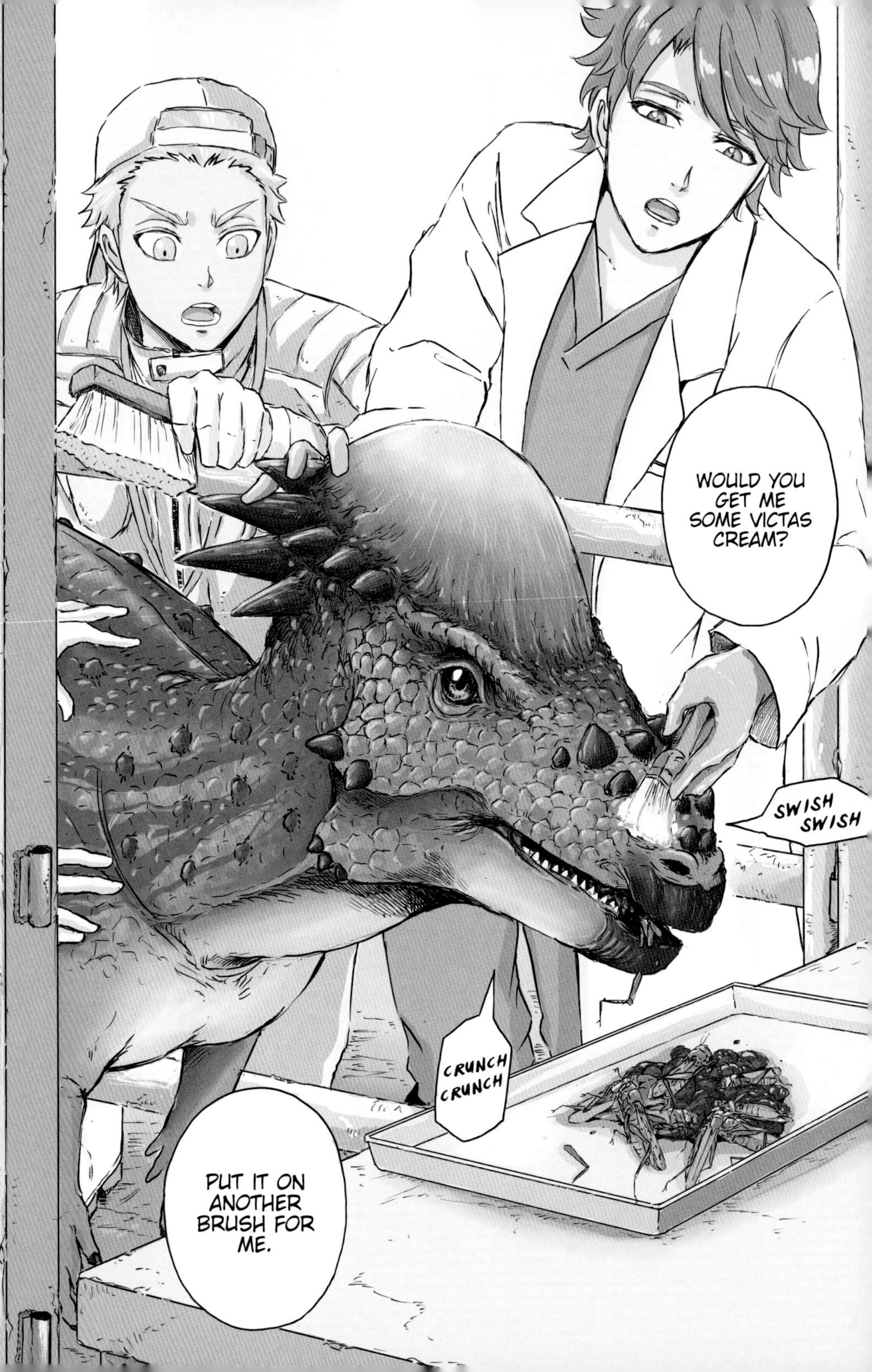
WOULD YOU GET ME SOME VICTAS CREAM?
SWISH SWISH
CRUNCH CRUNCH
PUT IT ON ANOTHER BRUSH FOR ME.

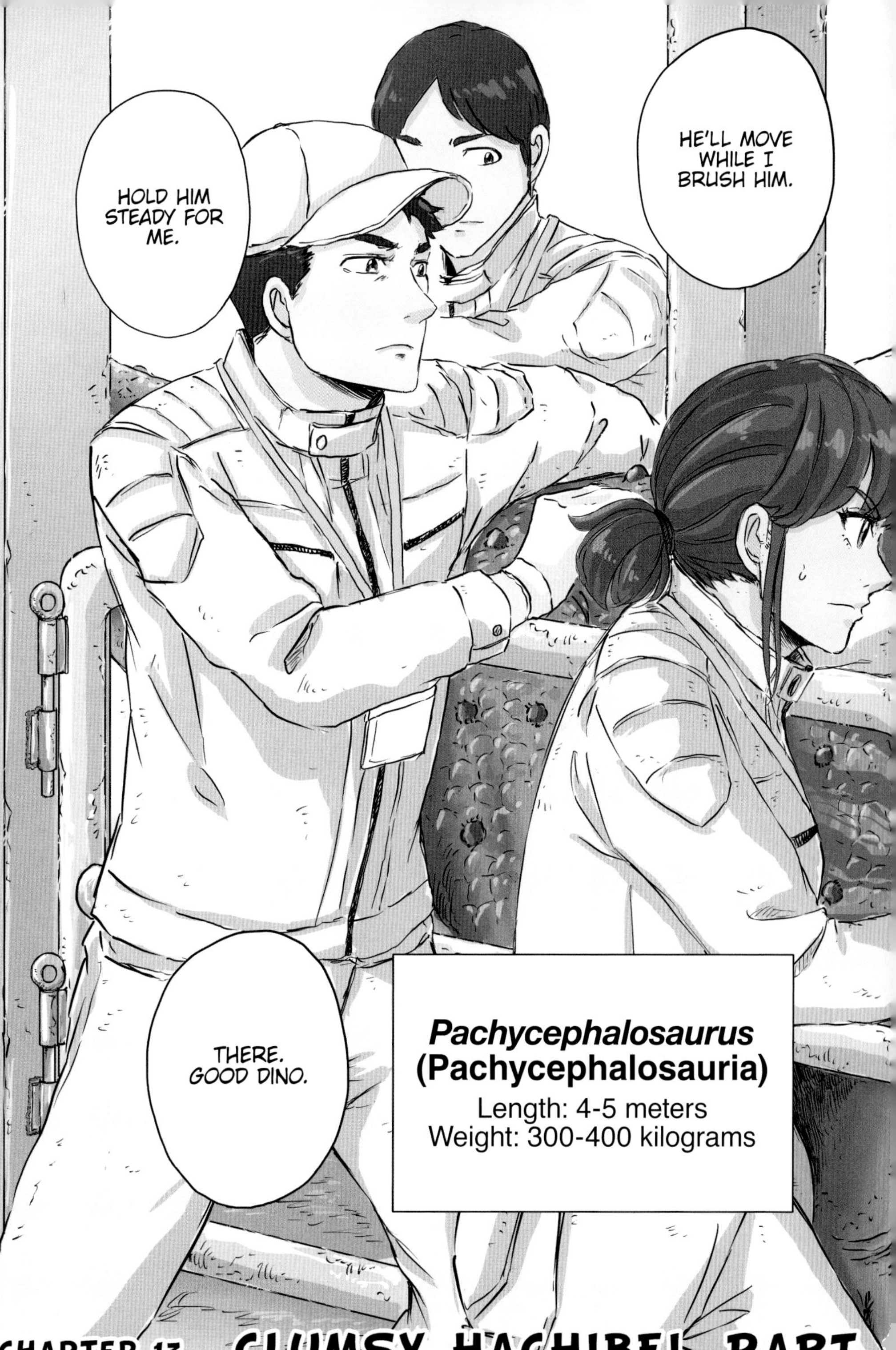
HE'LL MOVE WHILE I BRUSH HIM.
HOLD HIM STEADY FOR ME.
THERE. GOOD DINO.
Pachycephalosaurus (Pachycephalosauria)
Length: 4-5 meters
Weight: 300-400 kilograms

CHAPTER 13 CLUMSY HACHIBEI, PART

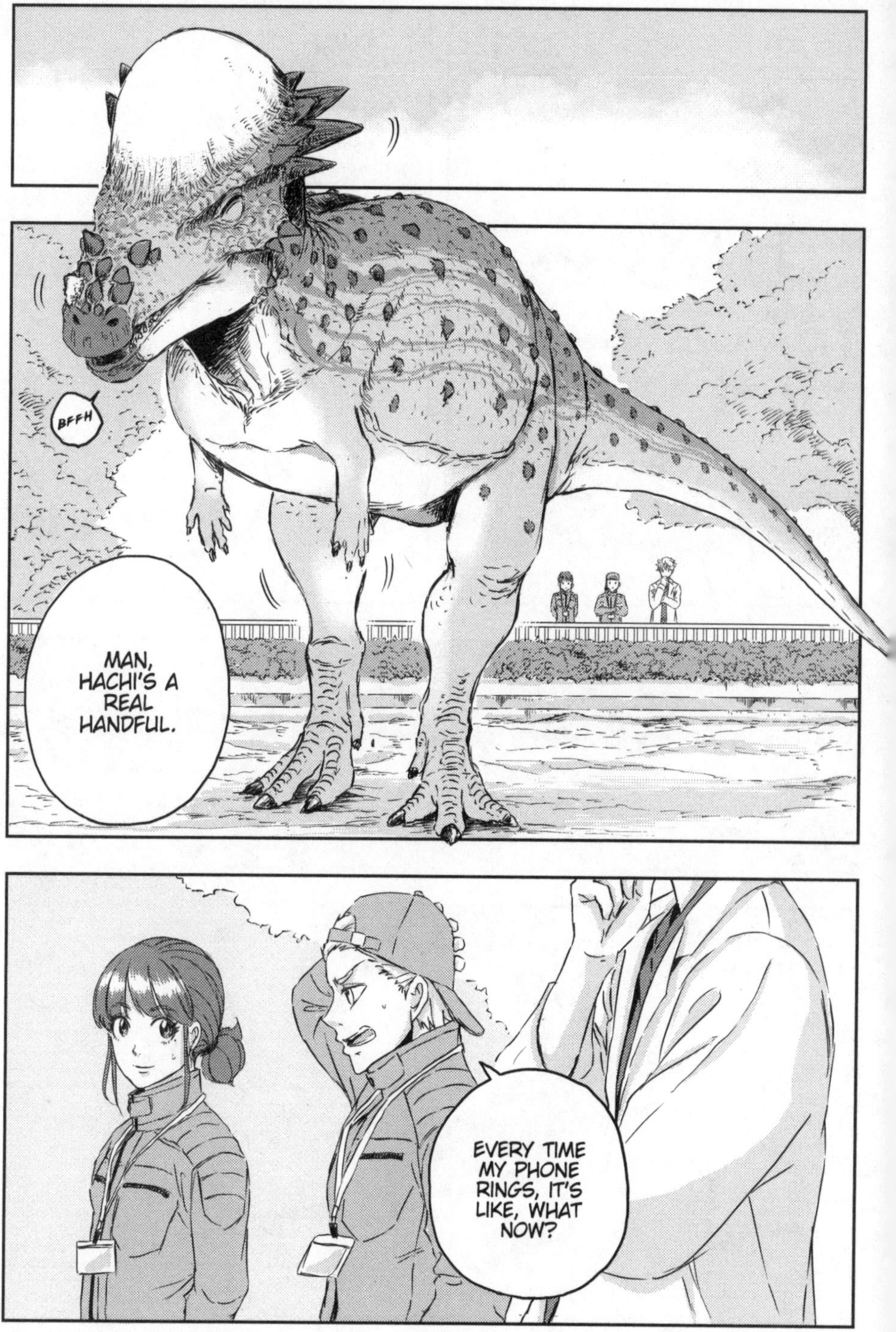
BFFH
MAN, HACHI'S A REAL HANDFUL.
EVERY TIME MY PHONE RINGS, IT'S LIKE, WHAT NOW?

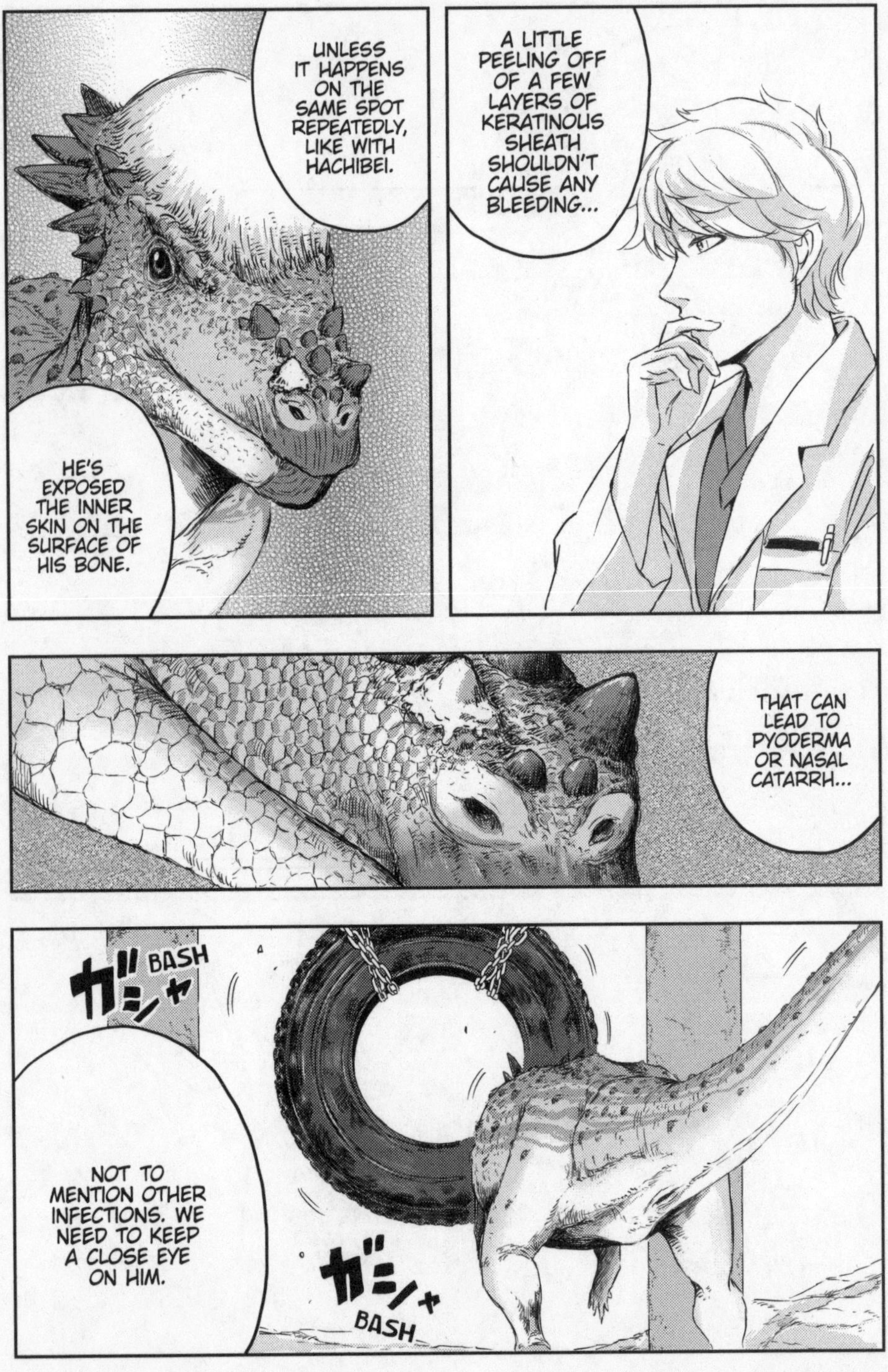
A LITTLE PEELING OFF OF A FEW LAYERS OF KERATINOUS SHEATH SHOULDN'T CAUSE ANY BLEEDING...
UNLESS IT HAPPENS ON THE SAME SPOT REPEATEDLY, LIKE WITH HACHIBEI.
HE'S EXPOSED THE INNER SKIN ON THE SURFACE OF HIS BONE.
THAT CAN LEAD TO PYODERMA OR NASAL CATARRH...
ガシャ BASH
NOT TO MENTION OTHER INFECTIONS. WE NEED TO KEEP A CLOSE EYE ON HIM.
ガシャ BASH

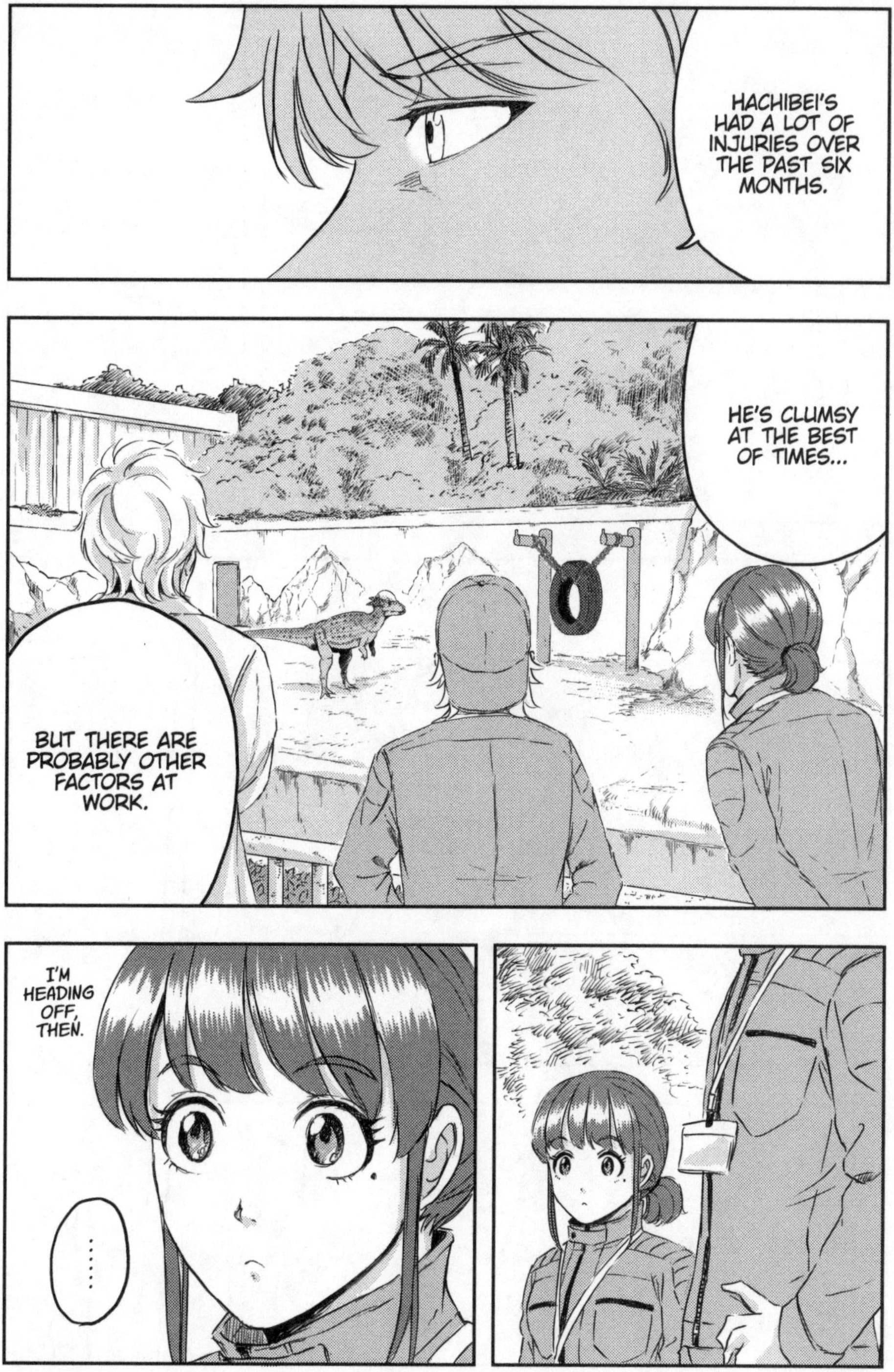
HACHIBEI'S HAD A LOT OF INJURIES OVER THE PAST SIX MONTHS.
HE'S CLUMSY AT THE BEST OF TIMES...
BUT THERE ARE PROBABLY OTHER FACTORS AT WORK.
I'M HEADING OFF, THEN.
......

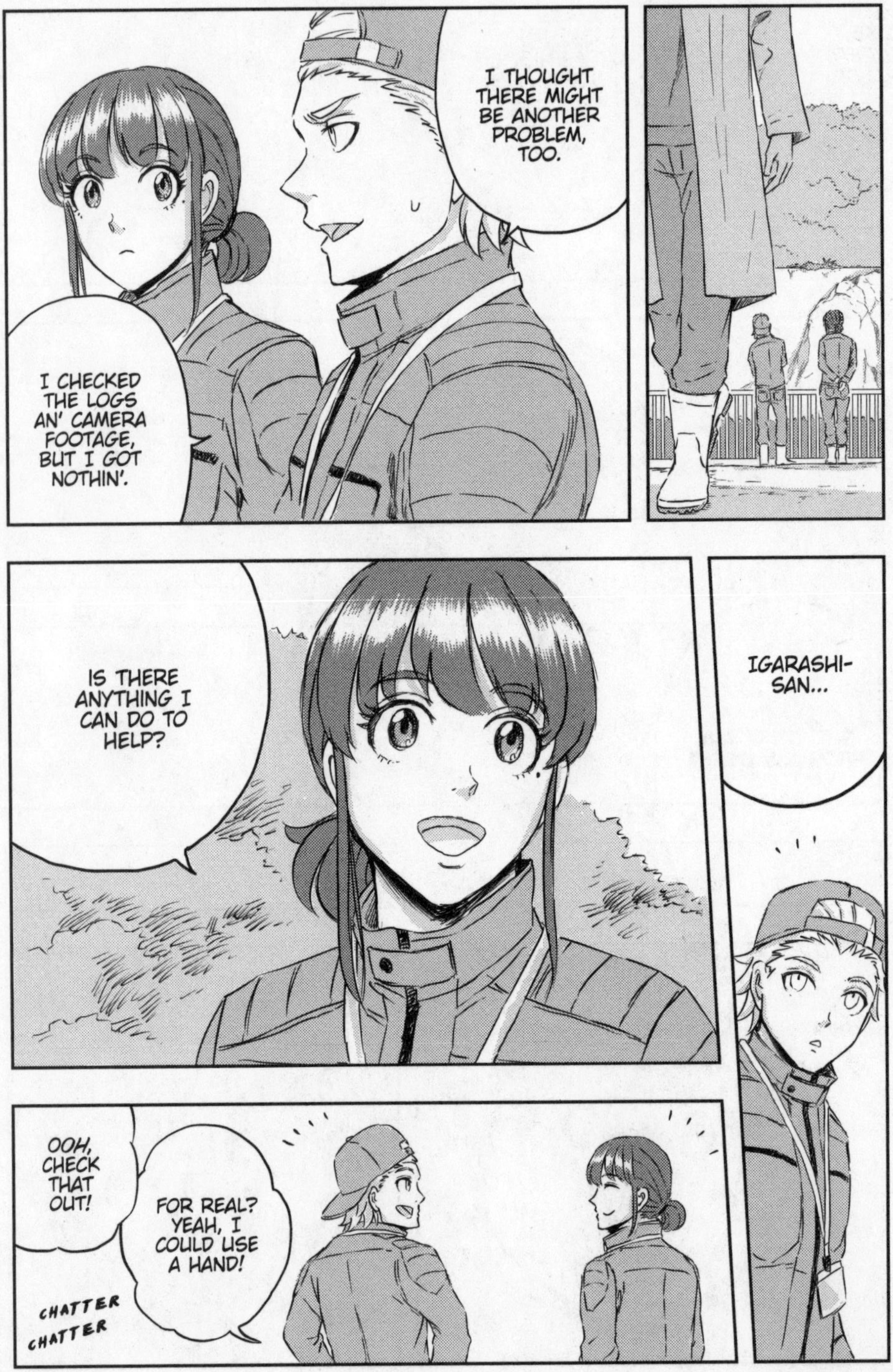
I THOUGHT THERE MIGHT BE ANOTHER PROBLEM, TOO.
I CHECKED THE LOGS AN' CAMERA FOOTAGE, BUT I GOT NOTHIN'.
IGARASHI-SAN...
IS THERE ANYTHING I CAN DO TO HELP?
FOR REAL? YEAH, I COULD USE A HAND!
OOH, CHECK THAT OUT!
CHATTER CHATTER

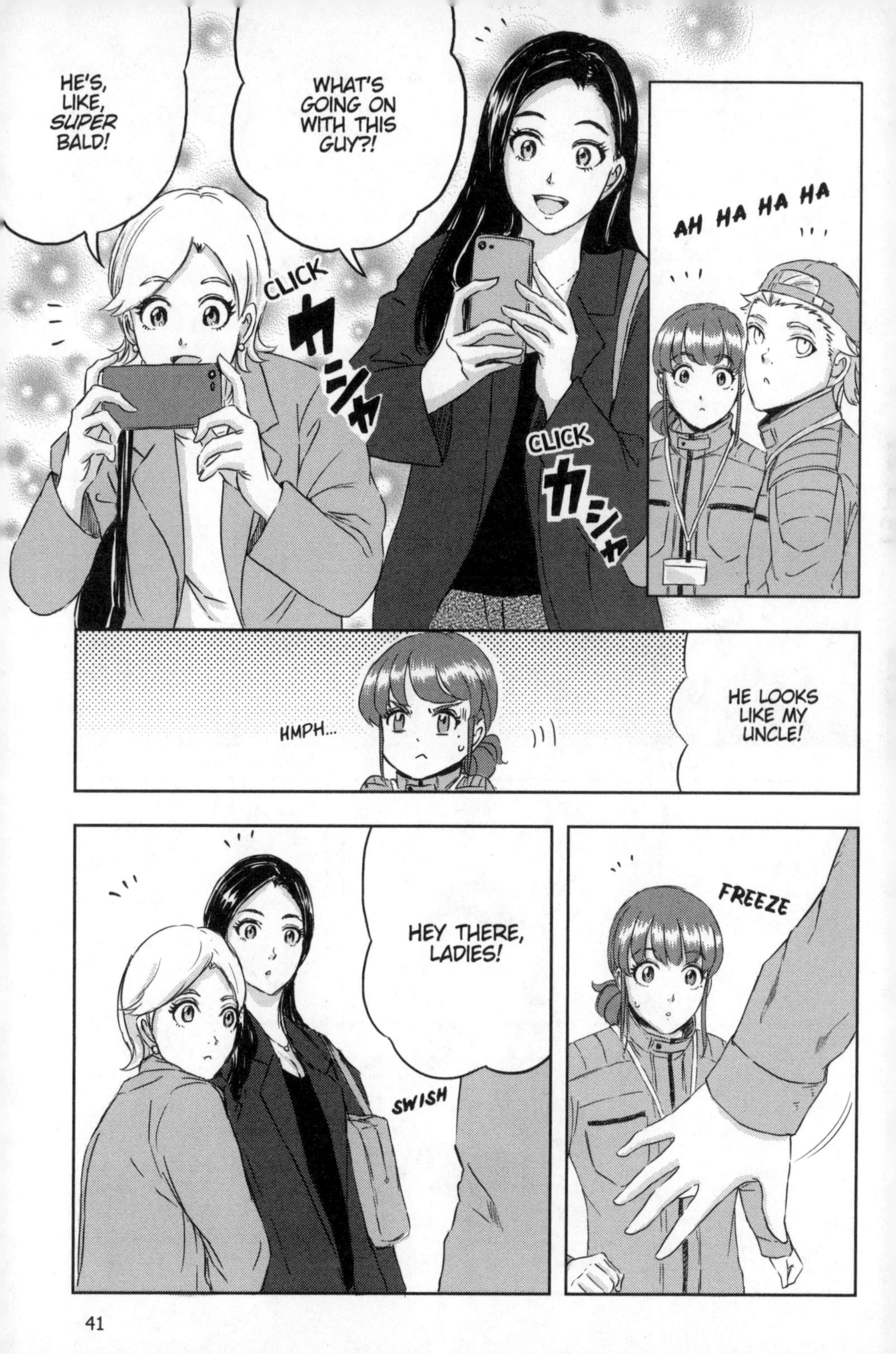
AH HA HA HA
WHAT'S GOING ON WITH THIS GUY?!
HE'S, LIKE, SUPER BALD!
CLICK
CLICK
HE LOOKS LIKE MY UNCLE!
HMPH...
FREEZE
HEY THERE, LADIES!
SWISH

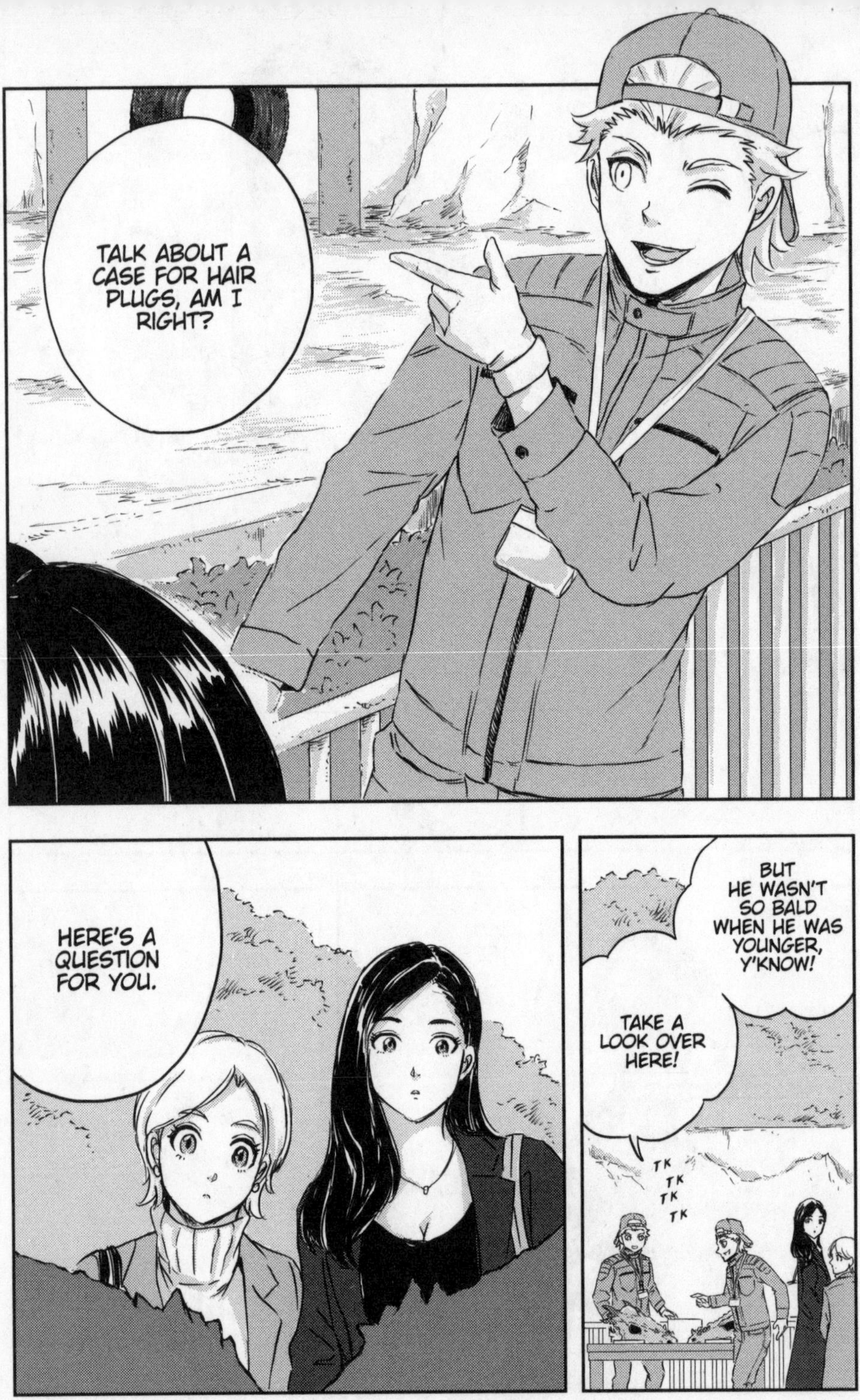
TALK ABOUT A CASE FOR HAIR PLUGS, AM I RIGHT?
BUT HE WASN'T SO BALD WHEN HE WAS YOUNGER, Y'KNOW!
TAKE A LOOK OVER HERE!
TK TK TK TK
HERE'S A QUESTION FOR YOU.

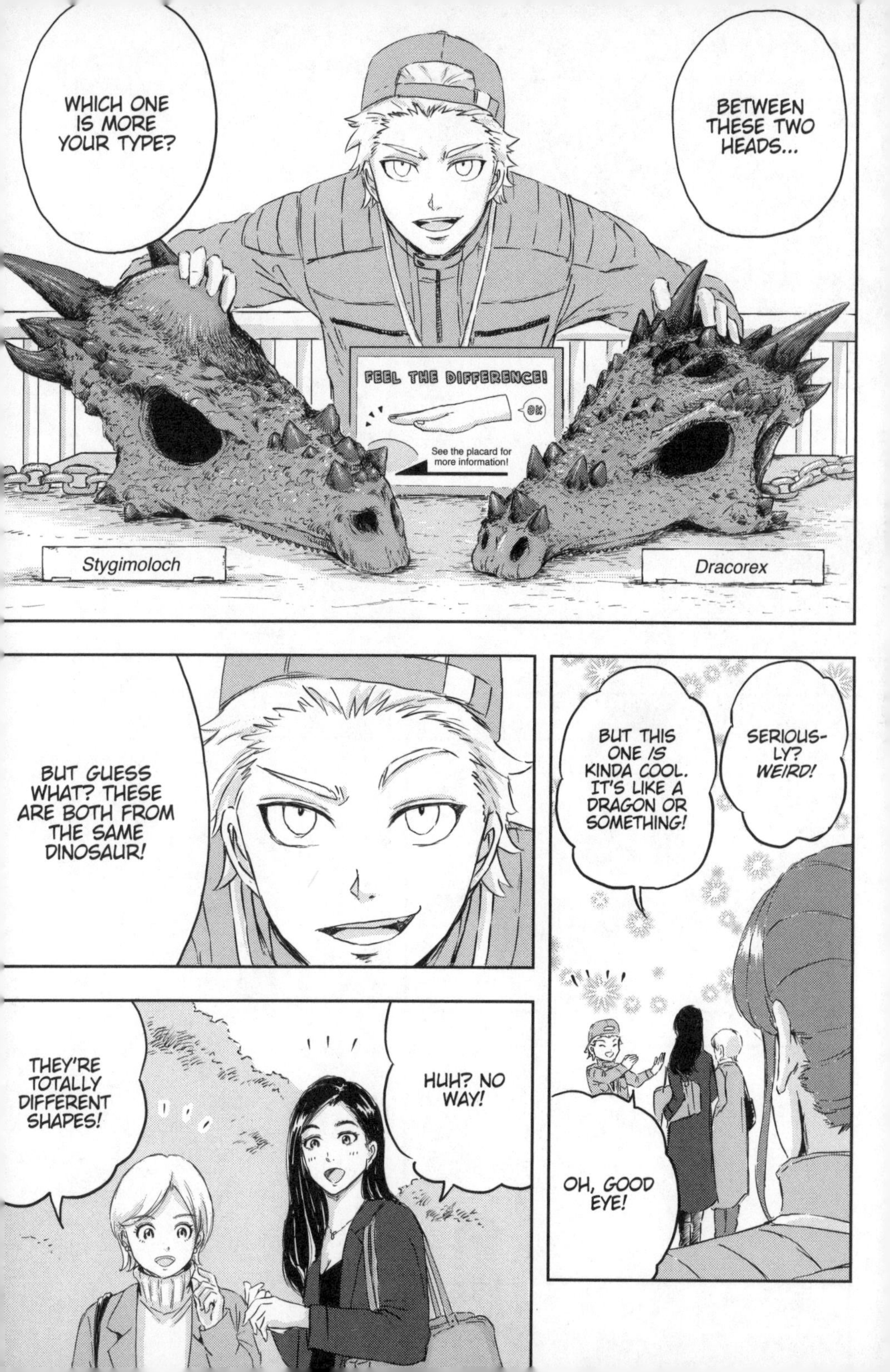
BETWEEN THESE TWO HEADS...
WHICH ONE IS MORE YOUR TYPE?
FEEL THE DIFFERENCE!
OK
See the placard for more information!
Stygimoloch
Dracorex
BUT GUESS WHAT? THESE ARE BOTH FROM THE SAME DINOSAUR!
HUH? NO WAY!
THEY'RE TOTALLY DIFFERENT SHAPES!
SERIOUS-LY? *WEIRD!*
BUT THIS ONE *IS* KINDA COOL. IT'S LIKE A DRAGON OR SOMETHING!
OH, GOOD EYE!

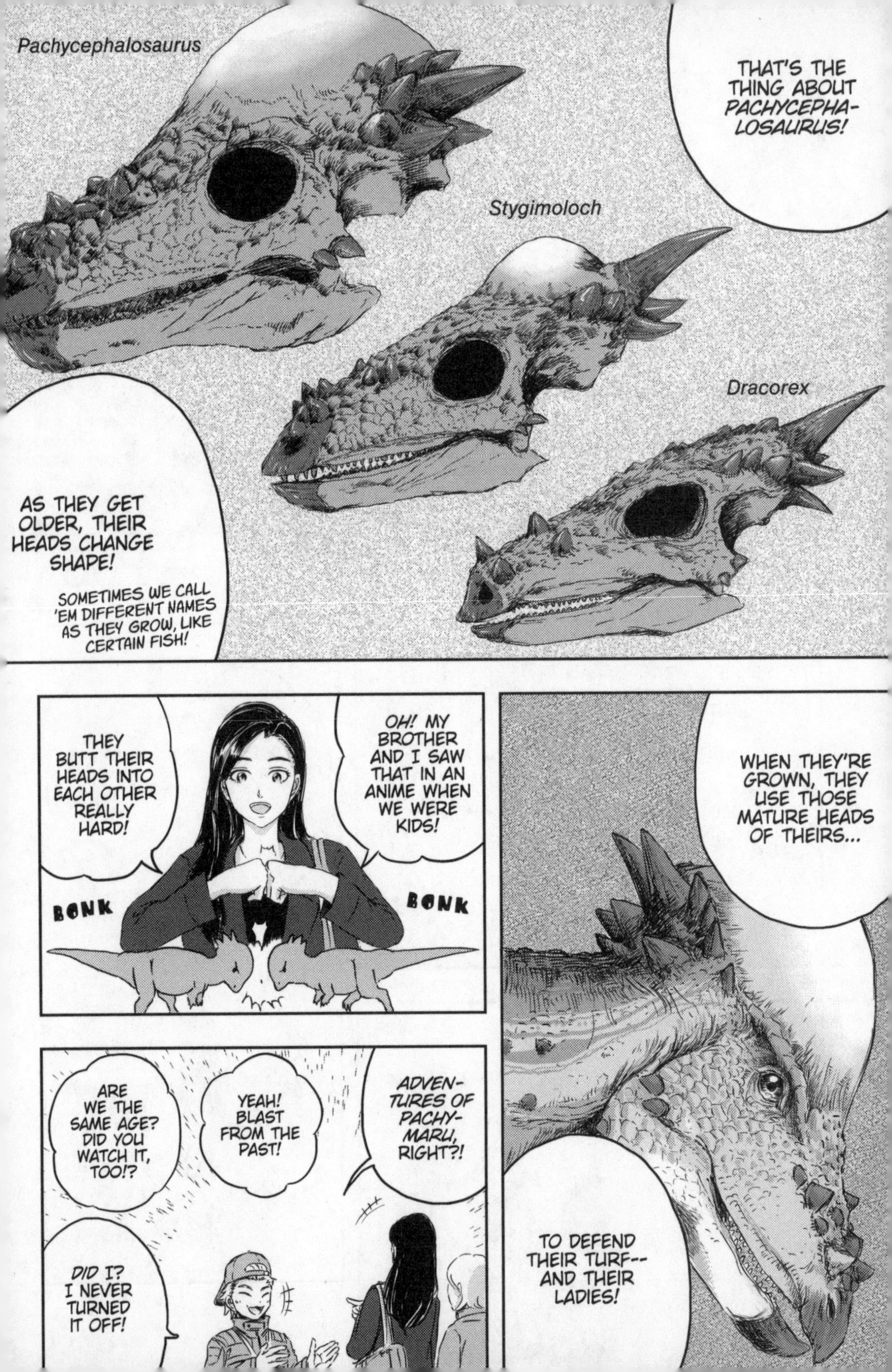
THAT'S THE THING ABOUT PACHYCEPHALOSAURUS!
Pachycephalosaurus
Stygimoloch
Dracorex
AS THEY GET OLDER, THEIR HEADS CHANGE SHAPE!
SOMETIMES WE CALL 'EM DIFFERENT NAMES AS THEY GROW, LIKE CERTAIN FISH!
WHEN THEY'RE GROWN, THEY USE THOSE MATURE HEADS OF THEIRS...
TO DEFEND THEIR TURF-- AND THEIR LADIES!
THEY BUTT THEIR HEADS INTO EACH OTHER REALLY HARD!
OH! MY BROTHER AND I SAW THAT IN AN ANIME WHEN WE WERE KIDS!
BONK
BONK
ADVENTURES OF PACHYMARU, RIGHT?!
YEAH! BLAST FROM THE PAST!
ARE WE THE SAME AGE? DID YOU WATCH IT, TOO!?
DID I? I NEVER TURNED IT OFF!

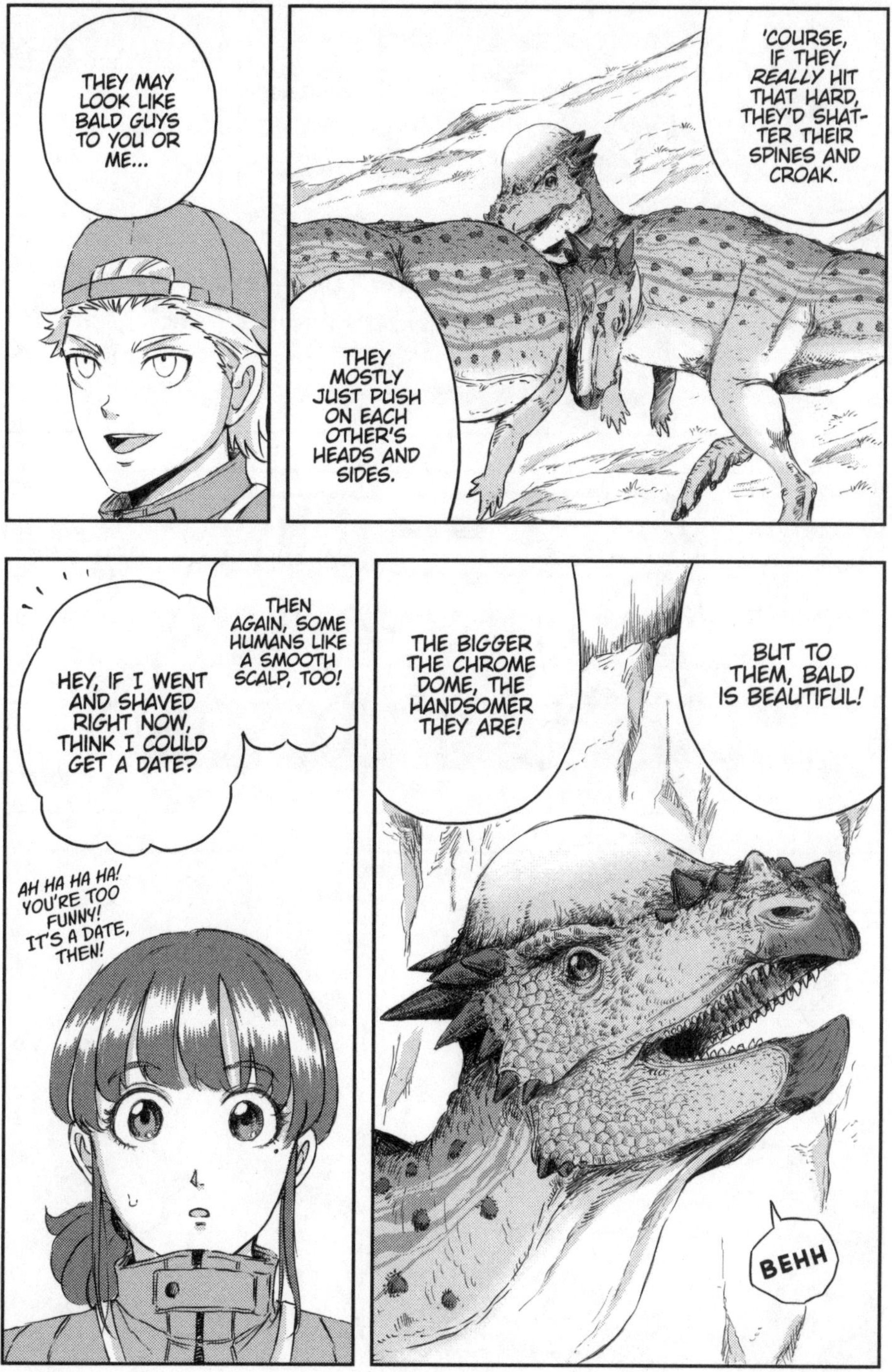
'COURSE, IF THEY REALLY HIT THAT HARD, THEY'D SHATTER THEIR SPINES AND CROAK.
THEY MOSTLY JUST PUSH ON EACH OTHER'S HEADS AND SIDES.
THEY MAY LOOK LIKE BALD GUYS TO YOU OR ME...
BUT TO THEM, BALD IS BEAUTIFUL!
THE BIGGER THE CHROME DOME, THE HANDSOMER THEY ARE!
BEHH
THEN AGAIN, SOME HUMANS LIKE A SMOOTH SCALP, TOO!
HEY, IF I WENT AND SHAVED RIGHT NOW, THINK I COULD GET A DATE?
AH HA HA HA! YOU'RE TOO FUNNY! IT'S A DATE, THEN!

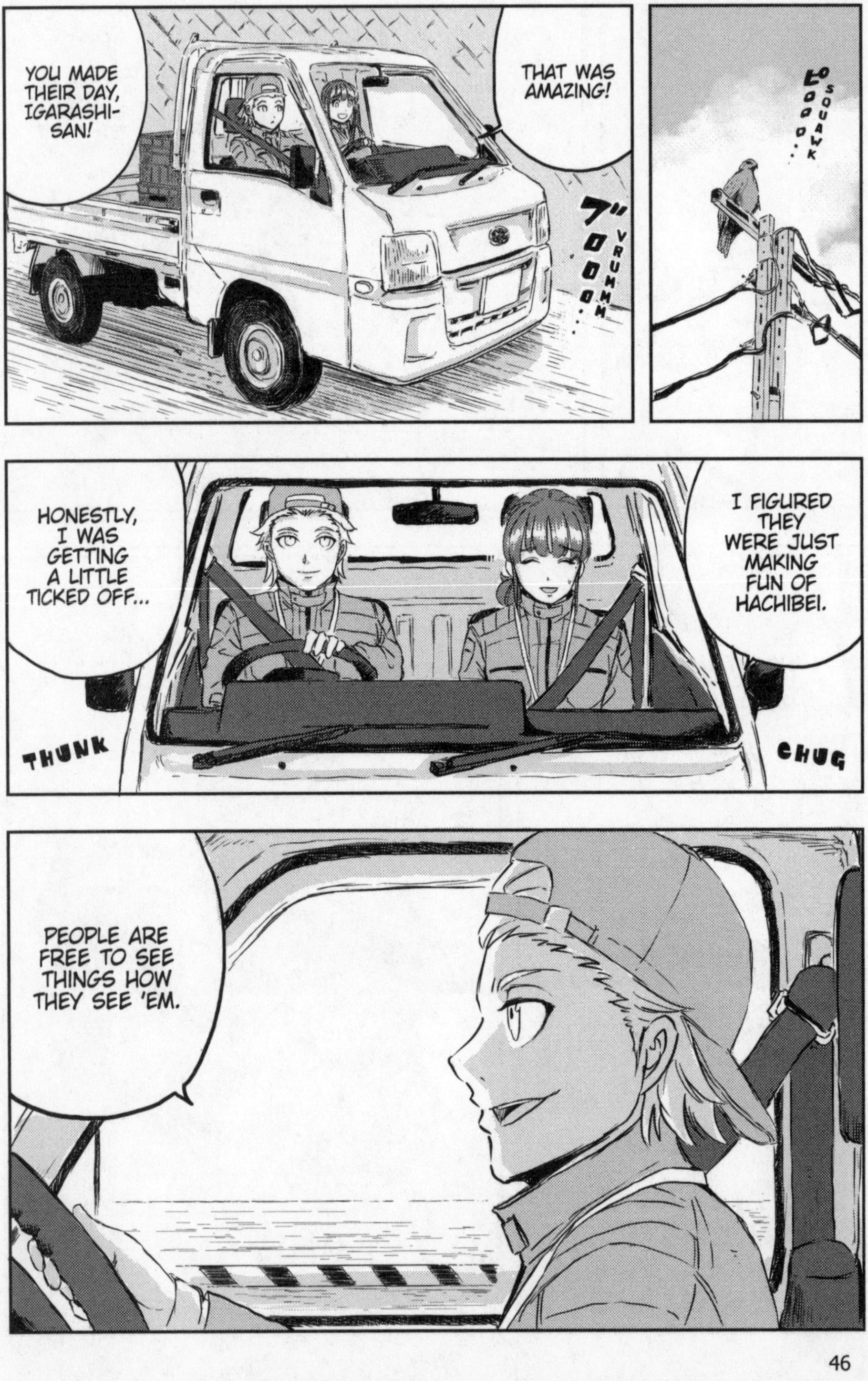
SQUAWK
THAT WAS AMAZING!
YOU MADE THEIR DAY, IGARASHI-SAN!
VRUMMM...
I FIGURED THEY WERE JUST MAKING FUN OF HACHIBEI.
HONESTLY, I WAS GETTING A LITTLE TICKED OFF...
CHUG
THUNK
PEOPLE ARE FREE TO SEE THINGS HOW THEY SEE 'EM.

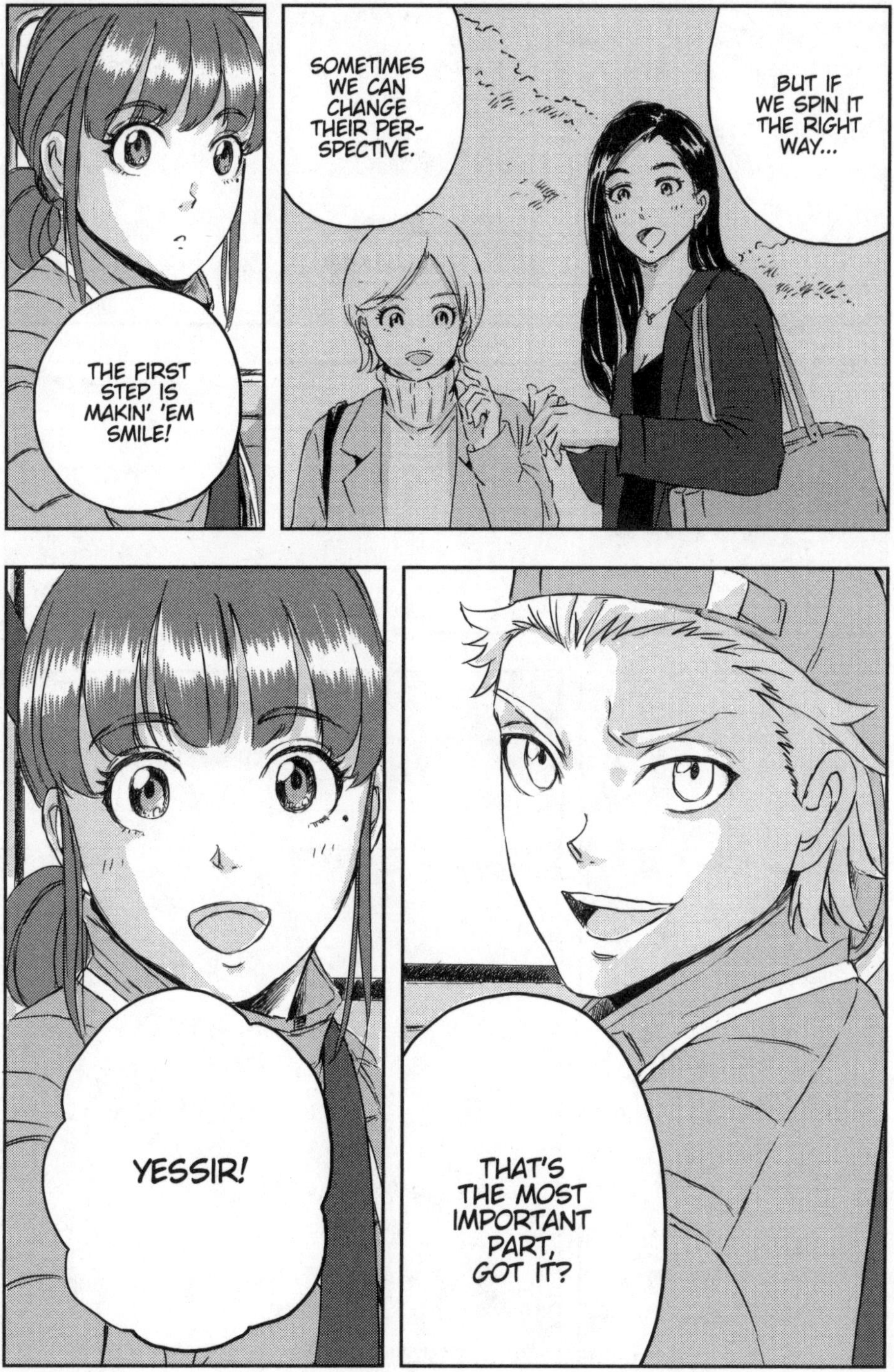
BUT IF WE SPIN IT THE RIGHT WAY...
SOMETIMES WE CAN CHANGE THEIR PER-SPECTIVE.
THE FIRST STEP IS MAKIN' 'EM SMILE!
THAT'S THE MOST IMPORTANT PART, GOT IT?
YESSIR!

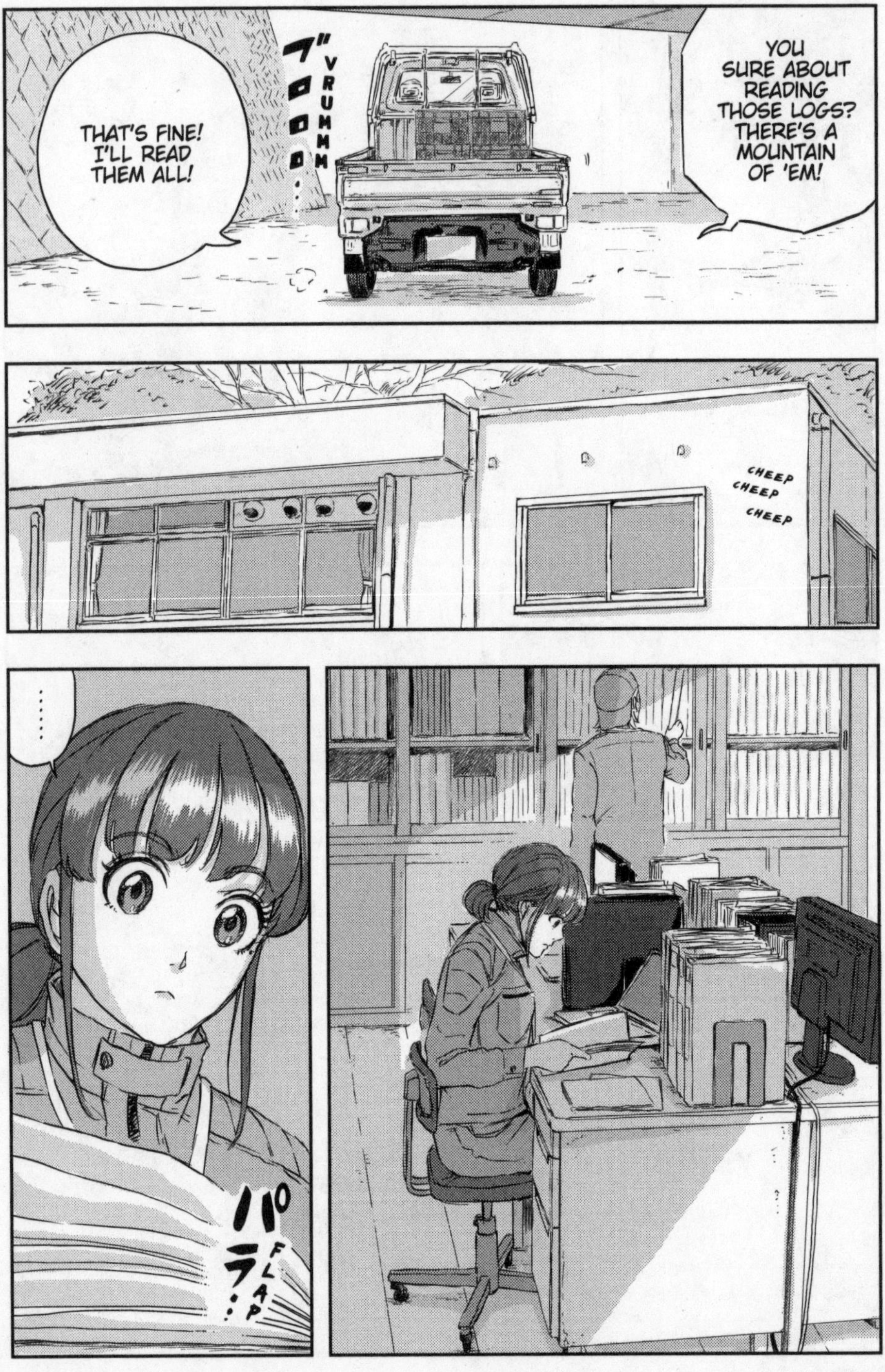
YOU SURE ABOUT READING THOSE LOGS? THERE'S A MOUNTAIN OF 'EM!
ブロロロ…
VRUMMM
THAT'S FINE! I'LL READ THEM ALL!
CHEEP
CHEEP
CHEEP
……
パラ…
FLAP

AH, YEAH. THAT WAS BEFORE YOU GOT HERE.

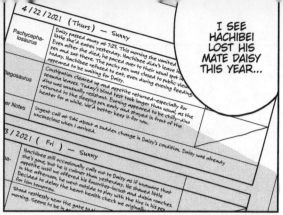

I SEE HACHIBEI LOST HIS MATE DAISY THIS YEAR...

4 / 22 / 2021 (Thurs) — Sunny

Pachycephalosaurus	Daisy passed away at 7:23. This morning she vomited a little she'd eaten yesterday. Even after she died, he paced over to their pen and sat there. The pen was closed to public view today. Hachibee refused to eat, even during evening feeding, appeared to be waiting for Daisy.
Stegosaurus	Constipation cleared up and appetite returned—especially for seaweed leaves. Today's blood test took longer than usual, dino also was unusually resistant. Evening appeared to be chilly, dino returned to the sleeping pen early and stayed in front of the heater for a while. We'd better keep it for now.
Other Notes	Urgent call at 5:46 about a sudden change in Daisy's condition. Daisy was already unconscious when I arrived.

3 / 2021 (Fri) — Sunny

Hachibee still occasionally calls out to Daisy as if unaware that she's gone, but he is calmer than yesterday. He showed little appetite until we offered his favorites—locust and dubia roaches. In the afternoon, he spent some time outside to play with the tire in his pen. Decided to delay the heart health check we originally planned for him tomorrow. Stood restlessly near the gate this morning. Seems to be in...

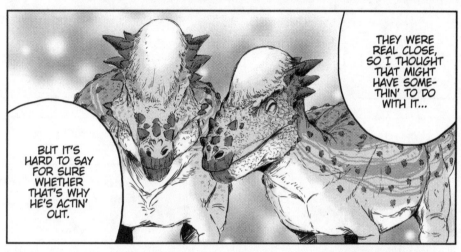

THEY WERE REAL CLOSE, SO I THOUGHT THAT MIGHT HAVE SOMETHIN' TO DO WITH IT...

BUT IT'S HARD TO SAY FOR SURE WHETHER THAT'S WHY HE'S ACTIN' OUT.

CAM02

GLANCE

I SEE...

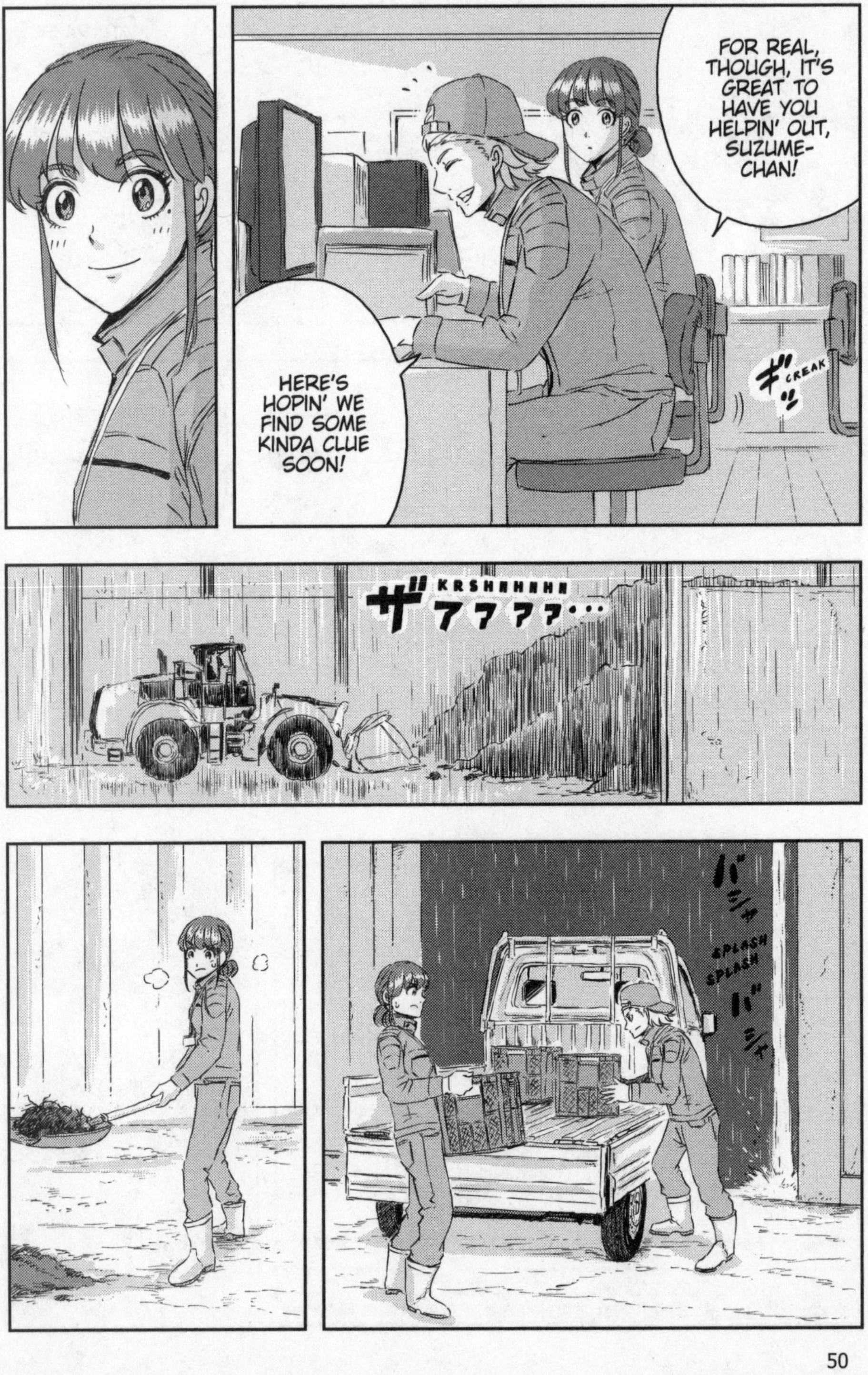
FOR REAL, THOUGH, IT'S GREAT TO HAVE YOU HELPIN' OUT, SUZUME-CHAN!
HERE'S HOPIN' WE FIND SOME KINDA CLUE SOON!
ギッ CREAK
ザァァァァ… KRSHHHHHHH
バシャ SPLASH
SPLASH バシャ

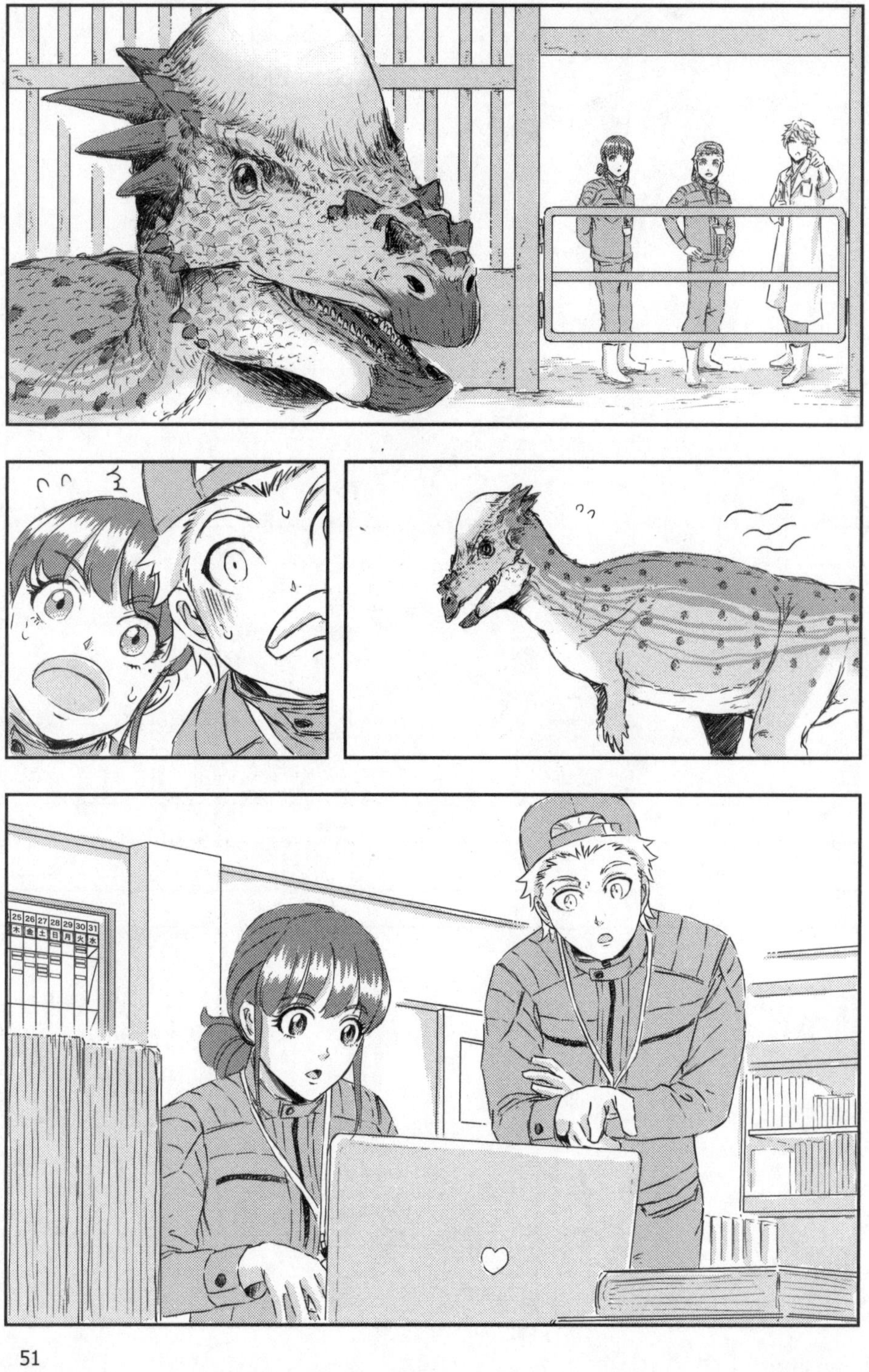
25 26 27 28 29 30 31
木 金 土 日 月 火 水

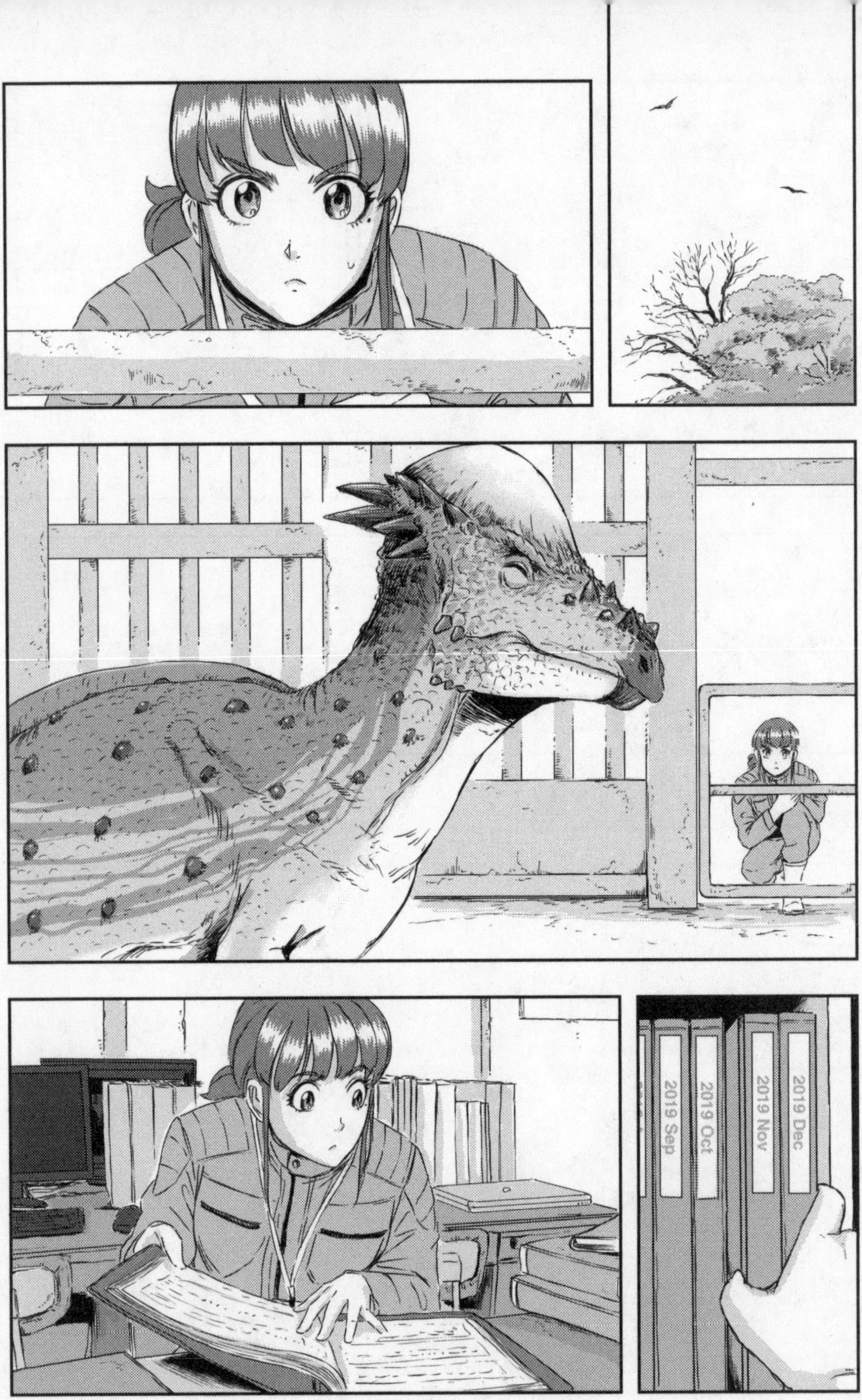
2019 Sep
2019 Oct
2019 Nov
2019 Dec

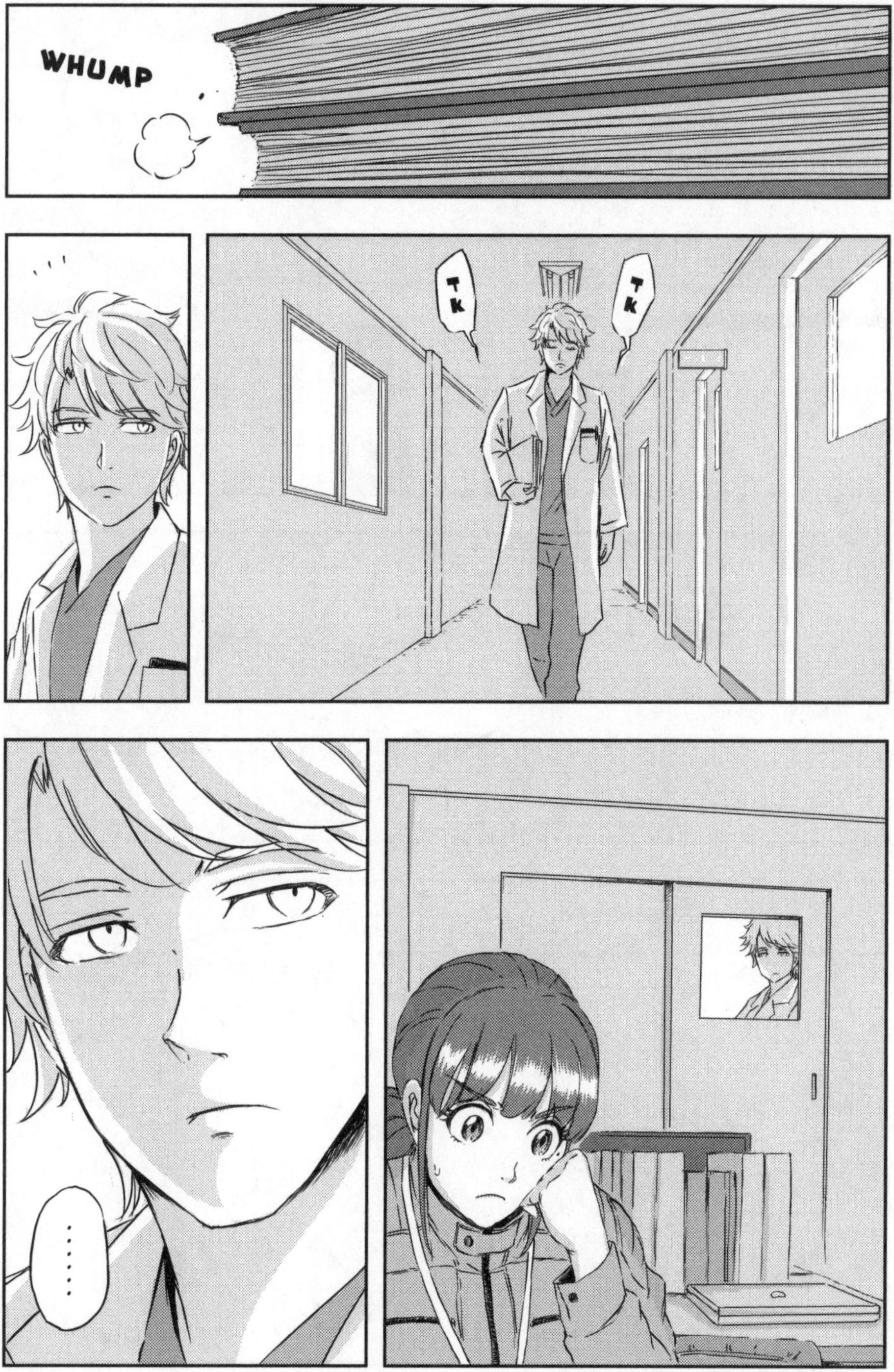
WHUMP
TK
TK
......

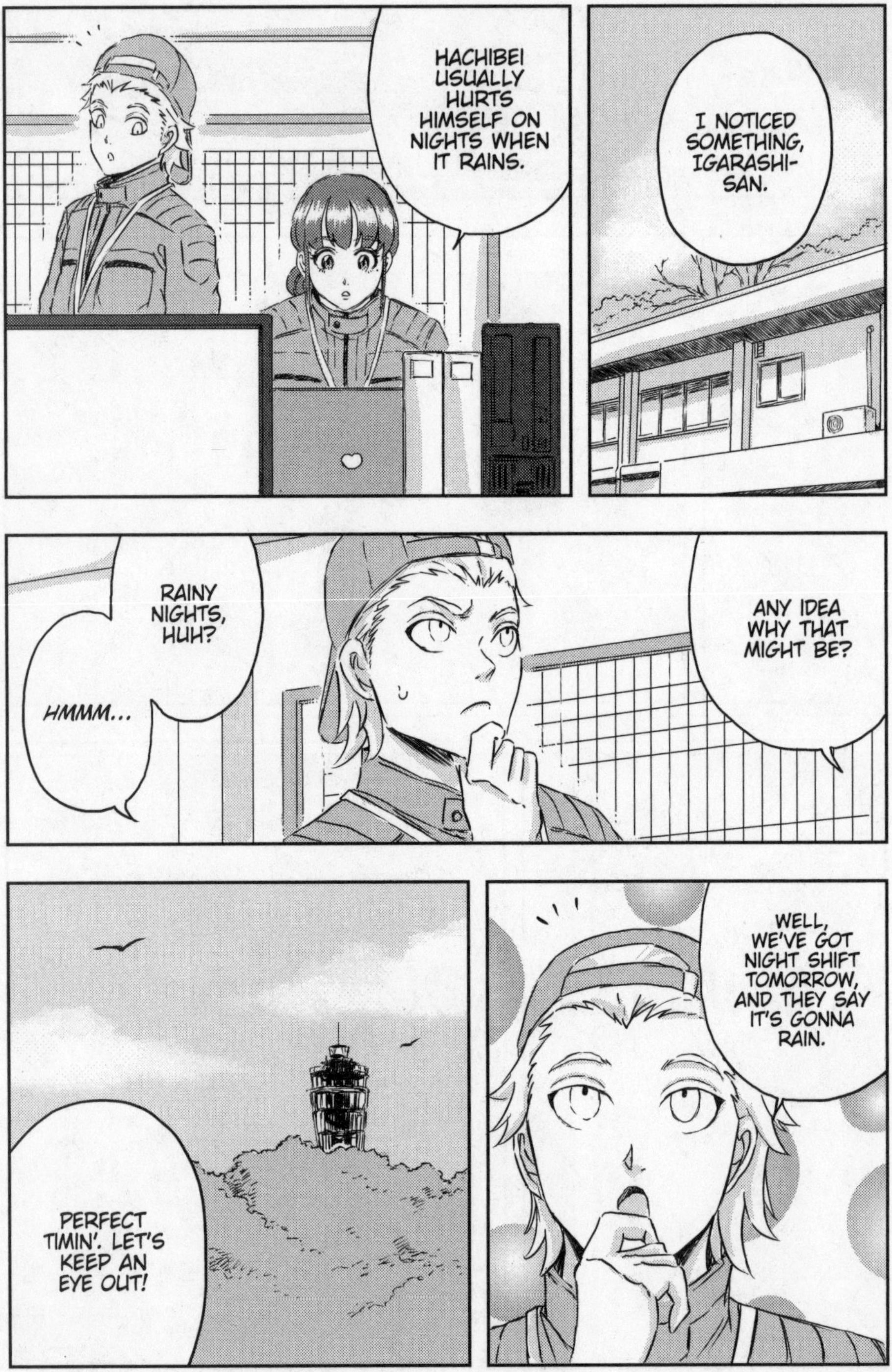
I NOTICED SOMETHING, IGARASHI-SAN.
HACHIBEI USUALLY HURTS HIMSELF ON NIGHTS WHEN IT RAINS.
ANY IDEA WHY THAT MIGHT BE?
RAINY NIGHTS, HUH?
HMMM...
WELL, WE'VE GOT NIGHT SHIFT TOMORROW, AND THEY SAY IT'S GONNA RAIN.
PERFECT TIMIN'. LET'S KEEP AN EYE OUT!

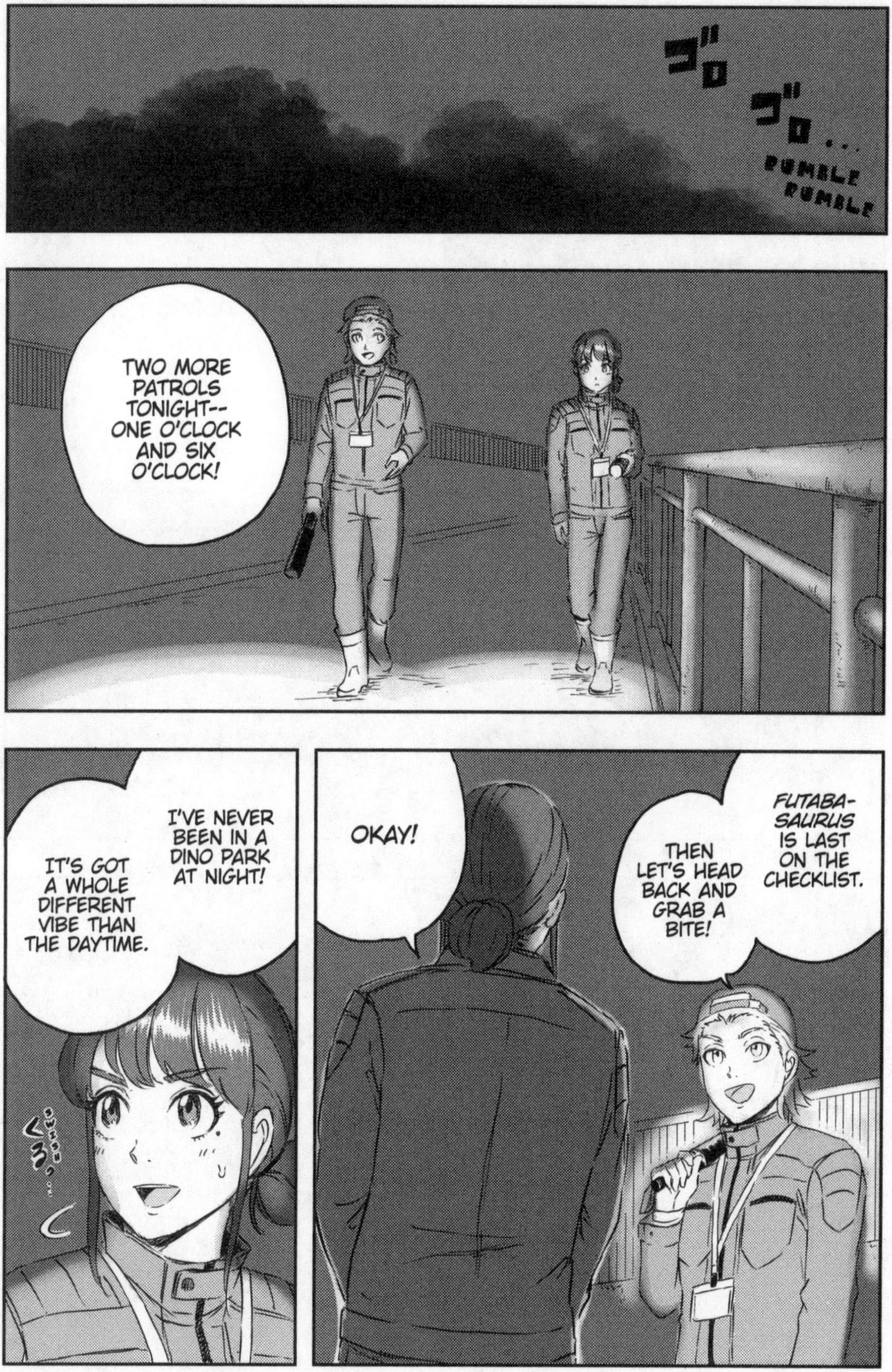
ゴロ ゴロ...
RUMBLE RUMBLE
TWO MORE PATROLS TONIGHT-- ONE O'CLOCK AND SIX O'CLOCK!
FUTABASAURUS IS LAST ON THE CHECKLIST.
THEN LET'S HEAD BACK AND GRAB A BITE!
OKAY!
I'VE NEVER BEEN IN A DINO PARK AT NIGHT!
IT'S GOT A WHOLE DIFFERENT VIBE THAN THE DAYTIME.

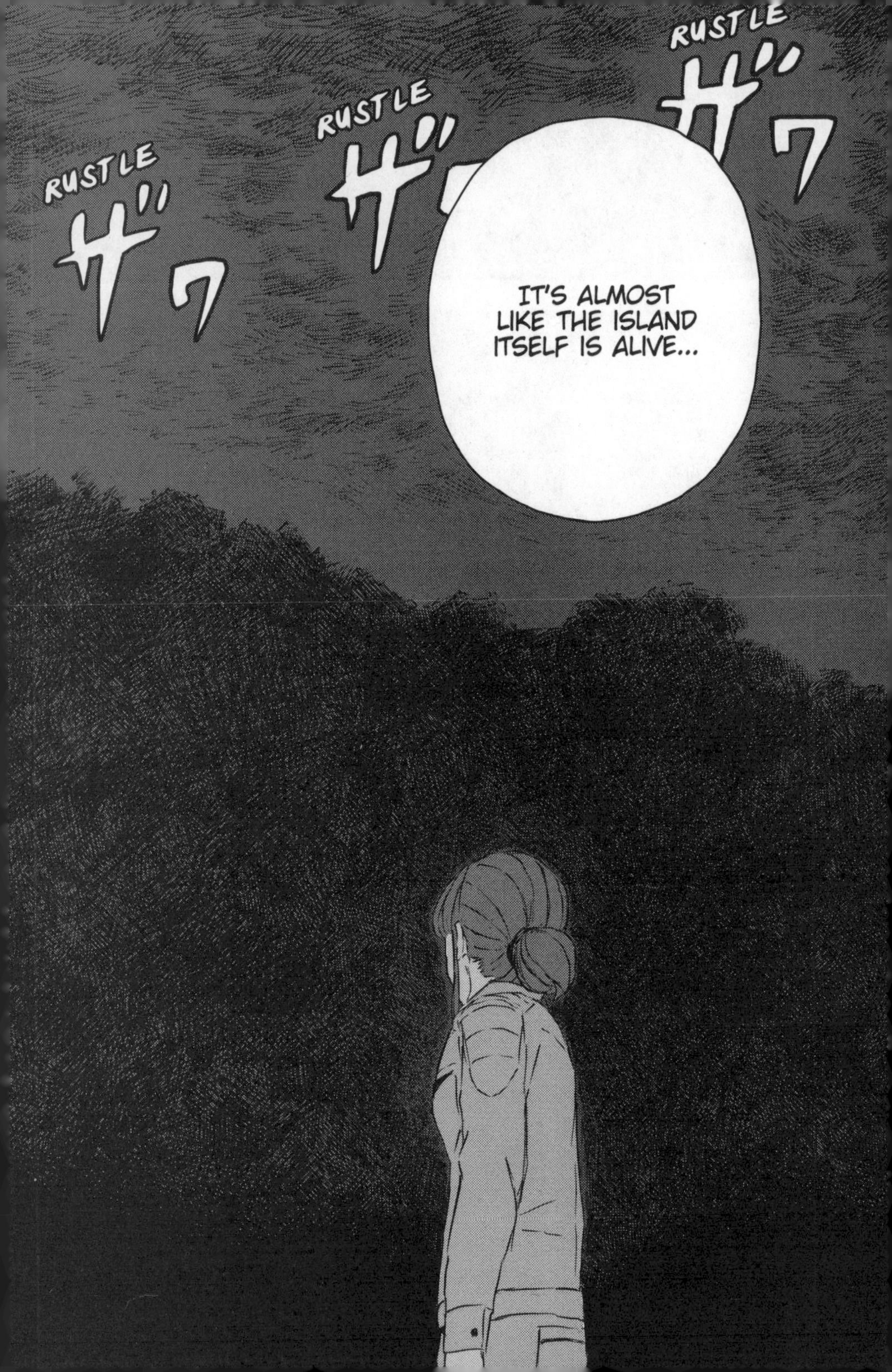
RUSTLE
ザワ
RUSTLE
ザワ
RUSTLE
ザワ
IT'S ALMOST LIKE THE ISLAND ITSELF IS ALIVE...

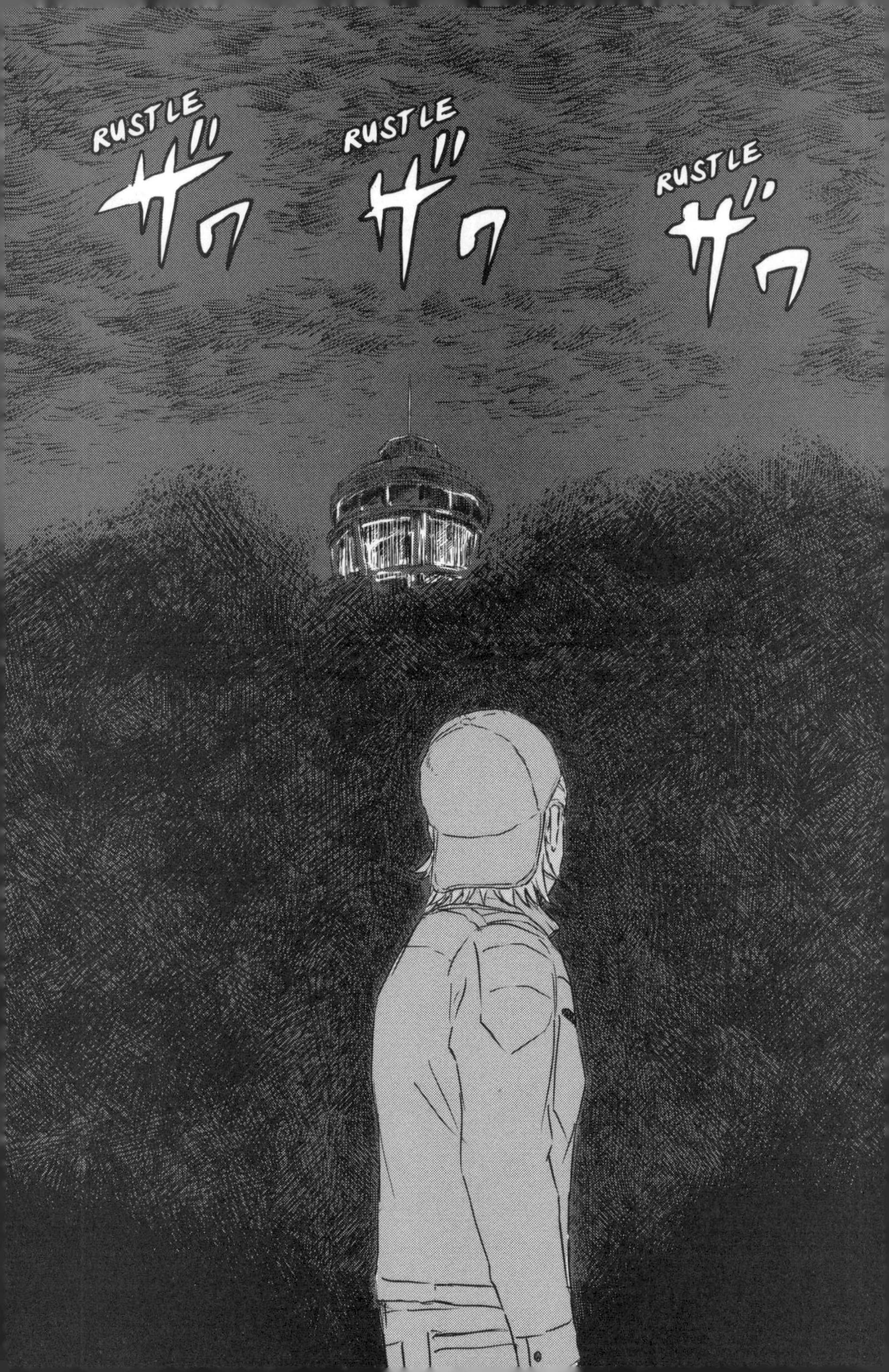
RUSTLE
ザワ
RUSTLE
ザワ
RUSTLE
ザワ

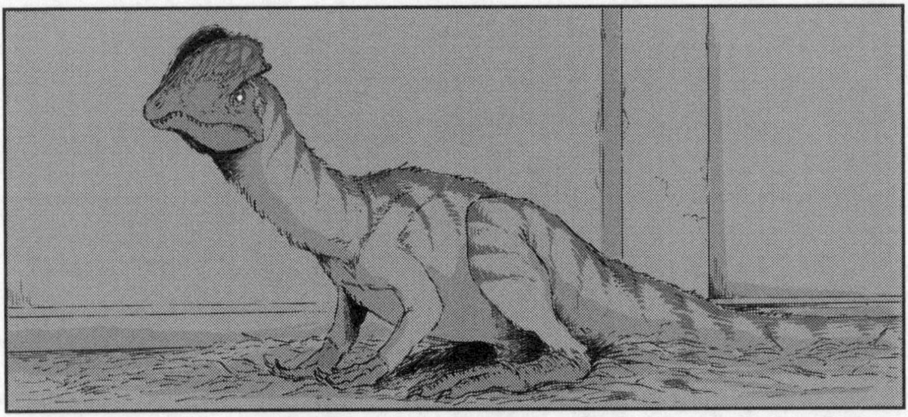
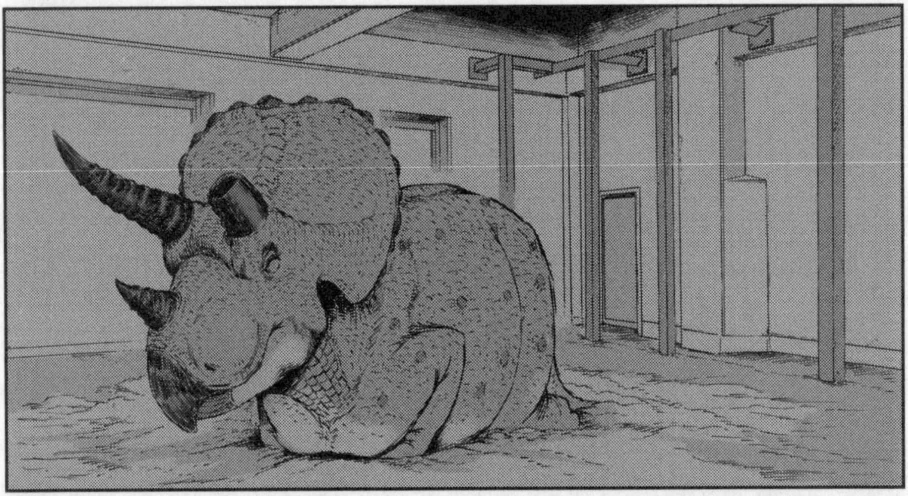
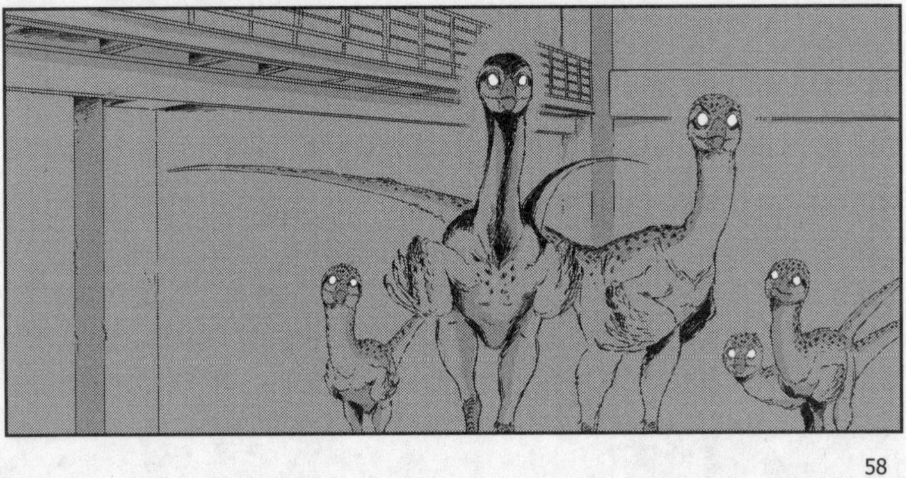

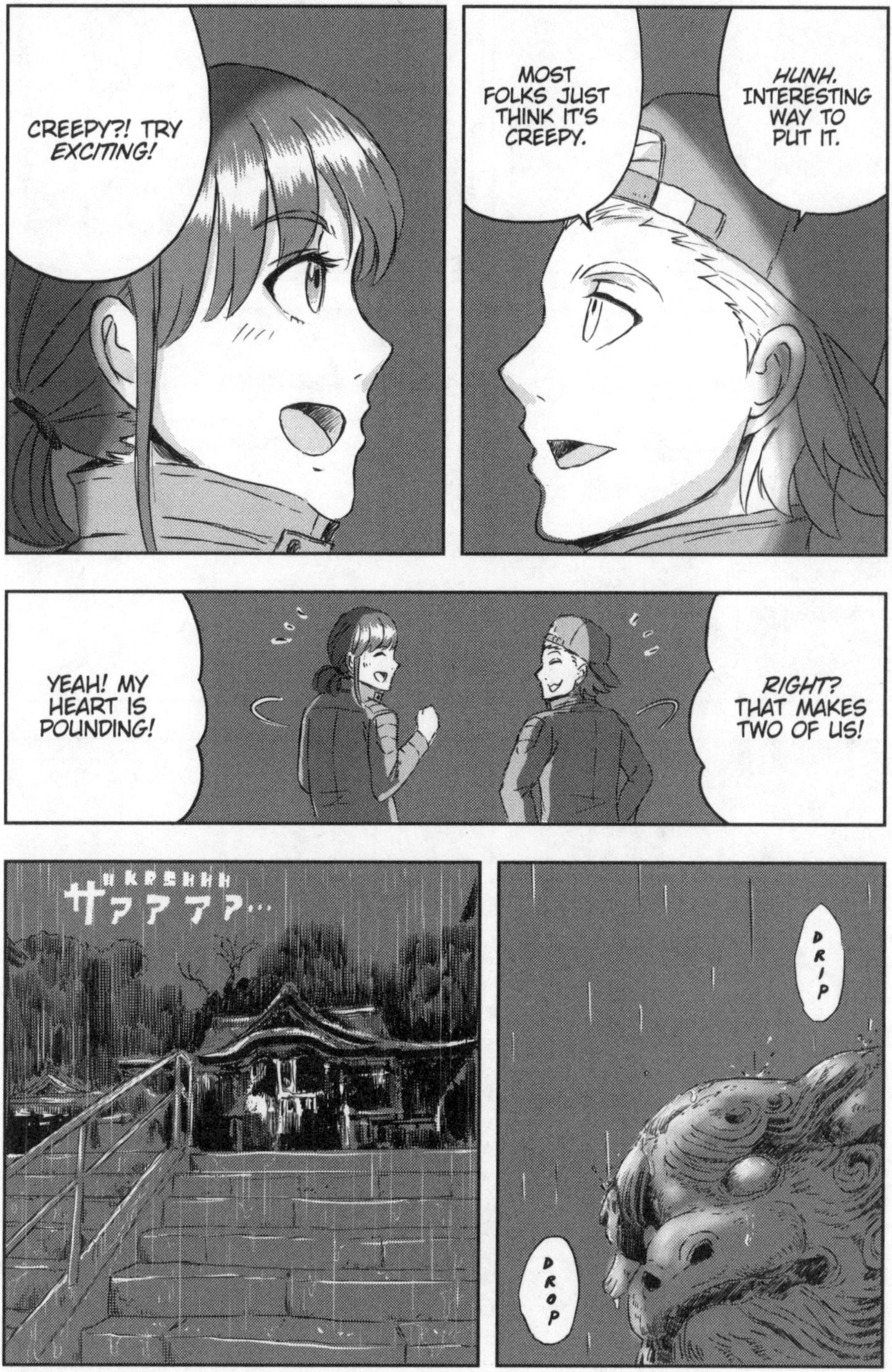
HUNH. INTERESTING WAY TO PUT IT.
MOST FOLKS JUST THINK IT'S CREEPY.
CREEPY?! TRY *EXCITING!*
RIGHT? THAT MAKES TWO OF US!
YEAH! MY HEART IS POUNDING!
DRIP
DROP
サァァァァ…

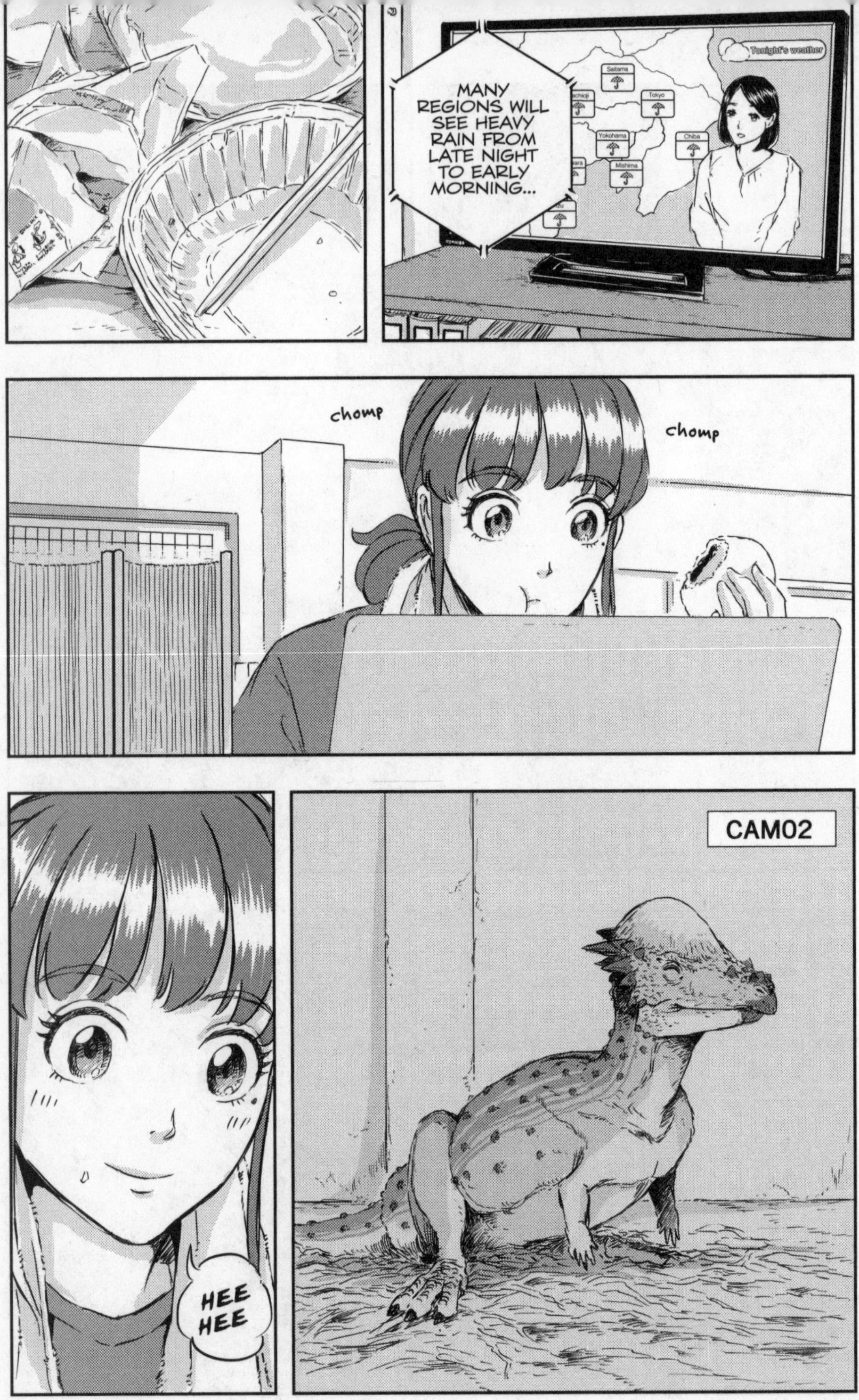
Tonight's weather
Saitama
Tokyo
Yokohama
Chiba
Mishima
MANY REGIONS WILL SEE HEAVY RAIN FROM LATE NIGHT TO EARLY MORNING...
chomp
chomp
CAM02
HEE HEE

OKAY!
I WILL!

AWRIGHT, I'M GET-TIN' SOME SHUT-EYE.

WE'VE GOT A WHILE 'TIL OUR NEXT PATROL.

REST UP IN THE NAP ROOM, 'KAY?

TICK

TOCK

EMPIRE

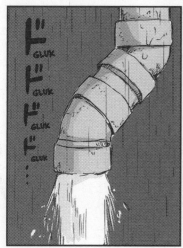

GLUK

GLUK

GLUK

...GLUK

ザ KRSSHHHHH
アァァァ..

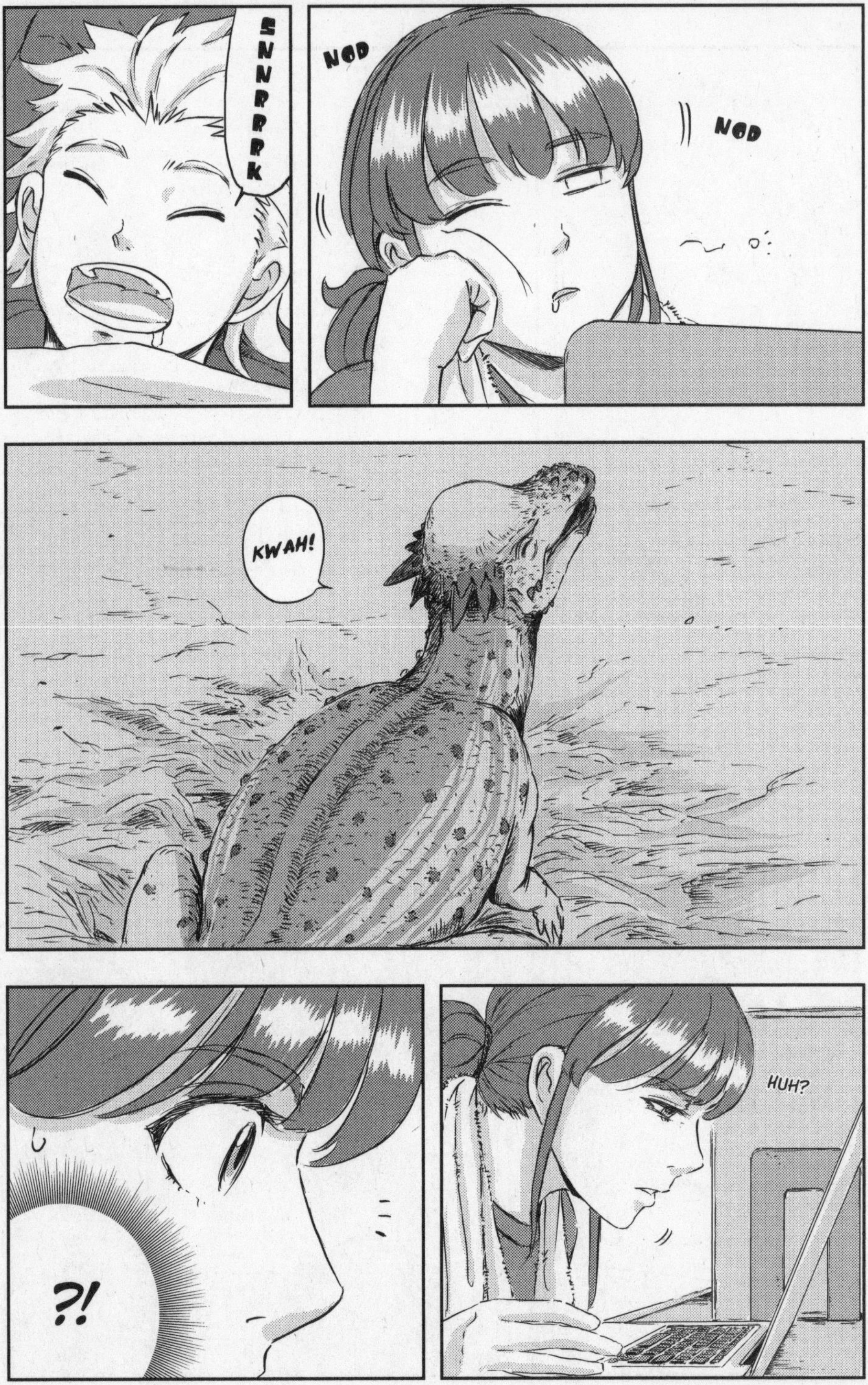
NOD
NOD
SNNRRRK
KWAH!
HUH?
?!

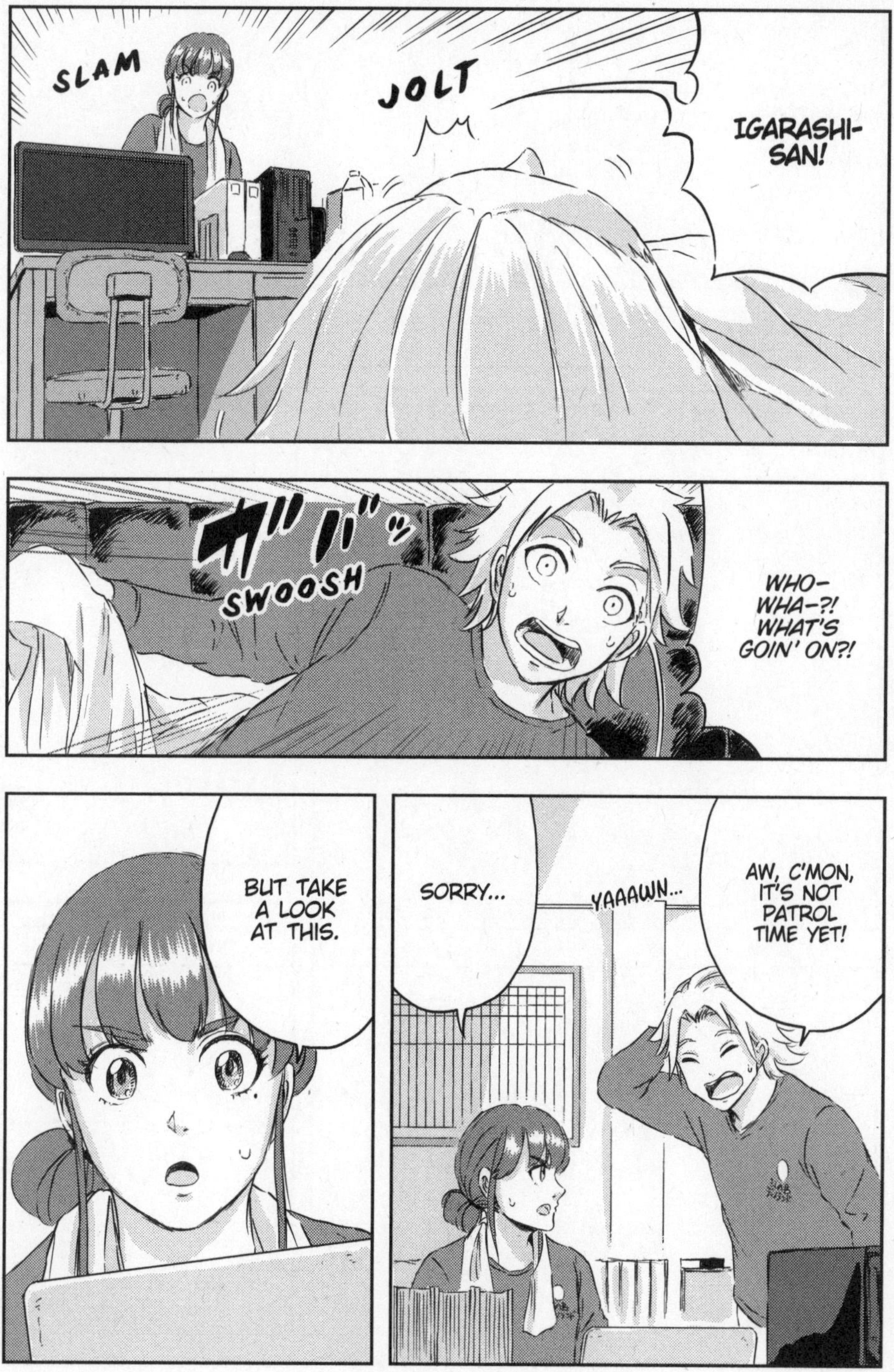
IGARASHI-SAN!
JOLT
SLAM
WHO-WHA-?! WHAT'S GOIN' ON?!
SWOOSH
AW, C'MON, IT'S NOT PATROL TIME YET!
YAAAWN...
SORRY...
BUT TAKE A LOOK AT THIS.

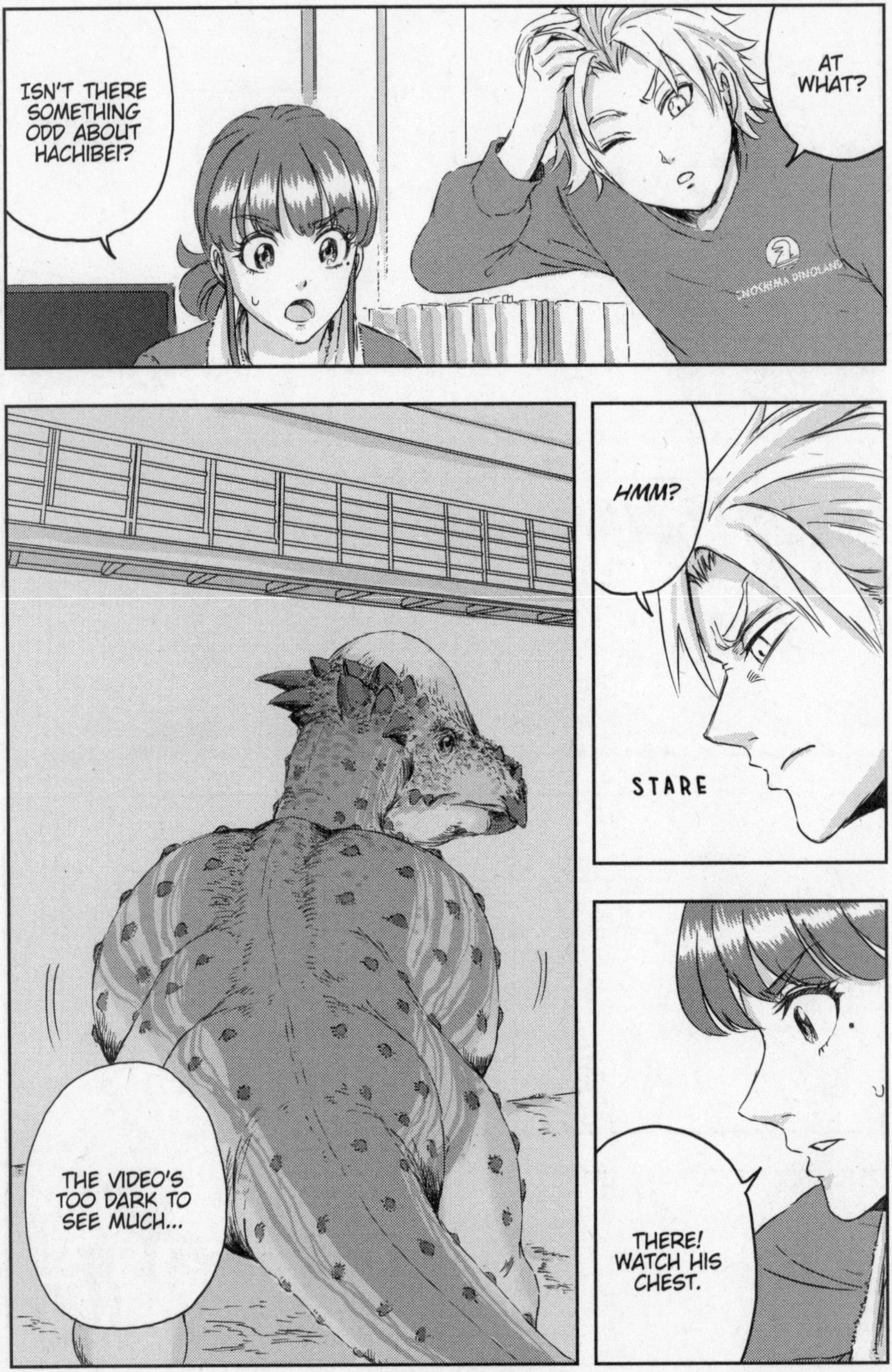
AT WHAT?
ISN'T THERE SOMETHING ODD ABOUT HACHIBEI?
HMM?
STARE
THERE! WATCH HIS CHEST.
THE VIDEO'S TOO DARK TO SEE MUCH...

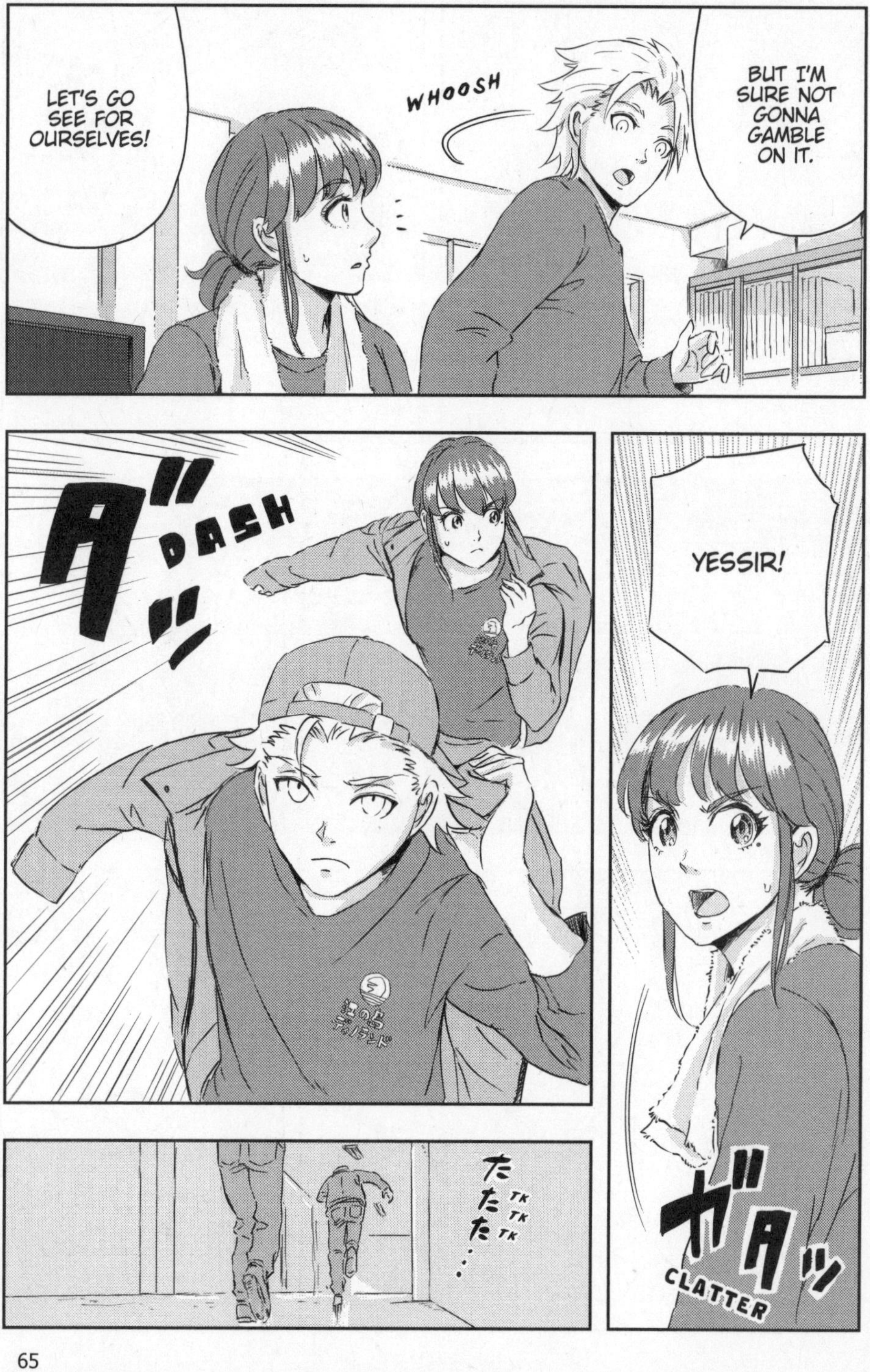
BUT I'M SURE NOT GONNA GAMBLE ON IT.
WHOOSH
LET'S GO SEE FOR OURSELVES!
YESSIR!
ガタッ
CLATTER
ダッ
DASH
たたた...
TK TK TK

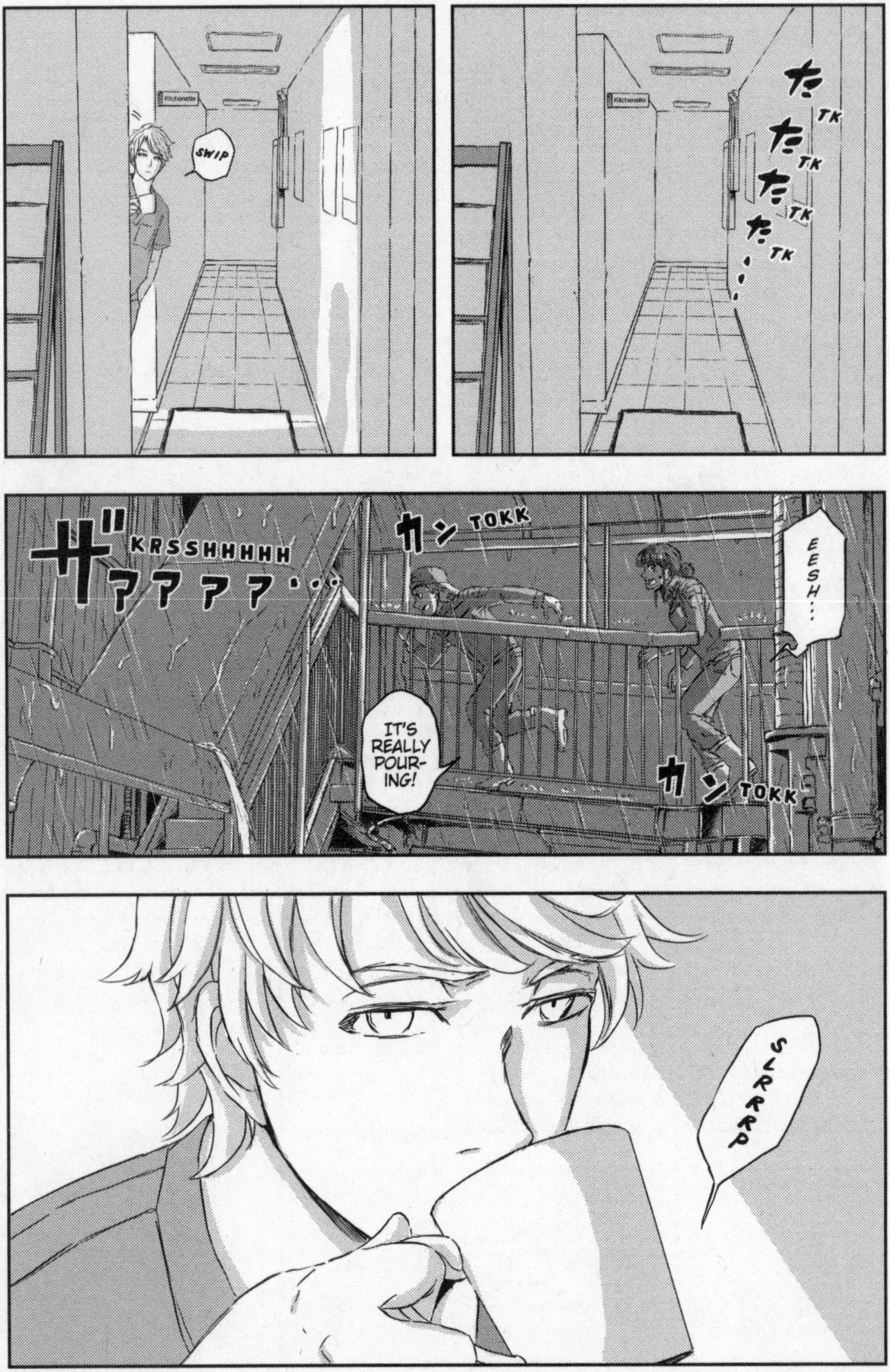
たたたた・・・
TK TK TK TK
Kitchenette
SWIP
EESH...
カン TOKK
ザァァァァ・・・ KRSSHHHHH
IT'S REALLY POURING!
カン TOKK
SLRRRP

Dr. Dino's Lab Log

FILE. 13 A Beguilingly Mysterious Dino

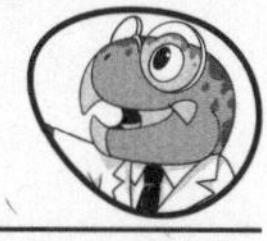

Hachibei the *Pachycephalosaurus* is a member of a clade called Pachycephalosauria. Let's break that down: "*Pachy*" means "thick," "*cephal*" means "head," and "*saur*" means "lizard." Just as the name suggests, the crowns of their heads are very thick—as you saw in the manga chapter you just read! Once you start learning where scientific names come from, you'll be able to start figuring out different animals' unique characteristics from those names alone. For example, the aforementioned "*pachy*" also appears in the names of the dinosaur *Pachyrhinosaurus* ("thick-nosed lizard") and the ammonite *Pachydiscus* ("thick disk").

Some pachycephalosaurs dwelled in what's now North America in the Maastrichtian age of the upper Cretaceous period. Scientists originally divided them into three genera—*Pachycephalosaurus, Stygimoloch,* and *Dracorex*—based on the shapes of their skulls. However, in the 2000s, a research team including the American paleontologists Jack Horner and Mark Goodwin put forth the hypothesis that these three dinosaurs were actually just different developmental stages of the same species. Their work had a major impact on how we view dinosaurs' growth cycles and the changes that came with them. If their hypothesis is correct, then as a *Pachycephalosaurus* grew, the ornamental spikes on the back of its skull gradually grew rounder and less sharp—which made it more appealing to other *Pachycephalosauruses,* if you get my drift. Wink wink, nudge nudge.

Even among dinosaurs as a whole, *Pachycephalosaurus* is particularly shrouded in mystery. Its overall shape remains something of a riddle. Plenty of specimens of their sturdy heads have been found, but comparatively little is known of their forelimbs (too bad—that's my favorite part!). In fact, their skeletal structure from the wrists down is a total enigma. Alas! When drawing them, we're forced to work from the standard dinosaur foundation of "five fingers, with claws on only three." At least for now...

On the other hand, we know that they're closely related to *Homalocephale* and similar genera, which is useful information when depicting their torsos and pelvises. The strangest part of all is that, compared to other bipedal dinosaurs, the point connecting their torsos and tails is rather broad, and their hip joints are positioned far out to the side.

Pachycephalosaurus forelimbs are rather short from the shoulders to the wrists, which suggests that they were bipedal. However, there has been no research into their walking posture thus far. Animals that walk on two legs must keep their legs under their centers of gravity, or else they'll fall over. The closer their hip joints are to that center of gravity when viewed from the front (in other words, the narrower the pelvis), the easier it is for them to shift balance between their legs and their hips, which translates to more stability during maneuvers like standing on one foot. But bipeds with their hip joints farther away from their spines must orient their trunks and angle their heels and toes properly to keep their legs under their centers of gravity. That might result in an exaggerated, pelvis-swinging, Marilyn Monroe-style walk... At least that's all I can imagine, judging from the bones. Someone, please do the research on this, already!

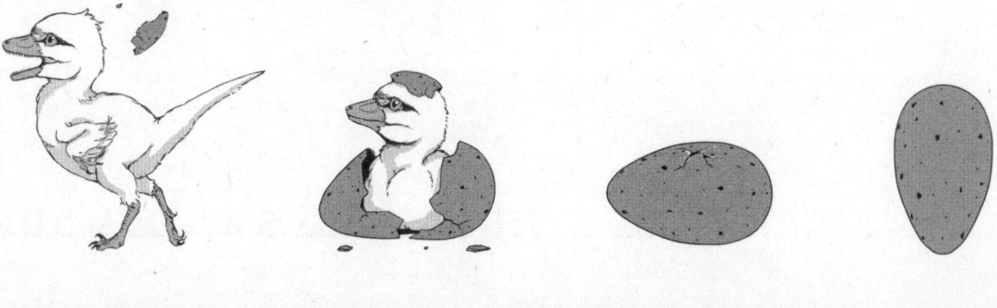

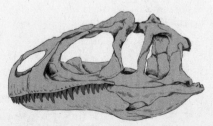

DINOSAUR SANCTUARY

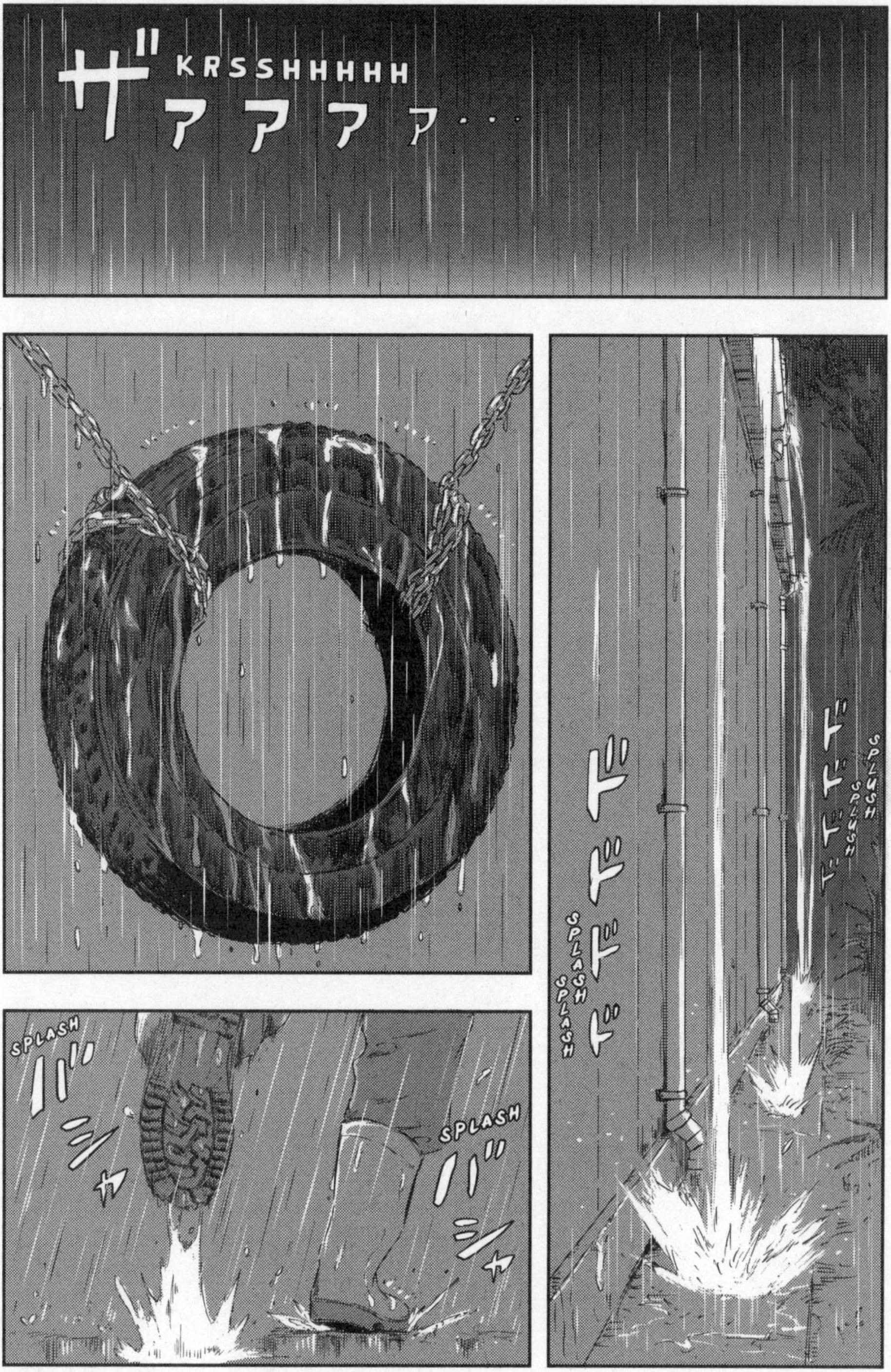
ザァアアァ...
KRSSHHHHHH
ドドドド
SPLASH
SPLUSH
SPLUSH
ドドドド
SPLASH
SPLASH
SPLASH
SPLASH
バシャ
SPLASH
バシャ

CHAPTER 14 CLUMSY HACHIBEI, PART 2

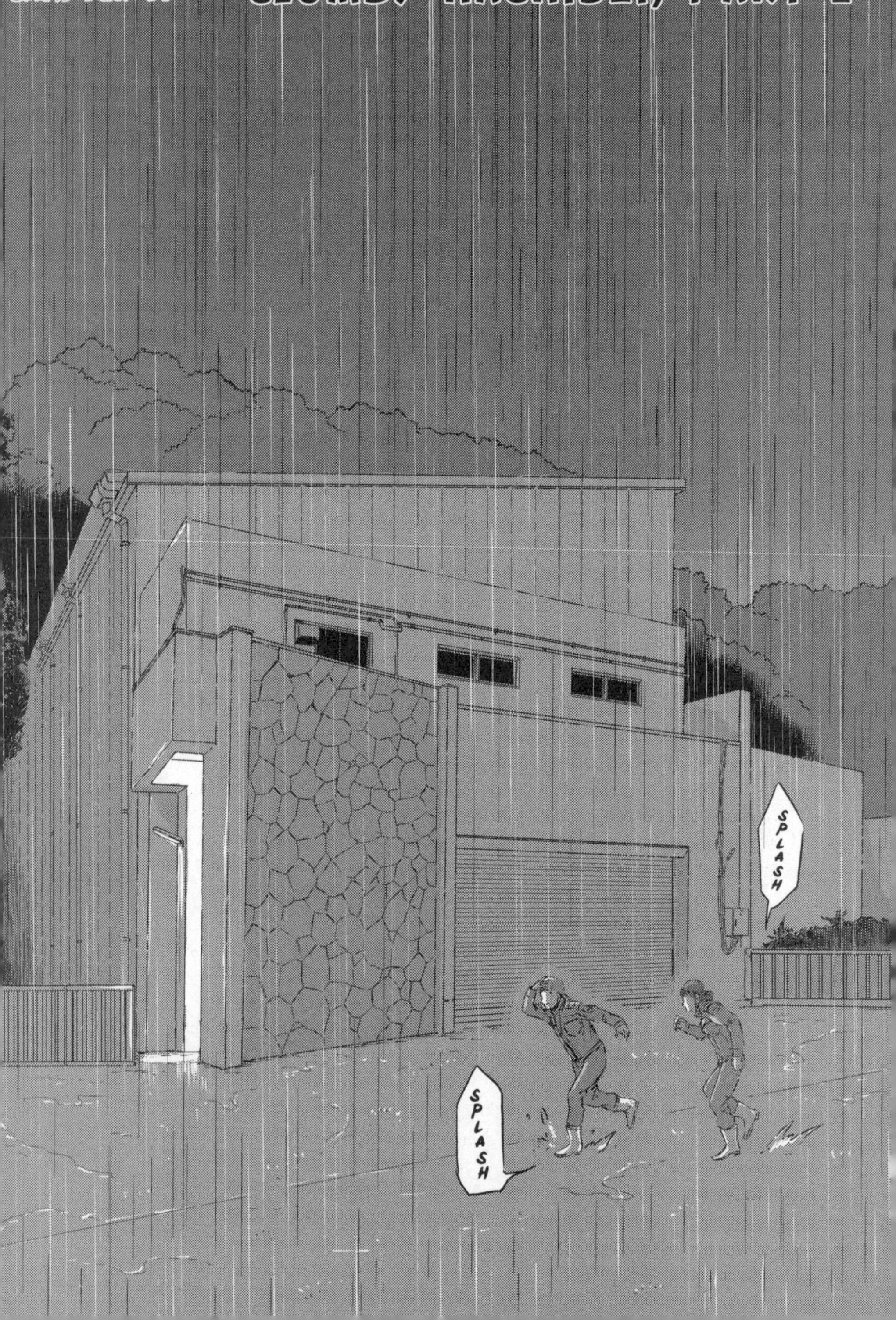
SPLASH
SPLASH

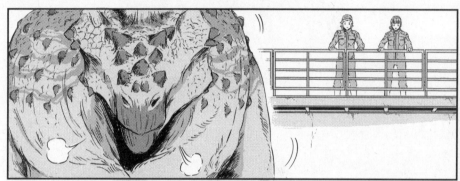

I KNEW IT...

SOMETHIN'S GOT HIM ALL SHOOK UP...

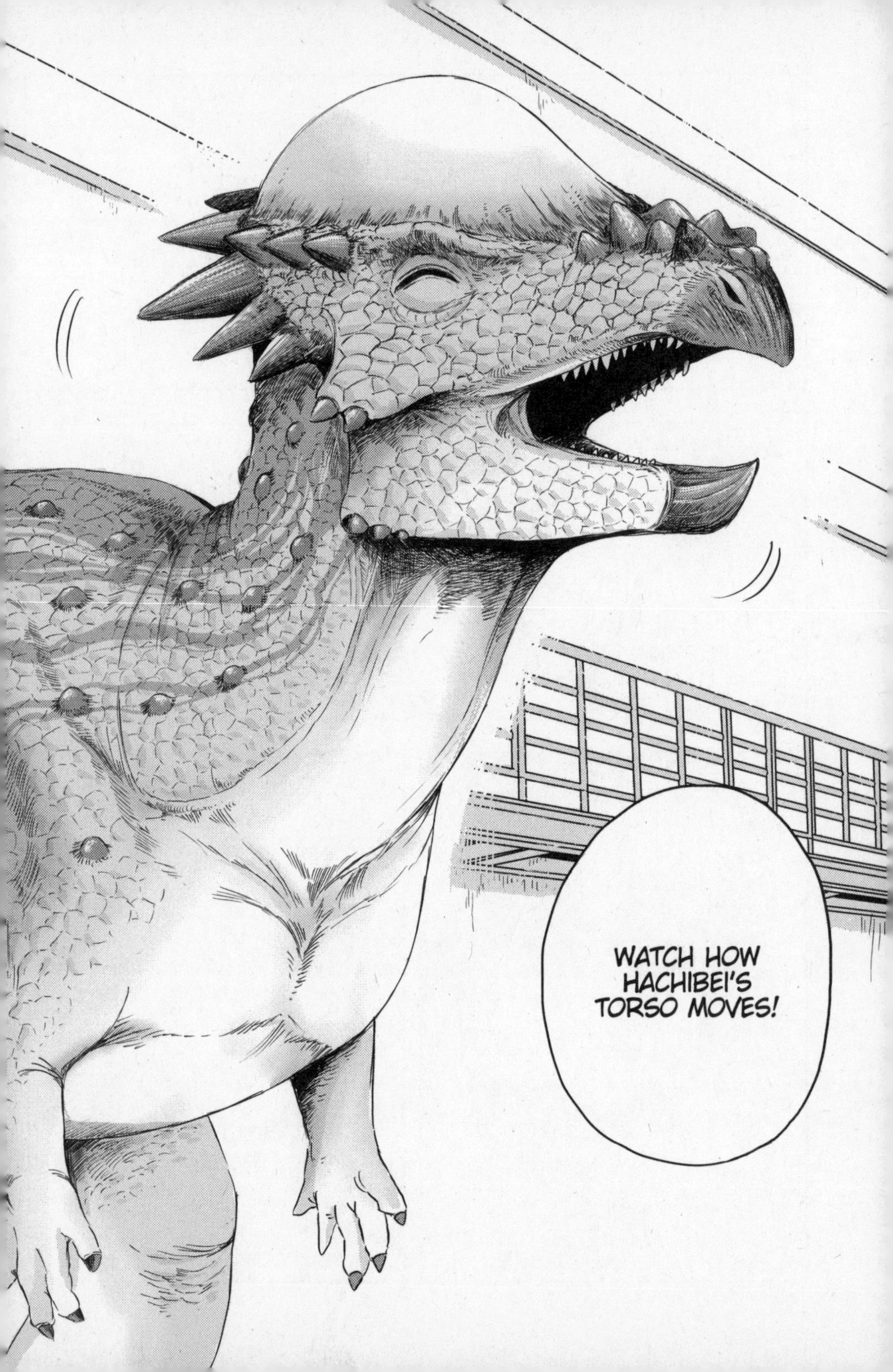
WATCH HOW HACHIBEI'S TORSO MOVES!

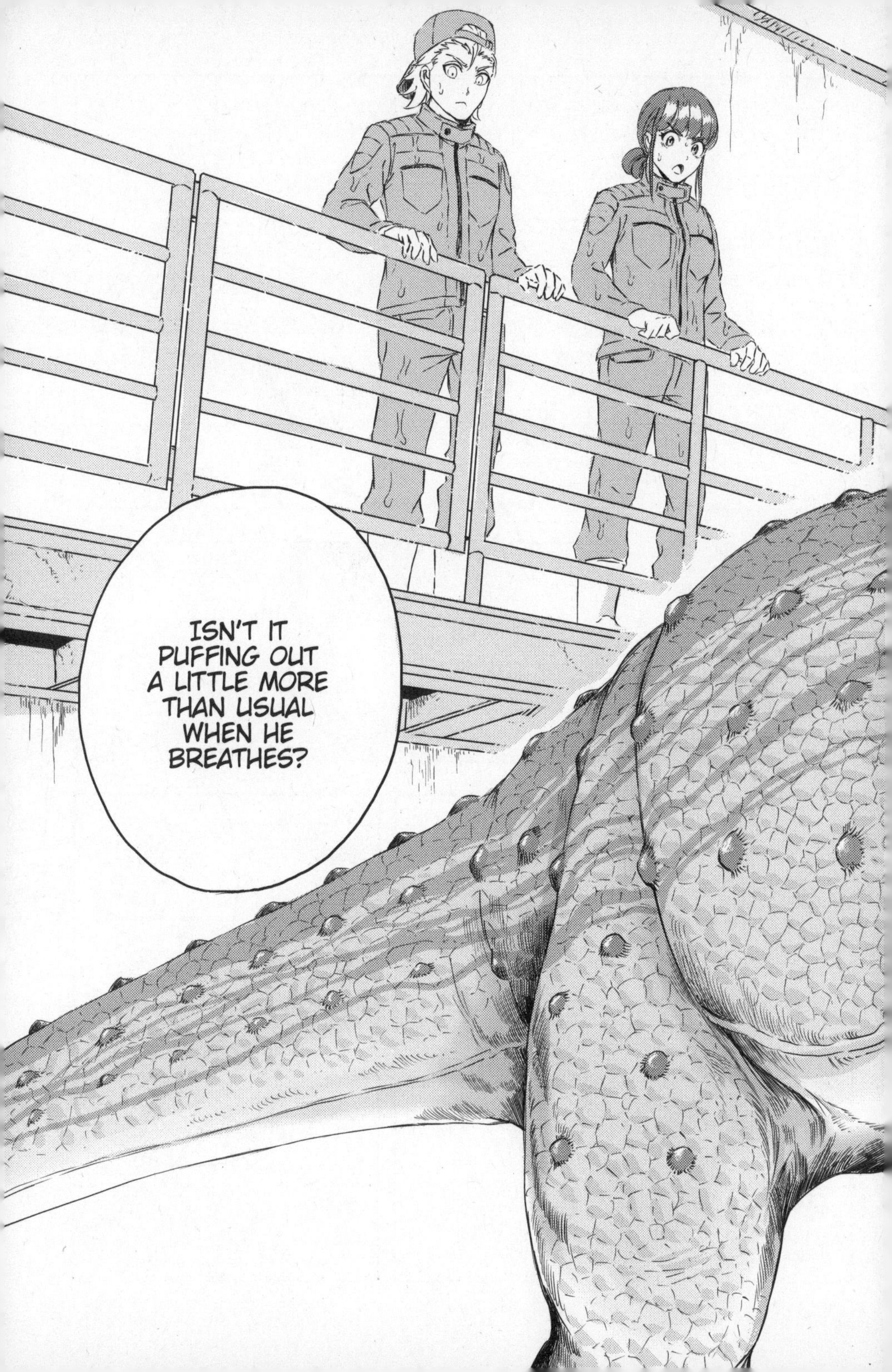
ISN'T IT PUFFING OUT A LITTLE MORE THAN USUAL WHEN HE BREATHES?

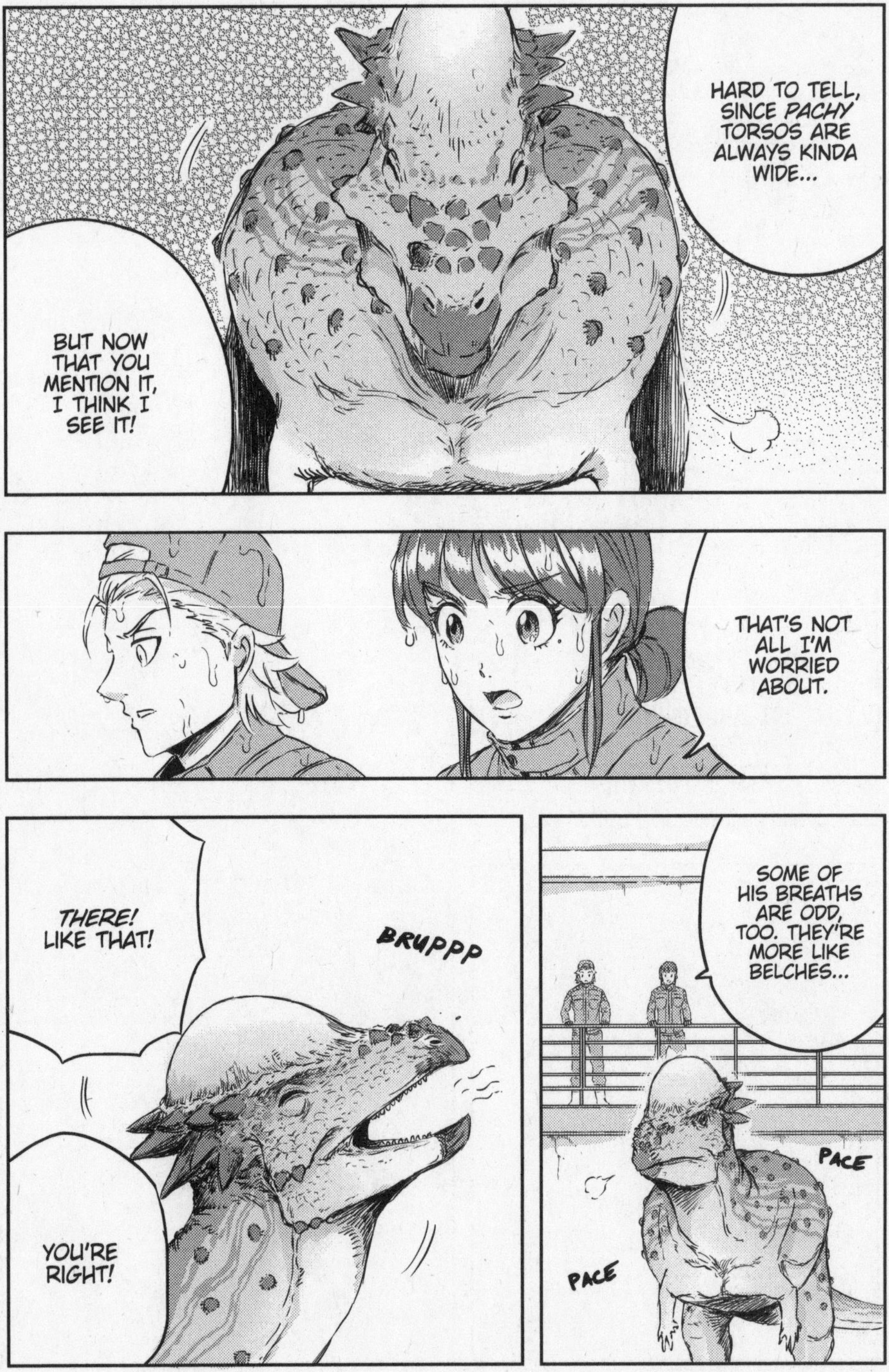
HARD TO TELL, SINCE *PACHY* TORSOS ARE ALWAYS KINDA WIDE...
BUT NOW THAT YOU MENTION IT, I THINK I SEE IT!
THAT'S NOT ALL I'M WORRIED ABOUT.
SOME OF HIS BREATHS ARE ODD, TOO. THEY'RE MORE LIKE BELCHES...
PACE
PACE
THERE! LIKE THAT!
BRUPPP
YOU'RE RIGHT!

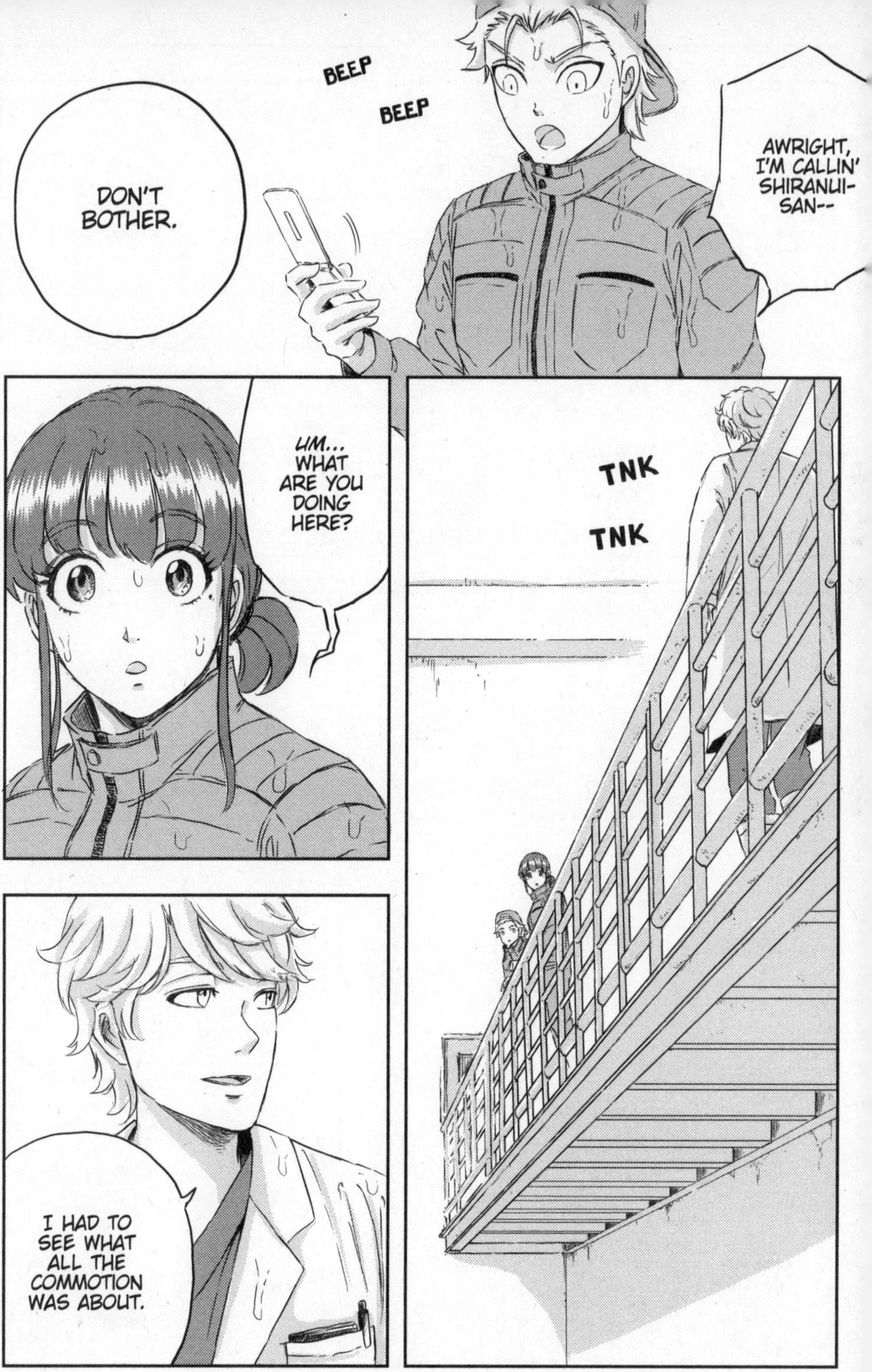
AWRIGHT, I'M CALLIN' SHIRANUI-SAN--
BEEP
BEEP
DON'T BOTHER.
TNK
TNK
UM... WHAT ARE YOU DOING HERE?
I HAD TO SEE WHAT ALL THE COMMOTION WAS ABOUT.

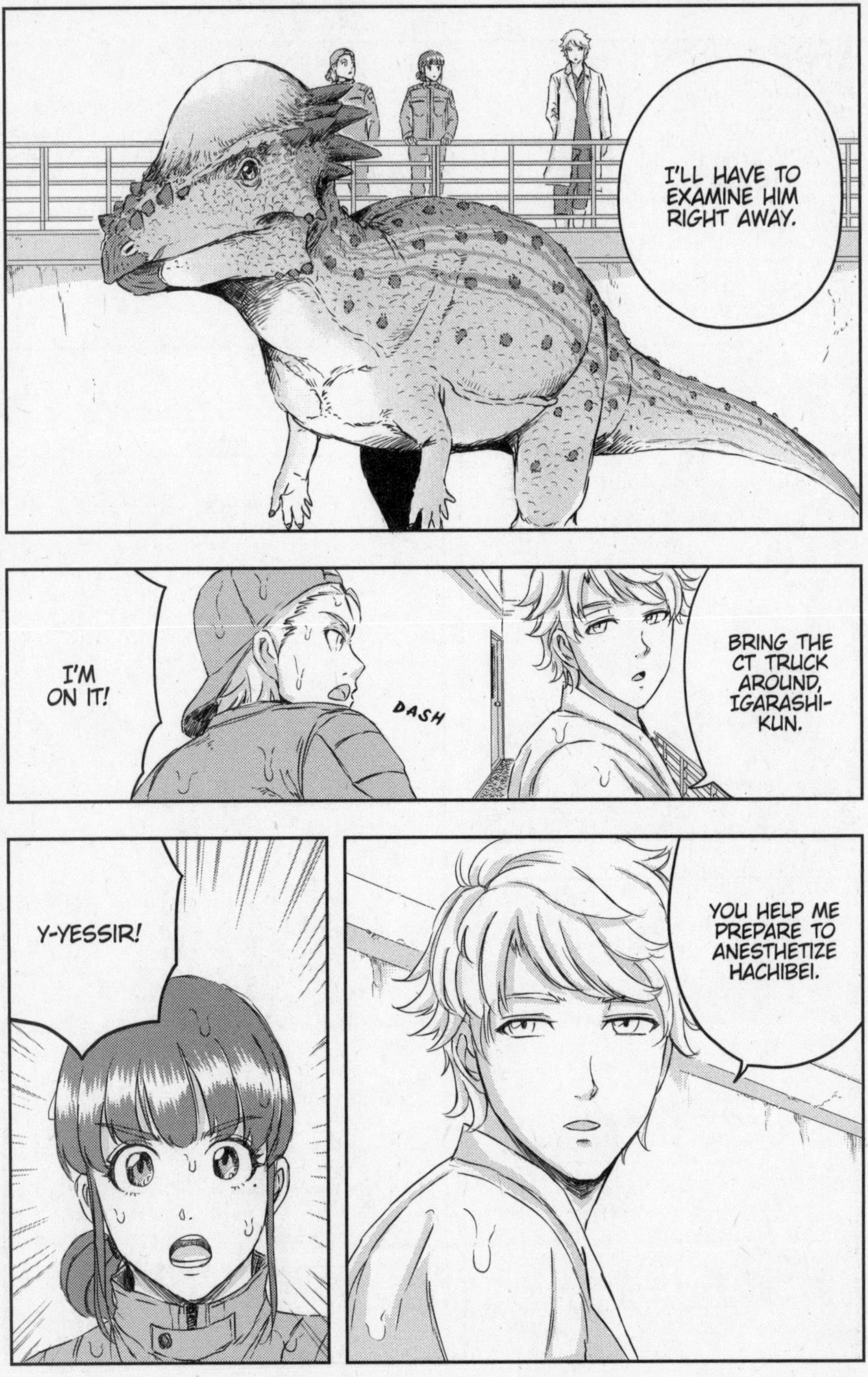
I'LL HAVE TO EXAMINE HIM RIGHT AWAY.
BRING THE CT TRUCK AROUND, IGARASHI-KUN.
I'M ON IT!
DASH
YOU HELP ME PREPARE TO ANESTHETIZE HACHIBEI.
Y-YESSIR!

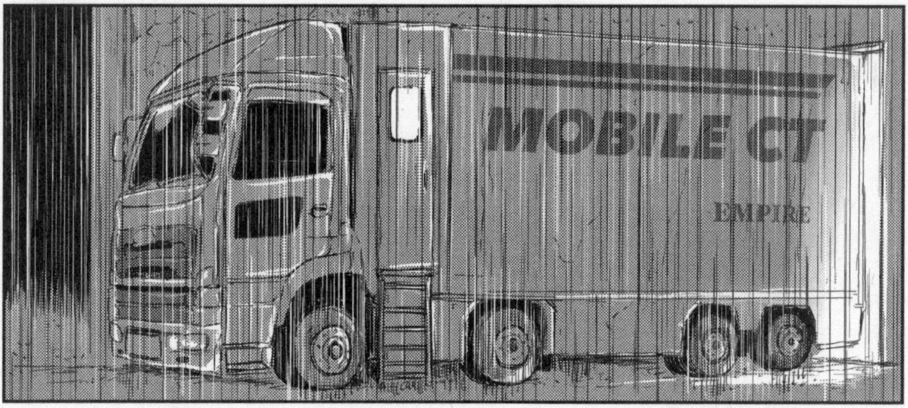
MOBILE CT
EMPIRE
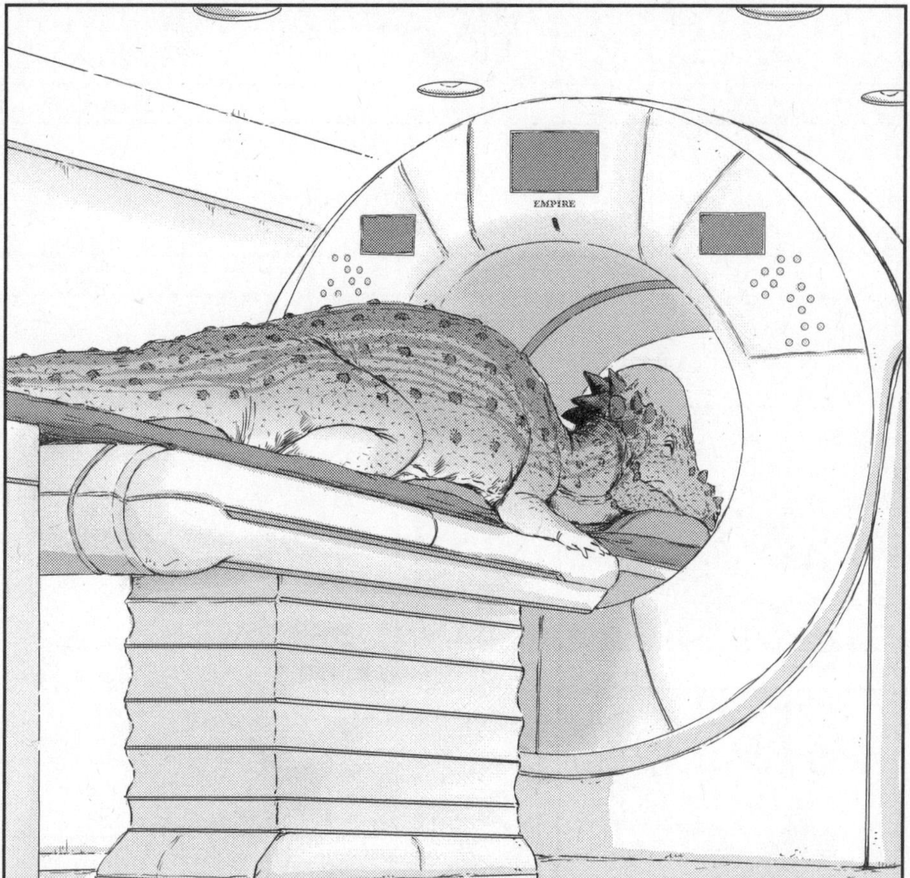
EMPIRE

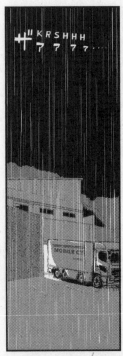

KRSHHH

Sign: Enoshima Shrine

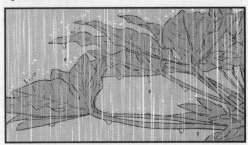

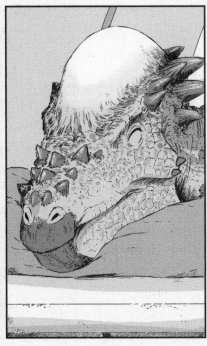

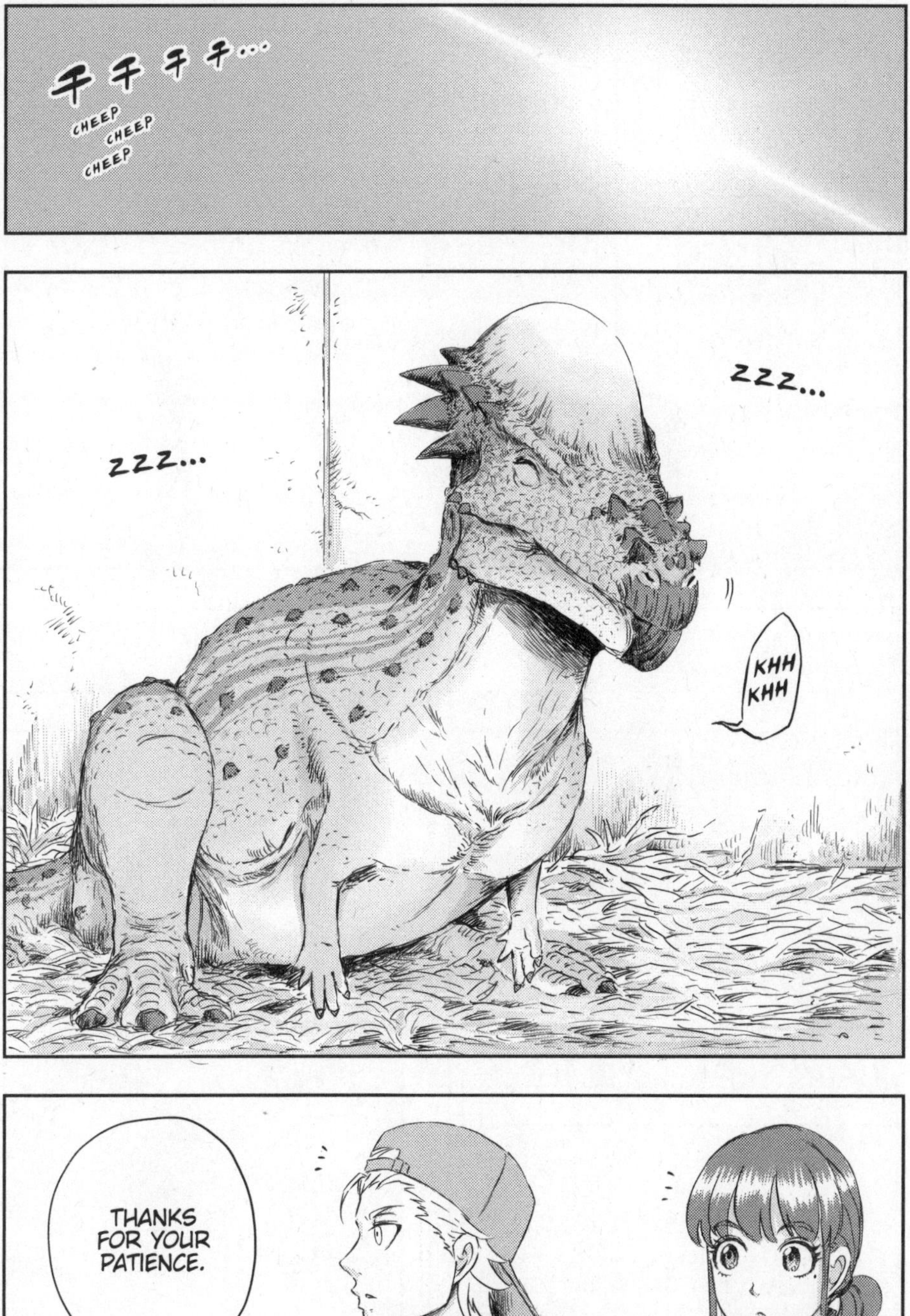
チチチチ…
CHEEP CHEEP CHEEP
ZZZ…
ZZZ…
KHH KHH
THANKS FOR YOUR PATIENCE.

I'VE GOT THE RESULTS OF THE SCAN.
TK
TK
IT SHOWED SIGNS OF LIGHT PNEUMONIA.
I BELIEVE IT STARTED WITH A NASAL CATARRH...
AS HIS INJURIES RESHAPED HIS NOSTRIL.
THE INFECTION LIKELY MOVED TO HIS LUNGS AS HE BREATHED.

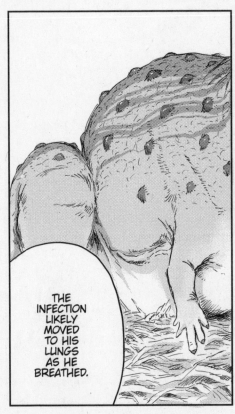

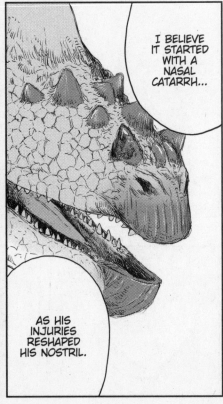

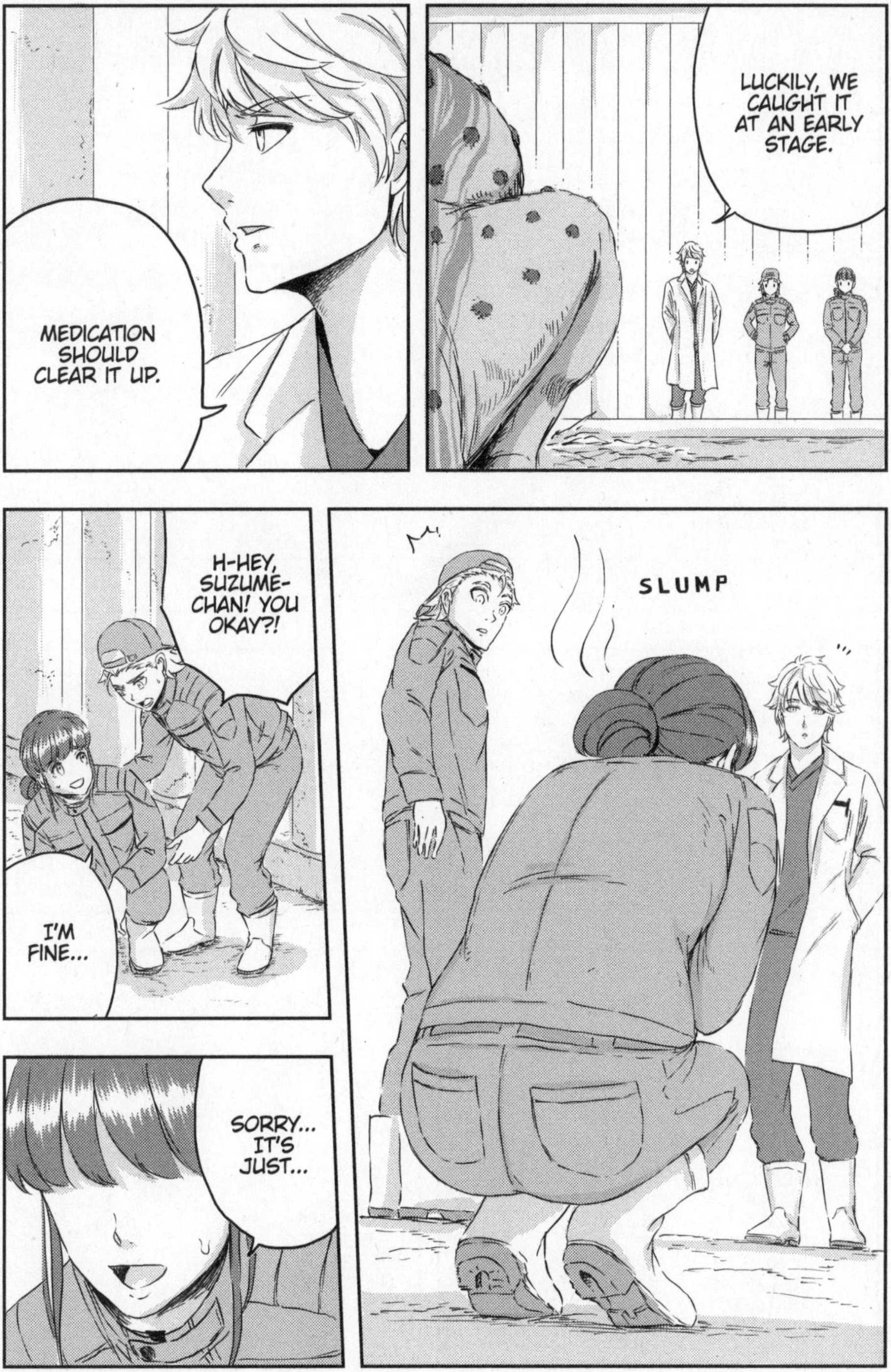
LUCKILY, WE CAUGHT IT AT AN EARLY STAGE.
MEDICATION SHOULD CLEAR IT UP.
SLUMP
H-HEY, SUZUME-CHAN! YOU OKAY?!
I'M FINE...
SORRY... IT'S JUST...

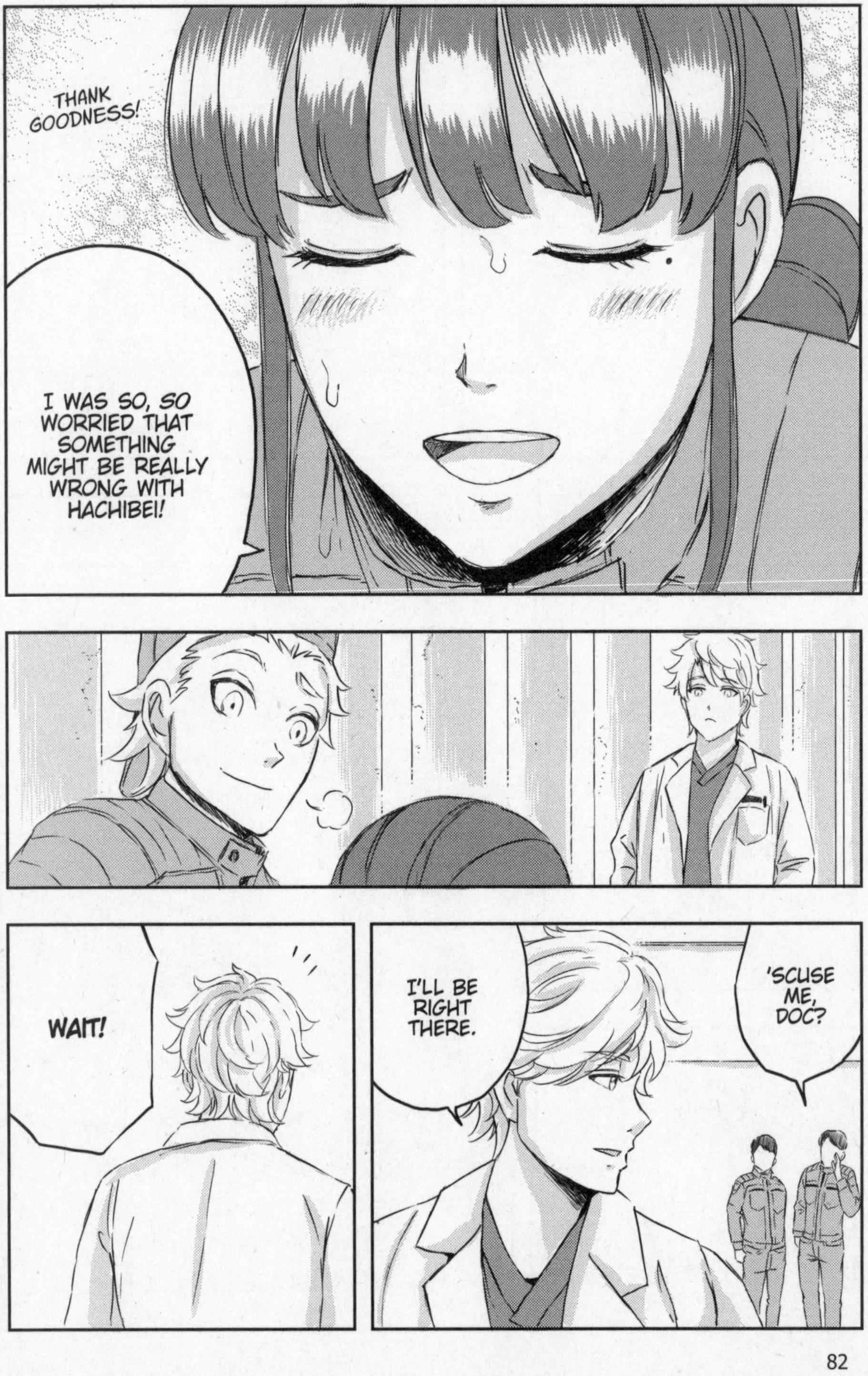
THANK GOODNESS!
I WAS SO, SO WORRIED THAT SOMETHING MIGHT BE REALLY WRONG WITH HACHIBEI!
'SCUSE ME, DOC?
I'LL BE RIGHT THERE.
WAIT!

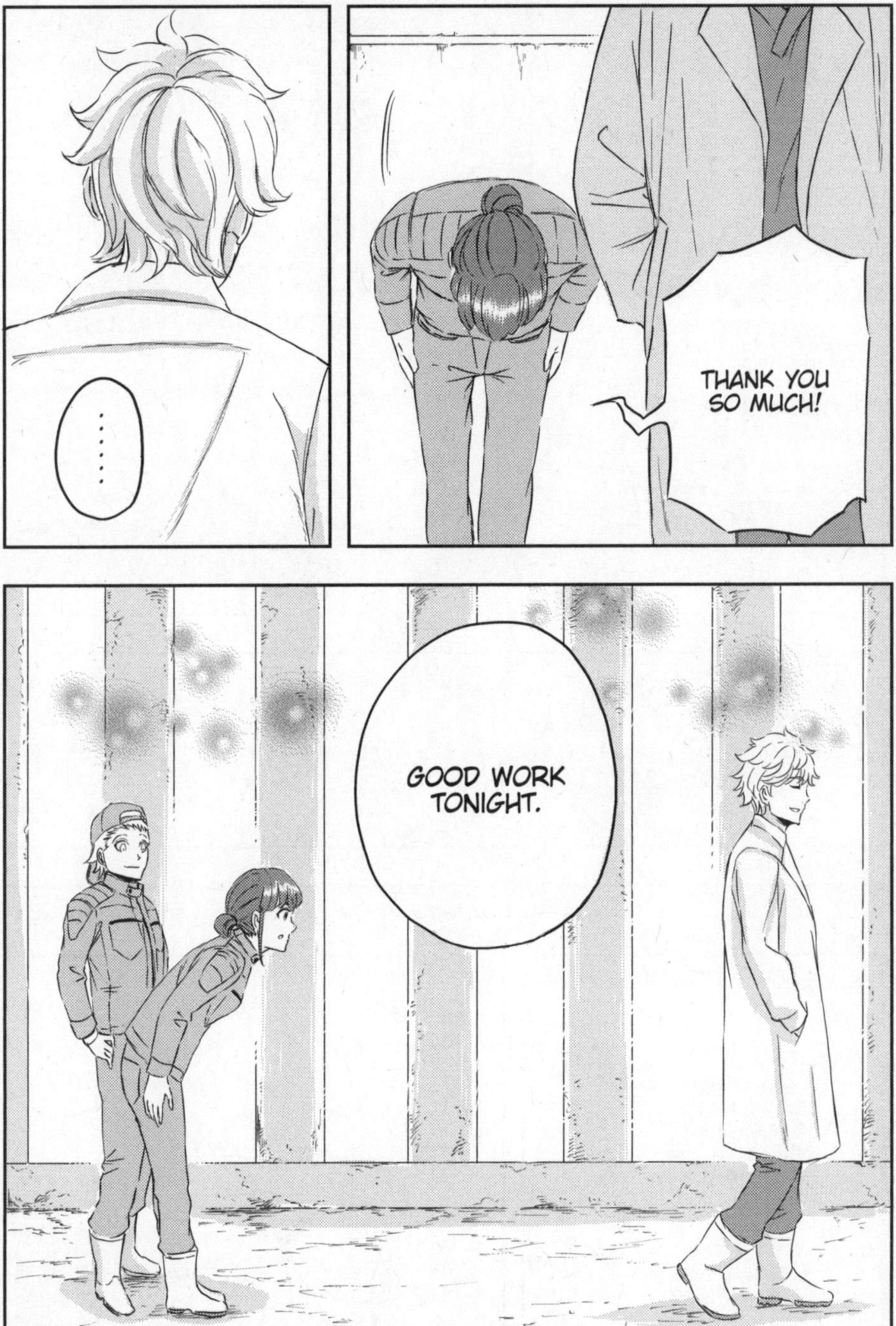
THANK YOU SO MUCH!
......
GOOD WORK TONIGHT.

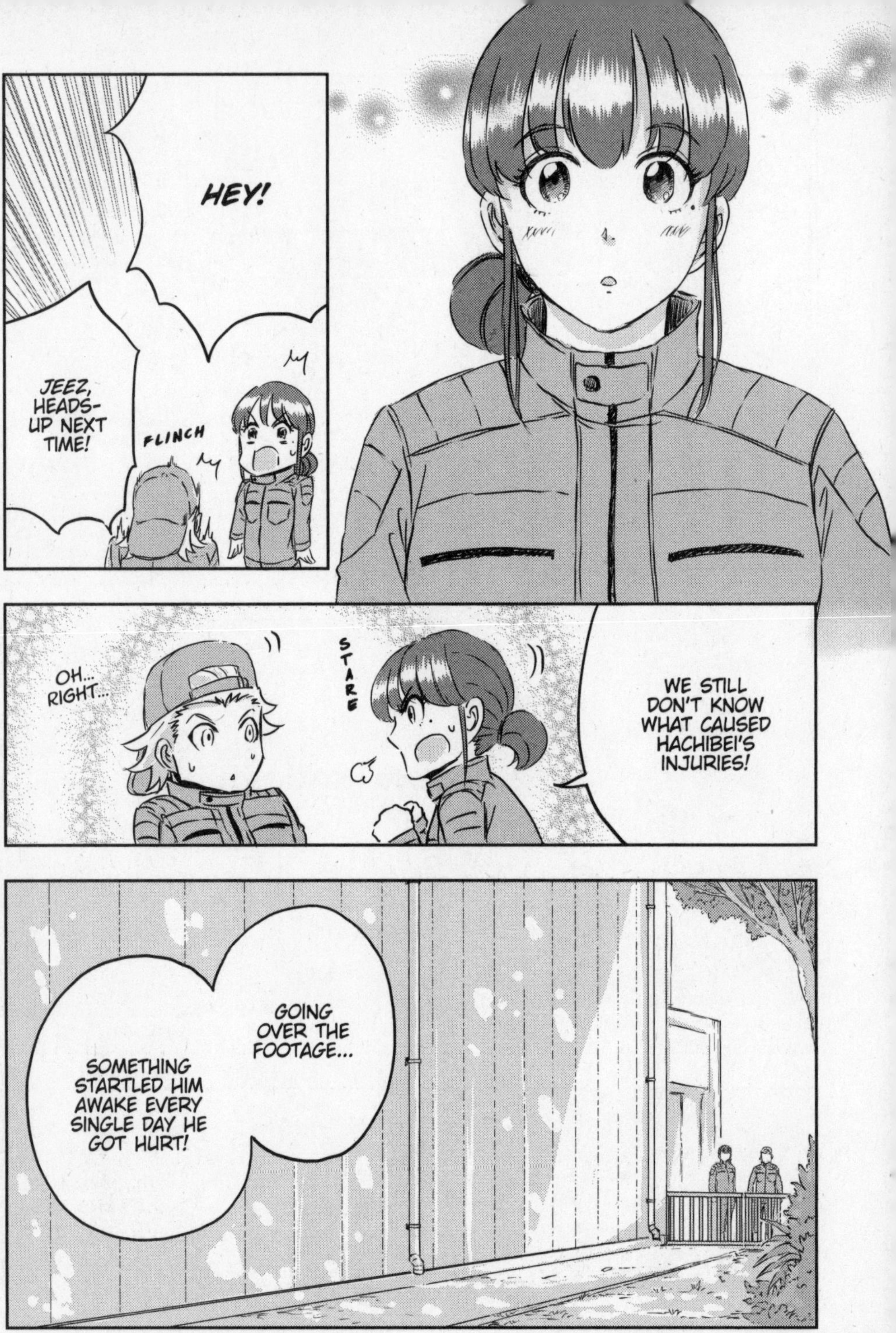
HEY!
FLINCH
JEEZ, HEADS-UP NEXT TIME!
WE STILL DON'T KNOW WHAT CAUSED HACHIBEI'S INJURIES!
STARE
OH... RIGHT...
GOING OVER THE FOOTAGE...
SOMETHING STARTLED HIM AWAKE EVERY SINGLE DAY HE GOT HURT!

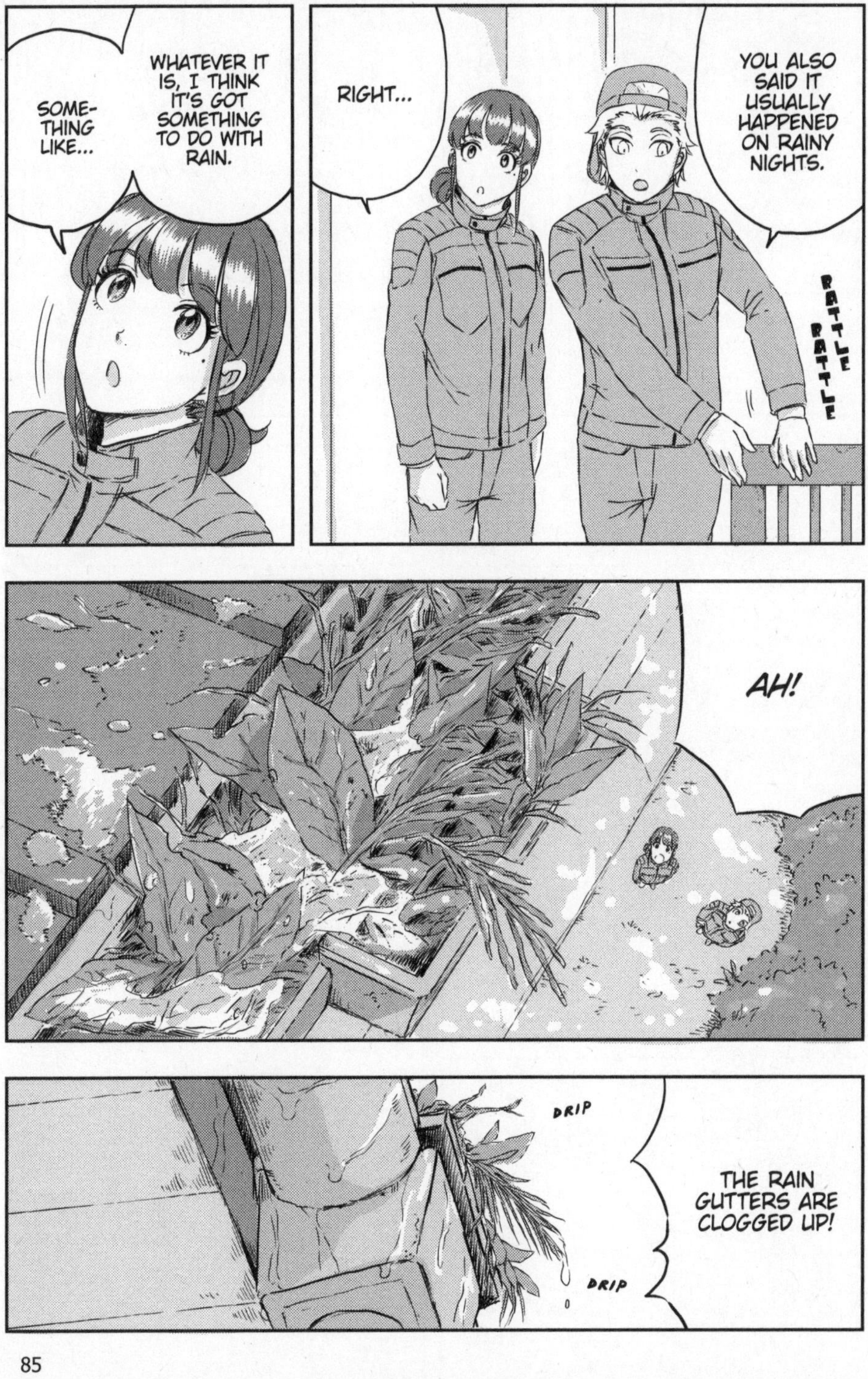
YOU ALSO SAID IT USUALLY HAPPENED ON RAINY NIGHTS.
RATTLE RATTLE
RIGHT...
WHATEVER IT IS, I THINK IT'S GOT SOMETHING TO DO WITH RAIN.
SOME-THING LIKE...
AH!
DRIP
DRIP
THE RAIN GUTTERS ARE CLOGGED UP!

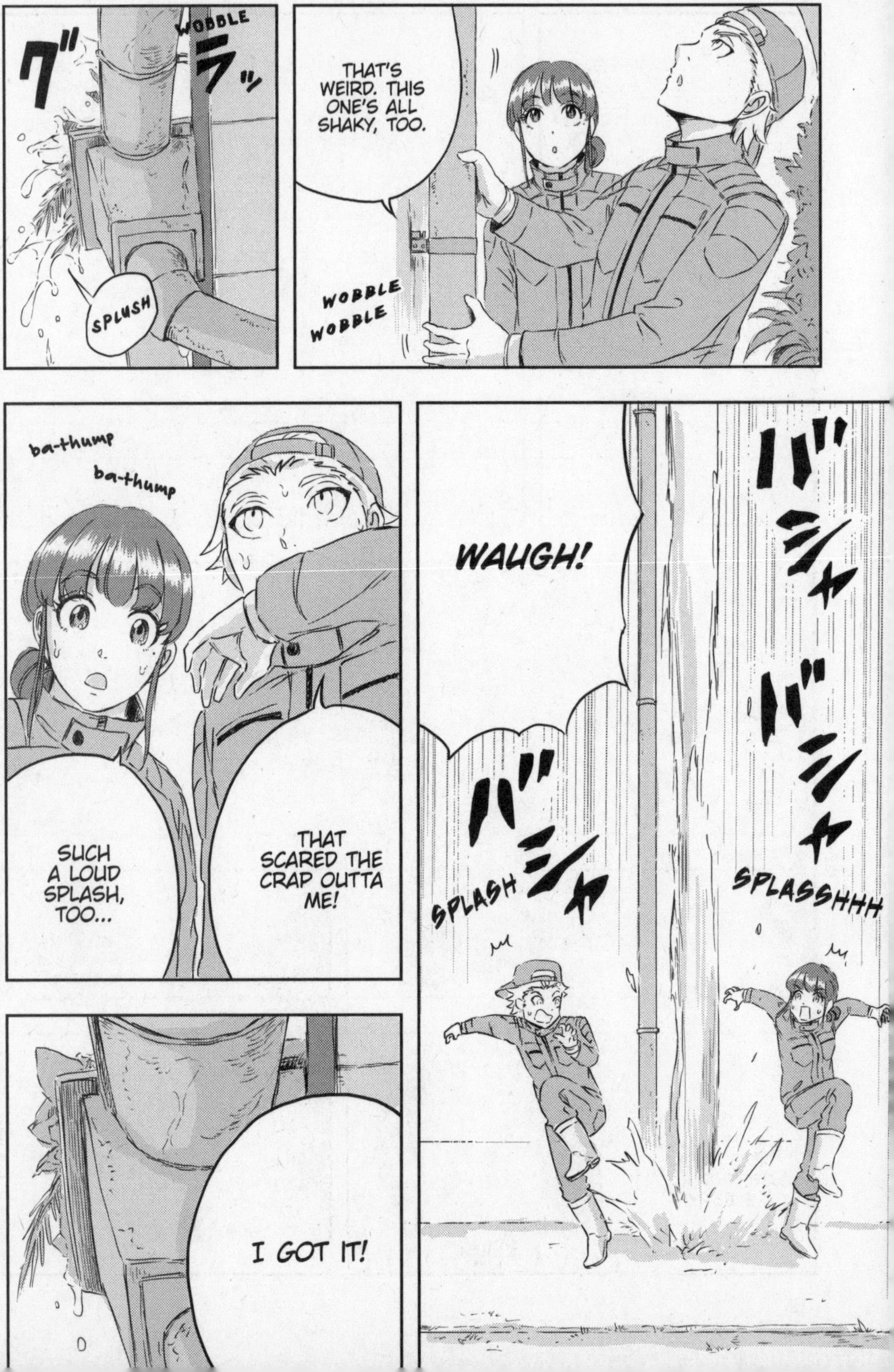
THAT'S WEIRD. THIS ONE'S ALL SHAKY, TOO.
WOBBLE WOBBLE
WOBBLE
グラッ
SPLUSH
バシャバシャ
SPLASSHHH
WAUGH!
バシャ
SPLASH
ba-thump ba-thump
THAT SCARED THE CRAP OUTTA ME!
SUCH A LOUD SPLASH, TOO...
I GOT IT!

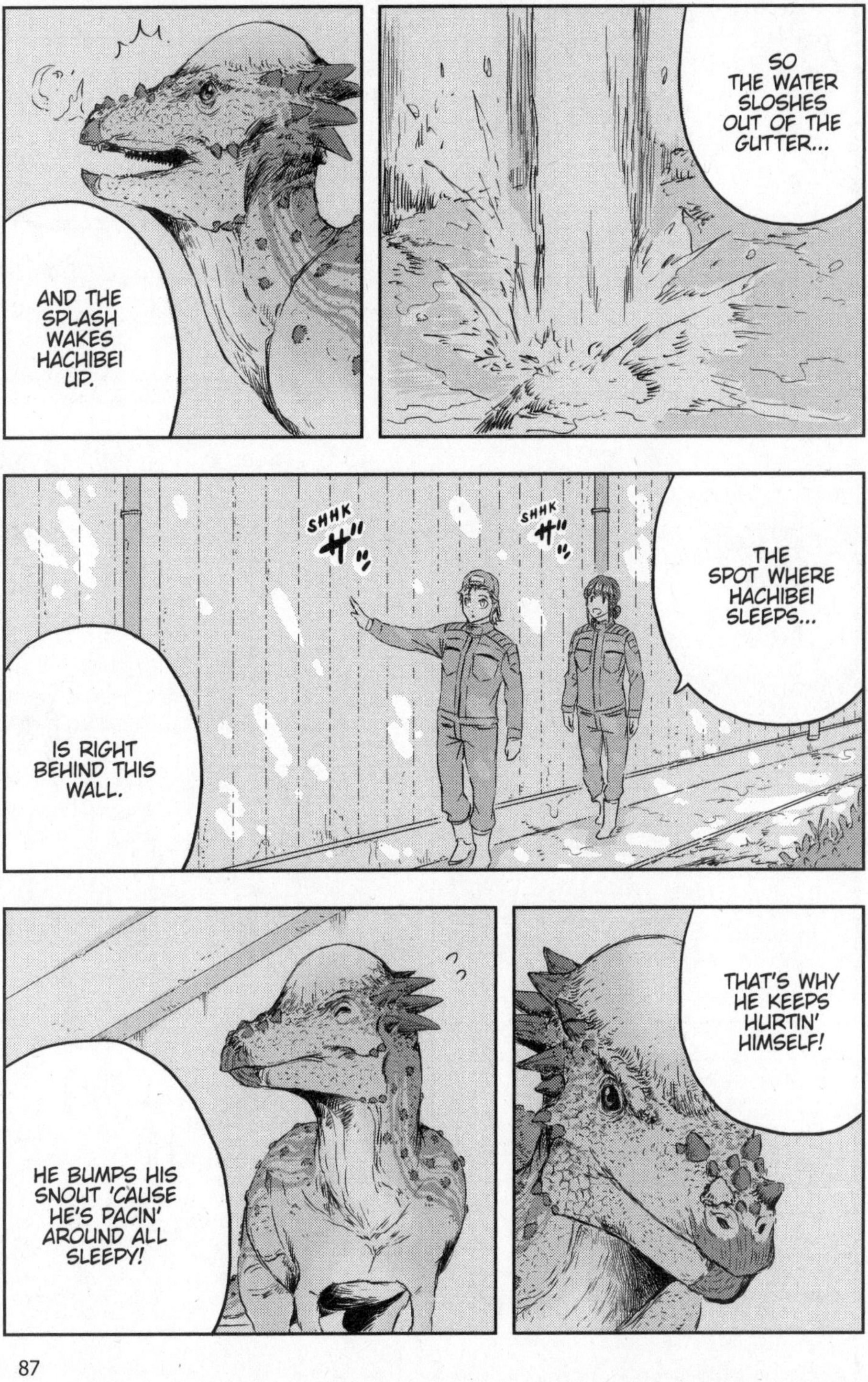
SO THE WATER SLOSHES OUT OF THE GUTTER...
AND THE SPLASH WAKES HACHIBEI UP.
THE SPOT WHERE HACHIBEI SLEEPS...
SHHK
SHHK
IS RIGHT BEHIND THIS WALL.
THAT'S WHY HE KEEPS HURTIN' HIMSELF!
HE BUMPS HIS SNOUT 'CAUSE HE'S PACIN' AROUND ALL SLEEPY!

AW, MAN! I CAN'T BELIEVE I DIDN'T NOTICE BEFORE!

HOW'D I MISS PUTTIN' THAT TOGETHER?

HACHIBEI STILL SLEEPS IN THAT SAME PLACE...

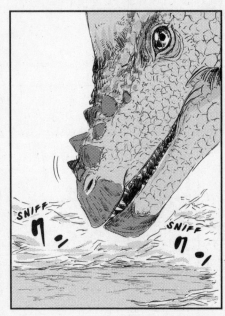

SNIFF

SNIFF

AND I THINK I CAN GUESS WHY!

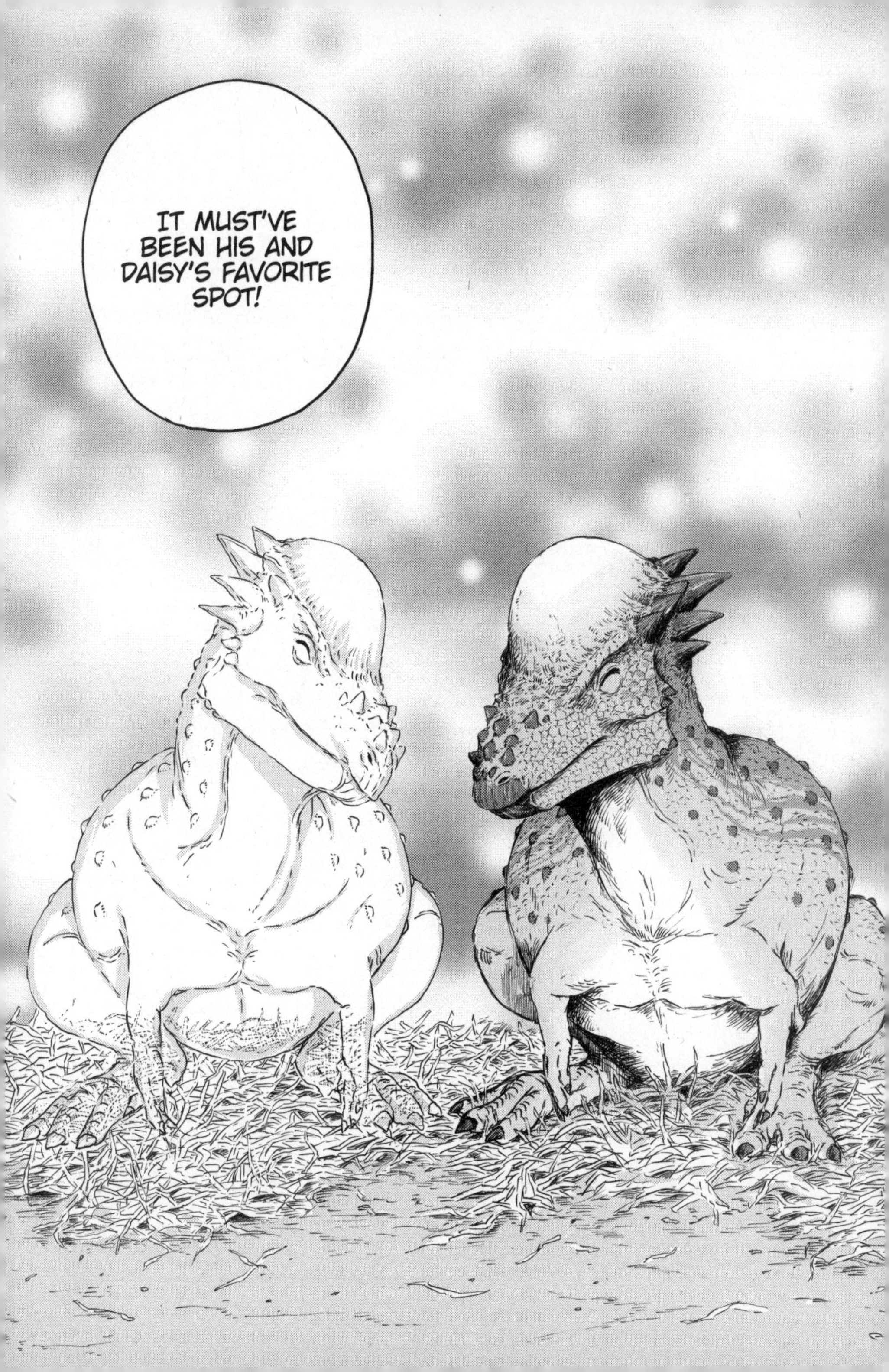
IT MUST'VE BEEN HIS AND DAISY'S FAVORITE SPOT!

Y'KNOW, I BET YOU'RE RIGHT.

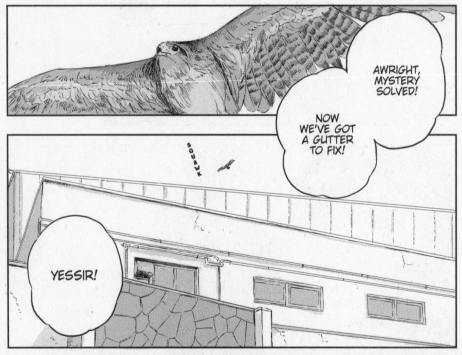

AWRIGHT, MYSTERY SOLVED!

NOW WE'VE GOT A GUTTER TO FIX!

YESSIR!

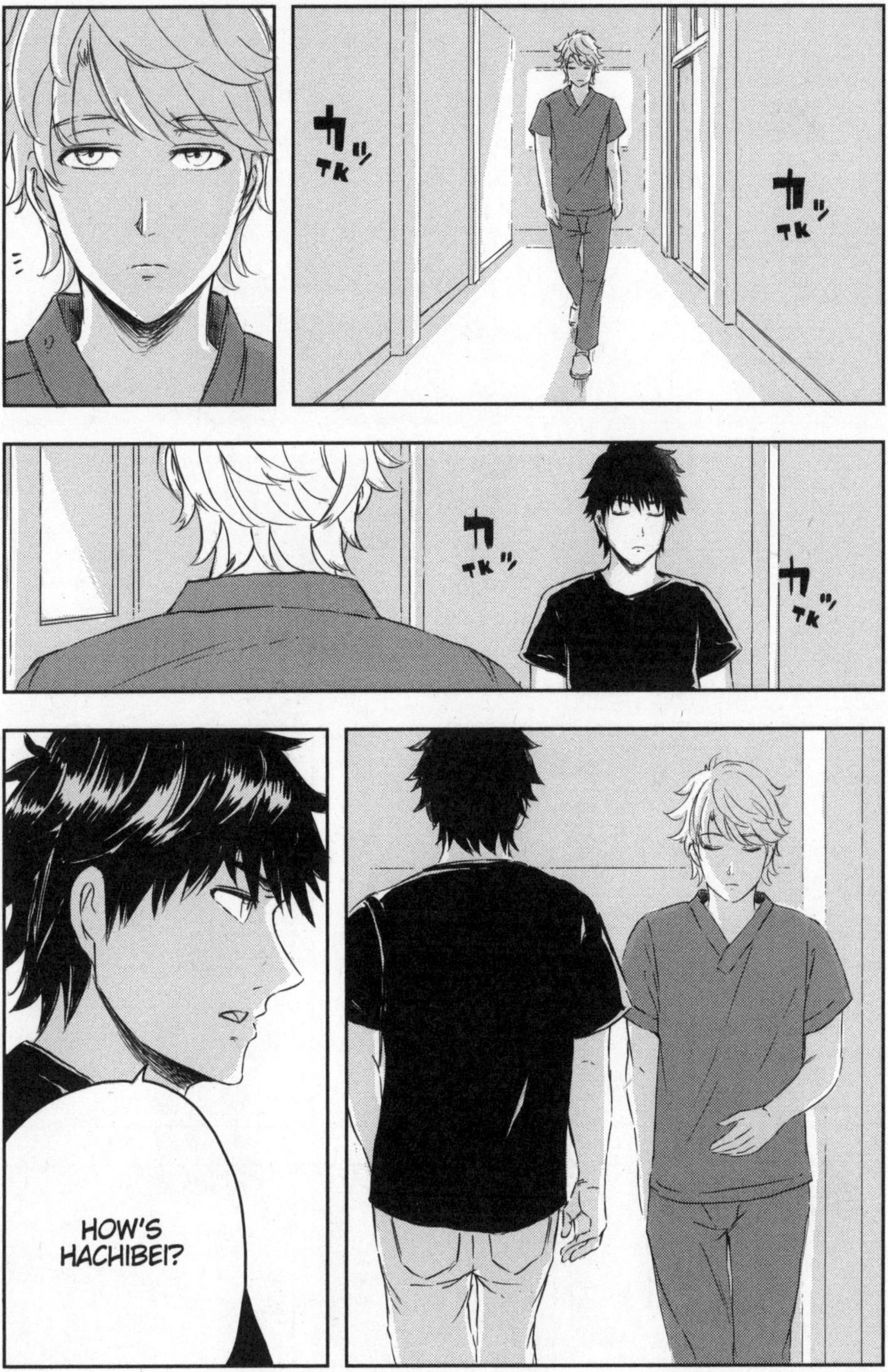
カッ TK
カッ TK
カッ TK
カッ TK
HOW'S HACHIBEI?

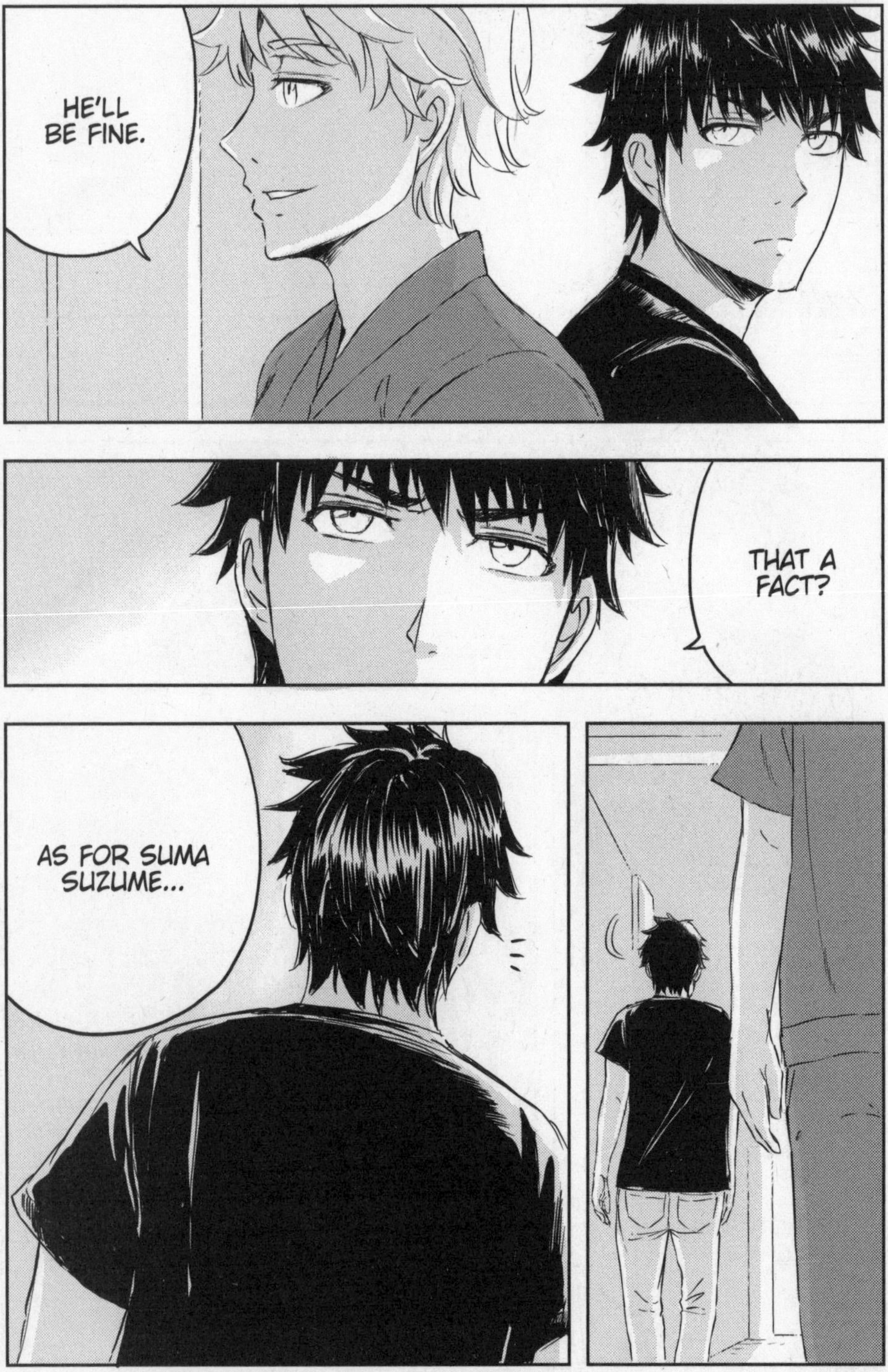
HE'LL BE FINE.
THAT A FACT?
AS FOR SUMA SUZUME...

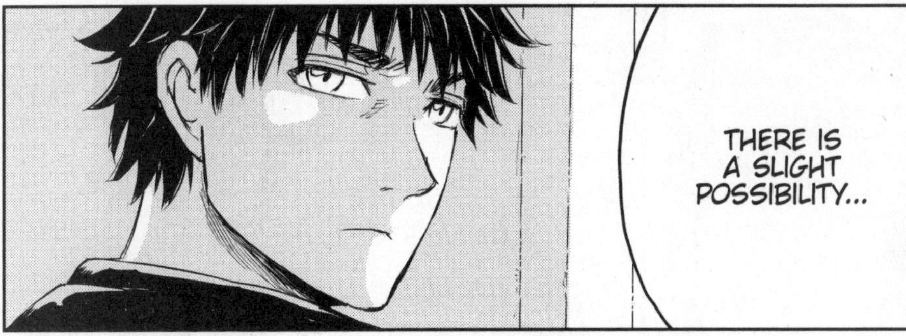
THERE IS A SLIGHT POSSIBILITY...
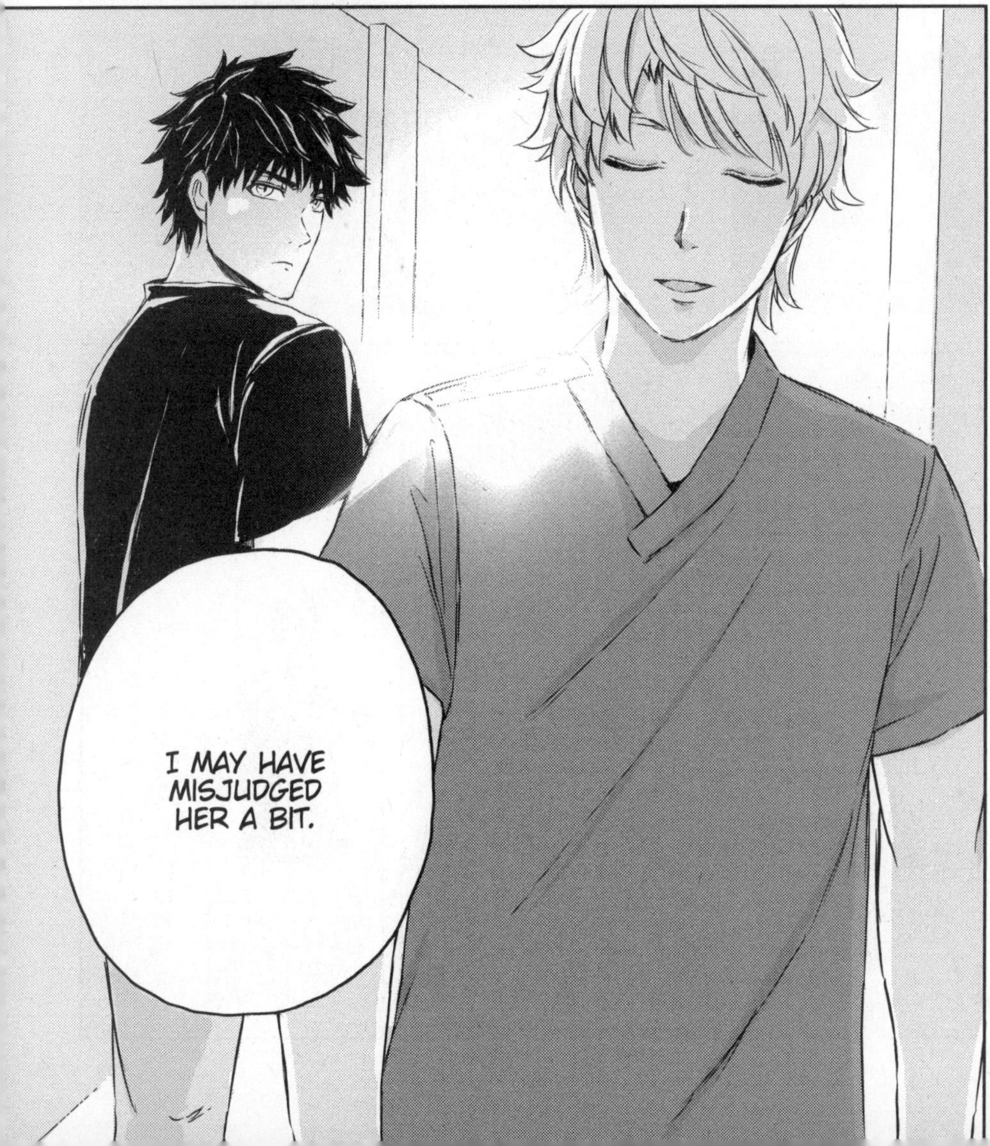
I MAY HAVE MISJUDGED HER A BIT.

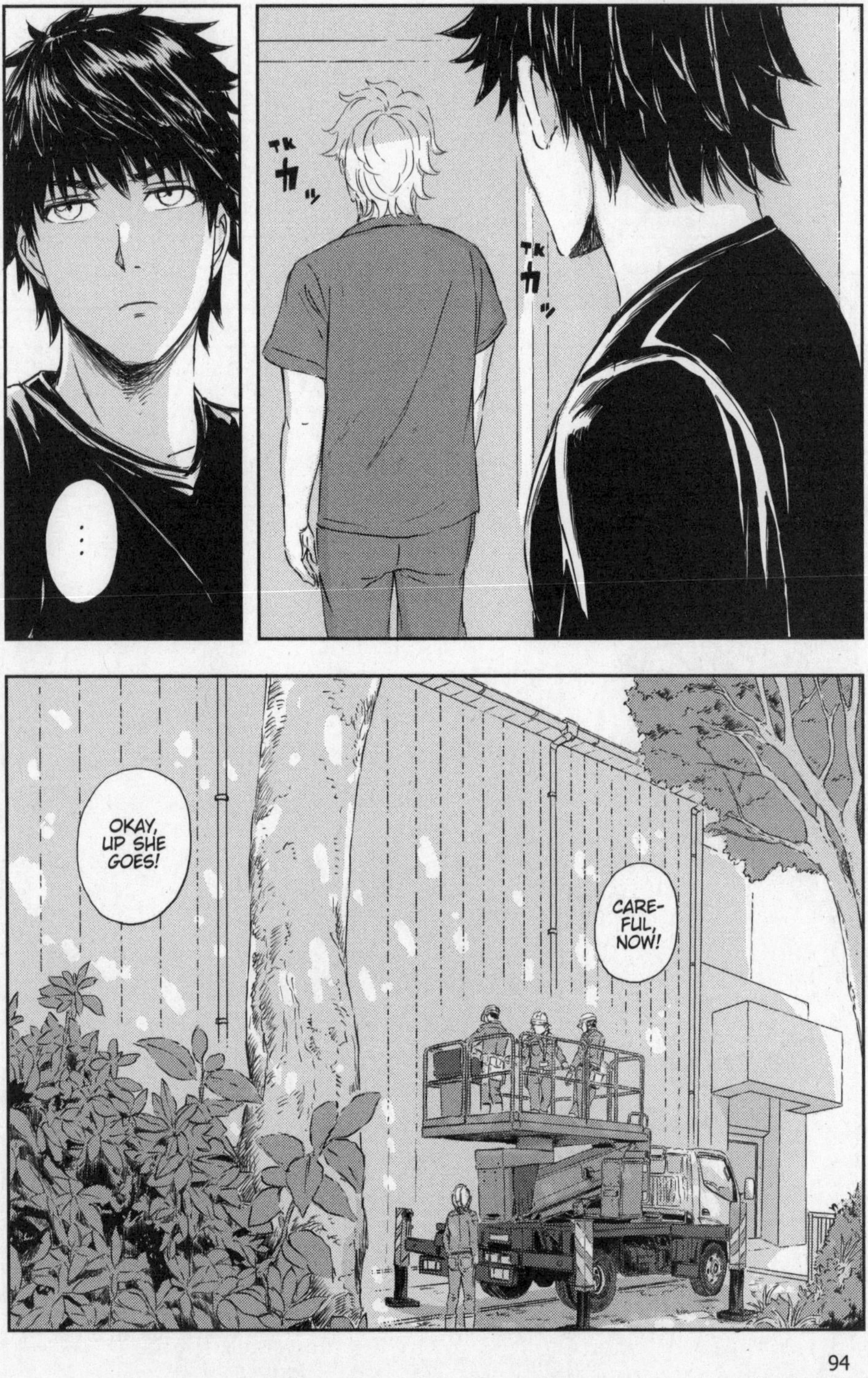
TK
カッ
TK
カッ
...
OKAY, UP SHE GOES!
CARE-FUL, NOW!

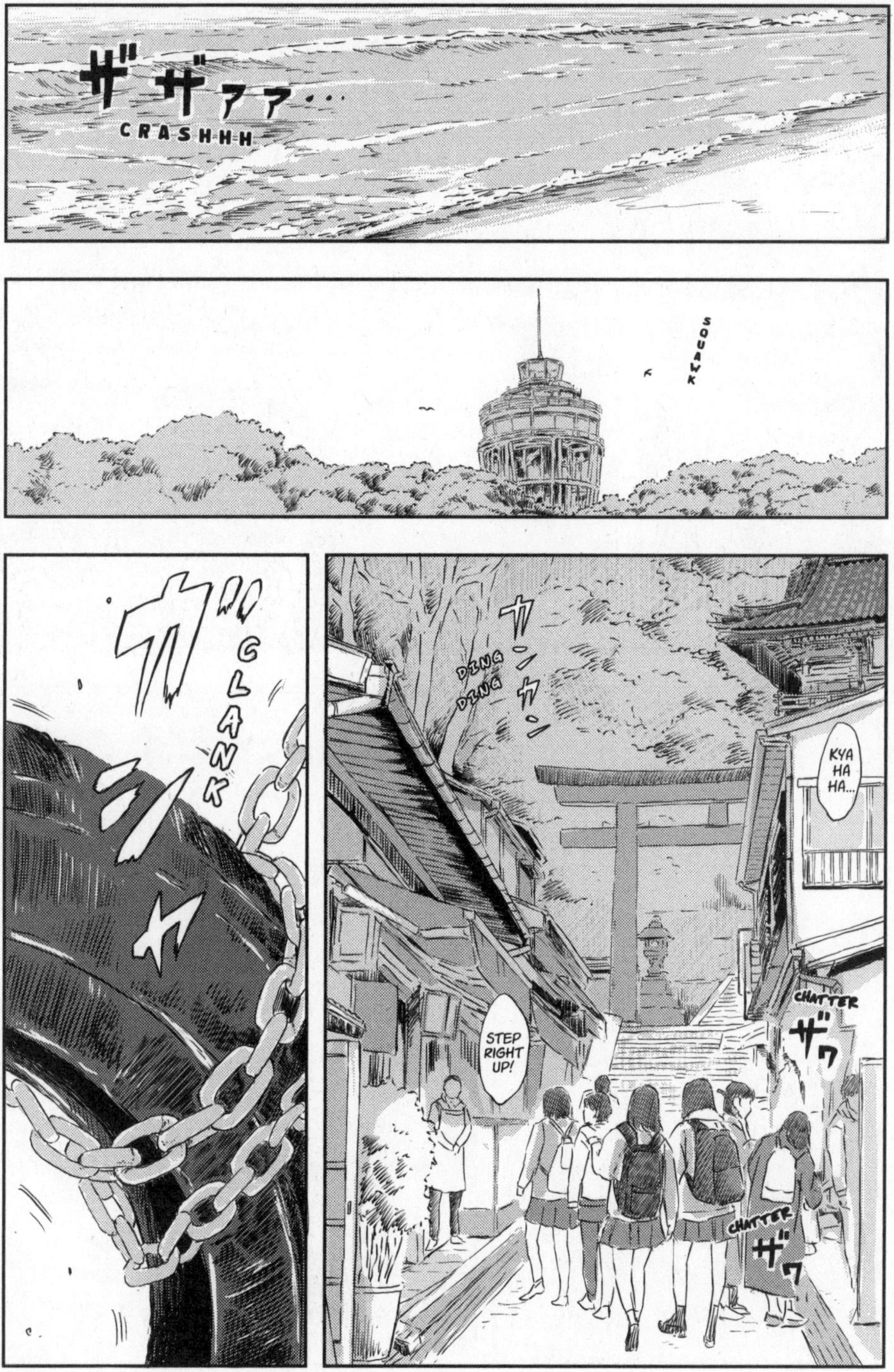

ザザァア…
CRASHHH
SQUAWK
カンカン
DING DING
KYA HA HA...
STEP RIGHT UP!
CHATTER
ザワ
CHATTER
ザワ
ガシャ
CLANK

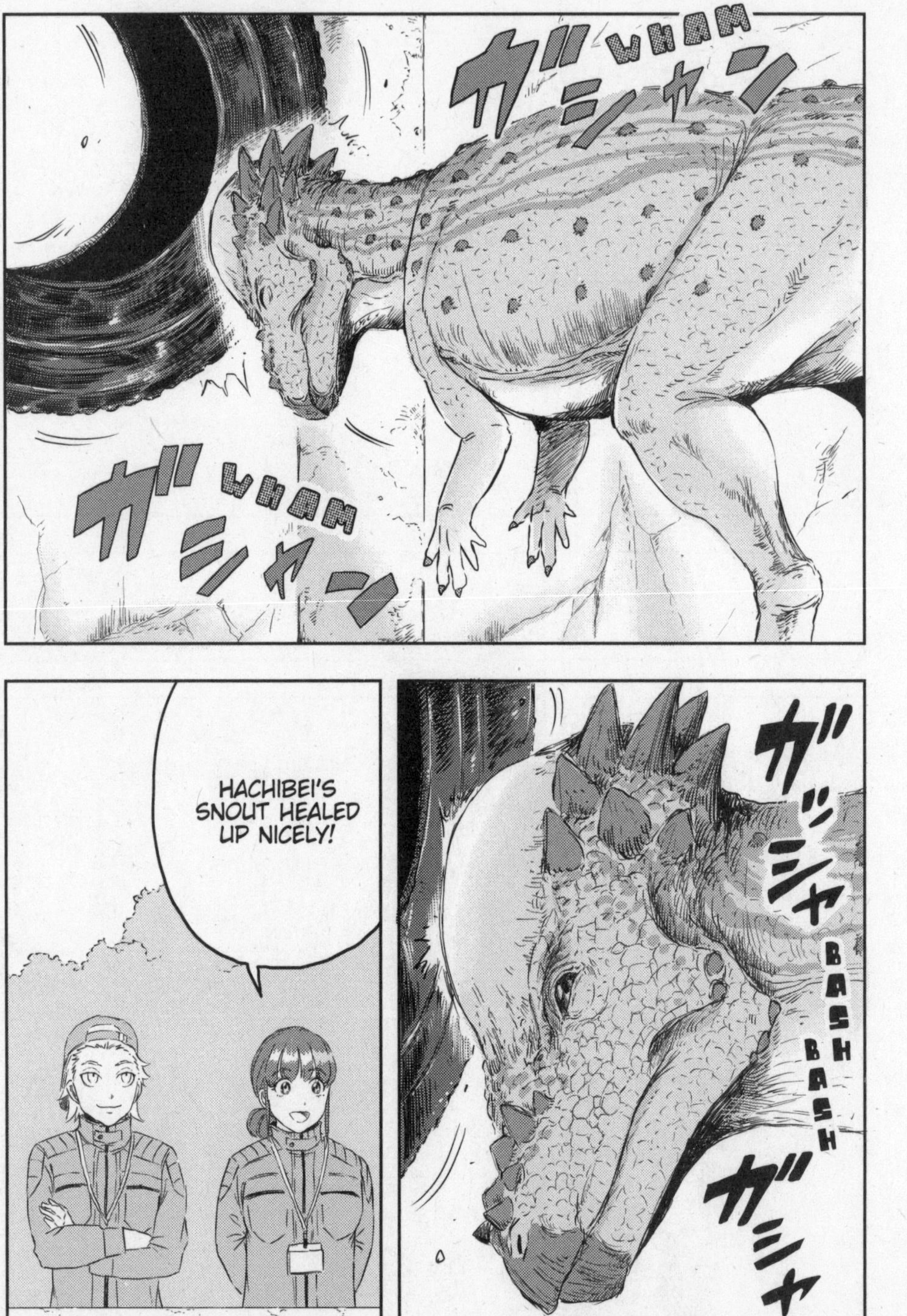
ガシャーン
WHAM
ガシャーン
WHAM
ガシャ
BASH
BASH
BASH
ガシャ
HACHIBEI'S SNOUT HEALED UP NICELY!

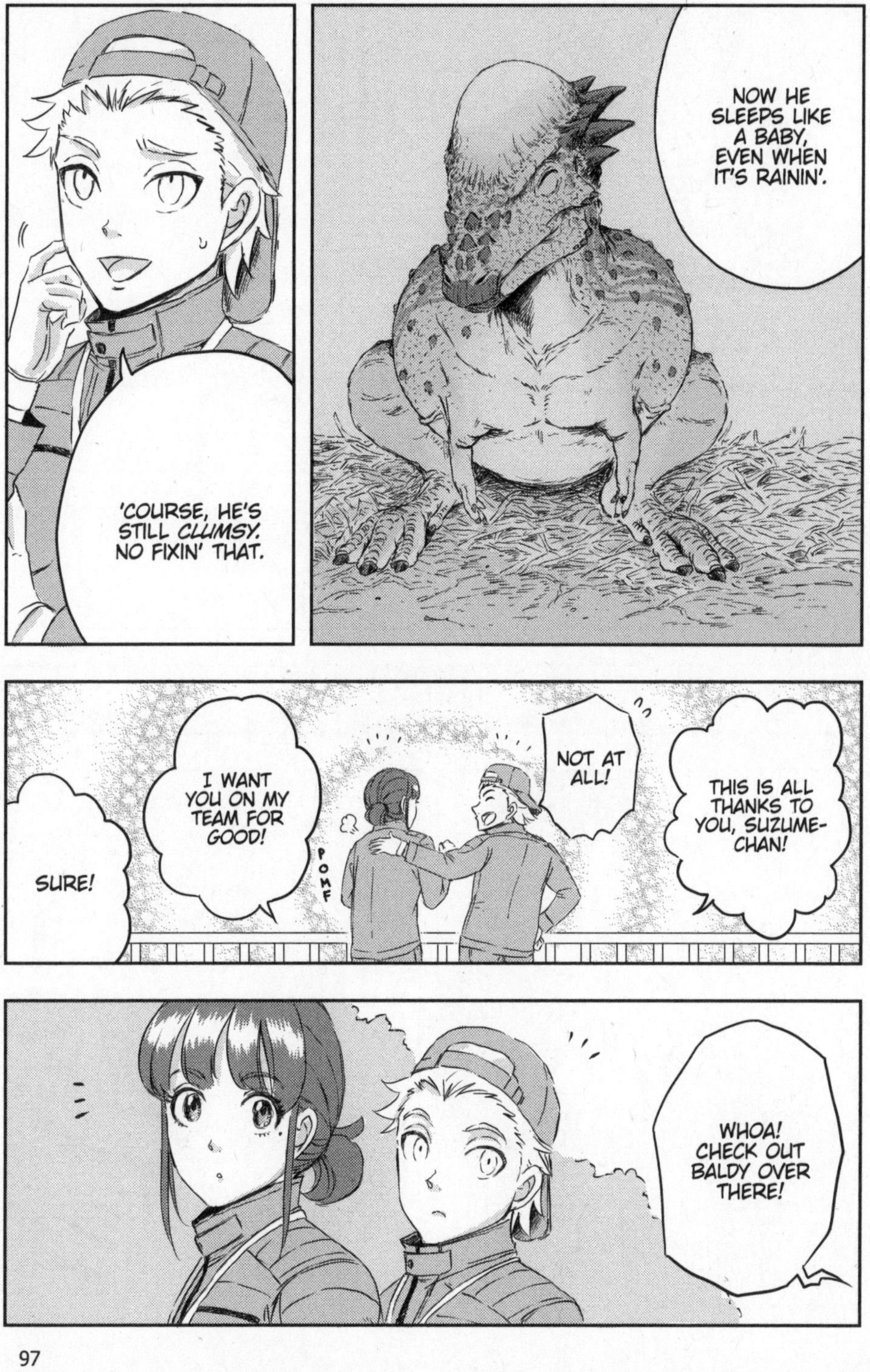
NOW HE SLEEPS LIKE A BABY, EVEN WHEN IT'S RAININ'.
'COURSE, HE'S STILL *CLUMSY*. NO FIXIN' THAT.
THIS IS ALL THANKS TO YOU, SUZUME-CHAN!
NOT AT ALL!
I WANT YOU ON MY TEAM FOR GOOD!
POMF
SURE!
WHOA! CHECK OUT BALDY OVER THERE!

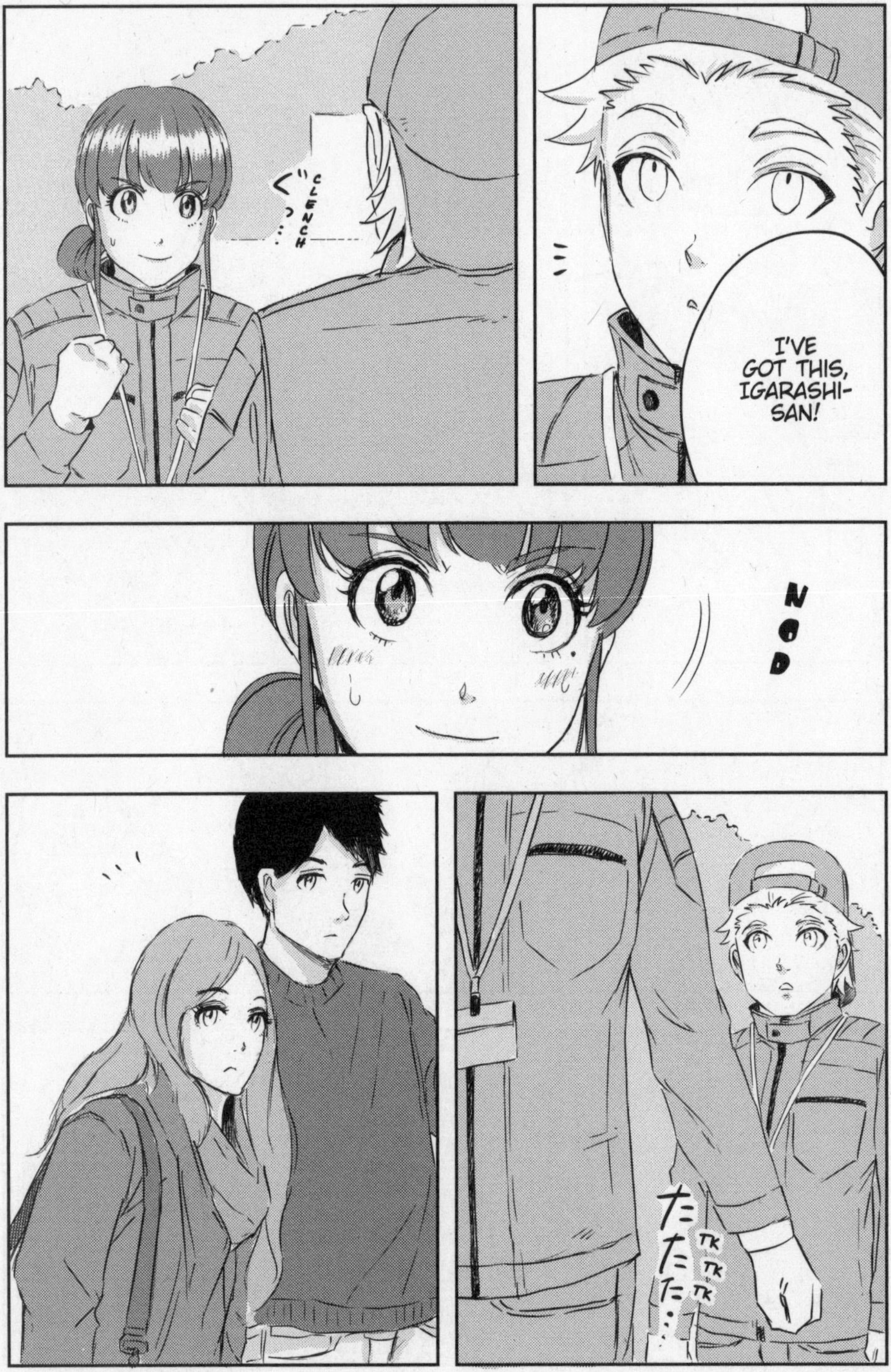
I'VE GOT THIS, IGARASHI-SAN!
くっ…
CLENCH
NOD
たたた…
TK TK TK

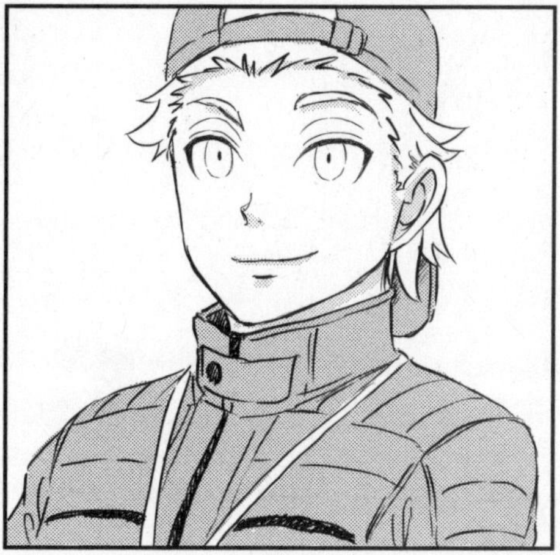

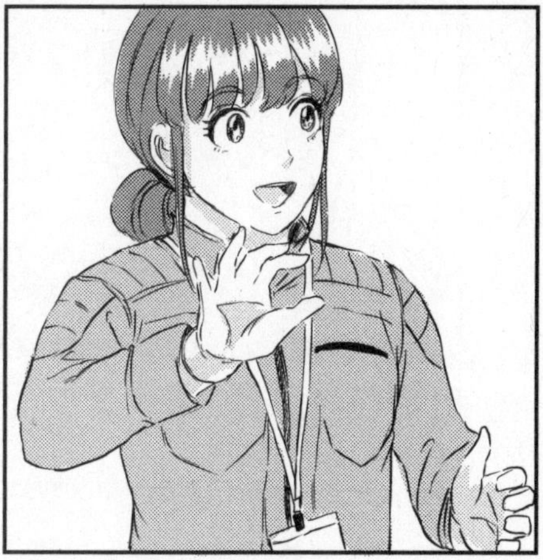

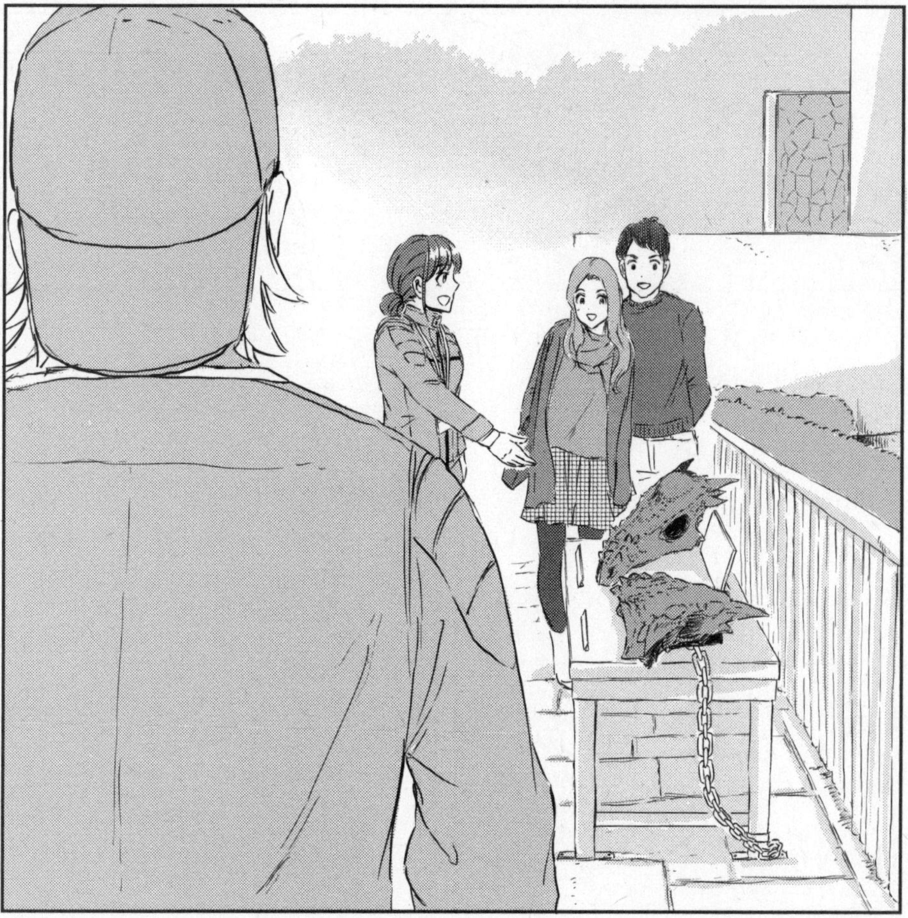

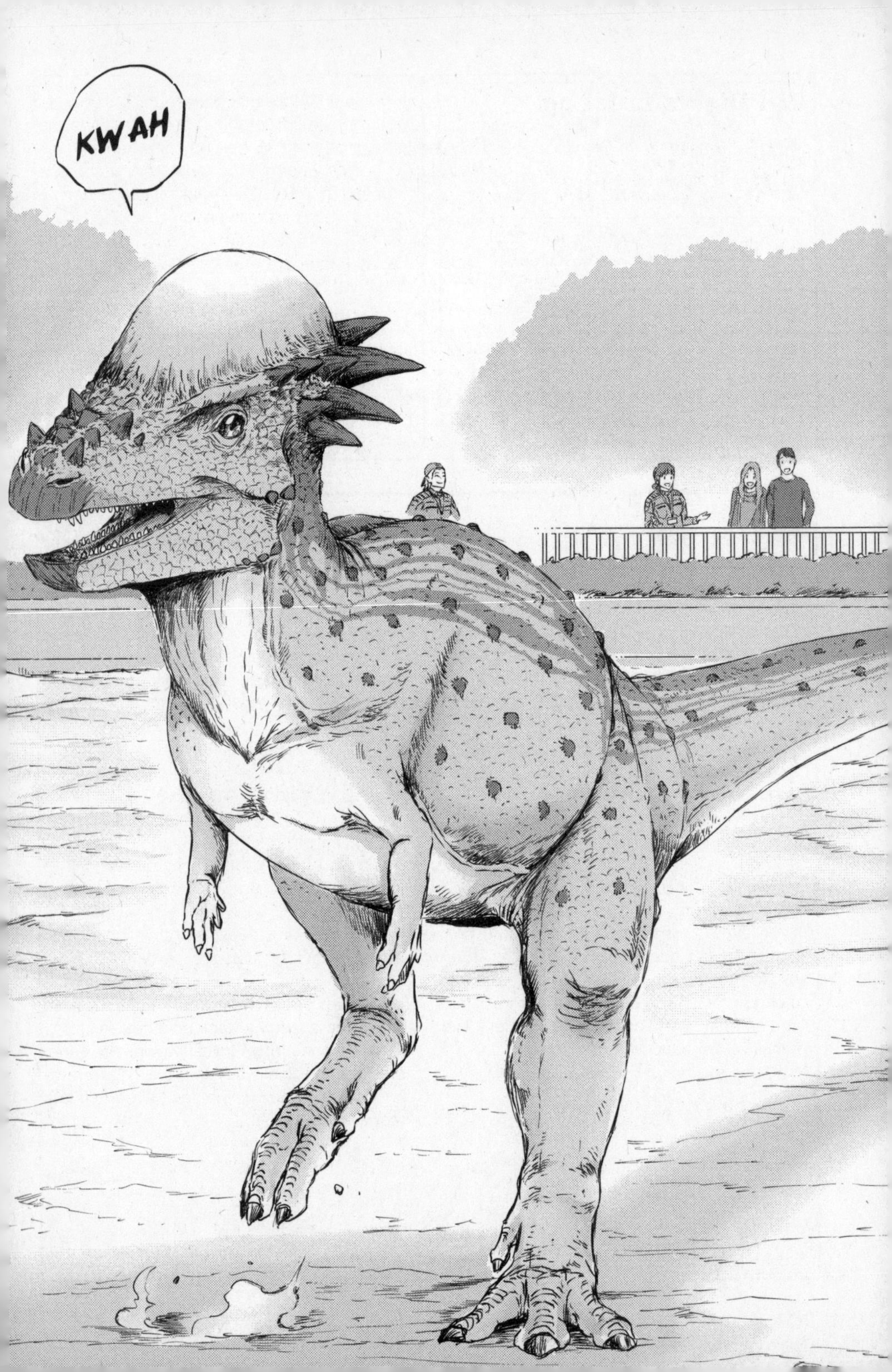
KWAH

Dr. Dino's Lab Log

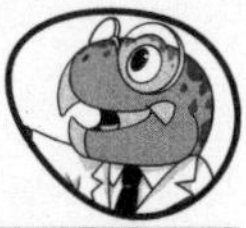

FILE. 14 Moving Up the Steps, or: A Journey of a Thousand Miles Starts with a Single CT Scan

Think back to when Roy the *Dilophosaurus* had an X-ray taken of his knee (volume 1, chapter 5, remember?). To make that happen, rays of radiation were sent through Roy's leg and into a detector. Finally, an image was made with tones that vary based on how hard it is for the rays to pass through different parts of his leg. Dense areas, such as bones and teeth, absorb a lot of those X-rays, and thus show up as white in the final image. Meanwhile, cartilage, muscles, and other less-absorbent parts show up as black.

When I was a student, I made X-ray images of dissected animal carcasses, developing the resulting film in the sour-smelling air of the museum's darkroom. (Ah, memories!) As everything's gotten more and more digital, we've mostly left the darkroom behind... Personally, though, I still prefer film to digital. Things just show up more clearly that way!

Anyway, this time around, Hachibei the *Pachycephalosaurus* had X-ray CT imaging done. The principles are basically the same: A volley of X-rays is passed through whole body, and the ray absorption rate distribution is shown with a 3D image, thanks to computerized tomography (hence "CT"). Both CT scans and conventional X-rays are often used to investigate parts of the body that we can't see from the outside. When making these images from living creatures, though, care must be taken to protect their bodies from X-ray radiation—especially their sensitive reproductive organs.

In an X-ray image, everything shows up in one place, from the outermost skin to the innermost part of the body. If an animal has thick skin, or dermal bones in its scales, those can get in the way and make it difficult to see the affected part of the body. (Like Hachibei's lungs, in this case.) Enter the CT scan, which is more effective at getting the whole picture with its three-dimensional images. Thanks to the CT scan, we saw a cross section of Hachibei's ribcage. The black parts of that image are his lungs, and his heart is likely visible somewhere below them.

Research into an animal's body doesn't stop at taking a CT scan. In fact, it barely *starts* there! The images that a CT scan creates are pixelated and in black and white. The work continues into 3D reconstruction, in which CT images are put together in layers to form a three-dimensional image. Necessary parts are filled in from hundreds, or even thousands, of images in this fairly mind-numbing process. Voxels—three-dimensional pixels—are split up and covered with triangular patches, forming polygonal shapes. That part might sound familiar to any of you who've gotten in on the recent 3D printing craze.

But 3D reconstruction isn't the end of the line, either! It's just a move up from step two to step three. The next few steps involve taking those new polygons and putting them to use in various types of research. In my case, I use polygonal bones to build computer models of joints and the areas around them. With those, I can look into how dinosaurs might have used their joints most effectively to move their muscles, for instance, or try to figure out how strong their bones were, based on the amount of stress they would have incurred with force applied to their complex shapes... Anyway, once those investigations are done, *then* we can finally say that the CT scan we took so long ago has yielded the sort of data that we call *results.*

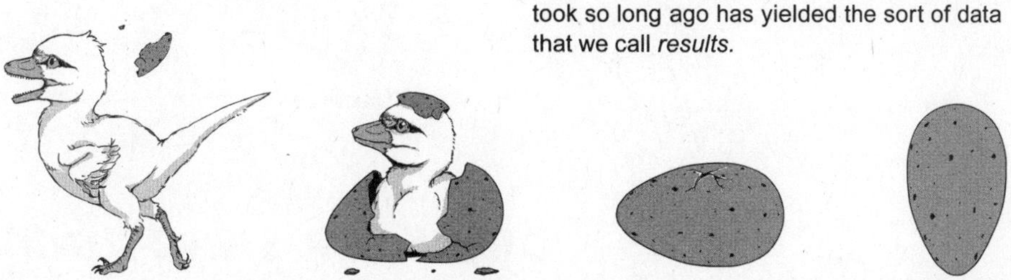

DINOSAUR SANCTUARY

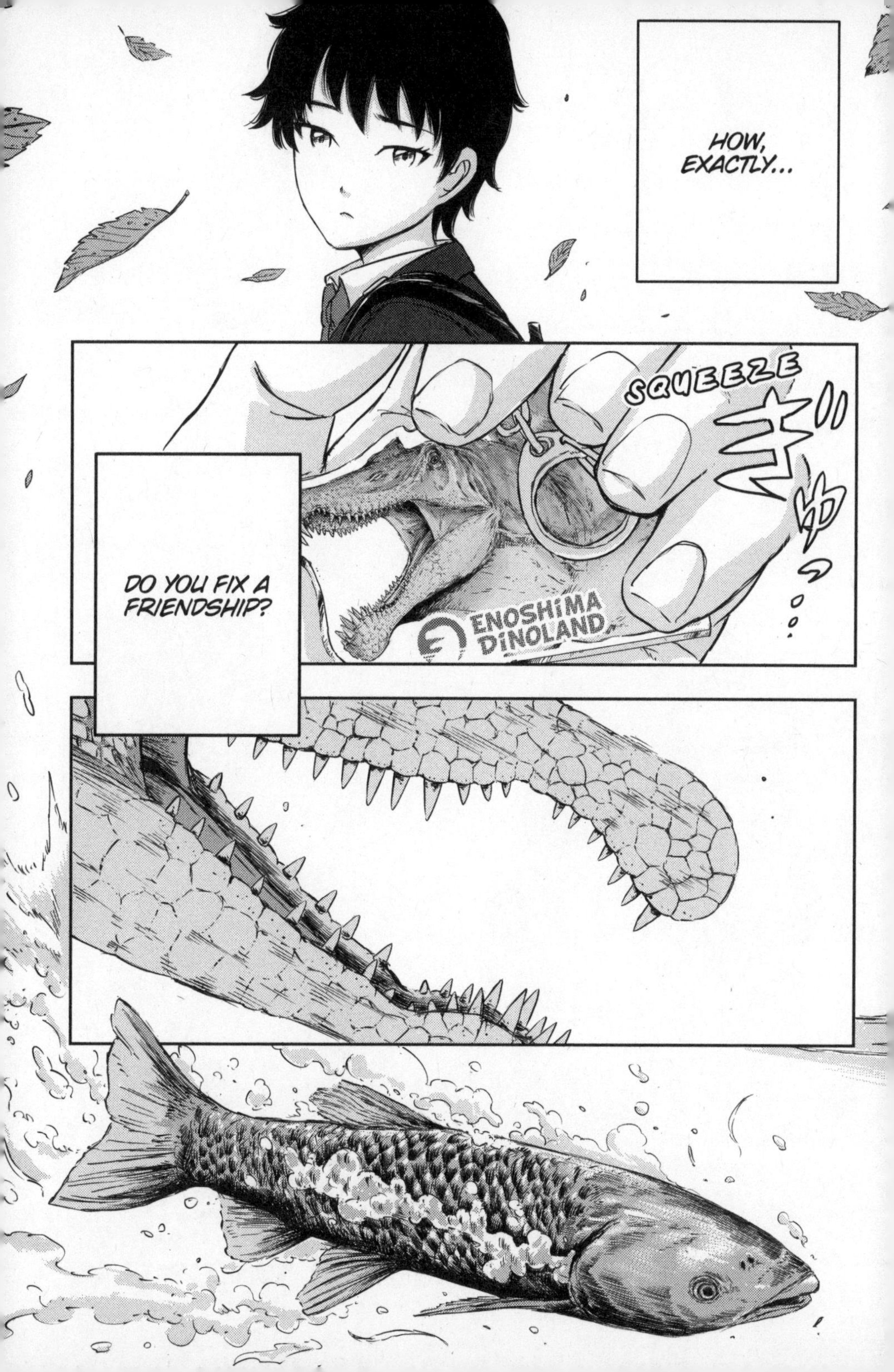
HOW, EXACTLY...
SQUEEZE
ぎゅっ
ENOSHIMA DINOLAND
DO YOU FIX A FRIENDSHIP?

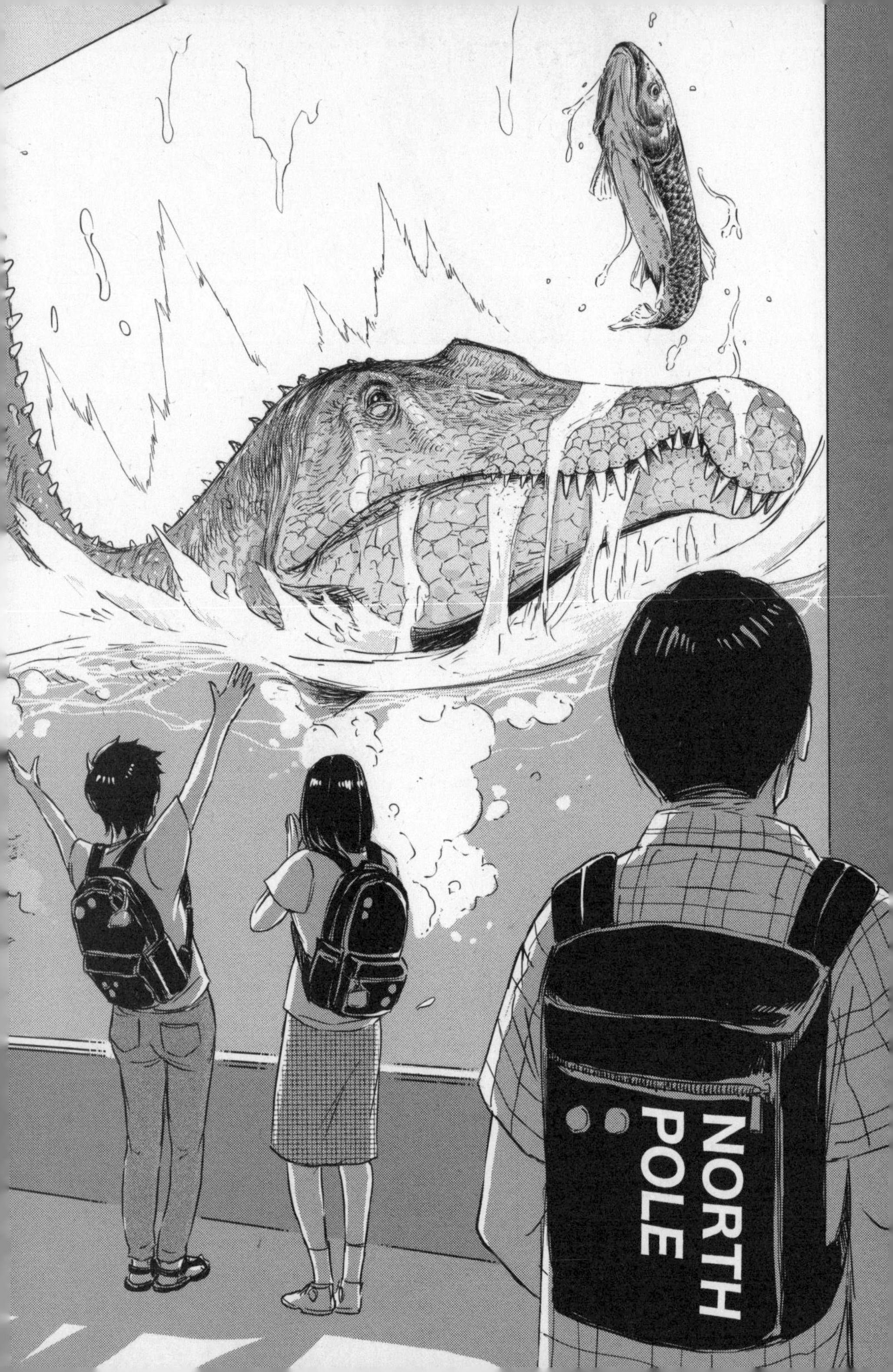
NORTH POLE

CHAPTER 15 DINO FANS FOREVER!

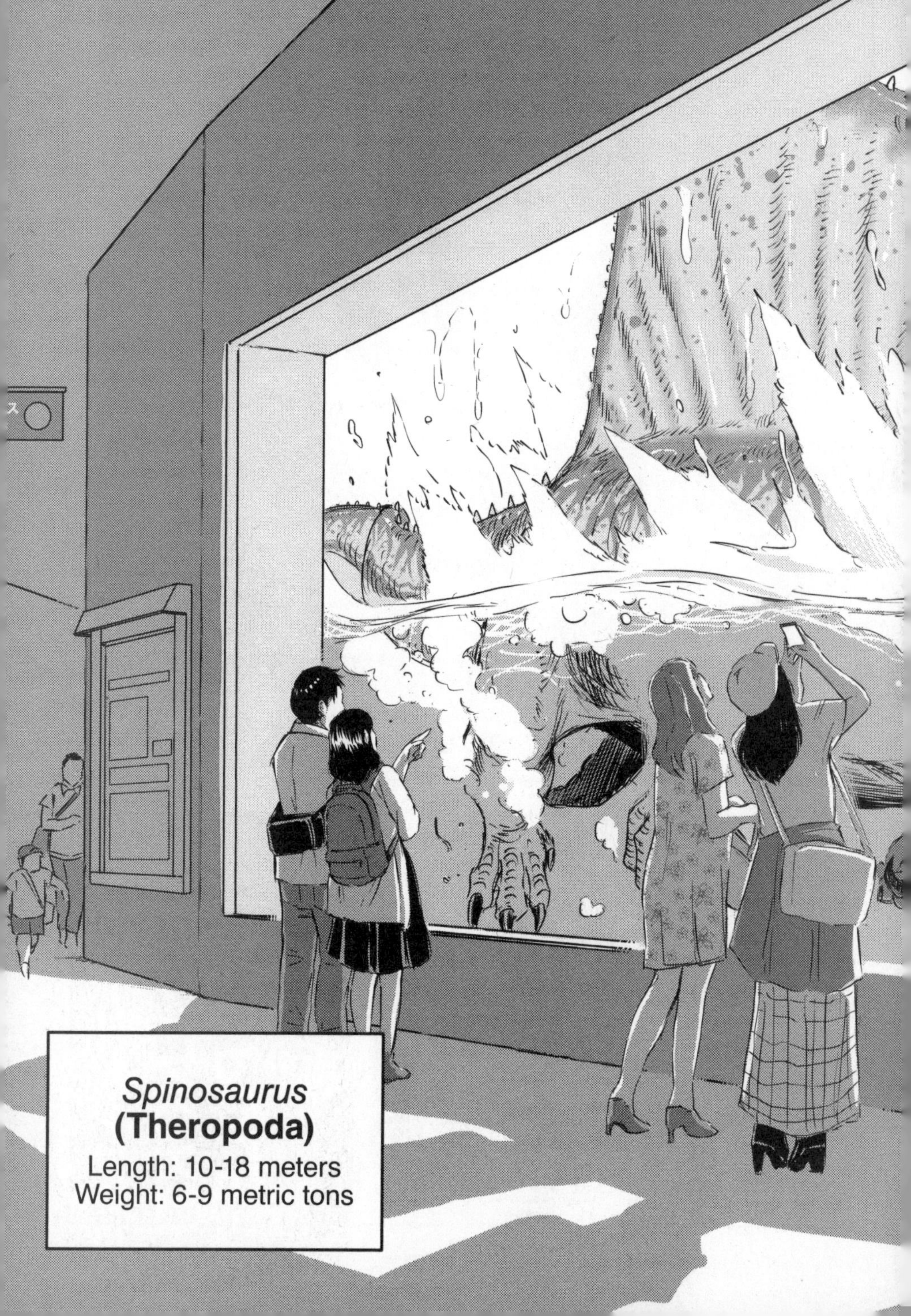
Spinosaurus
(Theropoda)
Length: 10-18 meters
Weight: 6-9 metric tons

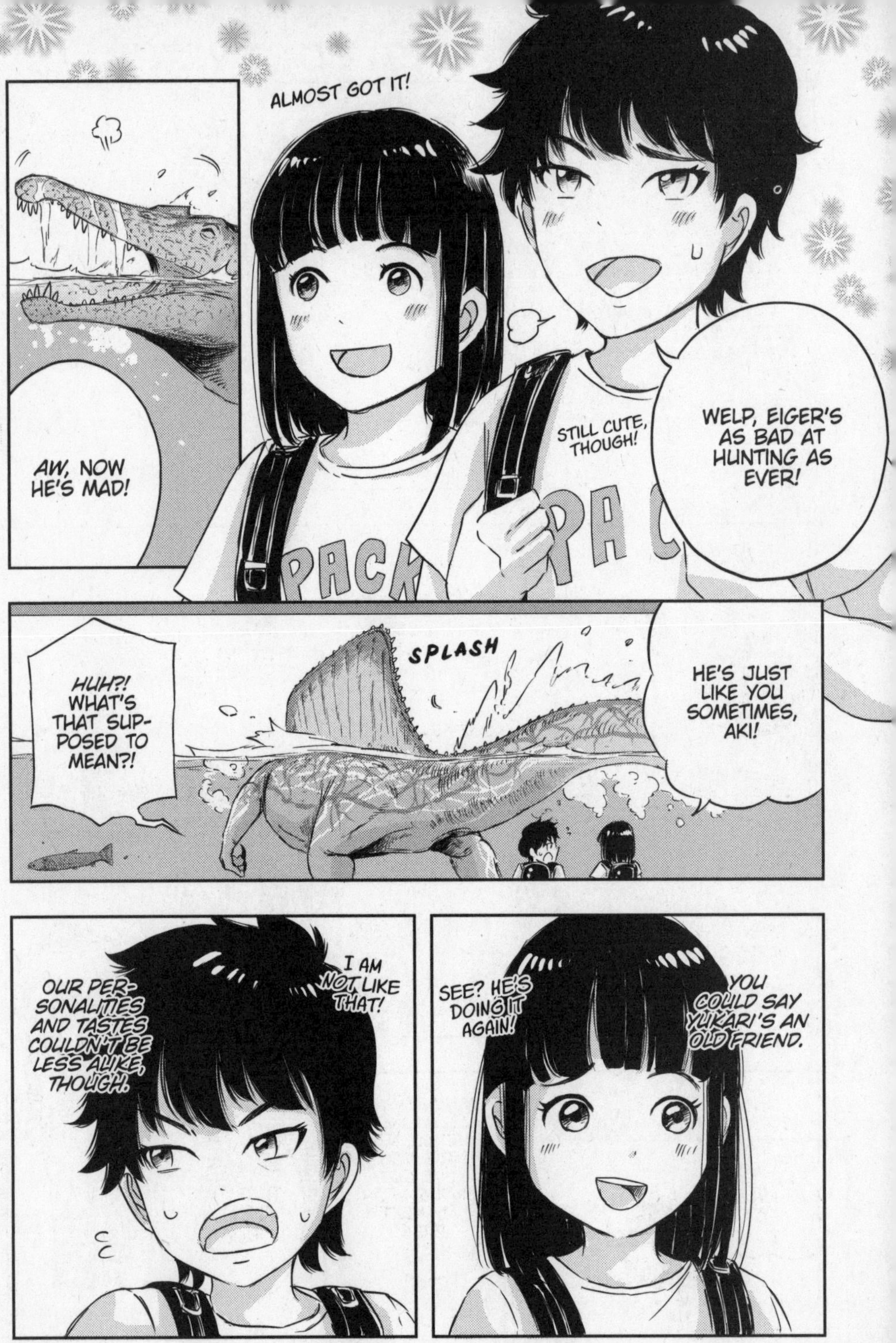
ALMOST GOT IT!
WELP, EIGER'S AS BAD AT HUNTING AS EVER!
STILL CUTE, THOUGH!
AW, NOW HE'S MAD!
HE'S JUST LIKE YOU SOMETIMES, AKI!
SPLASH
HUH?! WHAT'S THAT SUP-POSED TO MEAN?!
YOU COULD SAY YUKARI'S AN OLD FRIEND.
SEE? HE'S DOING IT AGAIN!
I AM NOT LIKE THAT!
OUR PER-SONALITIES AND TASTES COULDN'T BE LESS ALIKE, THOUGH.

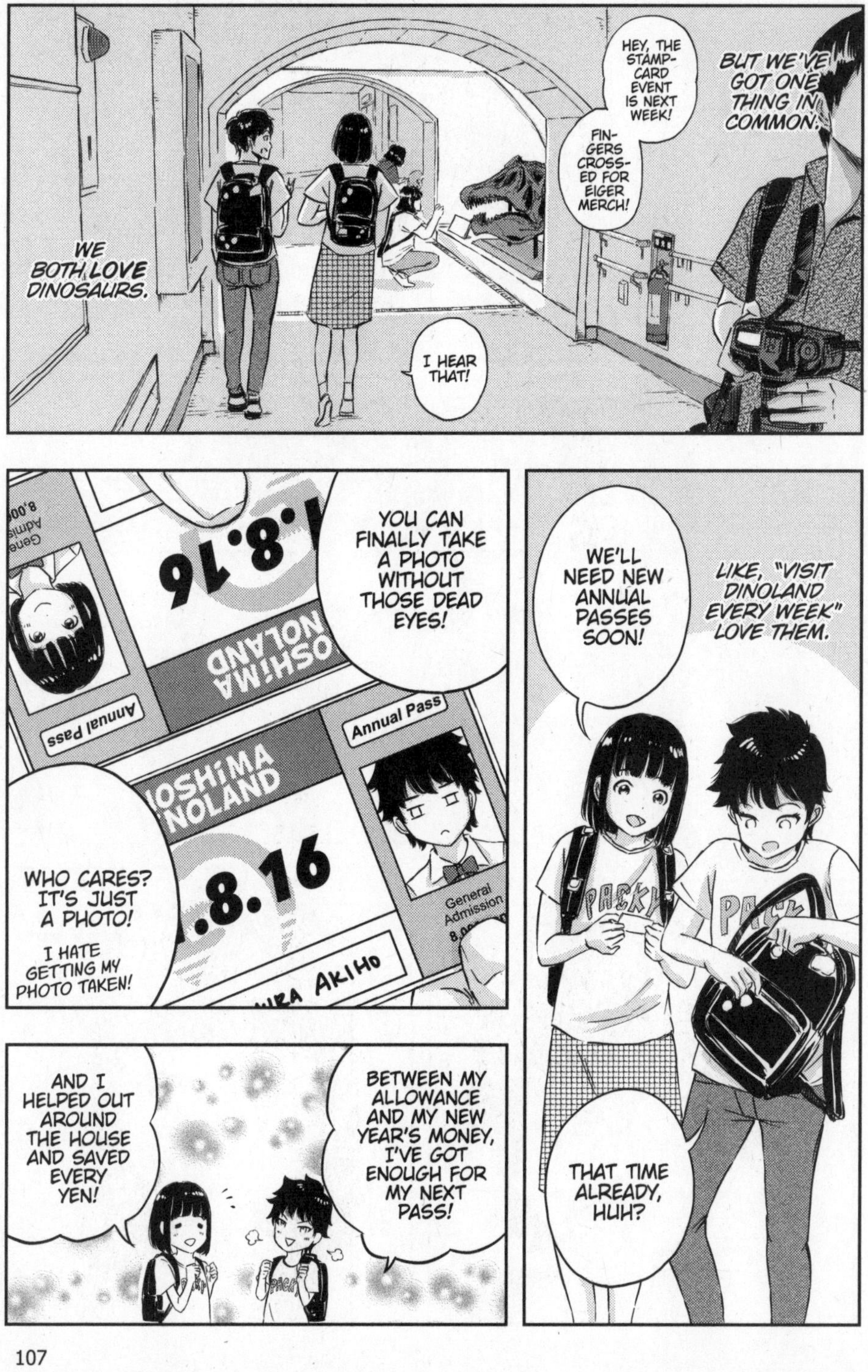
BUT WE'VE GOT ONE THING IN COMMON.
HEY, THE STAMP-CARD EVENT IS NEXT WEEK!
FIN-GERS CROSS-ED FOR EIGER MERCH!
WE BOTH LOVE DINOSAURS.
I HEAR THAT!
LIKE, "VISIT DINOLAND EVERY WEEK" LOVE THEM.
WE'LL NEED NEW ANNUAL PASSES SOON!
THAT TIME ALREADY, HUH?
YOU CAN FINALLY TAKE A PHOTO WITHOUT THOSE DEAD EYES!
Annual Pass
Annual Pass
General Admission
WHO CARES? IT'S JUST A PHOTO!
I HATE GETTING MY PHOTO TAKEN!
BETWEEN MY ALLOWANCE AND MY NEW YEAR'S MONEY, I'VE GOT ENOUGH FOR MY NEXT PASS!
AND I HELPED OUT AROUND THE HOUSE AND SAVED EVERY YEN!

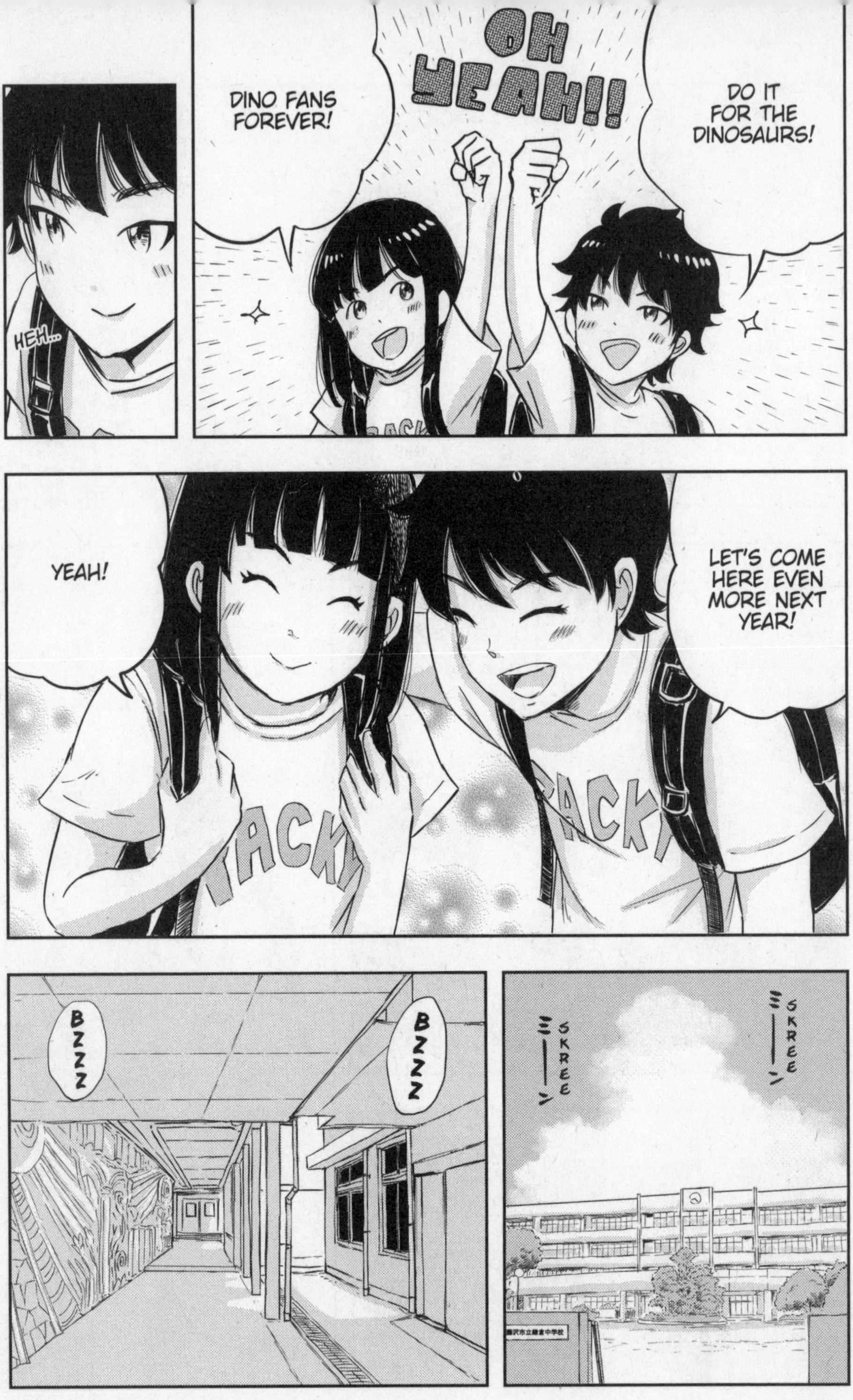
DO IT FOR THE DINOSAURS!
OH YEAH!!
DINO FANS FOREVER!
HEH...
LET'S COME HERE EVEN MORE NEXT YEAR!
YEAH!
SKREE
SKREE
BZZZ
BZZZ

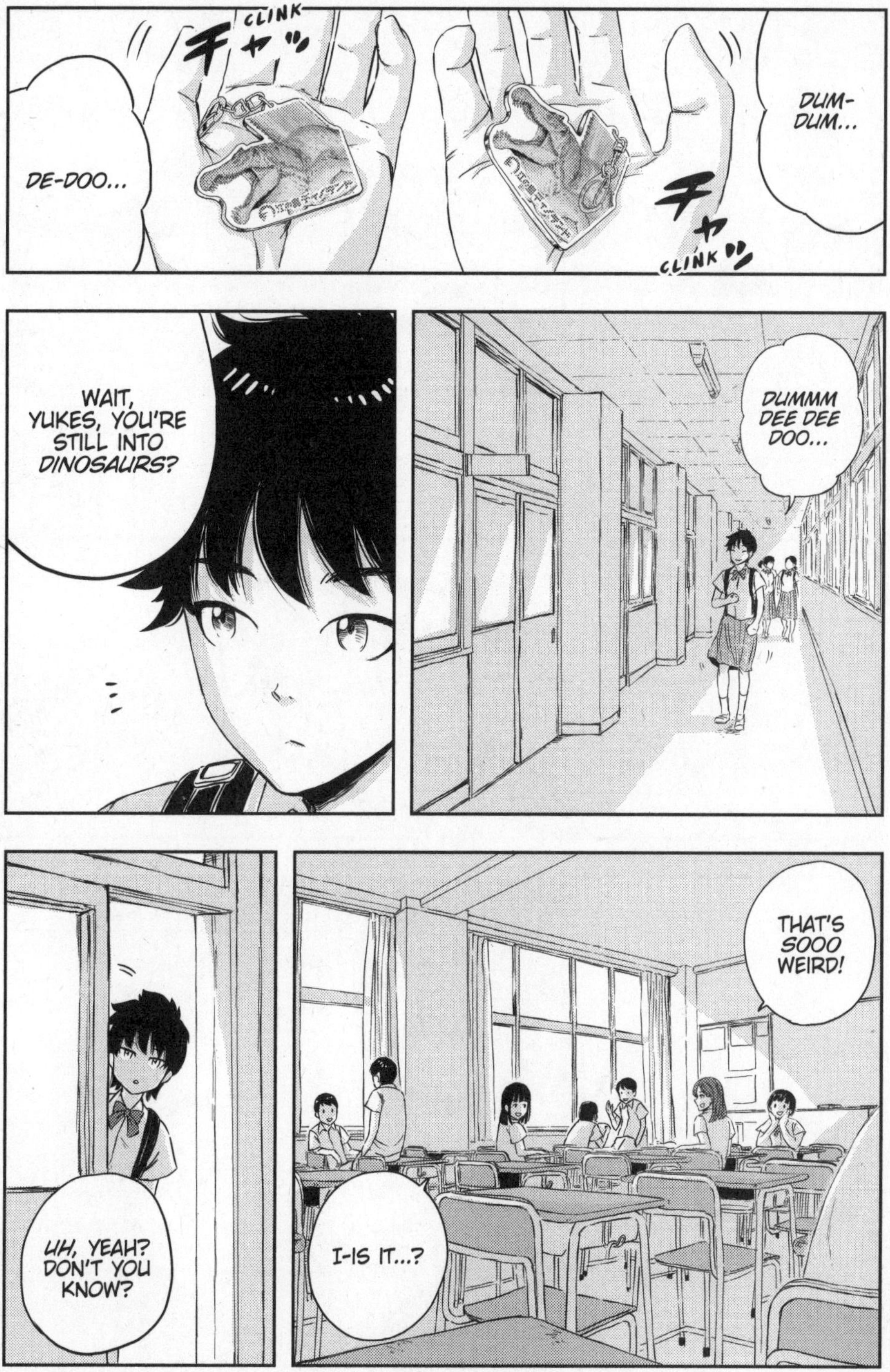

DUM-DUM...
チャ
CLINK
チャッ
CLINK
DE-DOO...
DUMMM DEE DEE DOO...
WAIT, YUKES, YOU'RE STILL INTO DINOSAURS?
THAT'S SOOO WEIRD!
I-IS IT...?
UH, YEAH? DON'T YOU KNOW?

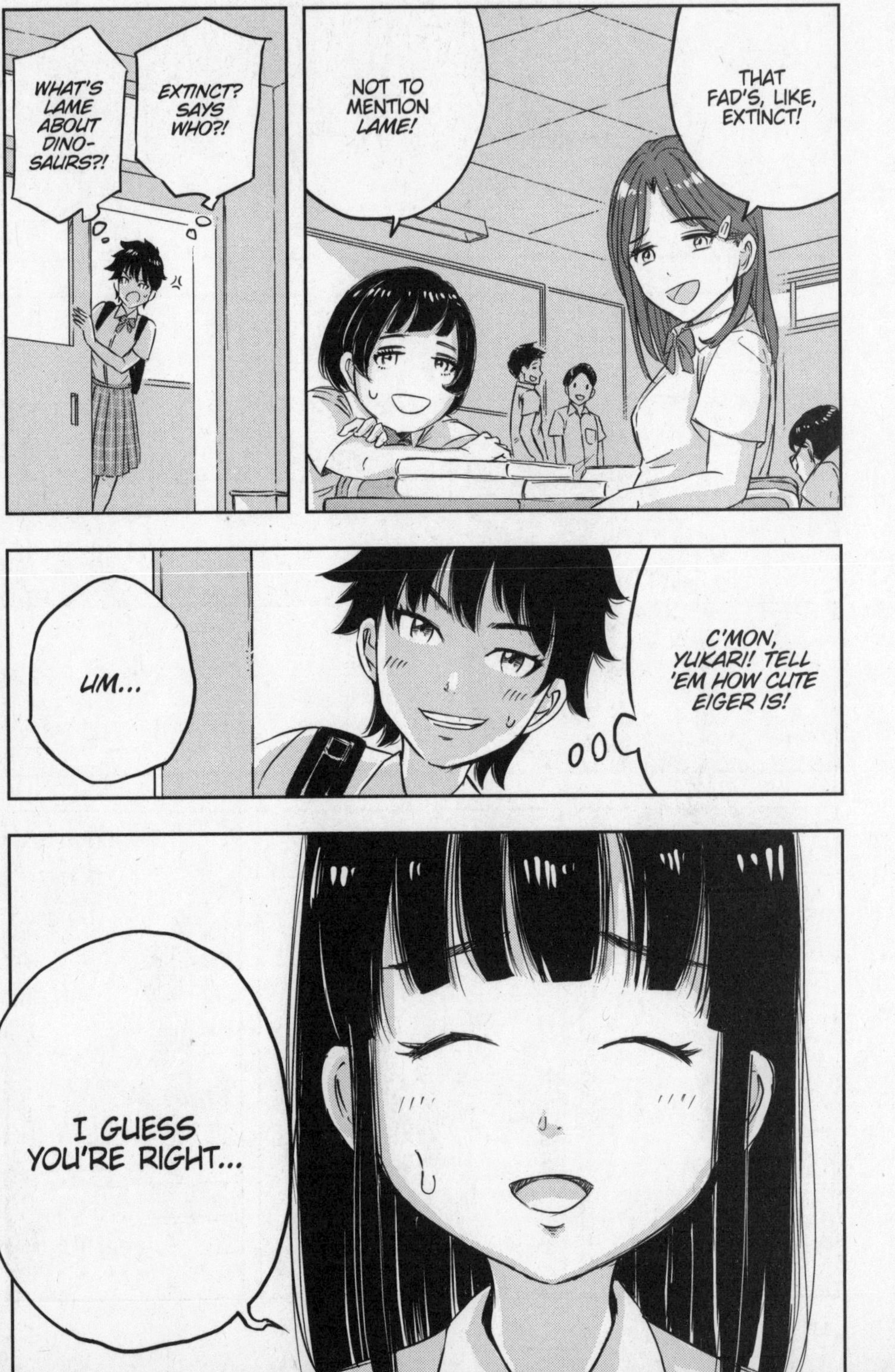
THAT FAD'S, LIKE, EXTINCT!
NOT TO MENTION LAME!
EXTINCT? SAYS WHO?!
WHAT'S LAME ABOUT DINO-SAURS?!
C'MON, YUKARI! TELL 'EM HOW CUTE EIGER IS!
UM...
I GUESS YOU'RE RIGHT...

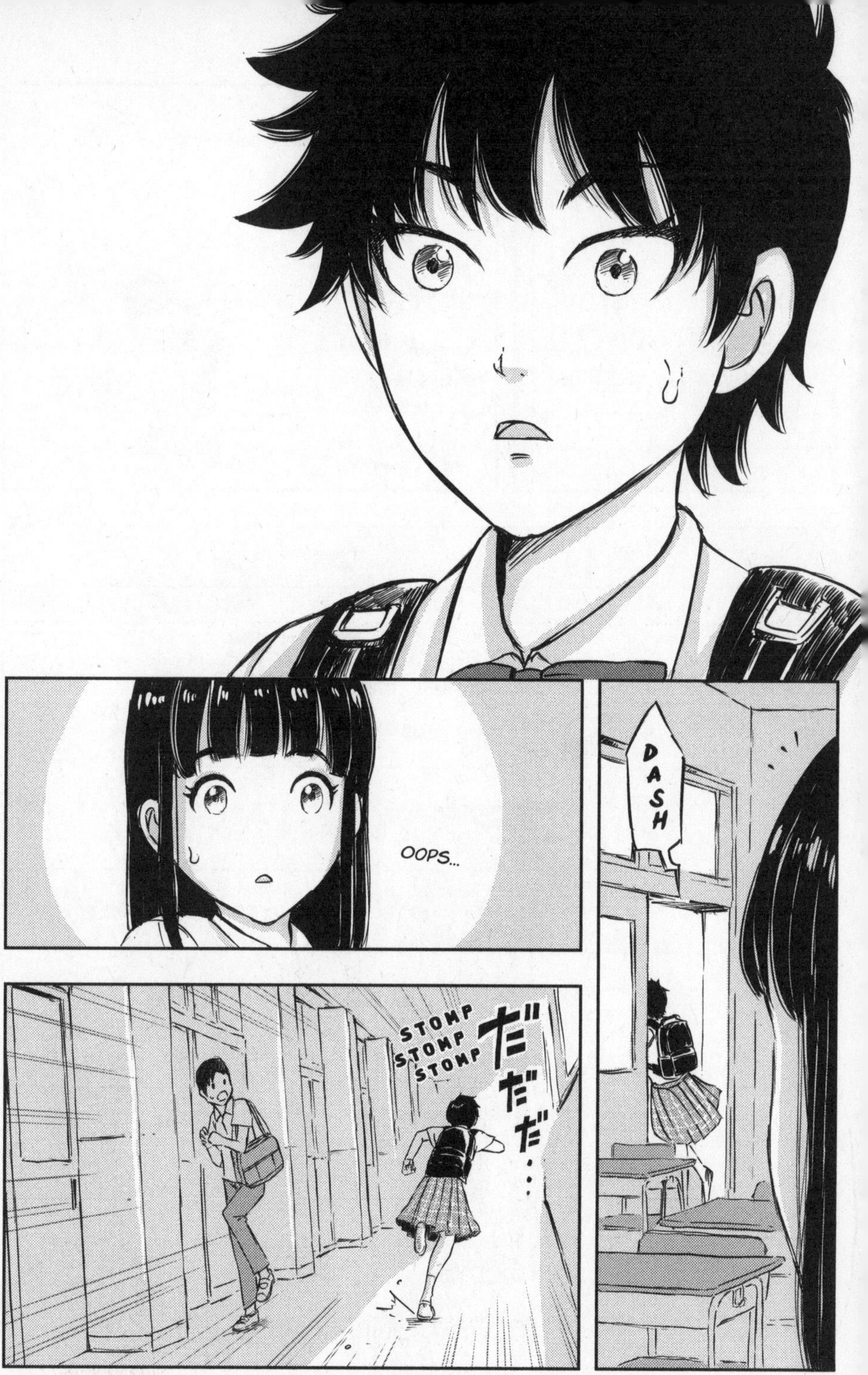
DASH
OOPS...
STOMP STOMP STOMP
だだだ…

だだだ…
STOMP
STOMP
STOMP

だだだだ
STOMP
STOMP
STOMP
STOMP

?

SLAM

· · · · · ·

squeeze

HAAH...
ハッ

ハッ

ハァ
HAAH...

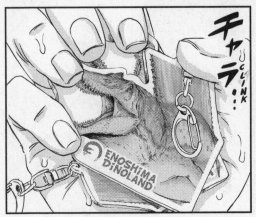

チャラ…
CLINK

ENOSHIMA
DINOLAND

SWOOSH

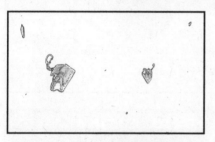

SKREE

SKREE

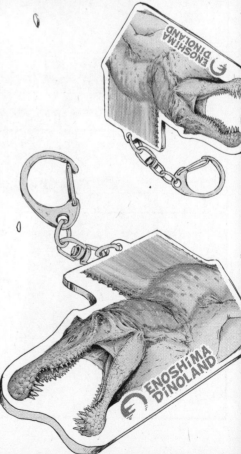

ENOSHIMA DINOLAND

ENOSHIMA DINOLAND

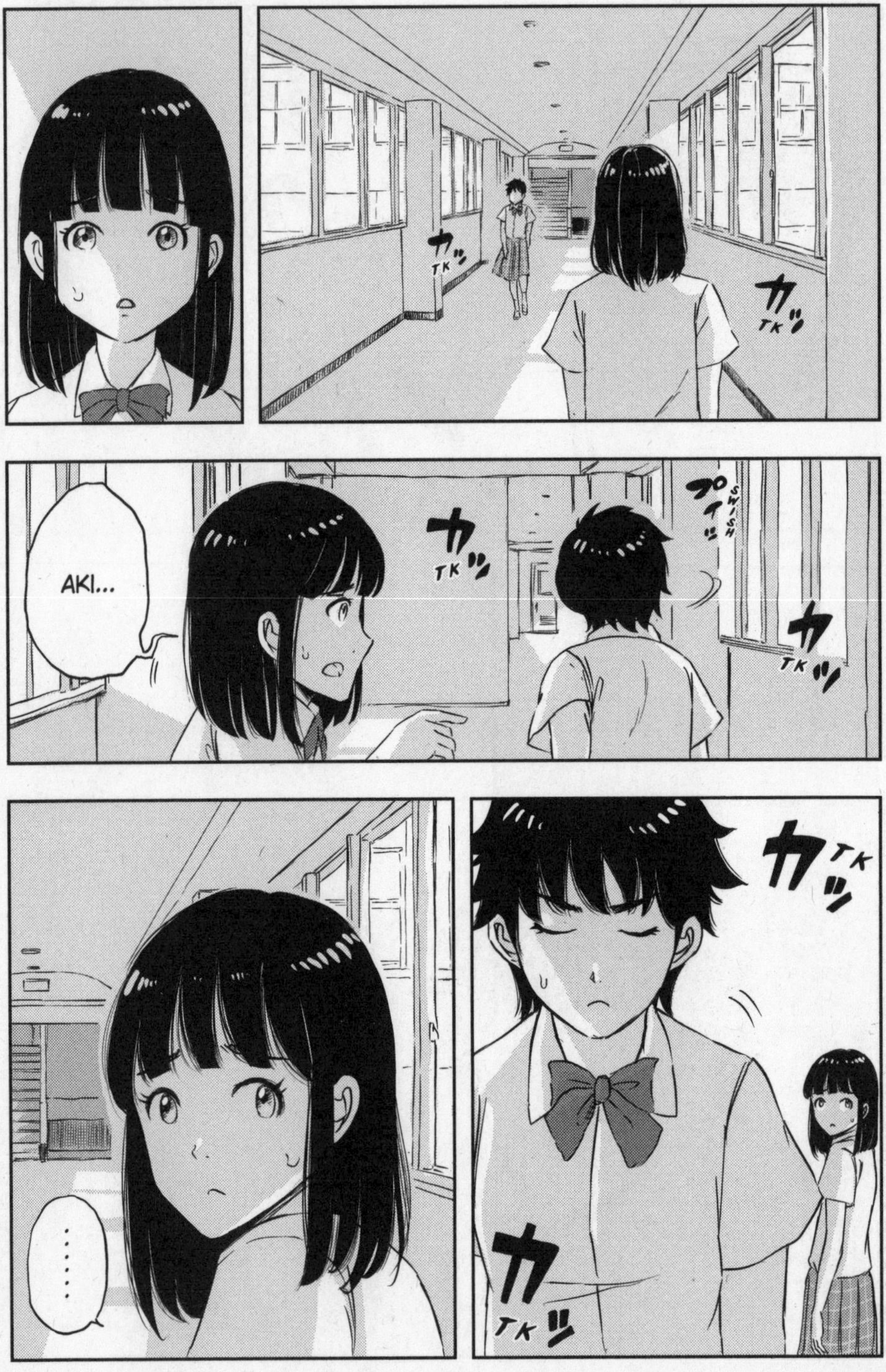
カッ TK
カッ TK
プイッ SWISH
カッ TK
カッ TK
AKI...
カッ TK
カッ TK
......

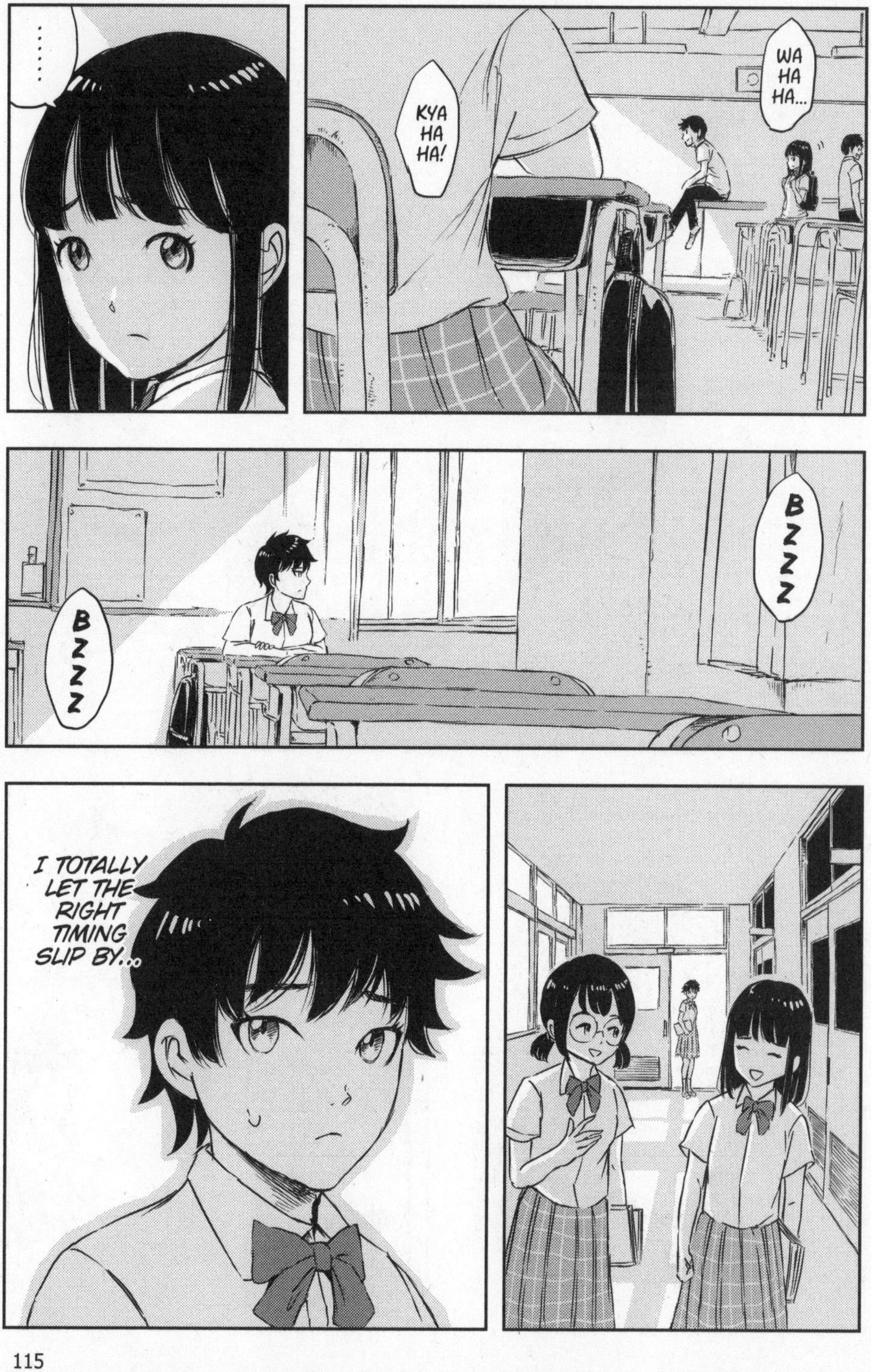
WA HA HA...
KYA HA HA!
......
BZZZ
BZZZ
I TOTALLY LET THE RIGHT TIMING SLIP BY...

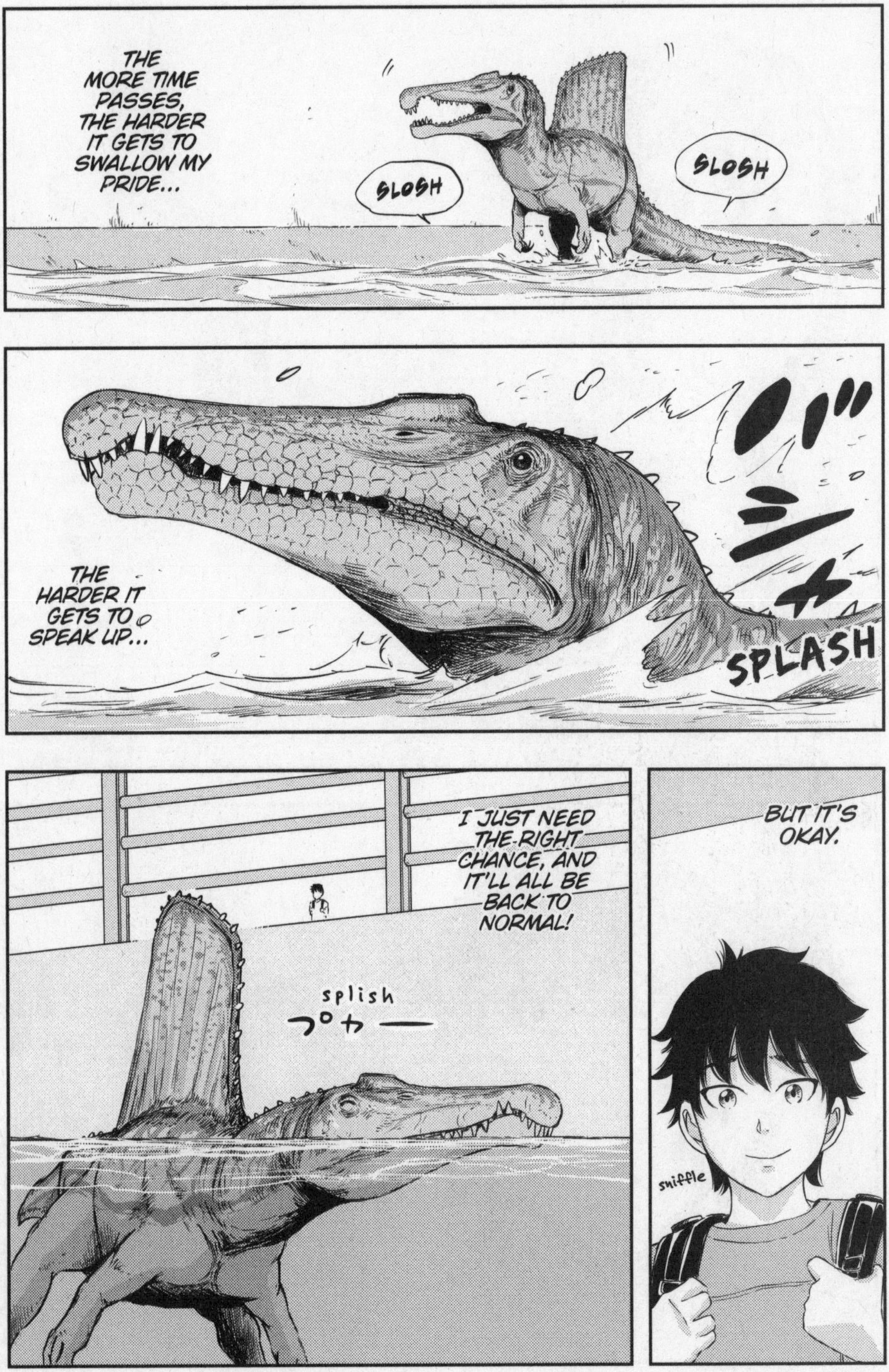
THE MORE TIME PASSES, THE HARDER IT GETS TO SWALLOW MY PRIDE...
SLOSH
SLOSH
SPLASH
THE HARDER IT GETS TO SPEAK UP...
BUT IT'S OKAY.
sniffle
I JUST NEED THE RIGHT CHANCE, AND IT'LL ALL BE BACK TO NORMAL!
splish

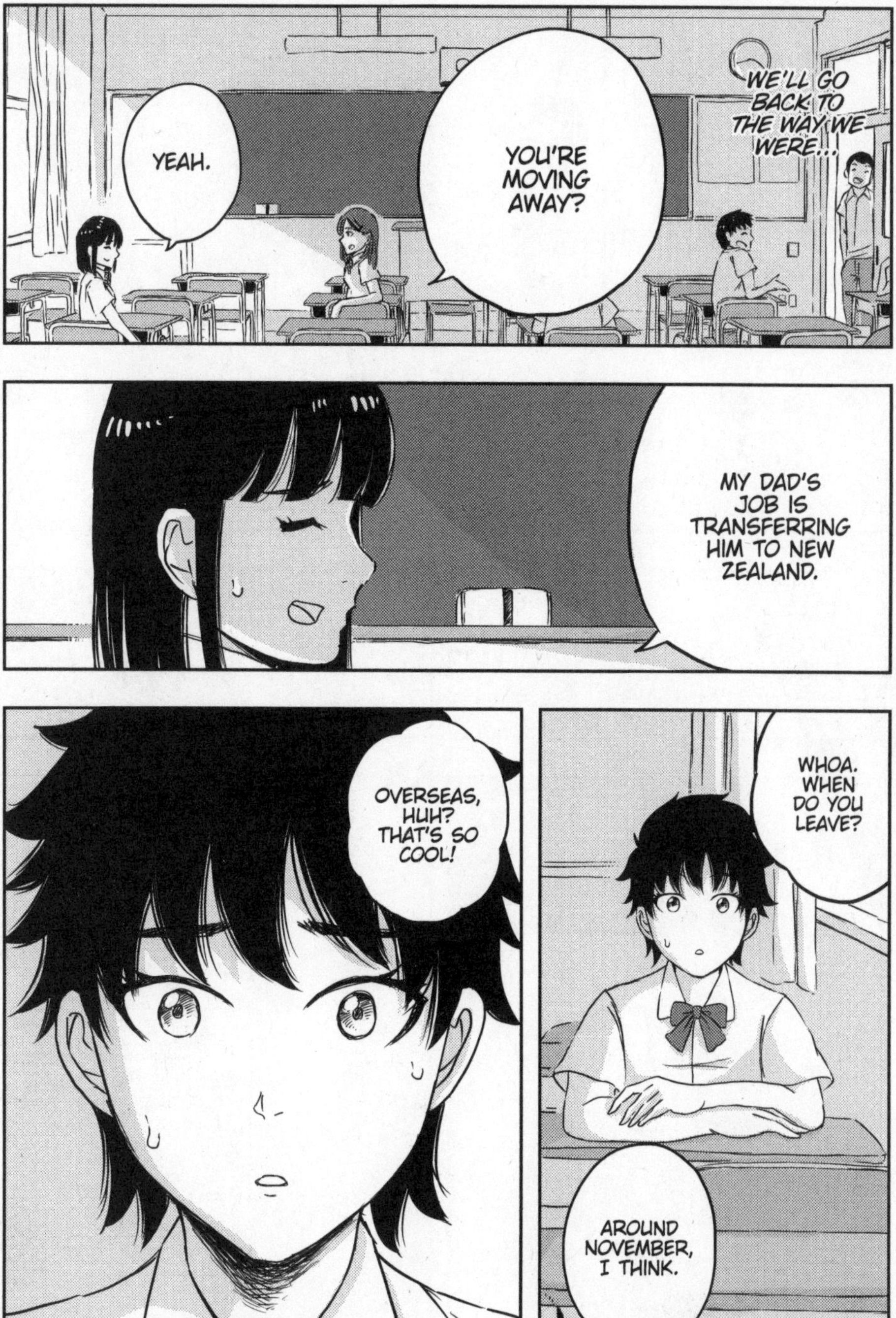
WE'LL GO BACK TO THE WAY WE WERE...
YOU'RE MOVING AWAY?
YEAH.
MY DAD'S JOB IS TRANSFERRING HIM TO NEW ZEALAND.
WHOA. WHEN DO YOU LEAVE?
AROUND NOVEMBER, I THINK.
OVERSEAS, HUH? THAT'S SO COOL!

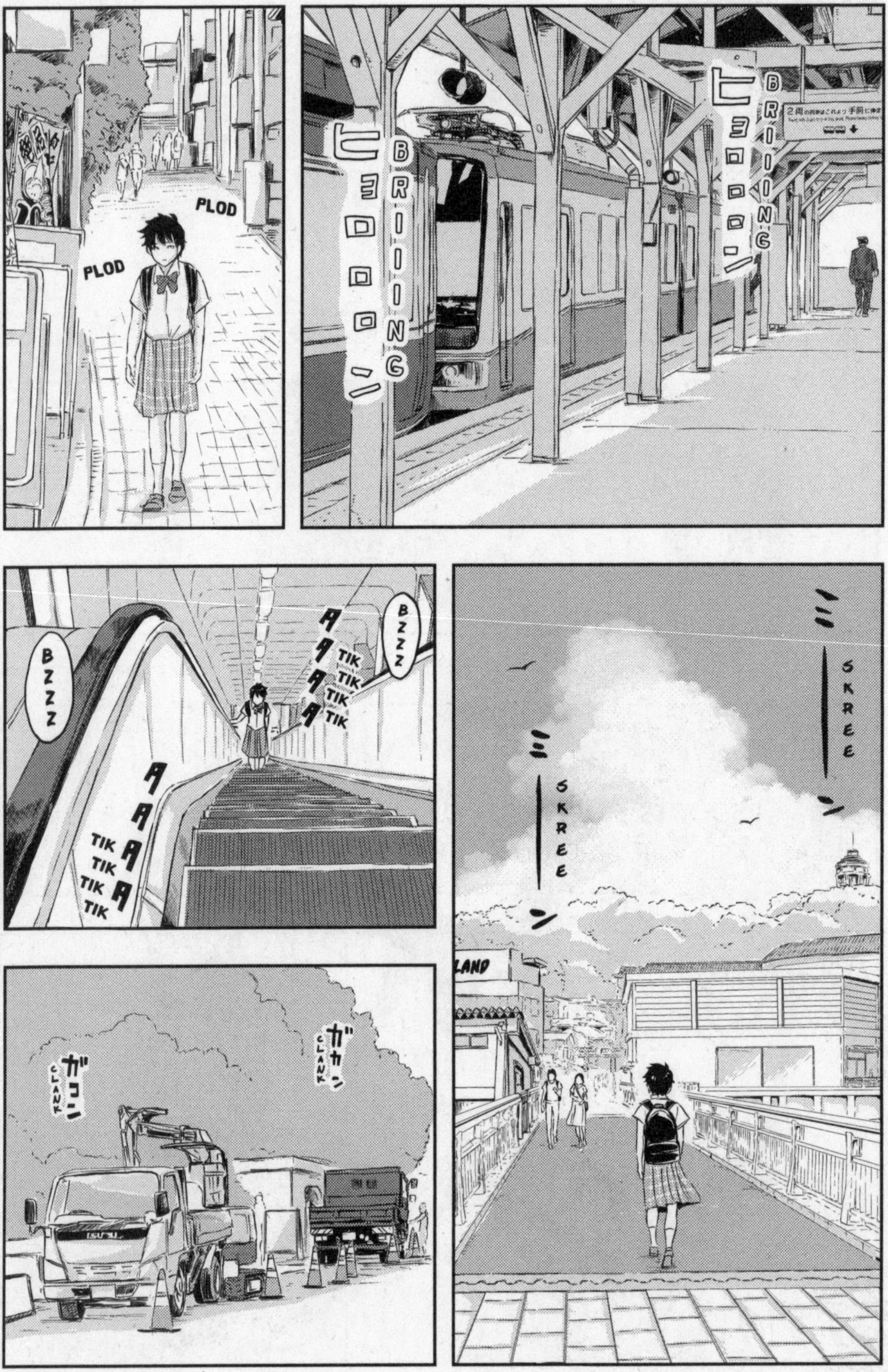
ヒョロロロ〜ン
BRIIING
ヒョロロロ〜ン
BRIIING
PLOD
PLOD
ミーーン
SKREE
ミーーン
SKREE
LAND
BZZZ
BZZZ
タタタタ
TIK TIK TIK TIK
タタタタ
TIK TIK TIK TIK
ガカン
CLANK
ガコン
CLANK

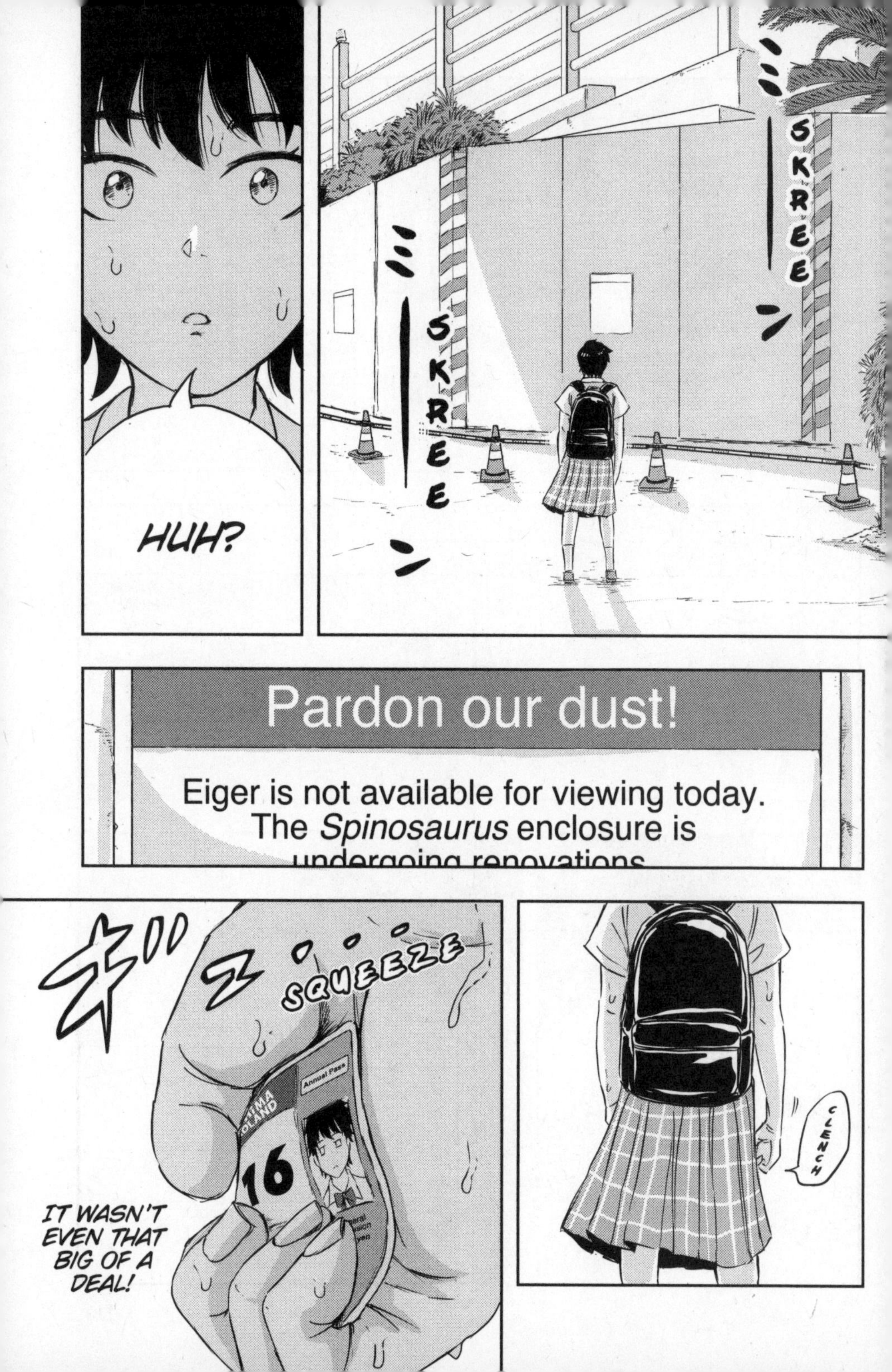
SKREE
SKREE
HUH?
Pardon our dust!
Eiger is not available for viewing today.
The Spinosaurus enclosure is
undergoing renovations
CLENCH
SQUEEZE
Annual Pass
16
IT WASN'T EVEN THAT BIG OF A DEAL!

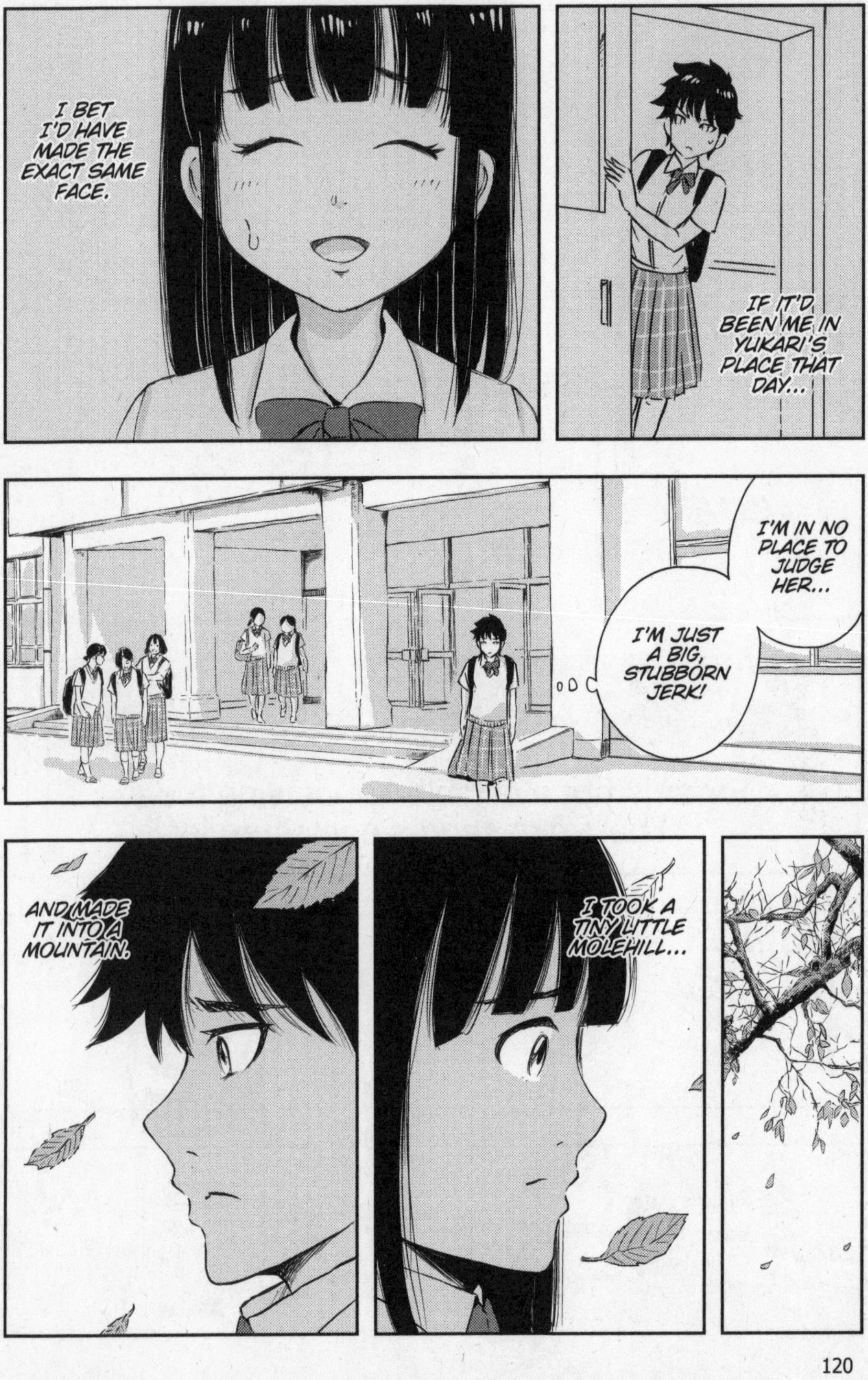
IF IT'D BEEN ME IN YUKARI'S PLACE THAT DAY...
I BET I'D HAVE MADE THE EXACT SAME FACE.
I'M IN NO PLACE TO JUDGE HER...
I'M JUST A BIG, STUBBORN JERK!
I TOOK A TINY LITTLE MOLEHILL...
AND MADE IT INTO A MOUNTAIN.

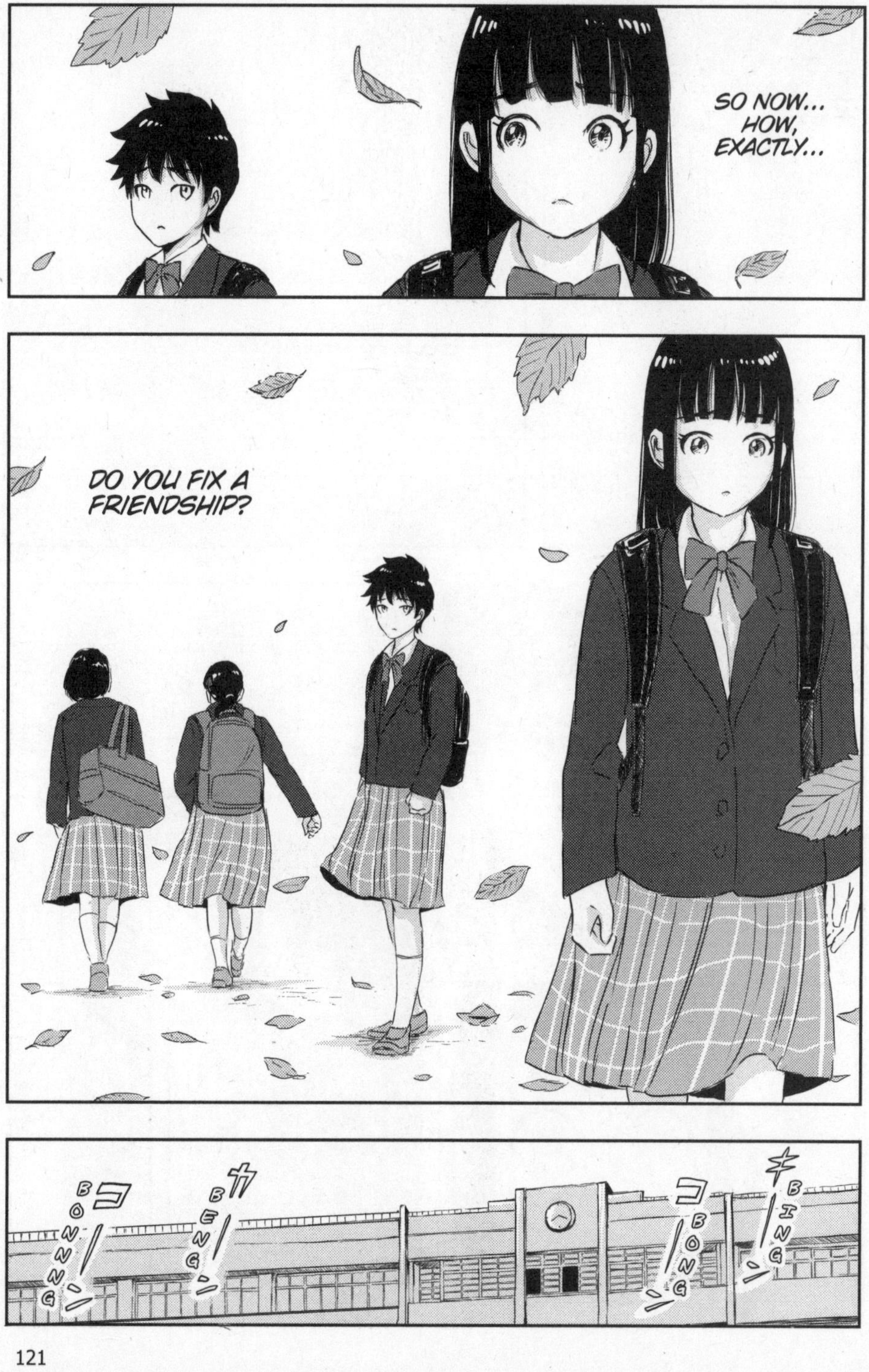
SO NOW... HOW, EXACTLY...
DO YOU FIX A FRIENDSHIP?
キ BING—
コ BONG—
カ BENG—
コ BONNNG—

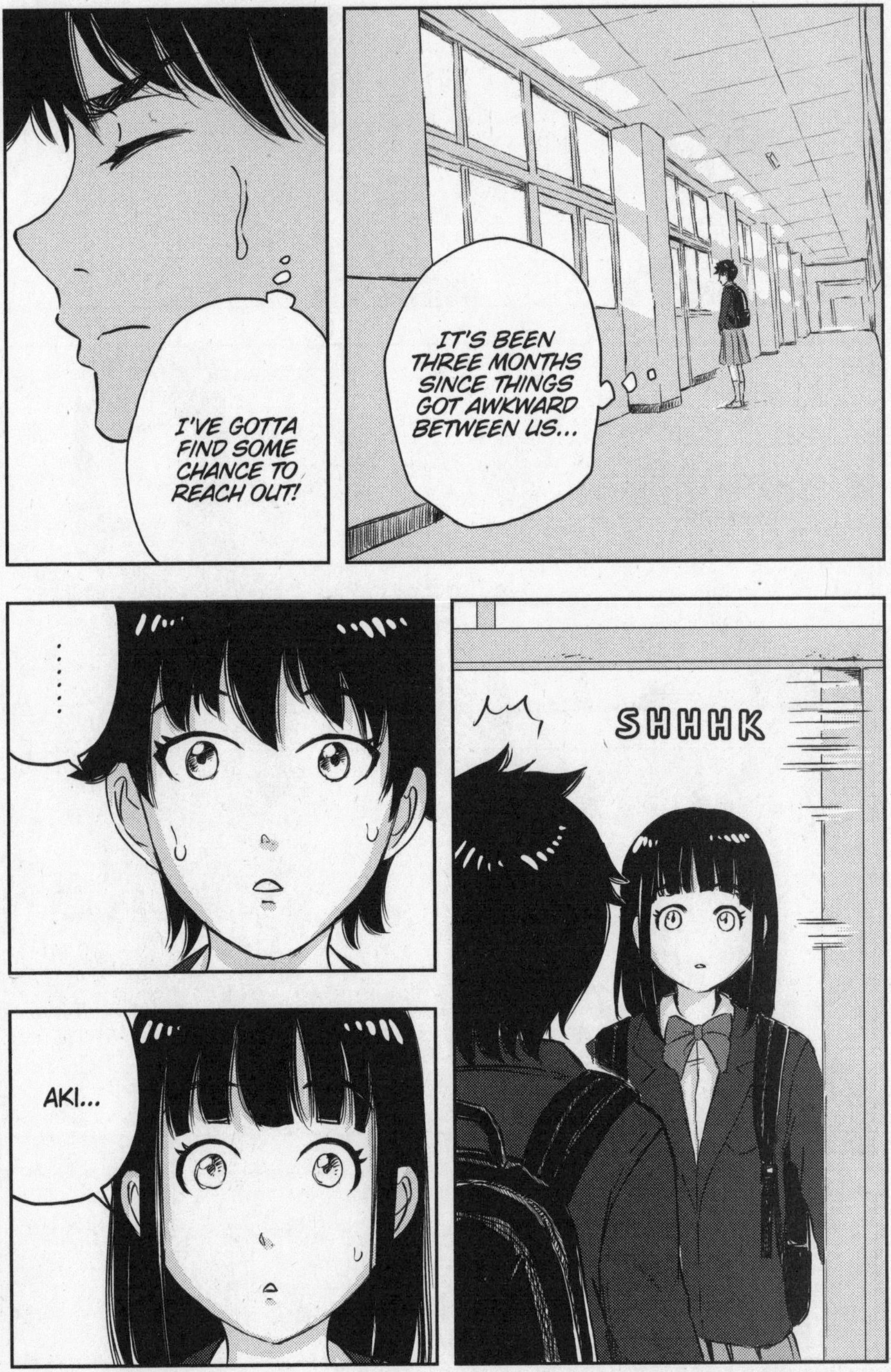
IT'S BEEN THREE MONTHS SINCE THINGS GOT AWKWARD BETWEEN US...
I'VE GOTTA FIND SOME CHANCE TO REACH OUT!
SHHHK
......
AKI...

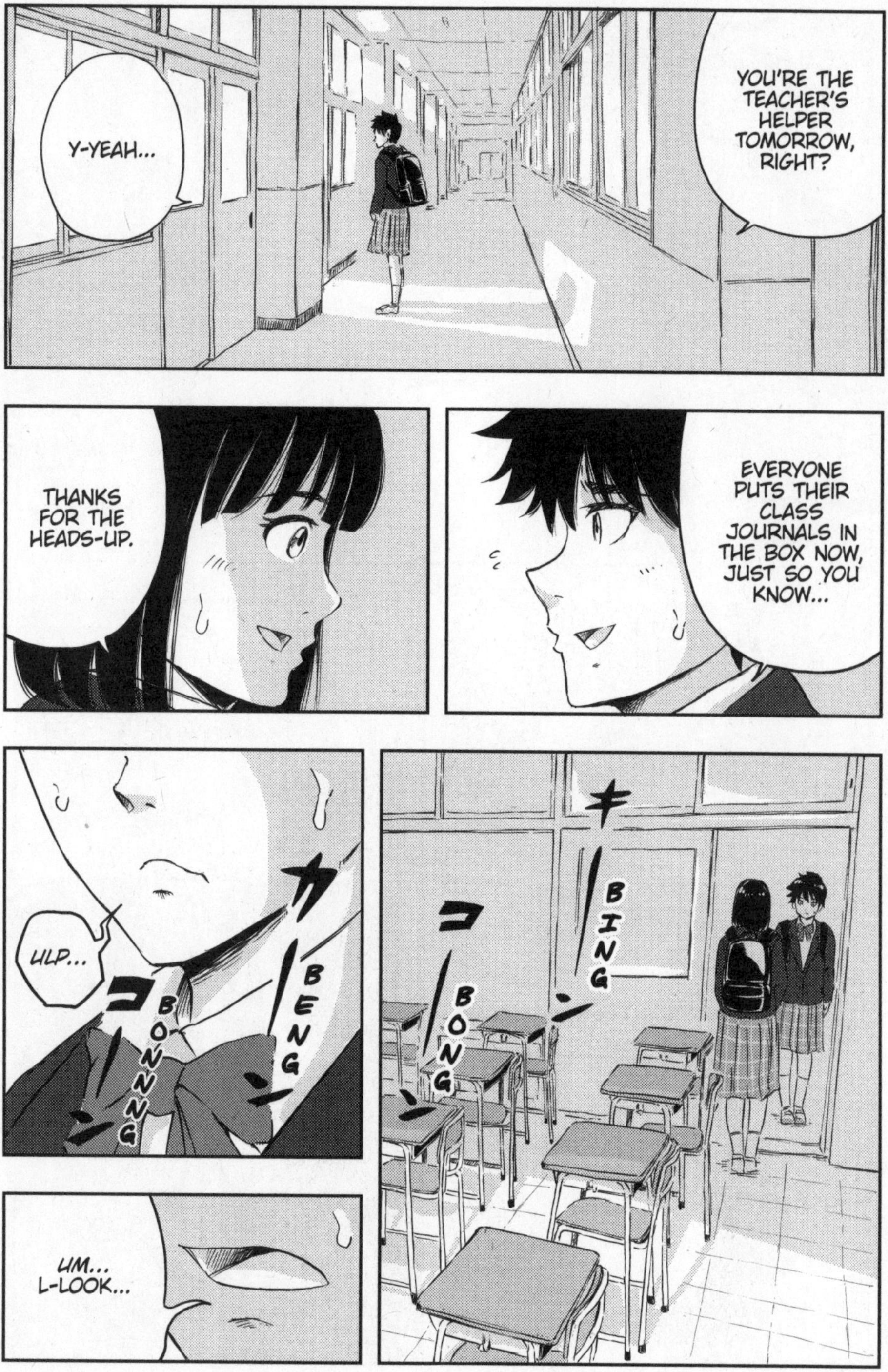
YOU'RE THE TEACHER'S HELPER TOMORROW, RIGHT?
Y-YEAH...
EVERYONE PUTS THEIR CLASS JOURNALS IN THE BOX NOW, JUST SO YOU KNOW...
THANKS FOR THE HEADS-UP.
BING
BONG
ULP...
BENG
BONNNG
UM... L-LOOK...

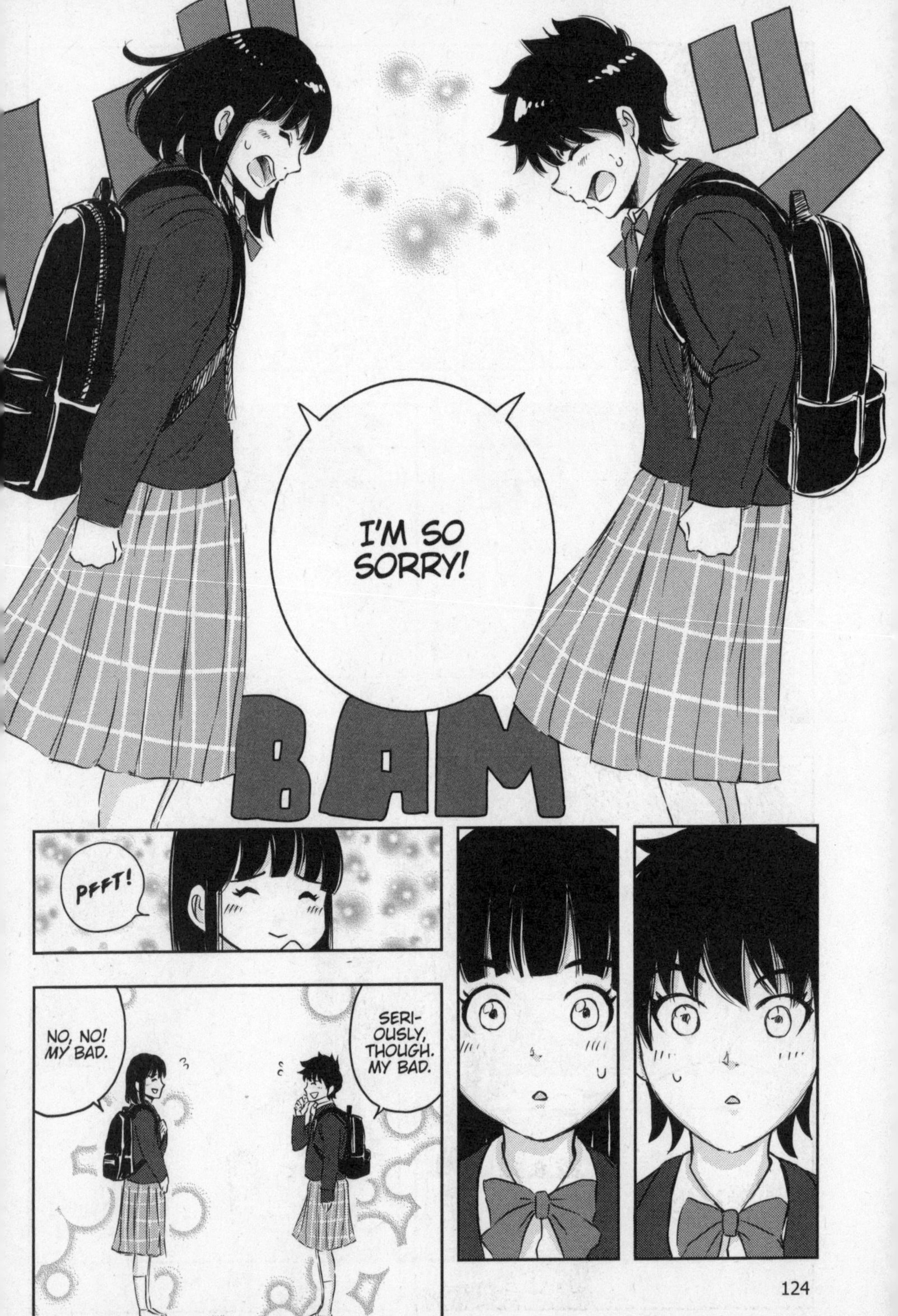
I'M SO SORRY!
BAM
PFFT!
SERI-OUSLY, THOUGH. MY BAD.
NO, NO! MY BAD.

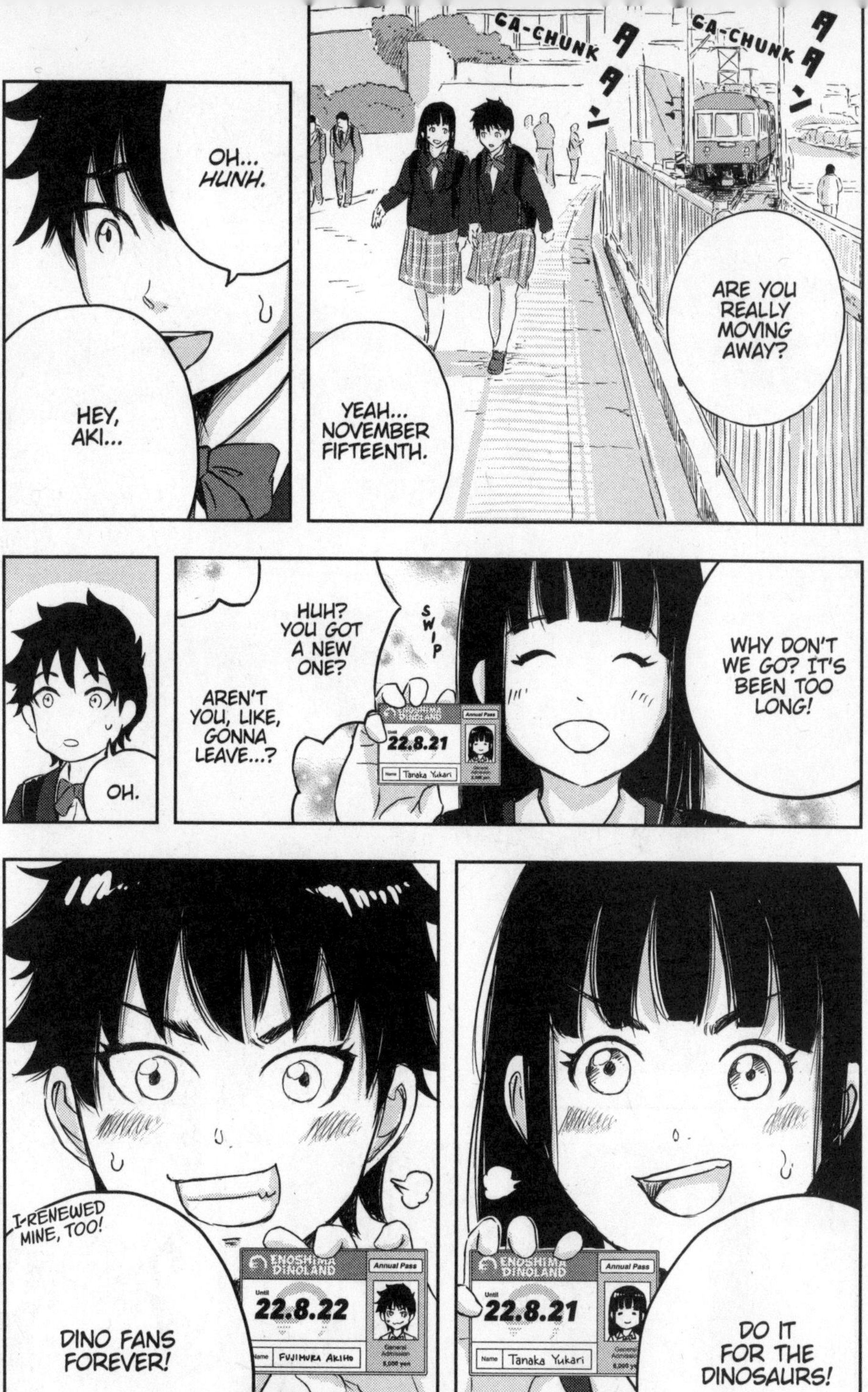
GA-CHUNK
タタン
GA-CHUNK
タタン
ARE YOU REALLY MOVING AWAY?
YEAH... NOVEMBER FIFTEENTH.
OH... HUNH.
HEY, AKI...
WHY DON'T WE GO? IT'S BEEN TOO LONG!
SWIP
HUH? YOU GOT A NEW ONE?
Annual Pass
Until
22.8.21
Name
Tanaka Yukari
AREN'T YOU, LIKE, GONNA LEAVE...?
OH.
DO IT FOR THE DINOSAURS!
ENOSHIMA DINOLAND
Annual Pass
Until
22.8.21
Name
Tanaka Yukari
I-RENEWED MINE, TOO!
ENOSHIMA DINOLAND
Annual Pass
Until
22.8.22
Name
FUJIMURA AKIHO
General Admission
8,000 yen
DINO FANS FOREVER!

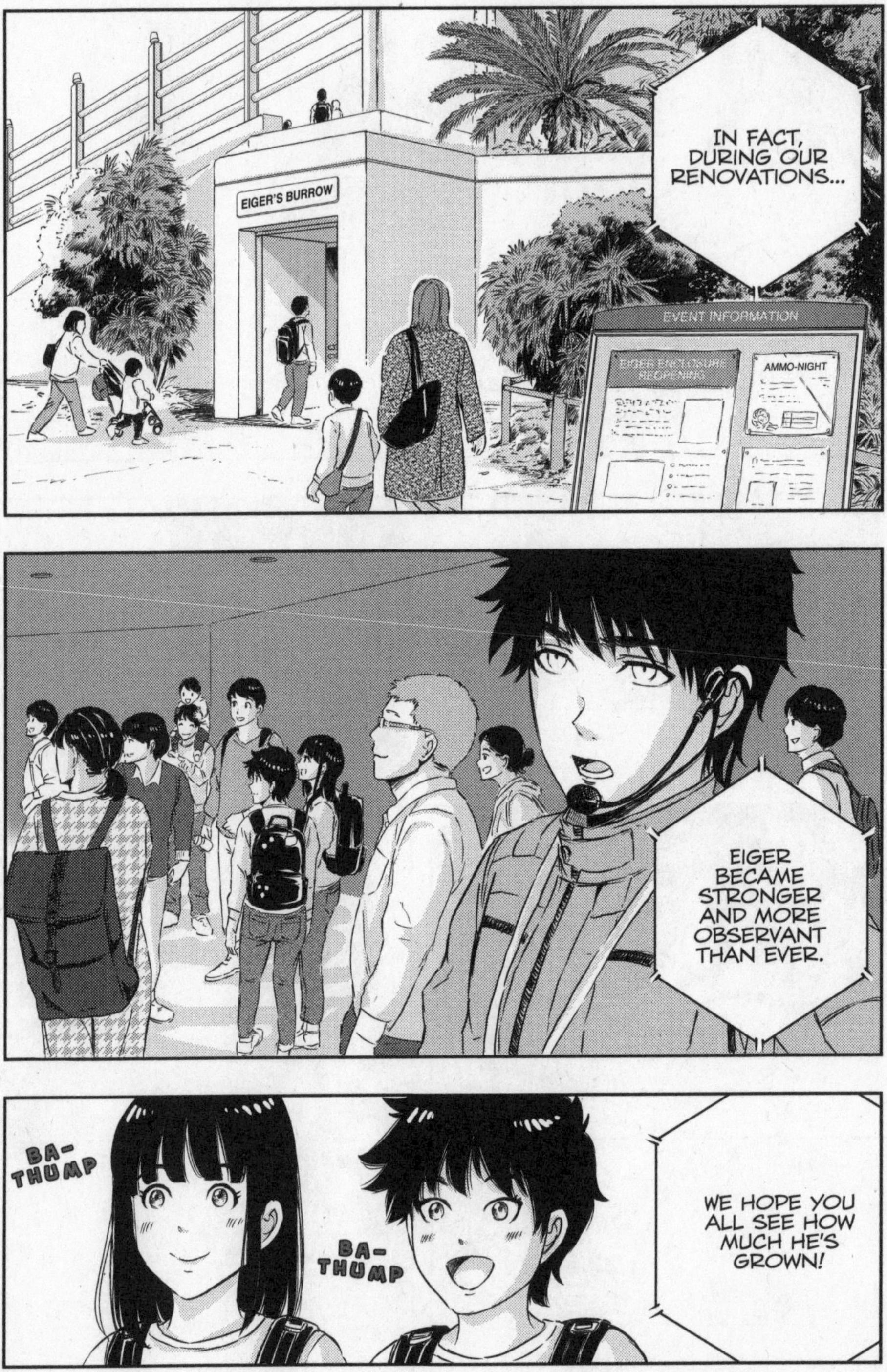
IN FACT, DURING OUR RENOVATIONS...
EVENT INFORMATION
AMMO-NIGHT
EIGER ENCLOSURE REOPENING
EIGER'S BURROW
EIGER BECAME STRONGER AND MORE OBSERVANT THAN EVER.
WE HOPE YOU ALL SEE HOW MUCH HE'S GROWN!
BA-THUMP
BA-THUMP

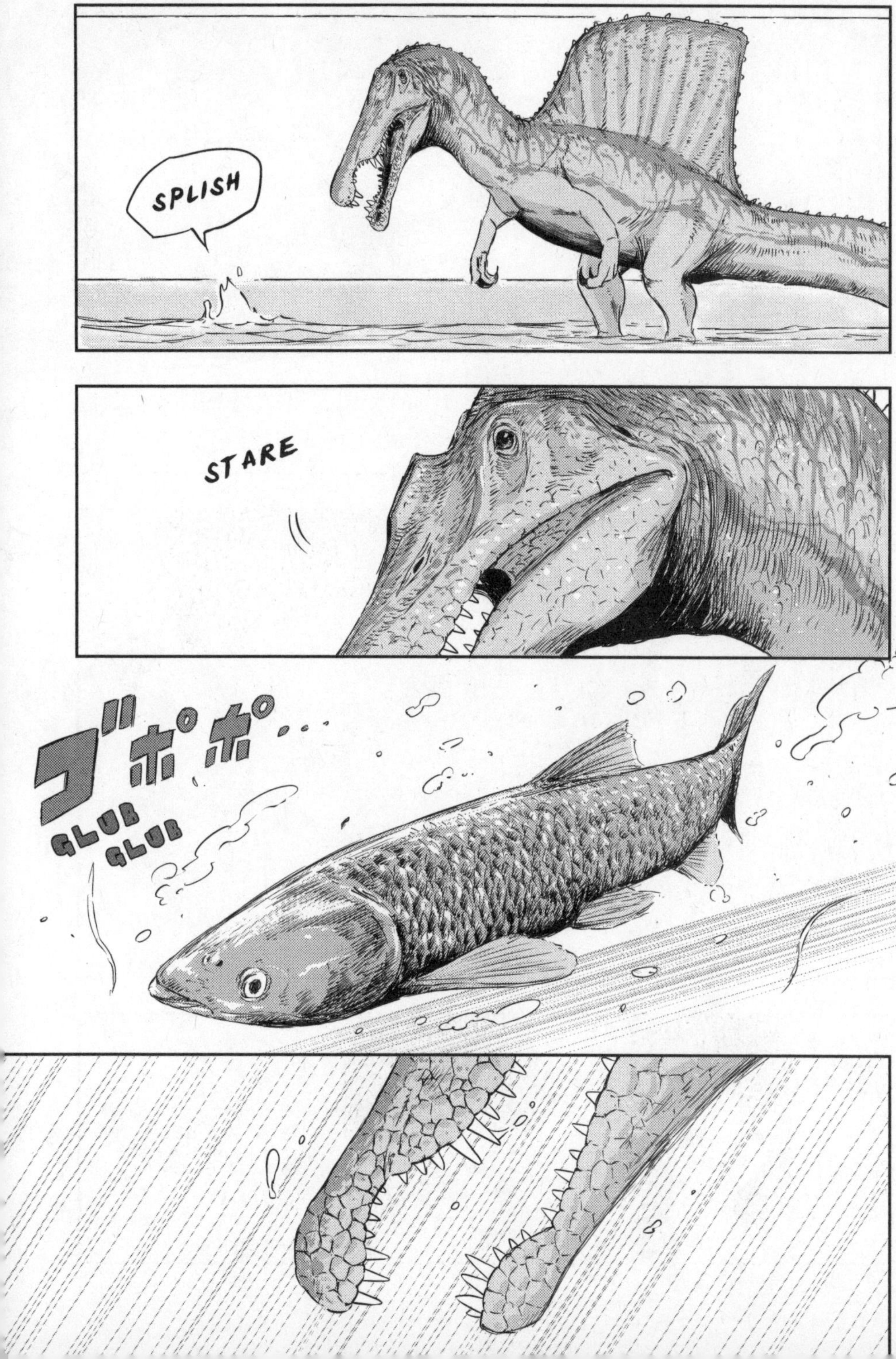
SPLISH
STARE
ゴポポ...
GLUB GLUB

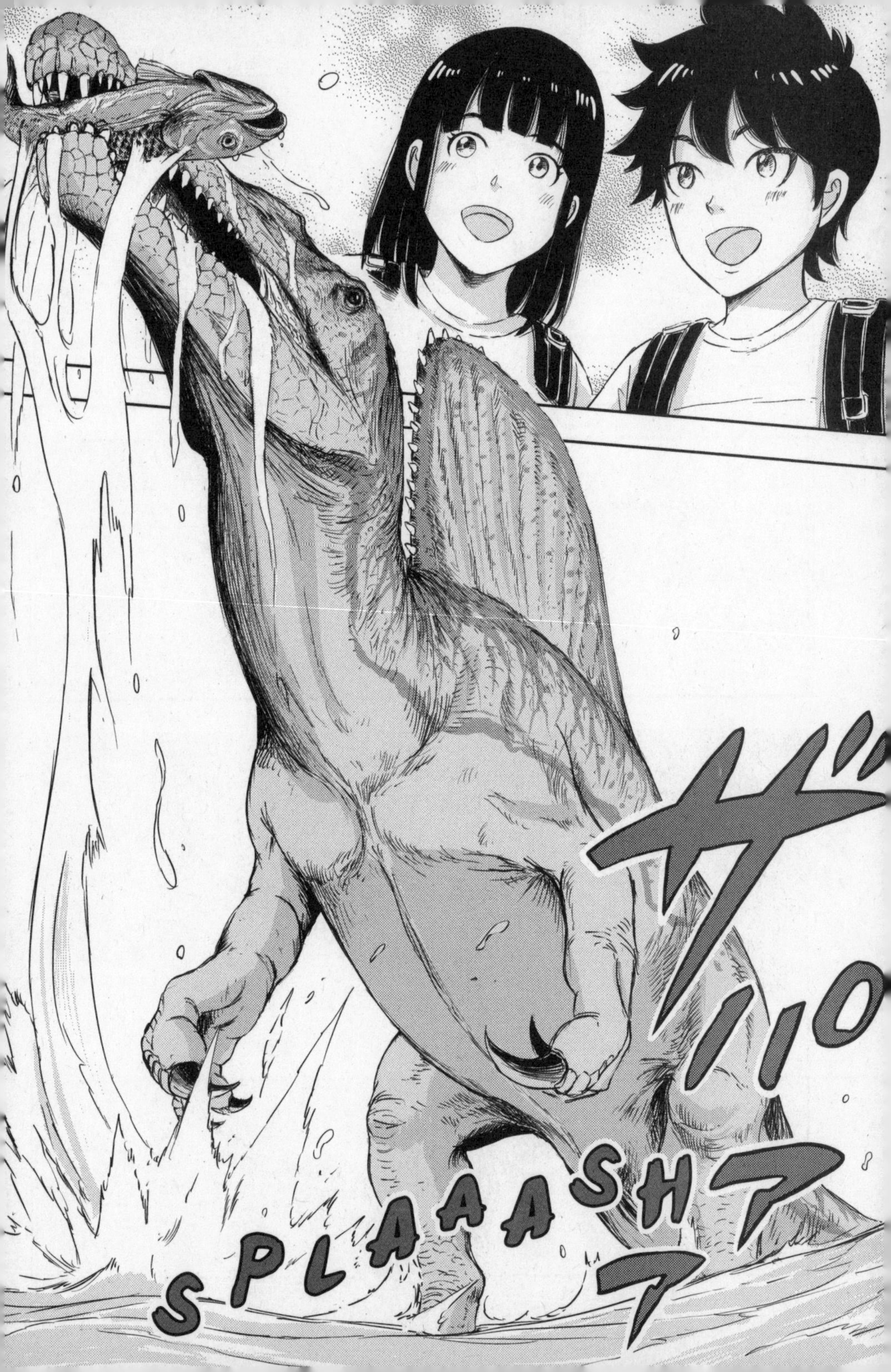
ザバァ
SPLAAASH

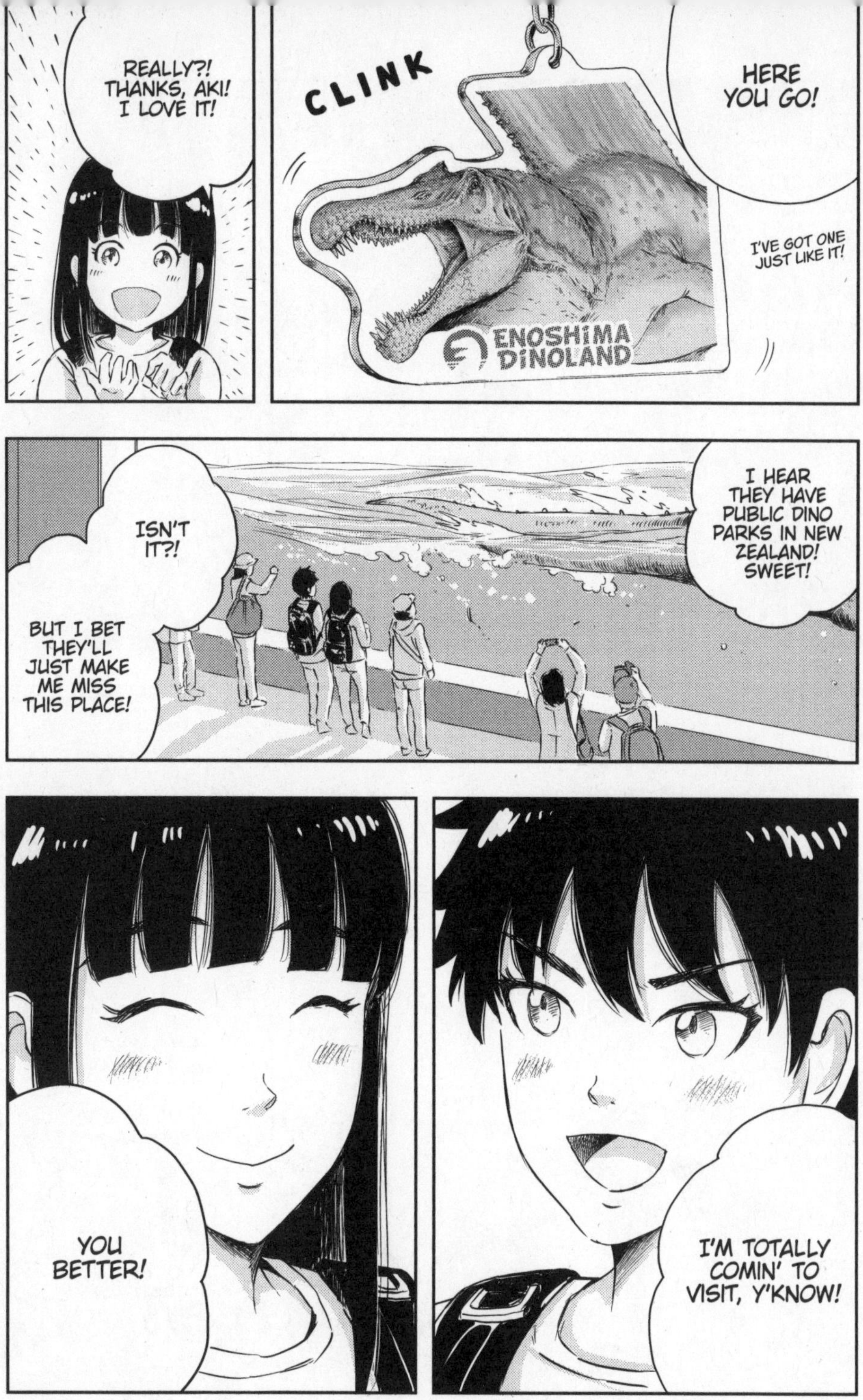
HERE YOU GO!
CLINK
ENOSHIMA DINOLAND
I'VE GOT ONE JUST LIKE IT!
REALLY?! THANKS, AKI! I LOVE IT!
I HEAR THEY HAVE PUBLIC DINO PARKS IN NEW ZEALAND! SWEET!
ISN'T IT?!
BUT I BET THEY'LL JUST MAKE ME MISS THIS PLACE!
I'M TOTALLY COMIN' TO VISIT, Y'KNOW!
YOU BETTER!

VRRRMMM
ゴオオオ...
SPLISH
プカ
SPLISH
プカ

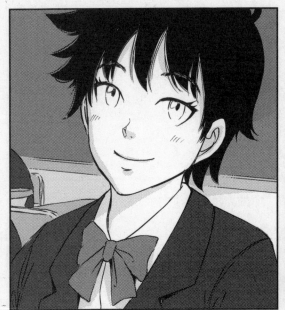

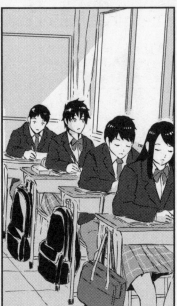

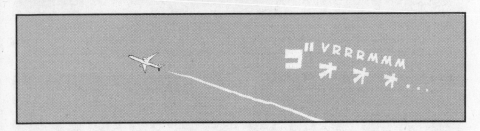

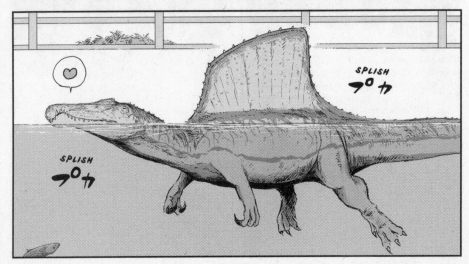

Dr. Dino's Lab Log

FILE. 15 Latest Isn't Always Best

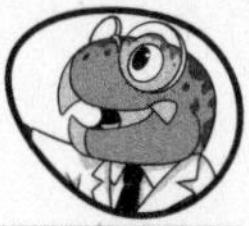

To get a paper published in a scientific journal, you have to convince both the journal's editorial board and your professional peers that the hypothesis you're putting forth is novel and probable. Researchers submit their papers to these journals, where they're evaluated by a few professional reviewers who are chosen by a board of editors—and it's (typically) a *very* strict evaluation. Then, based on the reviewers' feedback, the editors will decide whether to accept the paper or not. If a scientist has their work rejected, they have a choice: either submit the same paper elsewhere and try again, or start their research over in hopes of making their paper stronger. Either way, it goes through the same process of submission and review once again...until an editorial board deems it acceptable and, at last, it gets published.

All these reviews are made possible by the scientific community's spirit of volunteer work. Of course, it can be frustrating when peer readers rip your paper apart... But on the other hand, several specialists are spending their precious time—without being paid a cent!—in order to make your work the best that it can be. That's something to be very, very grateful for.

This peer review system isn't in place to guarantee that your conclusions are correct. But it has been devised, over the long history of scientific inquiry, to ensure some degree of quality in research.

Just so you know, the latest hot, new theories aren't given too terribly much weight here in the pages of *Dinosaur Sanctuary.* The newest ideas may have only flimsy evidence to support them so far, and I've taken care to use the information that I find most convincing at this point as I share my perspective with Kinoshita-sensei—along with as much actual reasoning as I can.

When a paleoecologist writes a paper to argue how they think an extinct animal lived, they typically arrange and present a wide variety of evidence in order to convince the reader that their hypothesis makes sense. To verify this, we rely on fossilized bones and observing the ways that living animals use their skeletons. If we suggest that a particular extinct animal performed a specific behavior, we then must consider what force that behavior would put on its skeleton, whether the animal's weight would be properly supported, and so on. Through this process of observation and estimation, we arrive at data that suggests numerically whether the animal could perform said behavior or not.

However, just because a theory has passed peer review, that doesn't mean it's okay to take it entirely as gospel. It's always possible that someone could use only evidence that happens to line up with their hypothesis in order to make it look stronger—even if performing the same analysis on other evidence might lead down a different, less convenient path. As much as it pains me to say it, there's no shortage of such papers out there. Others might make use of irrelevant analysis in order to make their claims.

The new, exciting conclusions of papers are often reported as the "latest theories," but if something has only been demonstrated in *one* paper, it's exactly that: *one* interpretation. The true essence of science lies in considering what each analysis takes for granted, what analytical methods it uses, how it arrives at its particular conclusion, and so on. It's important that we foster a culture in which readers grasp the assumptions, methods, and interpretations behind what they read and determine what seems like the most convincing theory for themselves. In order to do this, though, both scientists and scientific reporters must stay vigilant—and emphasize the *true essence* of scientific judgment, rather than just skip ahead to the flashy conclusions.

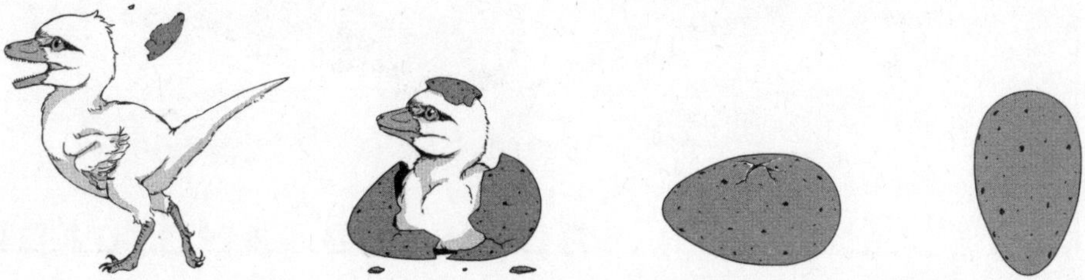

DINOSAUR SANCTUARY

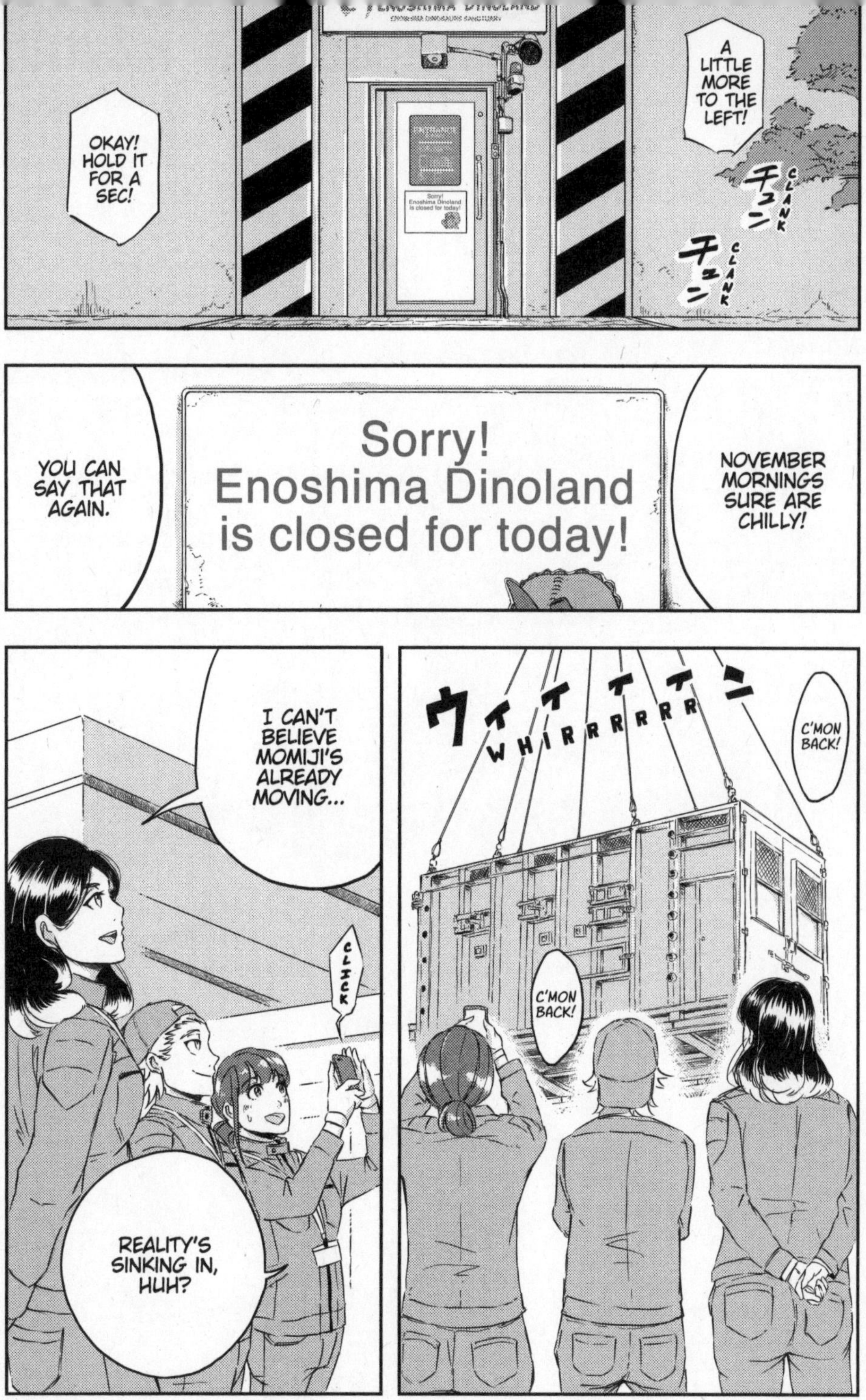
A LITTLE MORE TO THE LEFT!
チュン CLANK
チュン CLANK
OKAY! HOLD IT FOR A SEC!
NOVEMBER MORNINGS SURE ARE CHILLY!
Sorry! Enoshima Dinoland is closed for today!
YOU CAN SAY THAT AGAIN.
ウィイイイン WHIRRRRRR
C'MON BACK!
C'MON BACK!
I CAN'T BELIEVE MOMIJI'S ALREADY MOVING...
CLICK
REALITY'S SINKING IN, HUH?

CHAPTER 16 MOVING MOMIJI

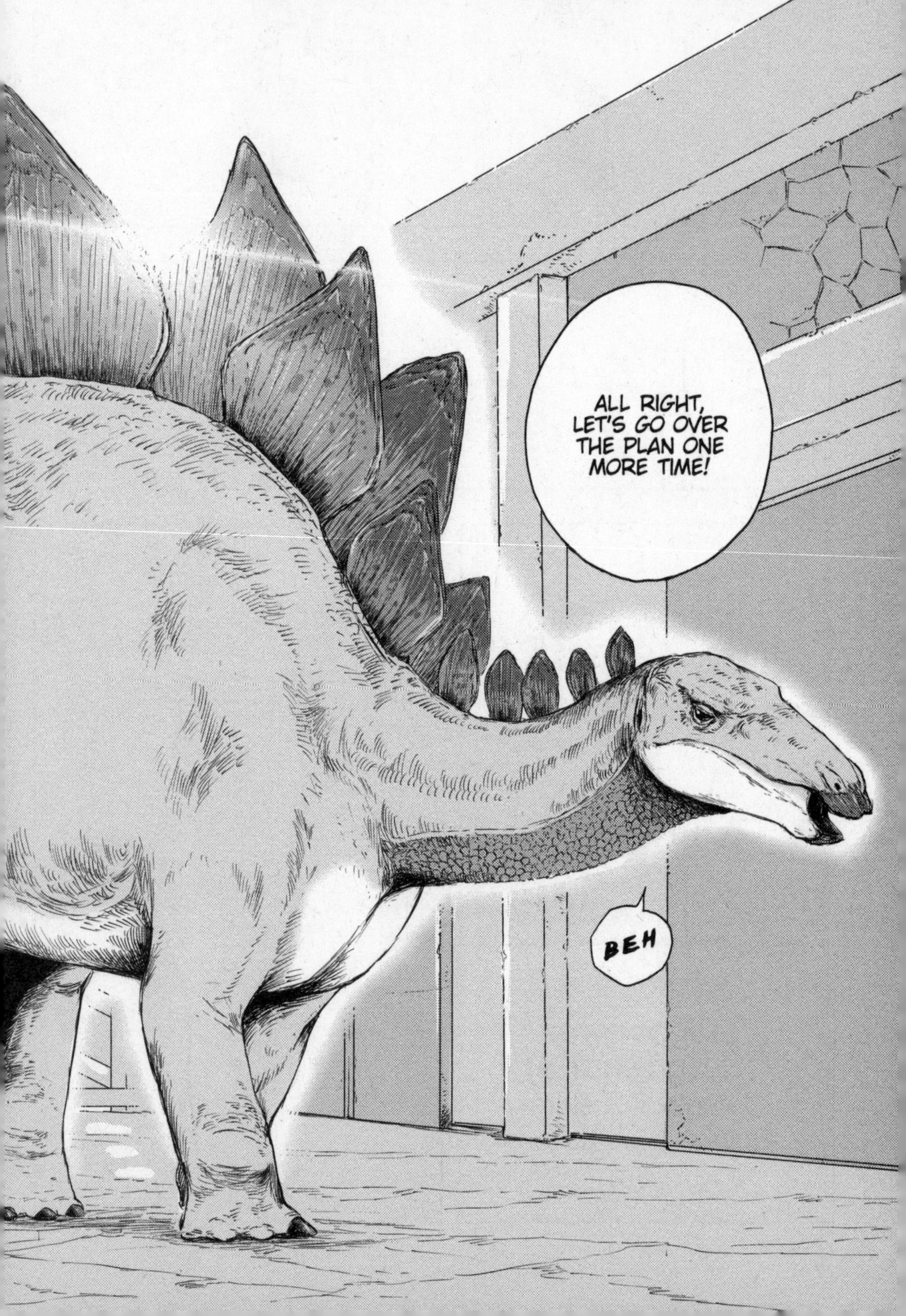
ALL RIGHT, LET'S GO OVER THE PLAN ONE MORE TIME!
BEH

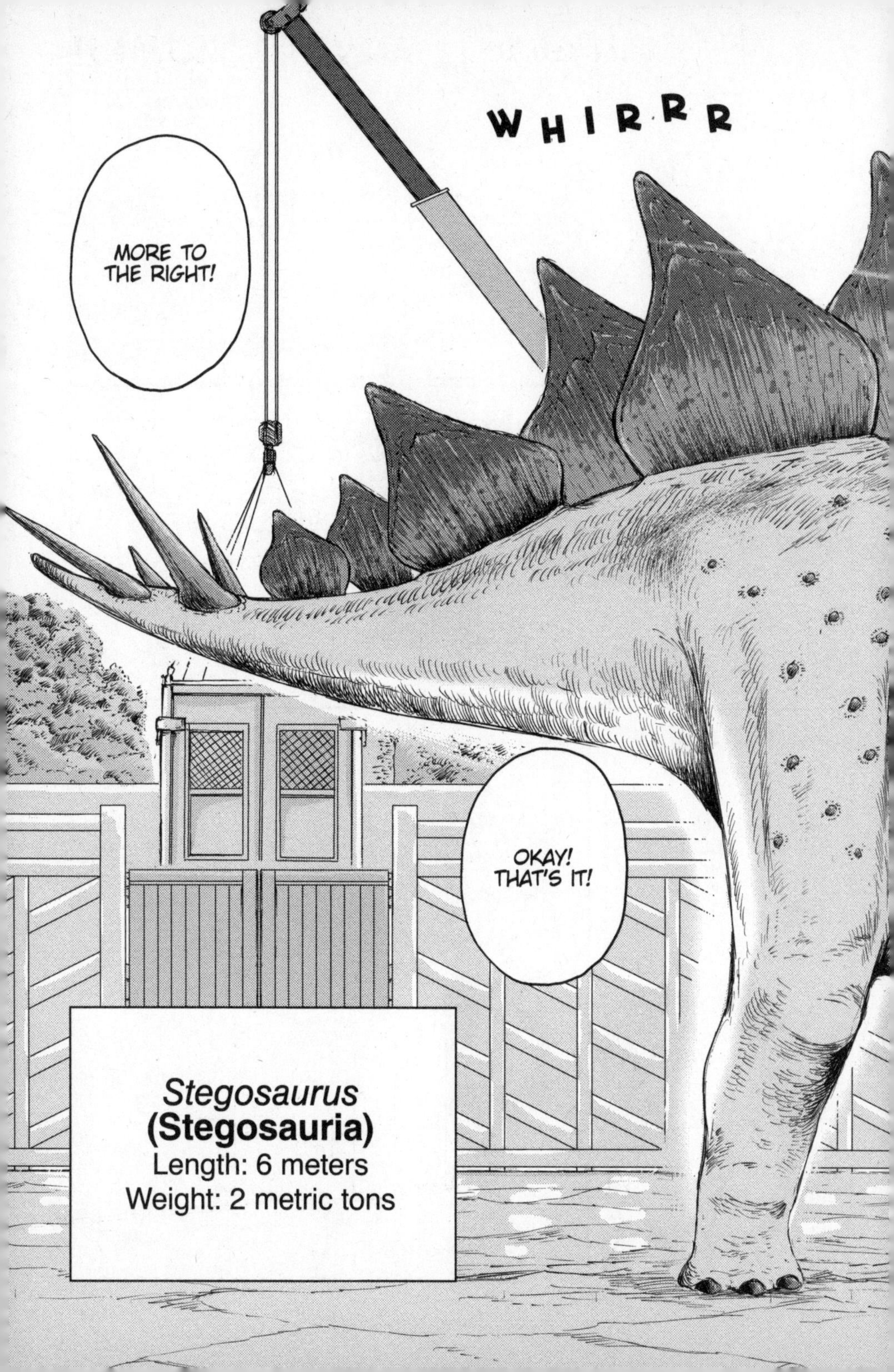
WHIRRR
MORE TO THE RIGHT!
OKAY! THAT'S IT!
Stegosaurus
(Stegosauria)
Length: 6 meters
Weight: 2 metric tons

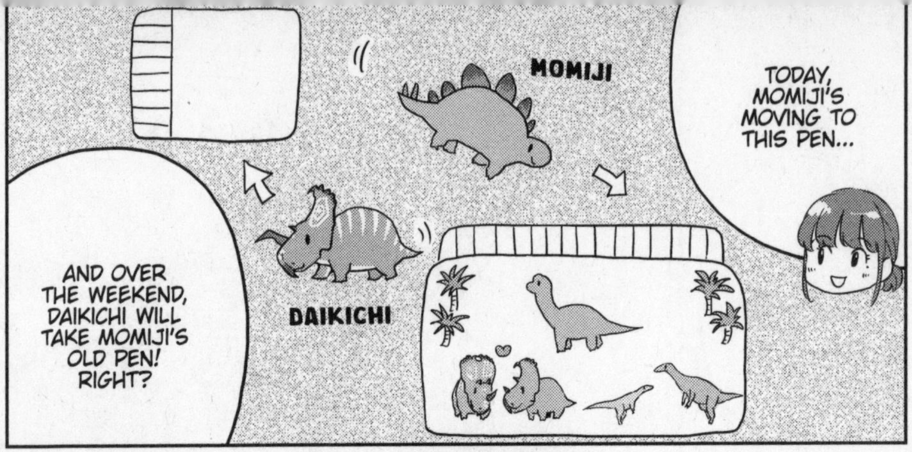
TODAY, MOMIJI'S MOVING TO THIS PEN...
MOMIJI
DAIKICHI
AND OVER THE WEEKEND, DAIKICHI WILL TAKE MOMIJI'S OLD PEN! RIGHT?

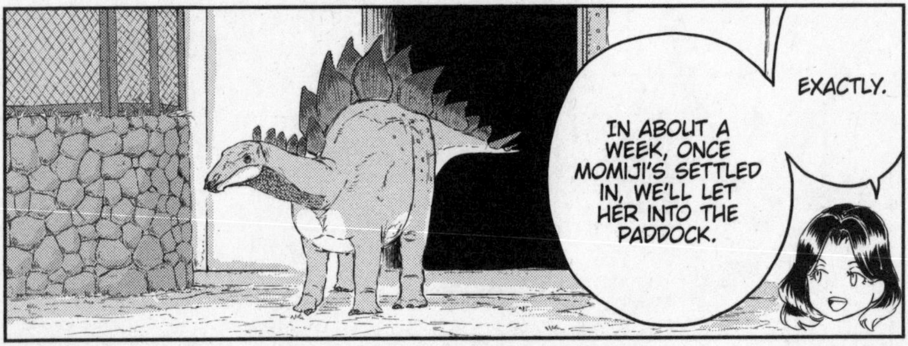
EXACTLY.
IN ABOUT A WEEK, ONCE MOMIJI'S SETTLED IN, WE'LL LET HER INTO THE PADDOCK.

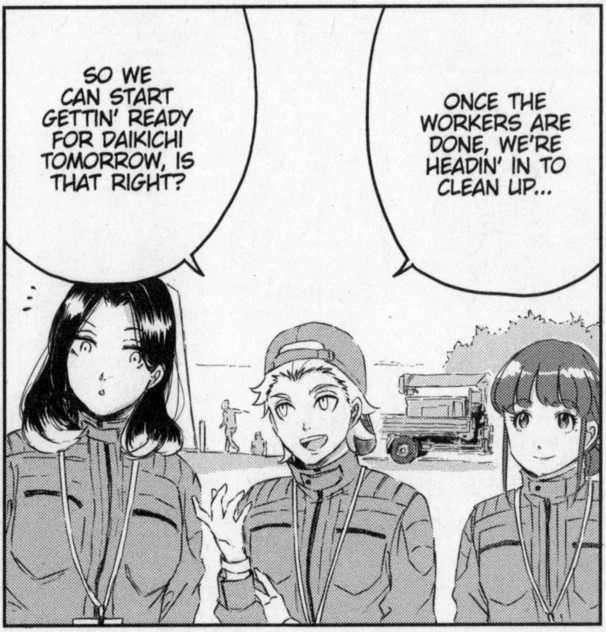
ONCE THE WORKERS ARE DONE, WE'RE HEADIN' IN TO CLEAN UP...
SO WE CAN START GETTIN' READY FOR DAIKICHI TOMORROW, IS THAT RIGHT?

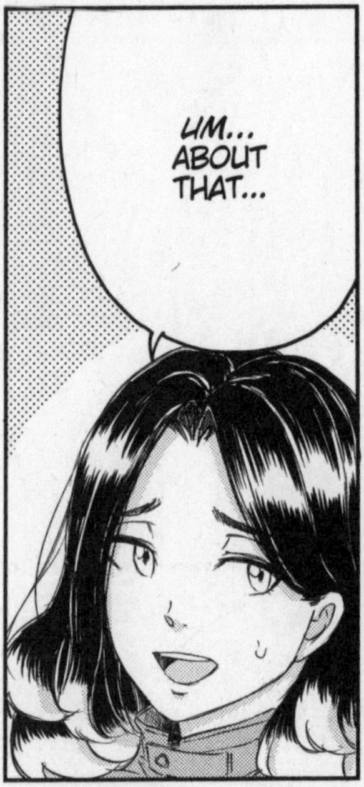
UM... ABOUT THAT...

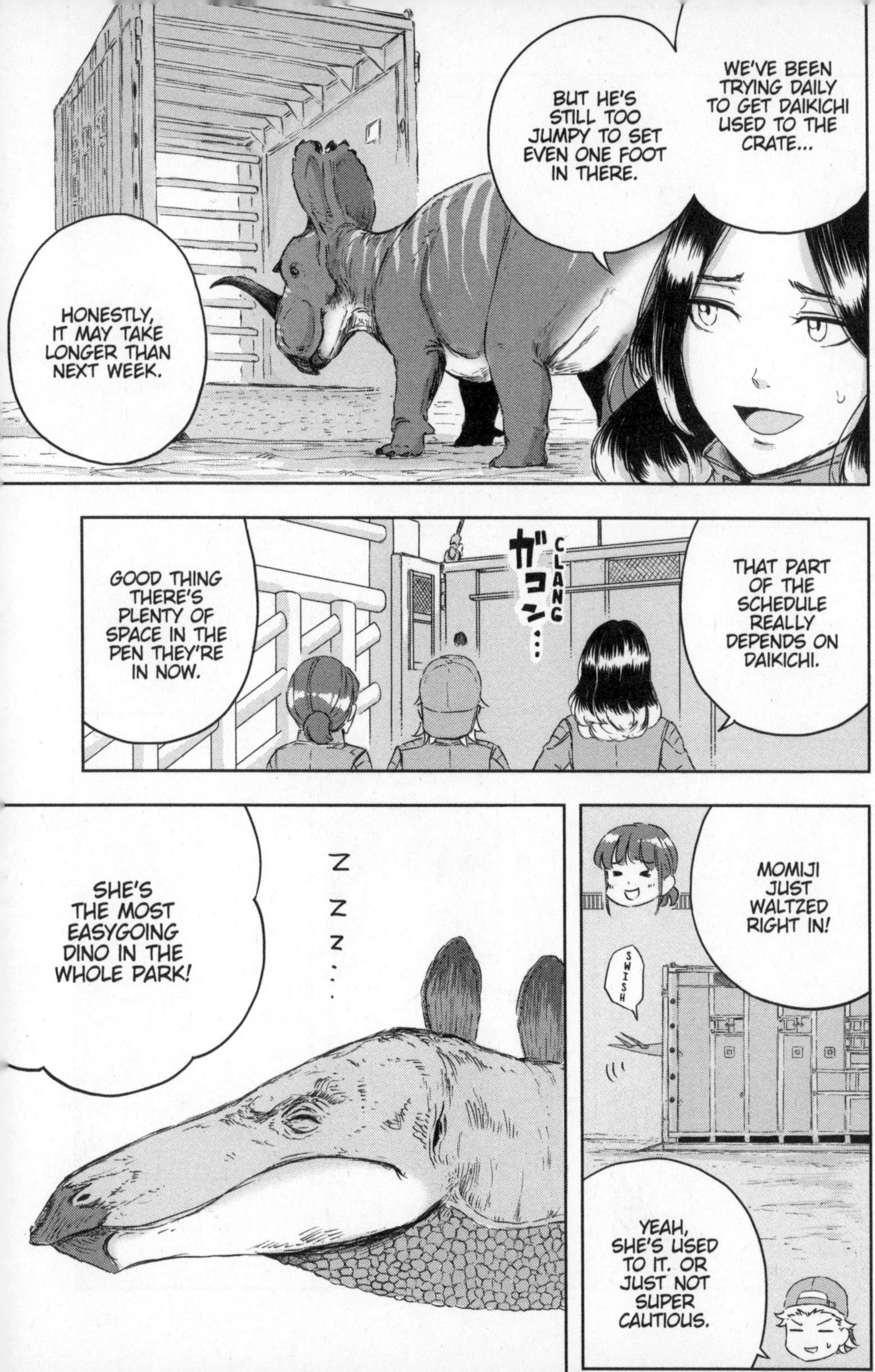
WE'VE BEEN TRYING DAILY TO GET DAIKICHI USED TO THE CRATE...
BUT HE'S STILL TOO JUMPY TO SET EVEN ONE FOOT IN THERE.
HONESTLY, IT MAY TAKE LONGER THAN NEXT WEEK.
THAT PART OF THE SCHEDULE REALLY DEPENDS ON DAIKICHI.
ガコン…
CLANG...
GOOD THING THERE'S PLENTY OF SPACE IN THE PEN THEY'RE IN NOW.
MOMIJI JUST WALTZED RIGHT IN!
SWISH
YEAH, SHE'S USED TO IT. OR JUST NOT SUPER CAUTIOUS.
Z Z Z...
SHE'S THE MOST EASYGOING DINO IN THE WHOLE PARK!

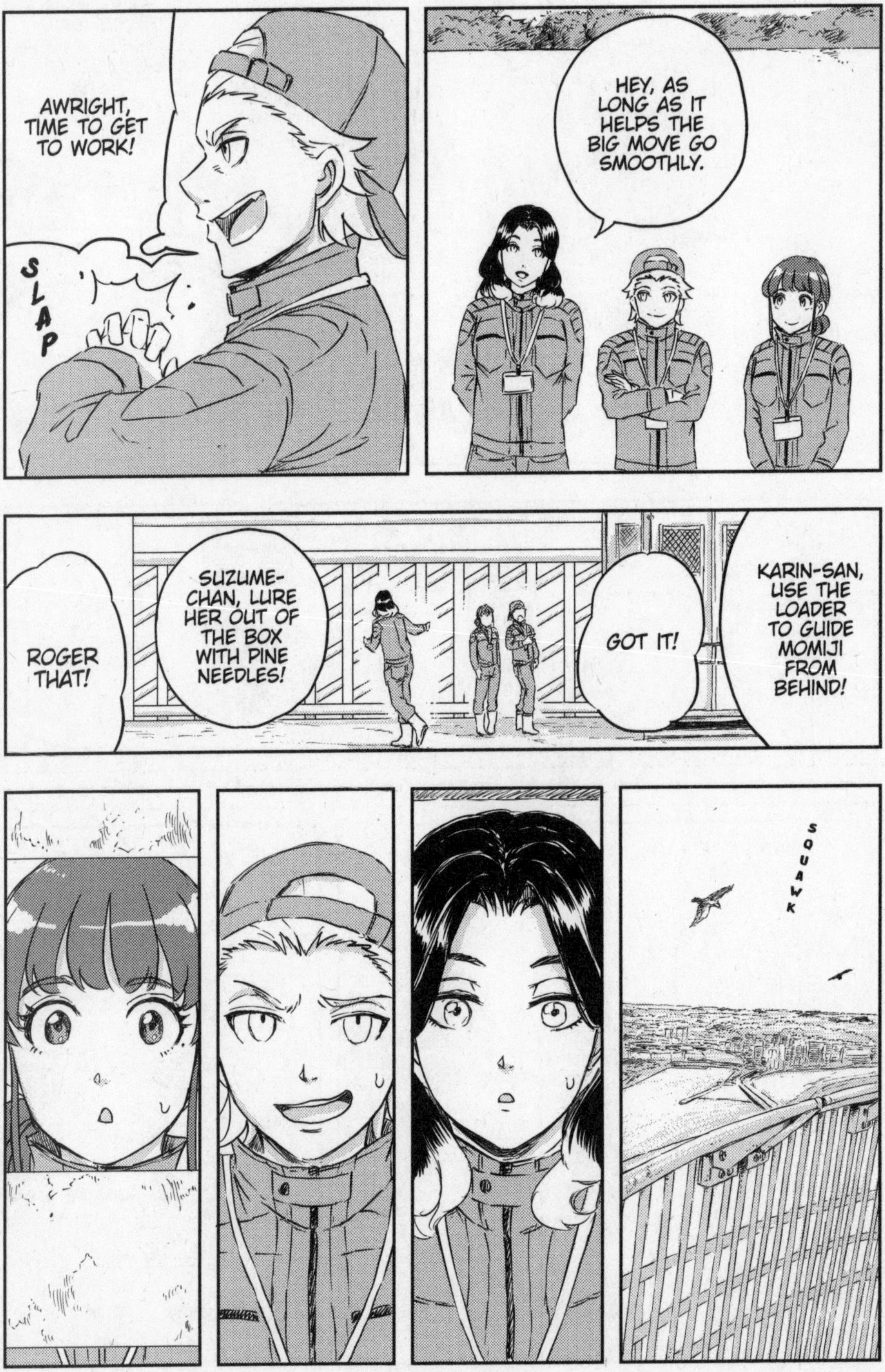
HEY, AS LONG AS IT HELPS THE BIG MOVE GO SMOOTHLY.
AWRIGHT, TIME TO GET TO WORK!
SLAP
KARIN-SAN, USE THE LOADER TO GUIDE MOMIJI FROM BEHIND!
GOT IT!
SUZUME-CHAN, LURE HER OUT OF THE BOX WITH PINE NEEDLES!
ROGER THAT!
SQUAWK

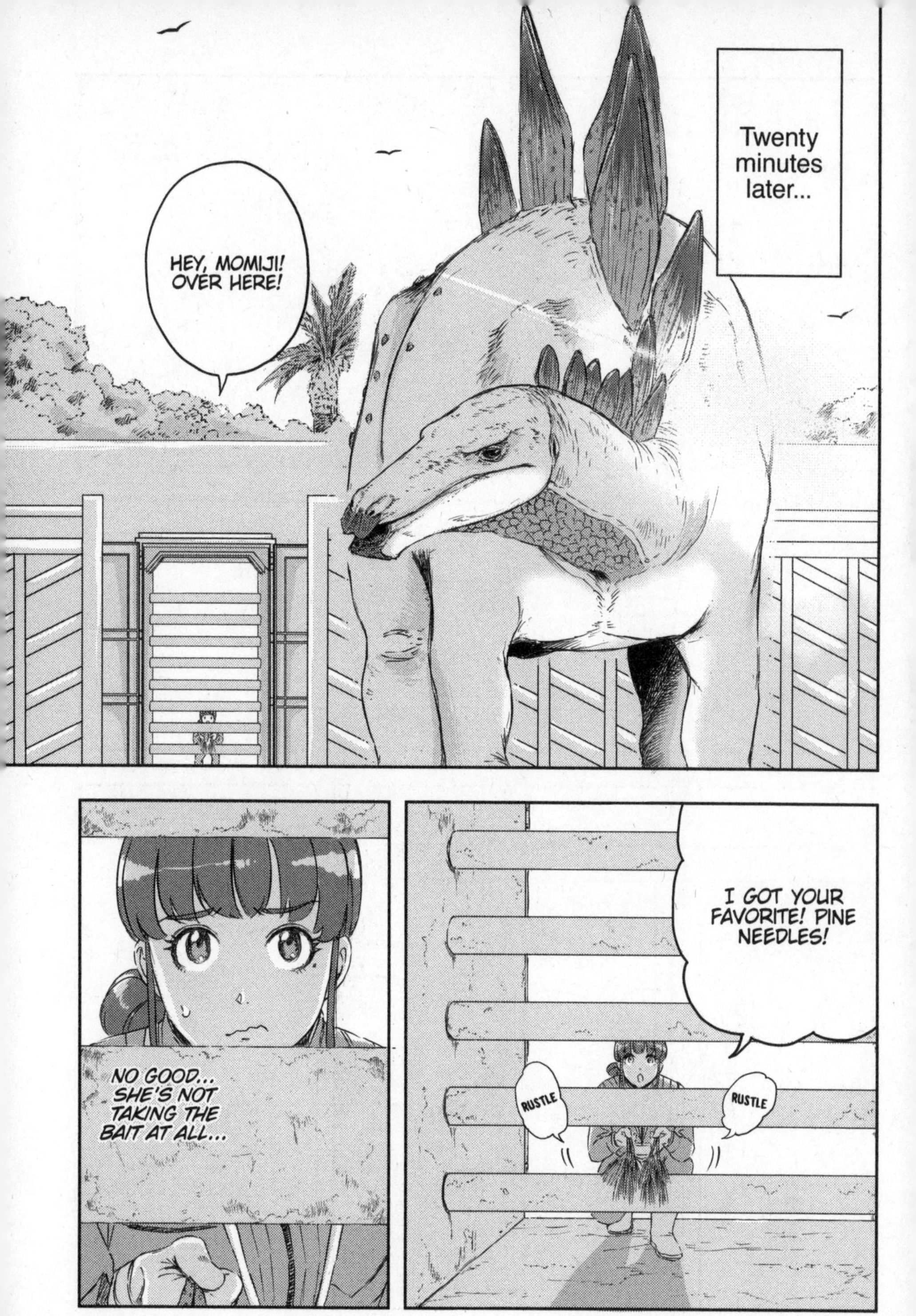
Twenty minutes later...
HEY, MOMIJI! OVER HERE!
I GOT YOUR FAVORITE! PINE NEEDLES!
RUSTLE
RUSTLE
NO GOOD... SHE'S NOT TAKING THE BAIT AT ALL...

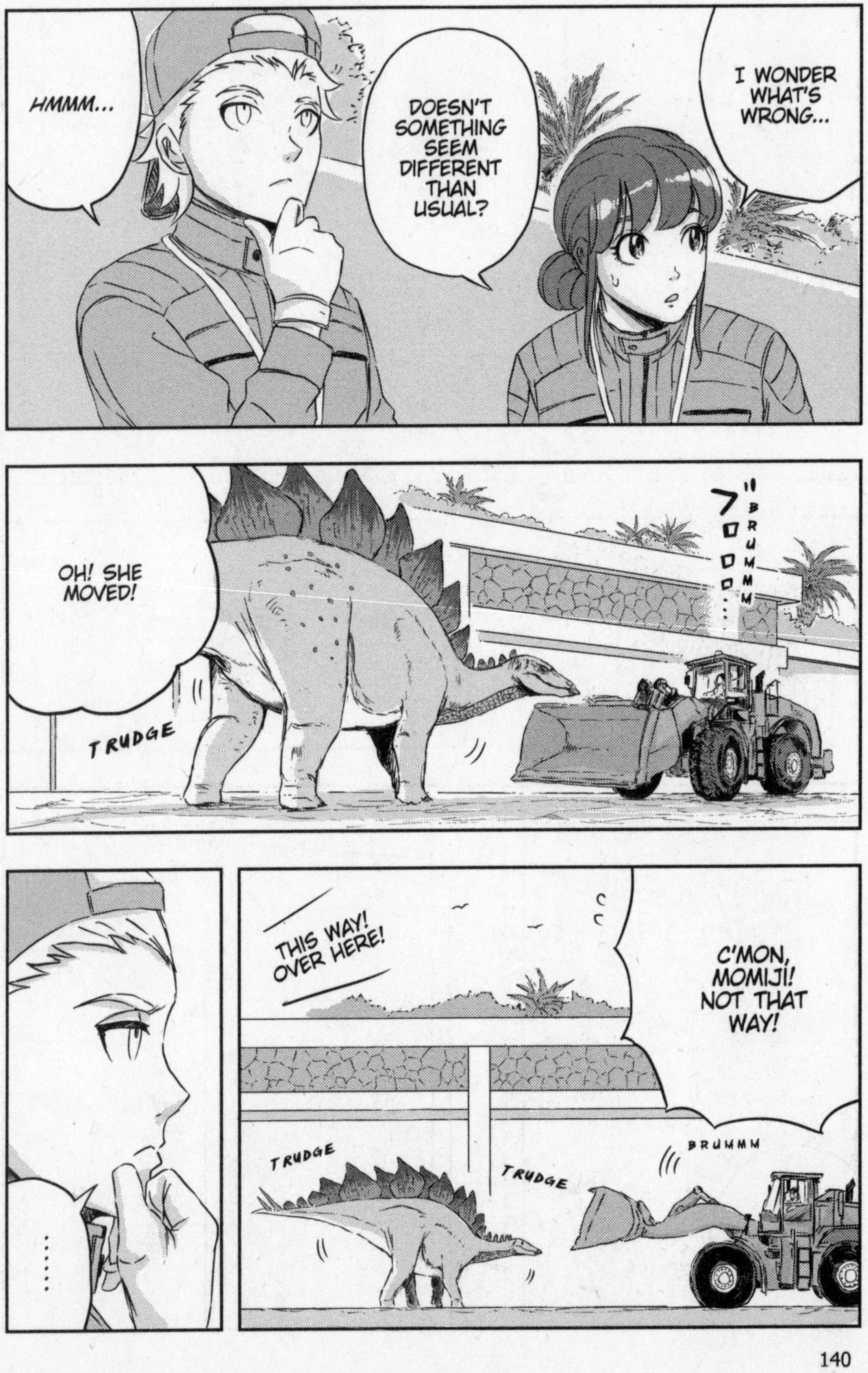
I WONDER WHAT'S WRONG...
DOESN'T SOMETHING SEEM DIFFERENT THAN USUAL?
HMMM...
ブロロロ...
BRUMMM
BRUMMM
OH! SHE MOVED!
TRUDGE
C'MON, MOMIJI! NOT THAT WAY!
THIS WAY! OVER HERE!
BRUMMM
TRUDGE
TRUDGE
......

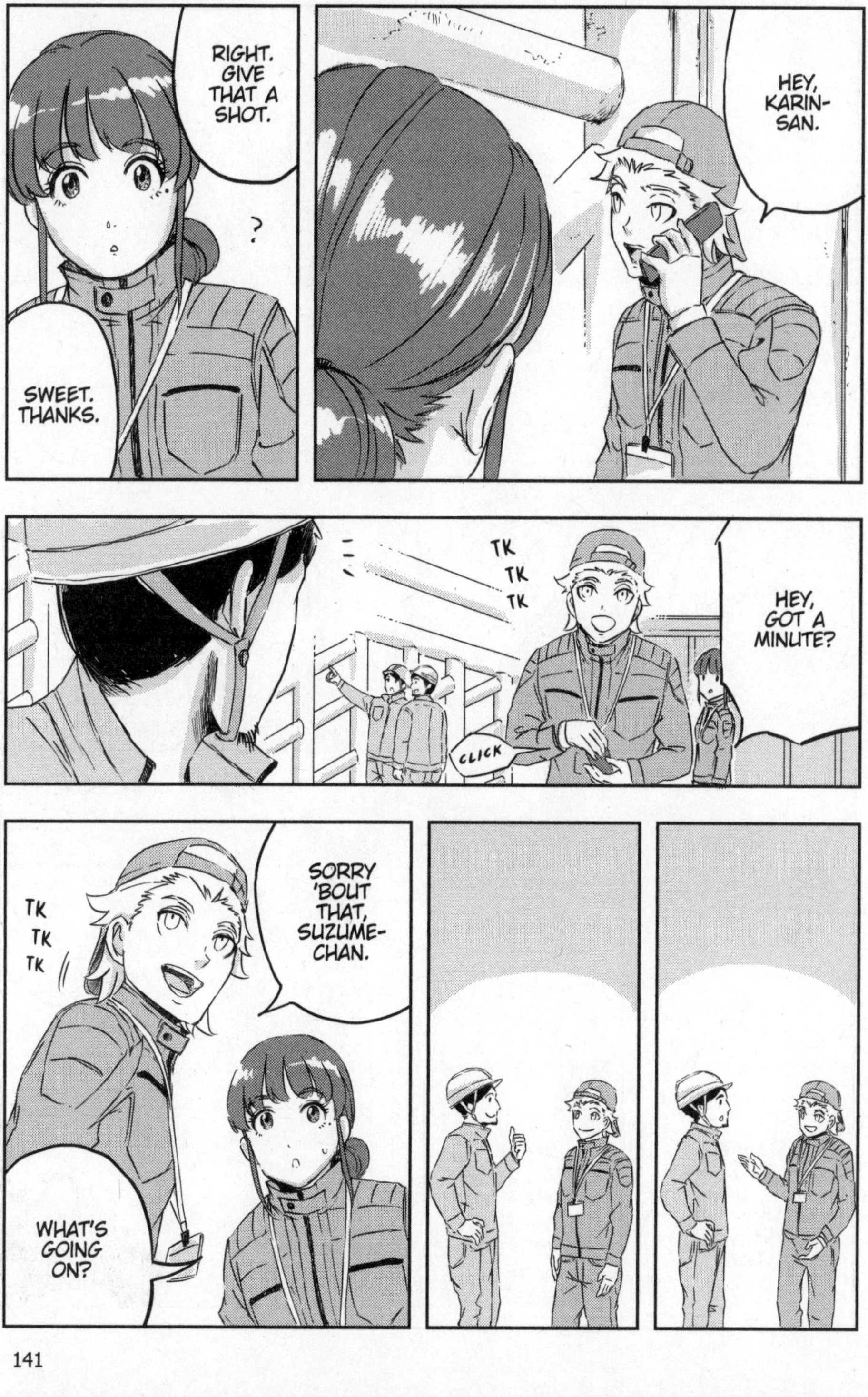
HEY, KARIN-SAN.
RIGHT. GIVE THAT A SHOT.
?
SWEET. THANKS.
HEY, GOT A MINUTE?
TK TK TK
CLICK
SORRY 'BOUT THAT, SUZUME-CHAN.
TK TK TK
WHAT'S GOING ON?

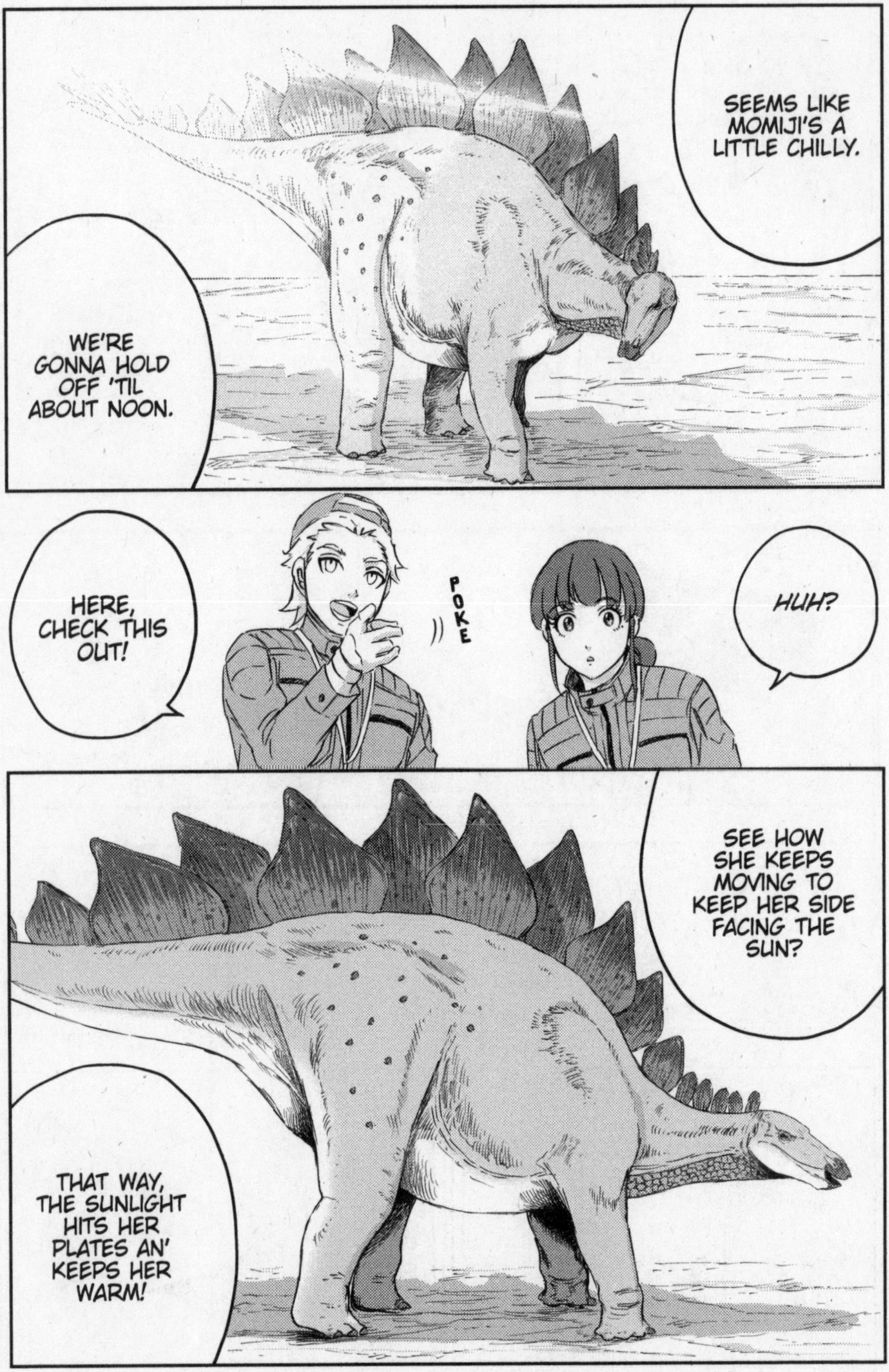
SEEMS LIKE MOMIJI'S A LITTLE CHILLY.
WE'RE GONNA HOLD OFF 'TIL ABOUT NOON.
HUH?
POKE
HERE, CHECK THIS OUT!
SEE HOW SHE KEEPS MOVING TO KEEP HER SIDE FACING THE SUN?
THAT WAY, THE SUNLIGHT HITS HER PLATES AN' KEEPS HER WARM!

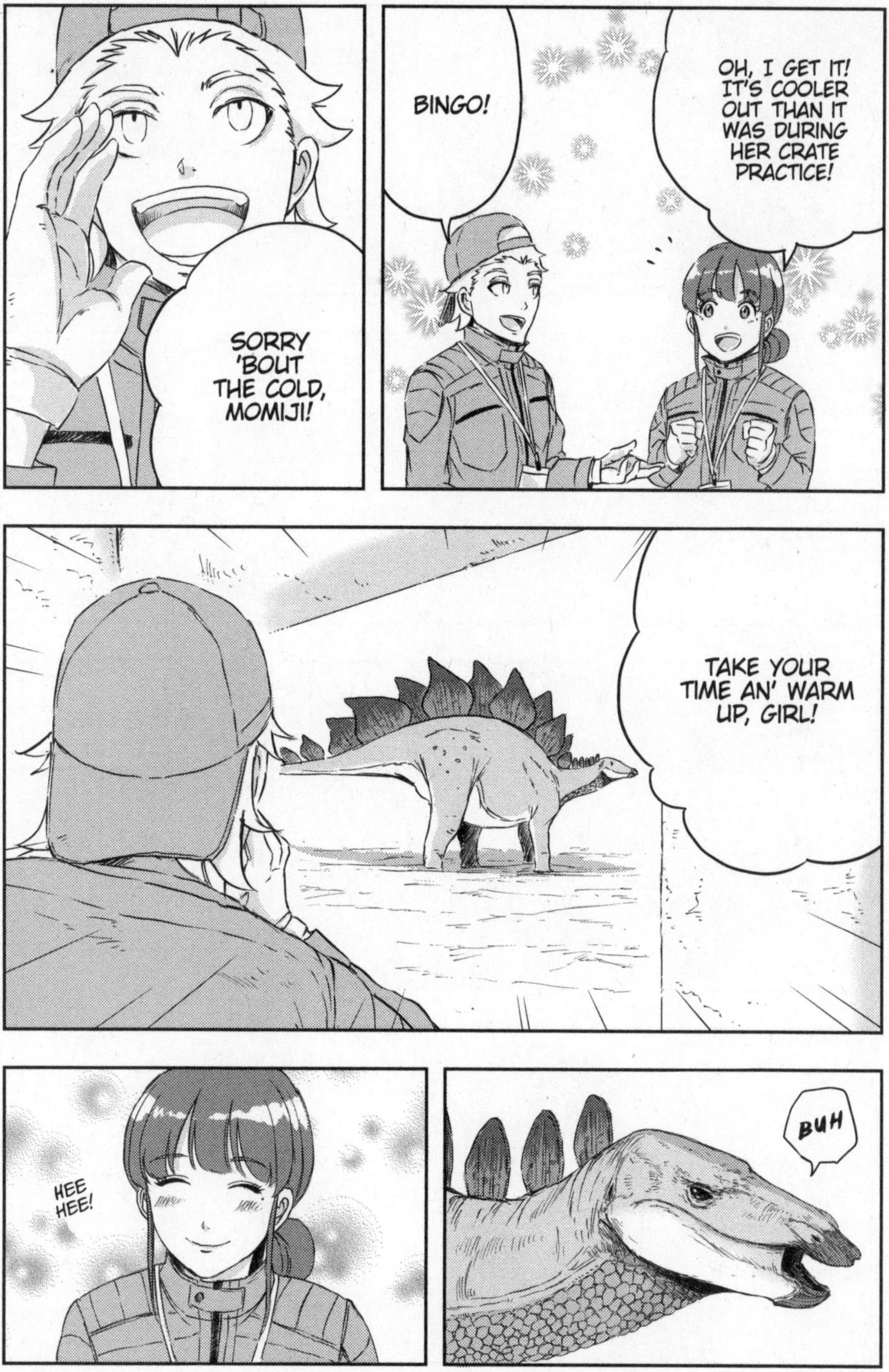
OH, I GET IT! IT'S COOLER OUT THAN IT WAS DURING HER CRATE PRACTICE!
BINGO!
SORRY 'BOUT THE COLD, MOMIJI!
TAKE YOUR TIME AN' WARM UP, GIRL!
BUH
HEE HEE!

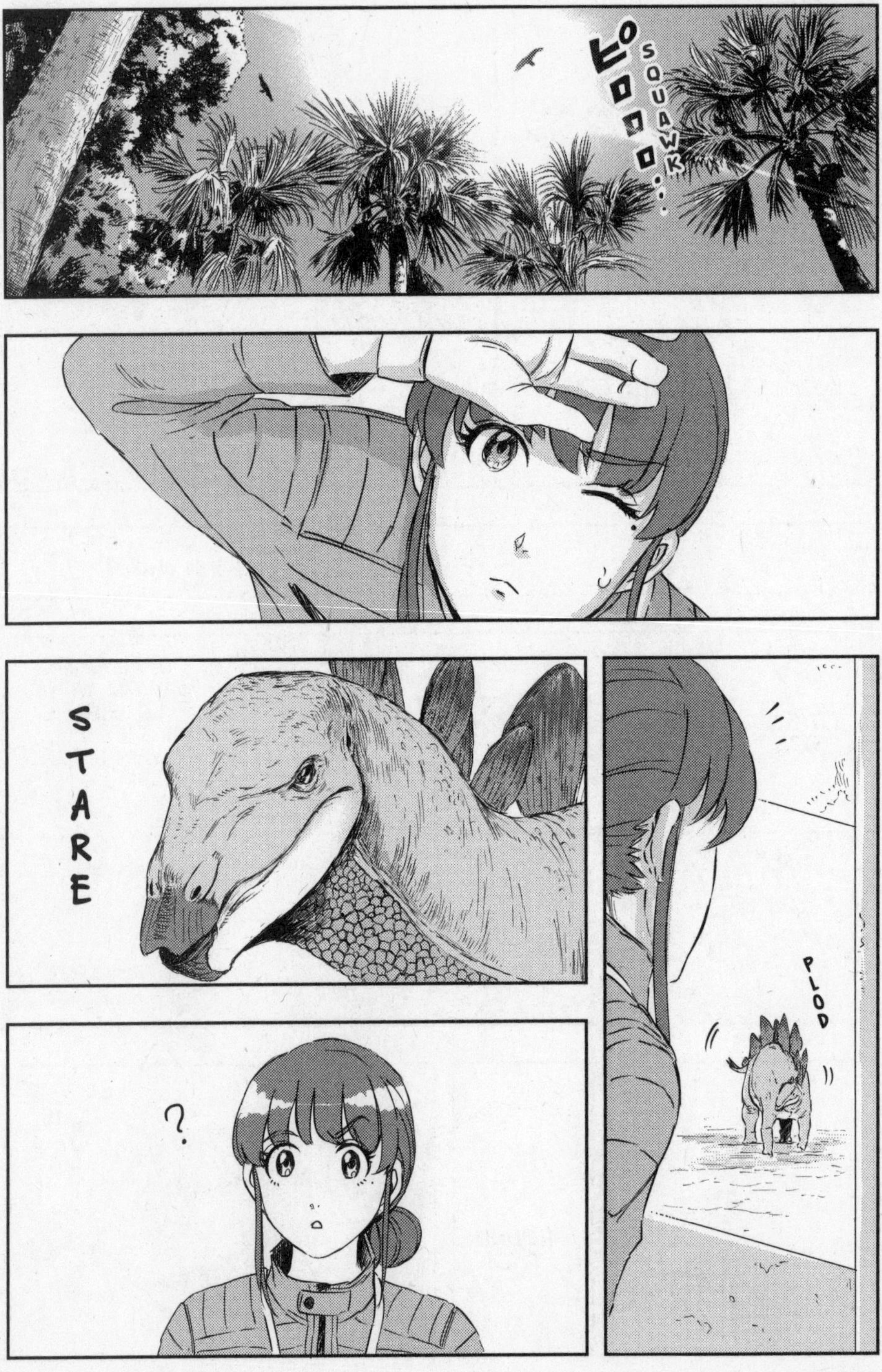
ピロロロ…
SQUAWK..
STARE
PLOD
?

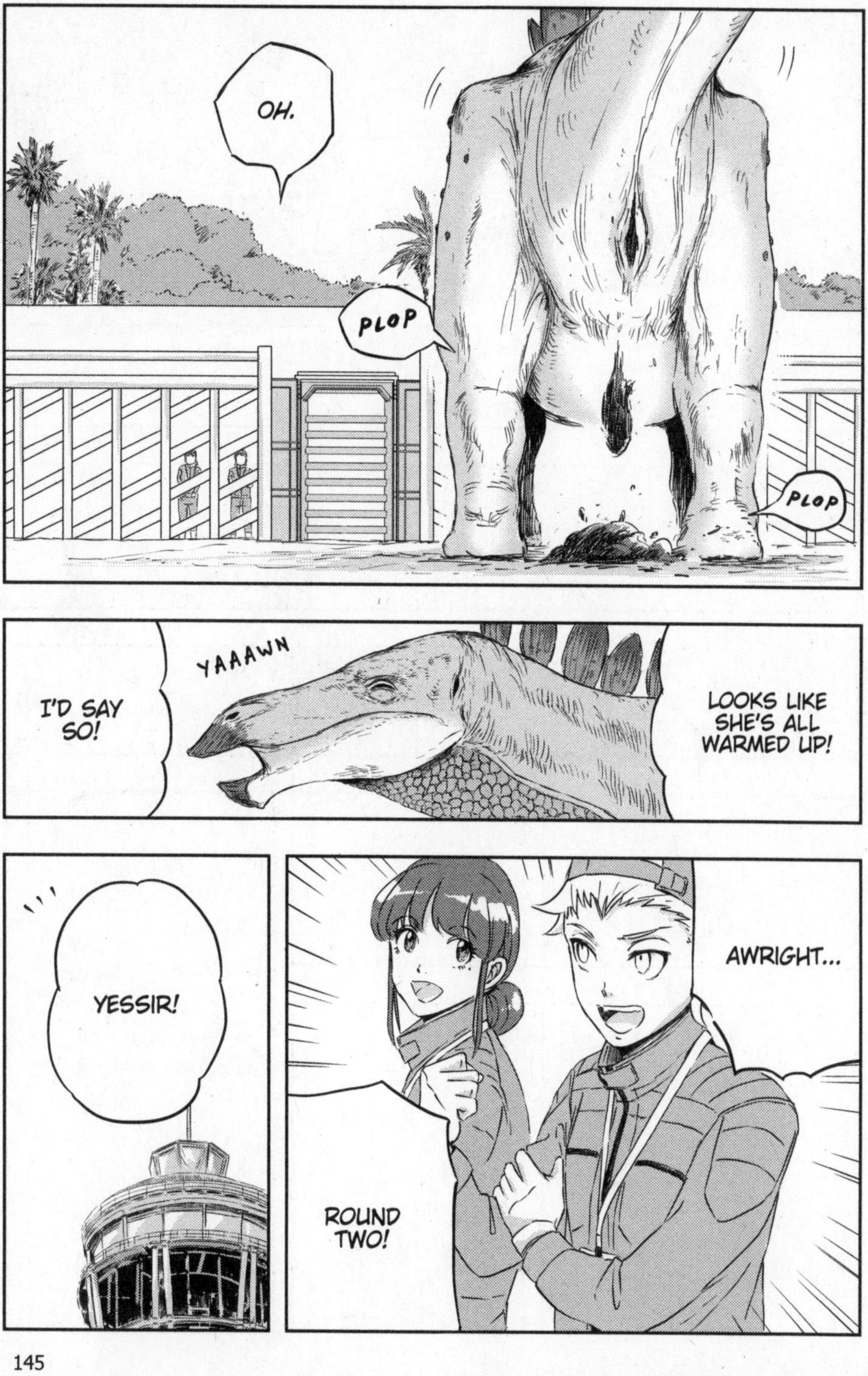
OH.
PLOP
PLOP
LOOKS LIKE SHE'S ALL WARMED UP!
YAAAWN
I'D SAY SO!
AWRIGHT...
ROUND TWO!
YESSIR!

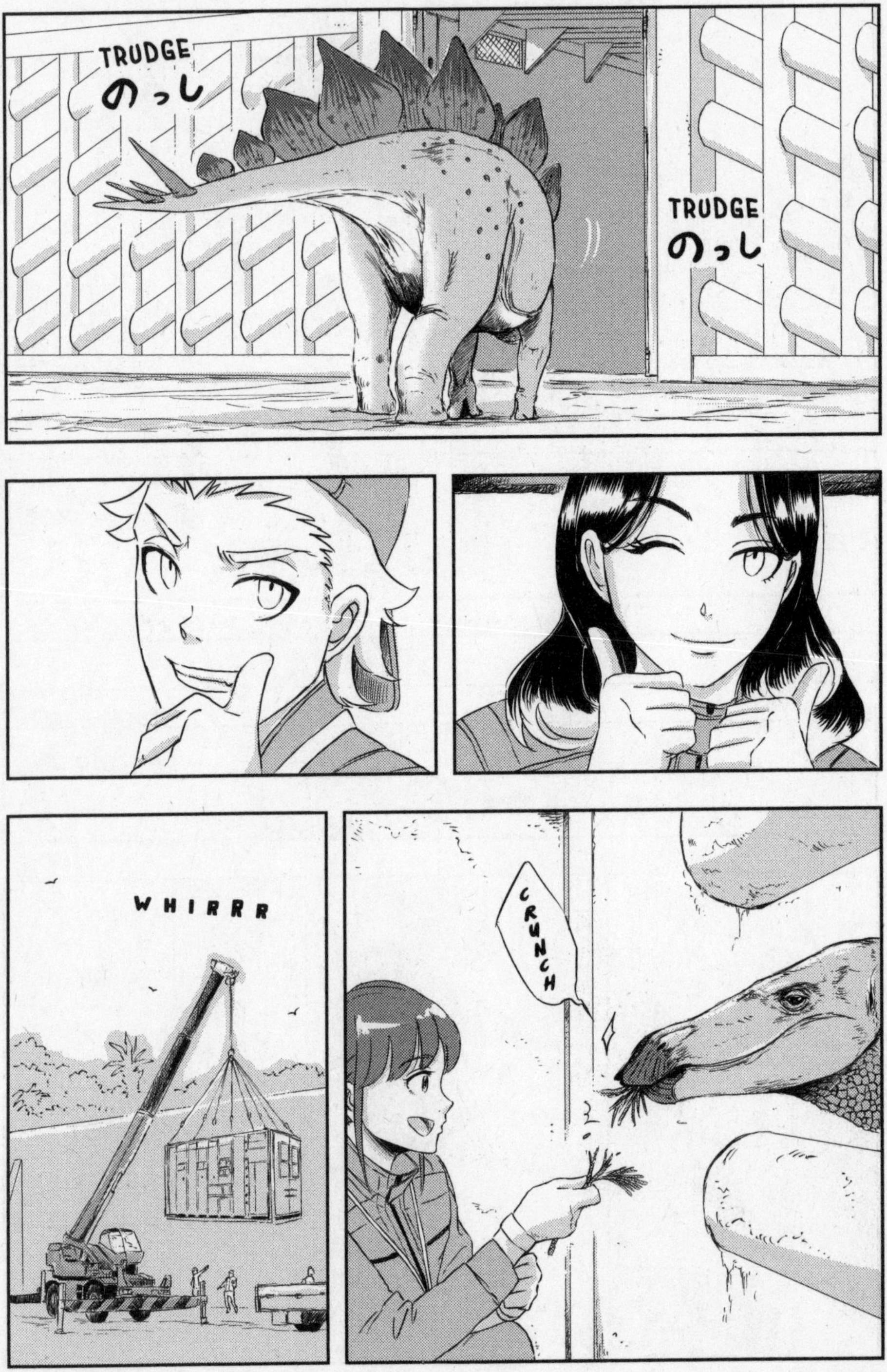
TRUDGE
のっし
TRUDGE
のっし
CRUNCH
WHIRRR

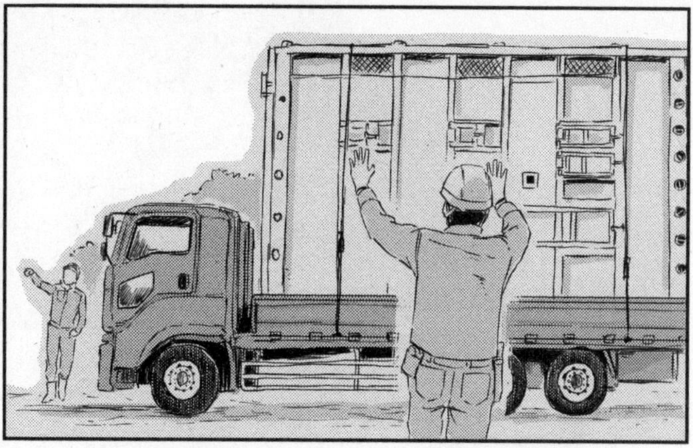

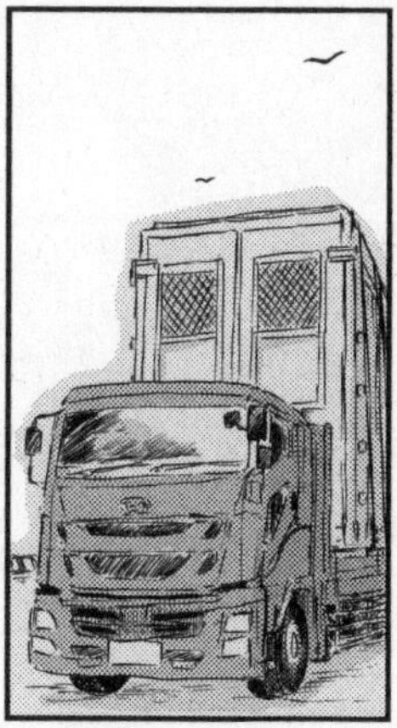

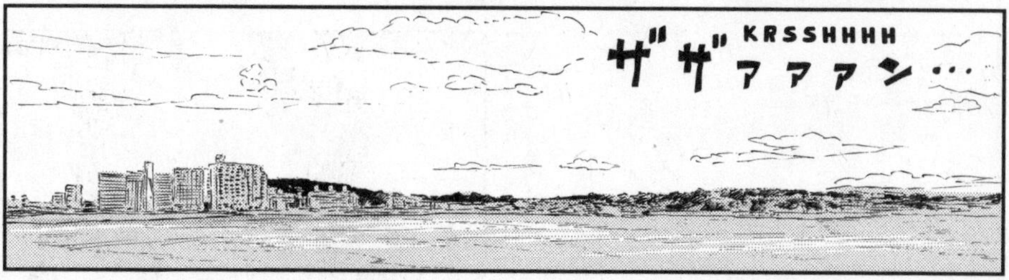
ザザァァァン…
KRSSHHHH

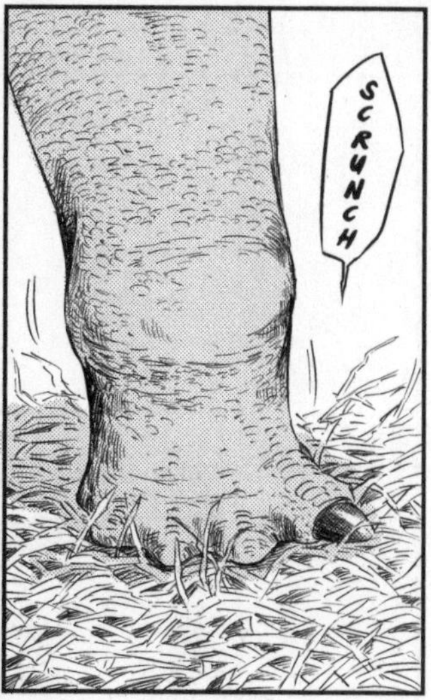
SCRUNCH

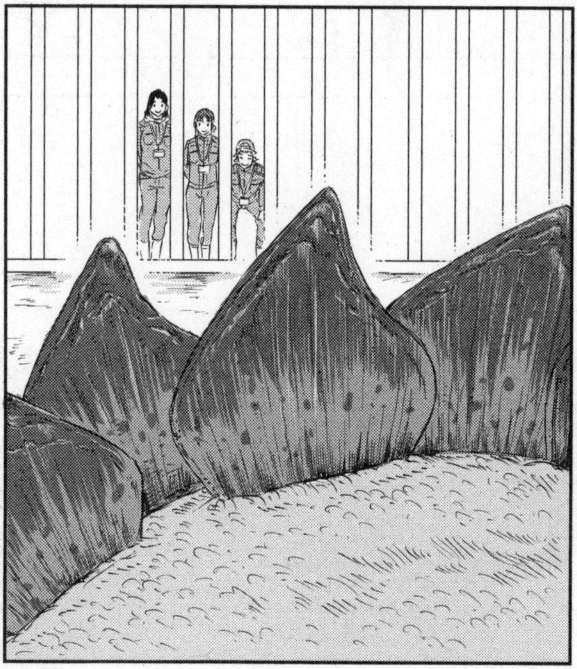

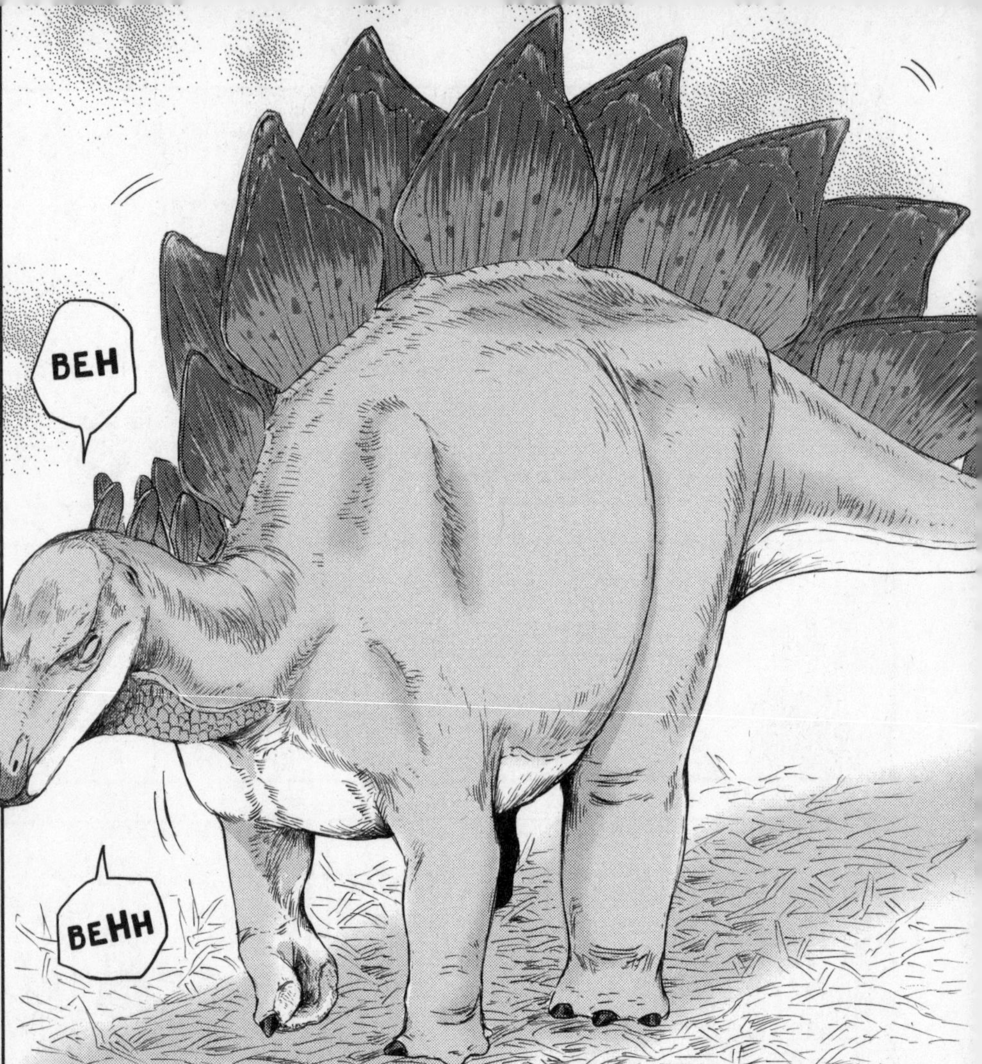
BEH
BEHH
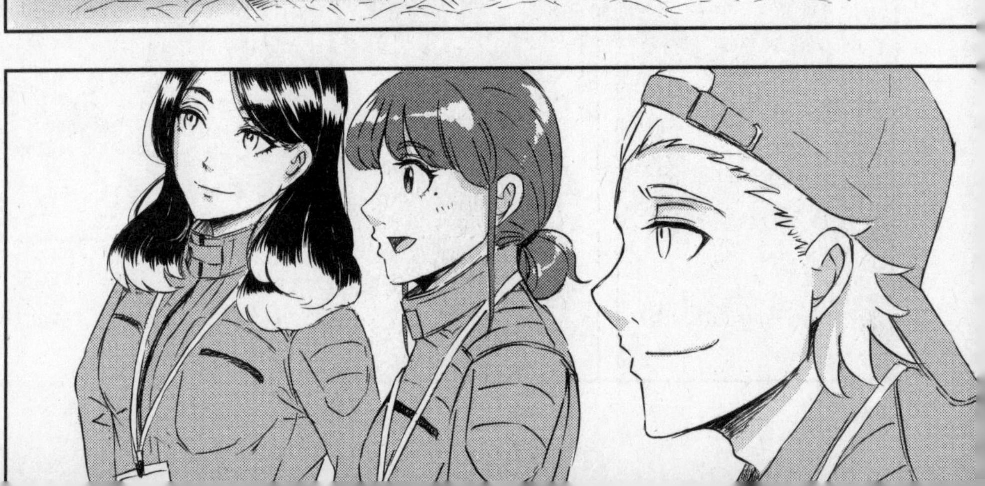

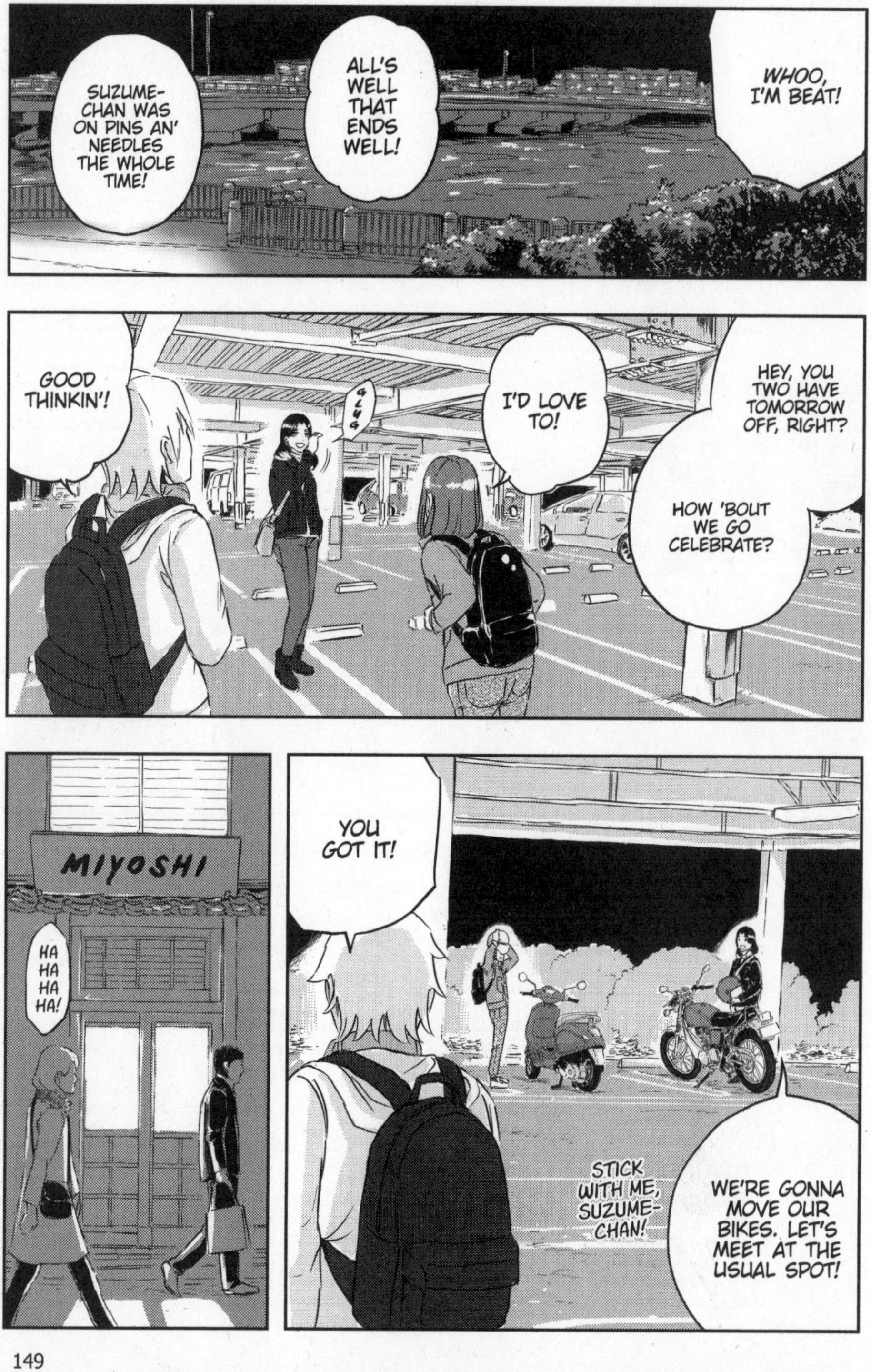
WHOO, I'M BEAT!
ALL'S WELL THAT ENDS WELL!
SUZUME-CHAN WAS ON PINS AN' NEEDLES THE WHOLE TIME!
HEY, YOU TWO HAVE TOMORROW OFF, RIGHT?
HOW 'BOUT WE GO CELEBRATE?
I'D LOVE TO!
GLUG
GOOD THINKIN'!
WE'RE GONNA MOVE OUR BIKES. LET'S MEET AT THE USUAL SPOT!
STICK WITH ME, SUZUME-CHAN!
YOU GOT IT!
MIYOSHI
HA HA HA HA!

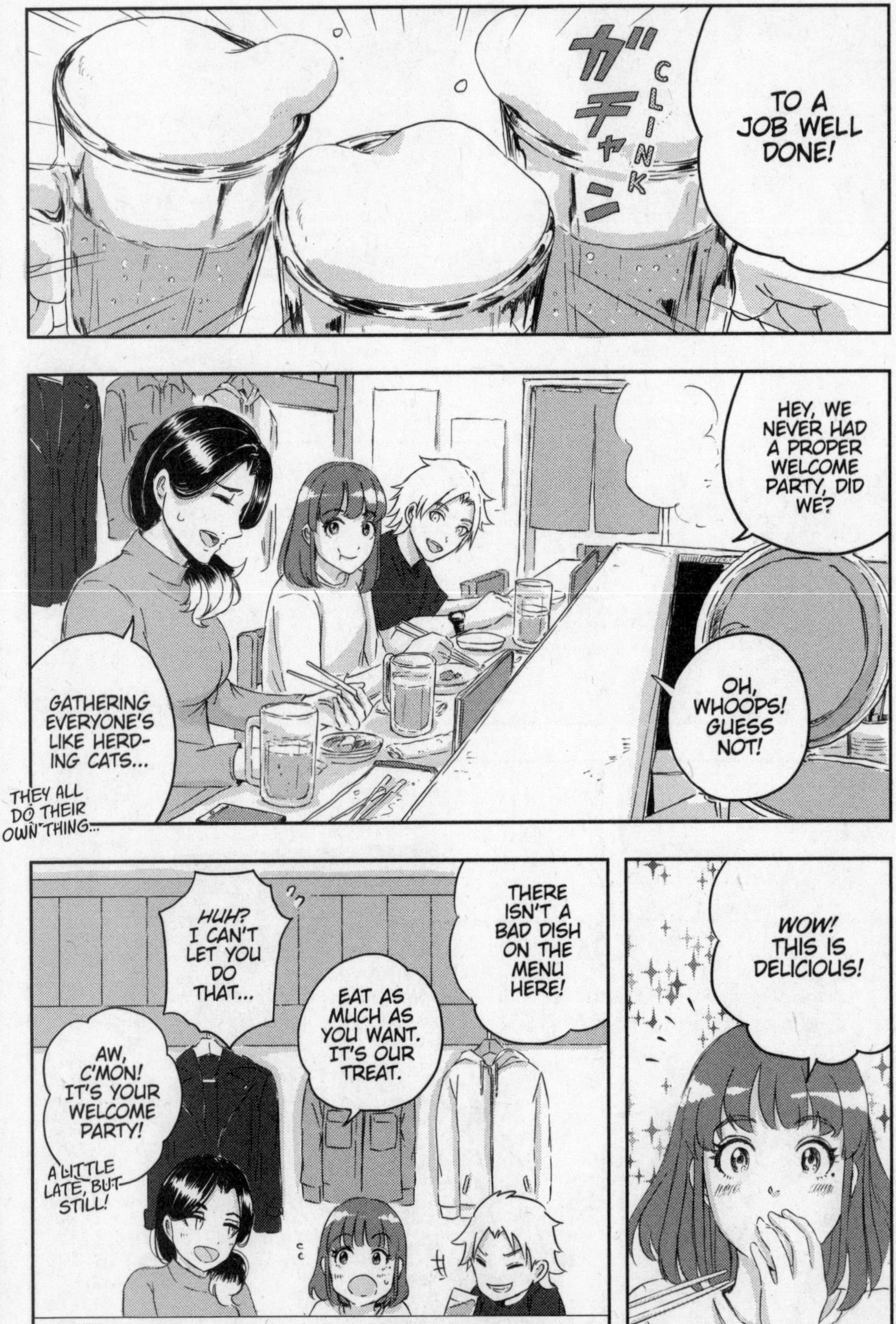
ガチャン
CLINK
TO A JOB WELL DONE!
HEY, WE NEVER HAD A PROPER WELCOME PARTY, DID WE?
OH, WHOOPS! GUESS NOT!
GATHERING EVERYONE'S LIKE HERDING CATS...
THEY ALL DO THEIR OWN THING...
WOW! THIS IS DELICIOUS!
THERE ISN'T A BAD DISH ON THE MENU HERE!
EAT AS MUCH AS YOU WANT. IT'S OUR TREAT.
HUH? I CAN'T LET YOU DO THAT...
AW, C'MON! IT'S YOUR WELCOME PARTY!
A LITTLE LATE, BUT STILL!

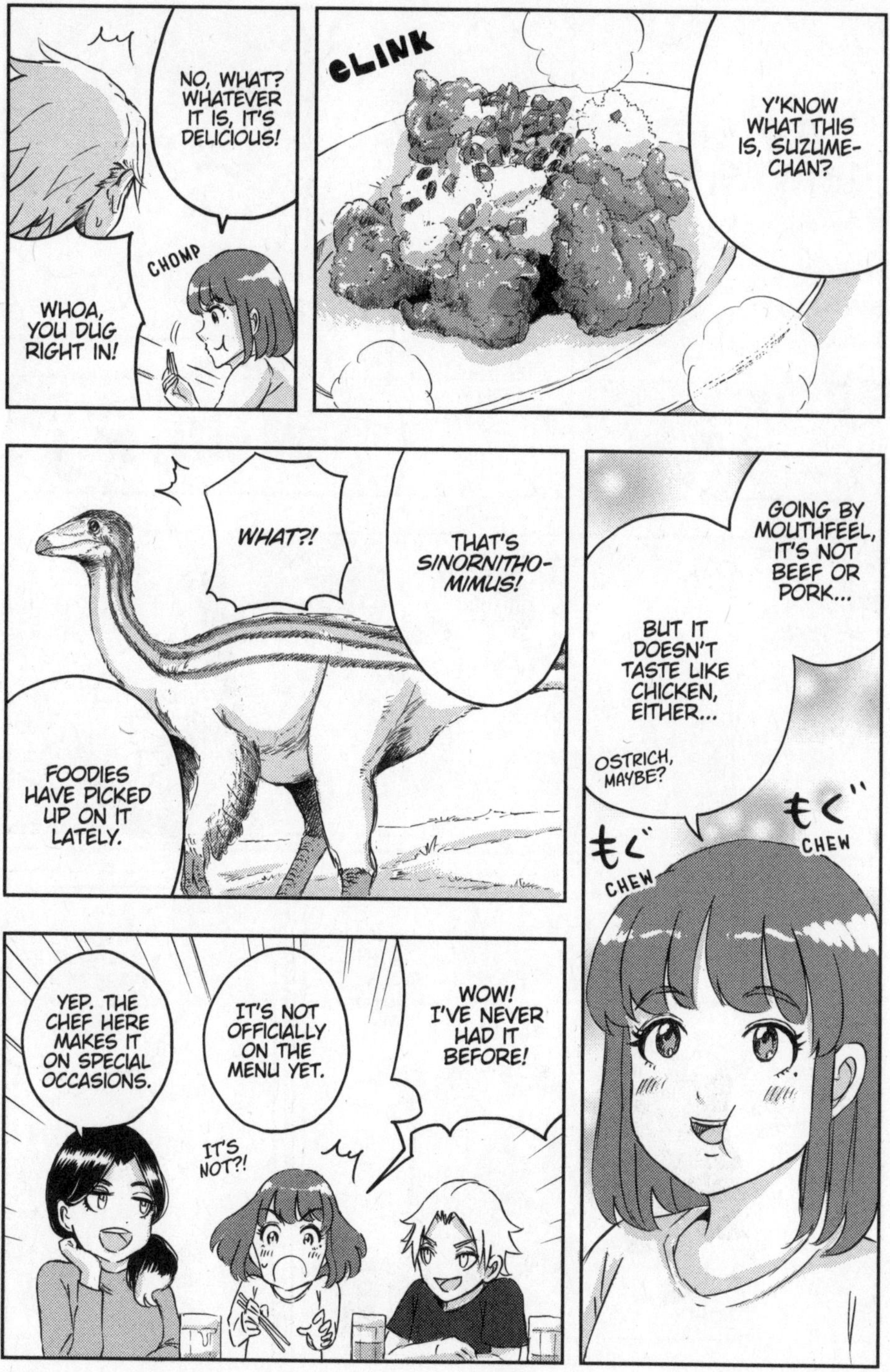
CLINK
Y'KNOW WHAT THIS IS, SUZUME-CHAN?
NO, WHAT? WHATEVER IT IS, IT'S DELICIOUS!
CHOMP
WHOA, YOU DUG RIGHT IN!
GOING BY MOUTHFEEL, IT'S NOT BEEF OR PORK...
BUT IT DOESN'T TASTE LIKE CHICKEN, EITHER...
OSTRICH, MAYBE?
もぐ
CHEW
もぐ
CHEW
THAT'S SINORNITHO-MIMUS!
WHAT?!
FOODIES HAVE PICKED UP ON IT LATELY.
WOW! I'VE NEVER HAD IT BEFORE!
IT'S NOT OFFICIALLY ON THE MENU YET.
YEP. THE CHEF HERE MAKES IT ON SPECIAL OCCASIONS.
IT'S NOT?!

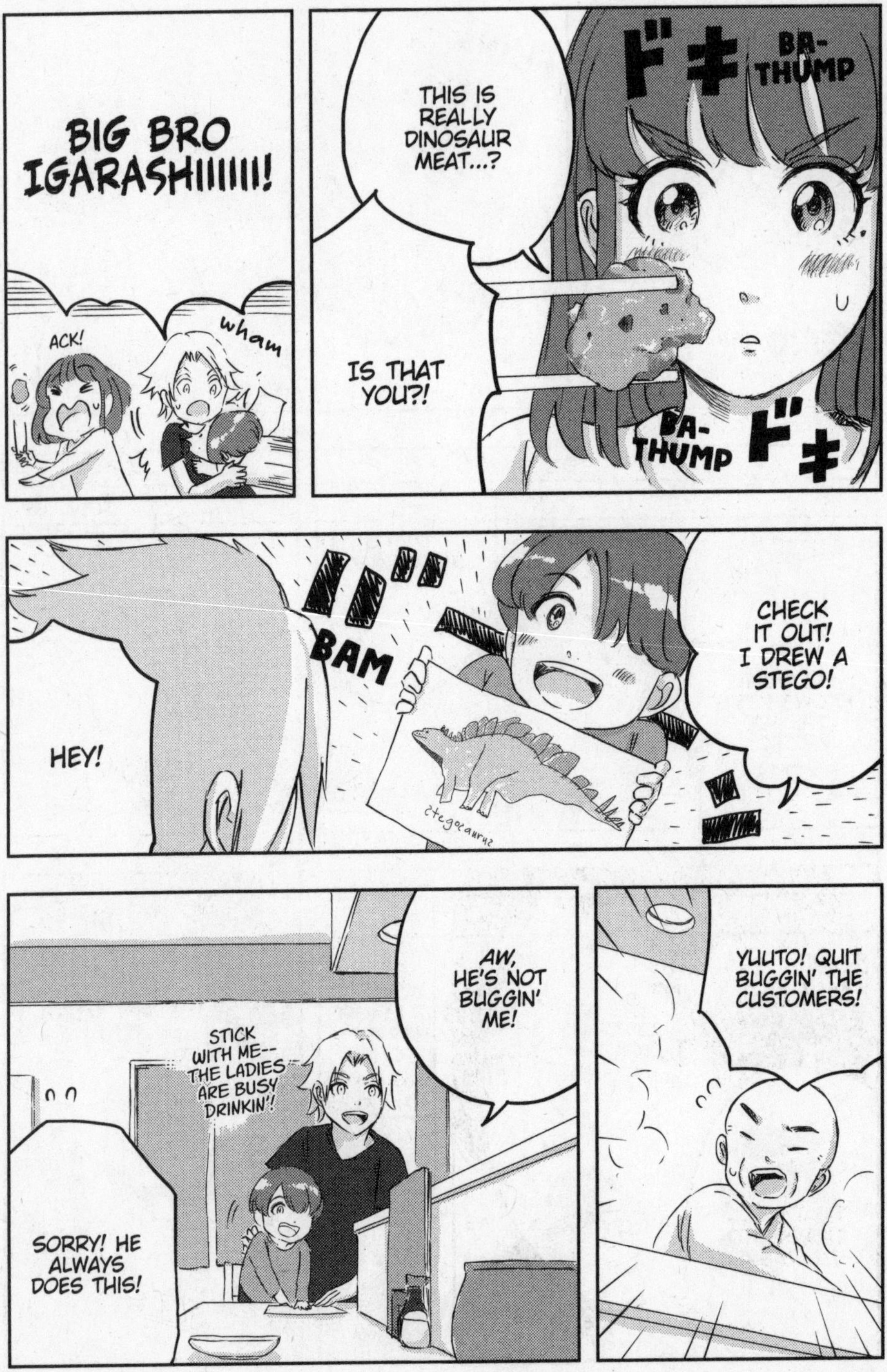
THIS IS REALLY DINOSAUR MEAT...?
ドキ BA-THUMP
IS THAT YOU?!
BA-THUMP ドキ
BIG BRO IGARASHIIIIIII!
wham
ACK!
CHECK IT OUT! I DREW A STEGO!
BAM
HEY!
YUUTO! QUIT BUGGIN' THE CUSTOMERS!
AW, HE'S NOT BUGGIN' ME!
STICK WITH ME-- THE LADIES ARE BUSY DRINKIN'!
SORRY! HE ALWAYS DOES THIS!

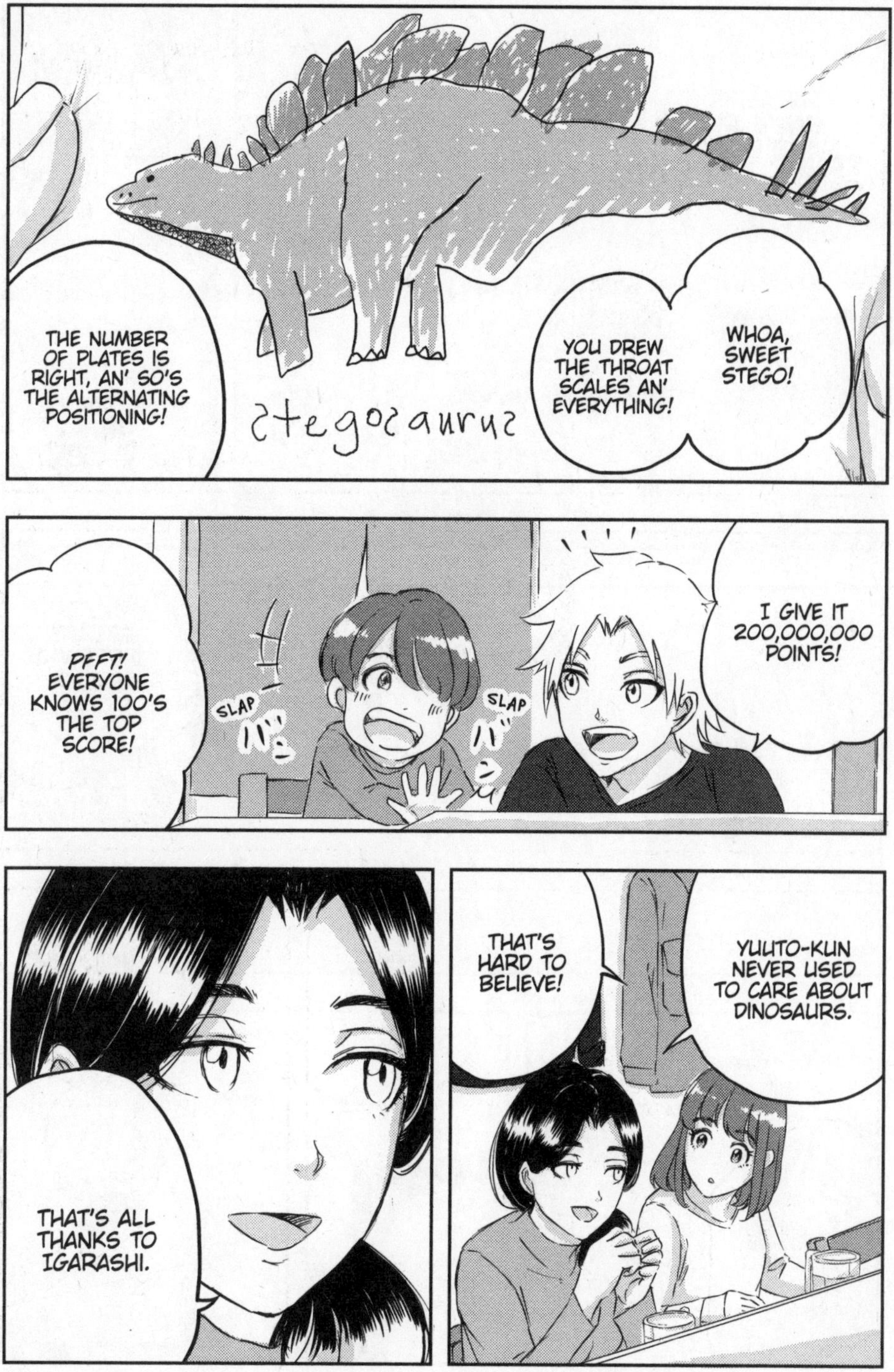
WHOA, SWEET STEGO!
YOU DREW THE THROAT SCALES AN' EVERYTHING!
THE NUMBER OF PLATES IS RIGHT, AN' SO'S THE ALTERNATING POSITIONING!
Stegosaurus
I GIVE IT 200,000,000 POINTS!
SLAP
バッ
SLAP
バッ
PFFT! EVERYONE KNOWS 100'S THE TOP SCORE!
YUUTO-KUN NEVER USED TO CARE ABOUT DINOSAURS.
THAT'S HARD TO BELIEVE!
THAT'S ALL THANKS TO IGARASHI.

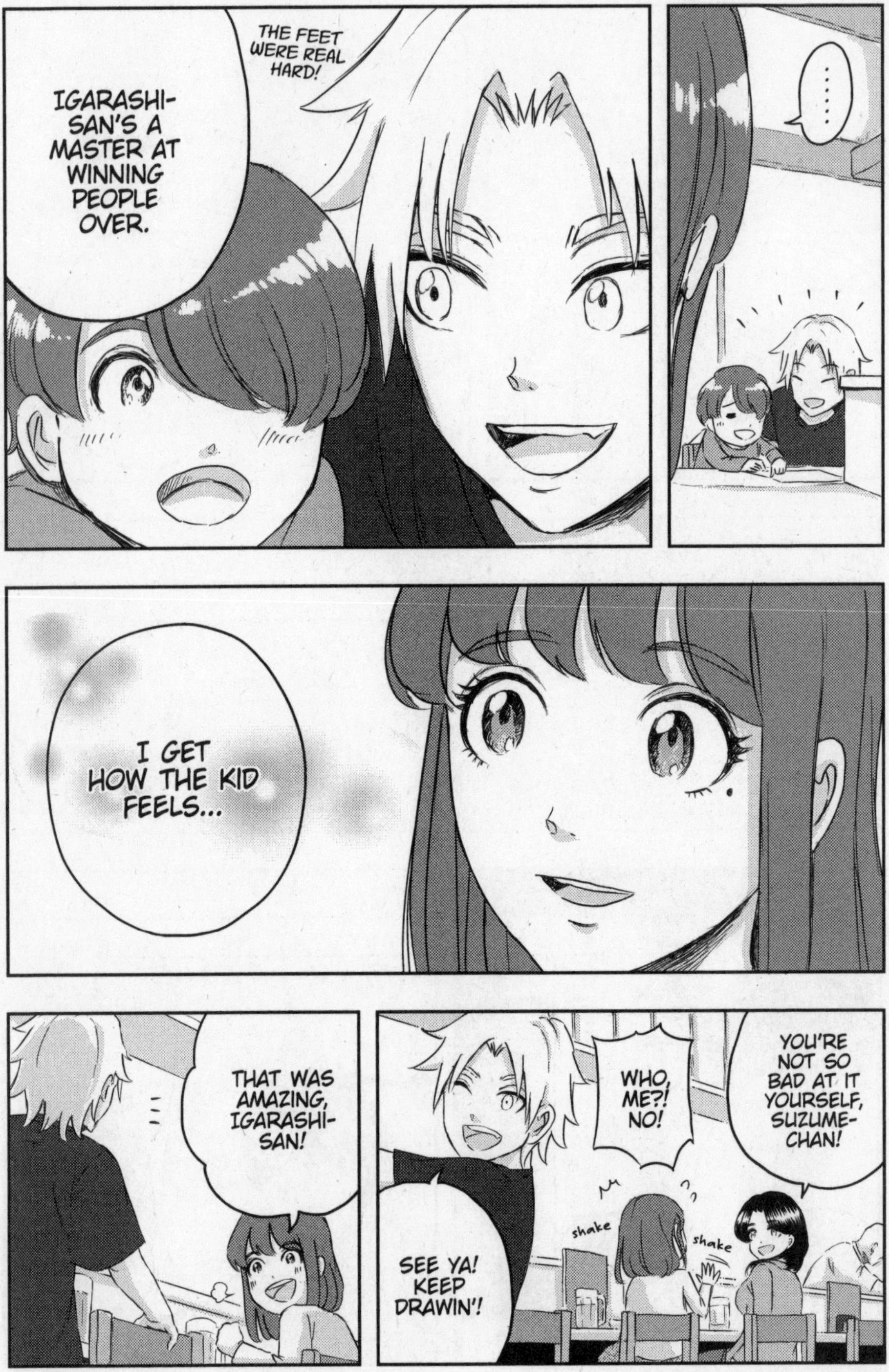
……
THE FEET WERE REAL HARD!
IGARASHI-SAN'S A MASTER AT WINNING PEOPLE OVER.
I GET HOW THE KID FEELS...
YOU'RE NOT SO BAD AT IT YOURSELF, SUZUME-CHAN!
WHO, ME?! NO!
shake
shake
SEE YA! KEEP DRAWIN'!
THAT WAS AMAZING, IGARASHI-SAN!

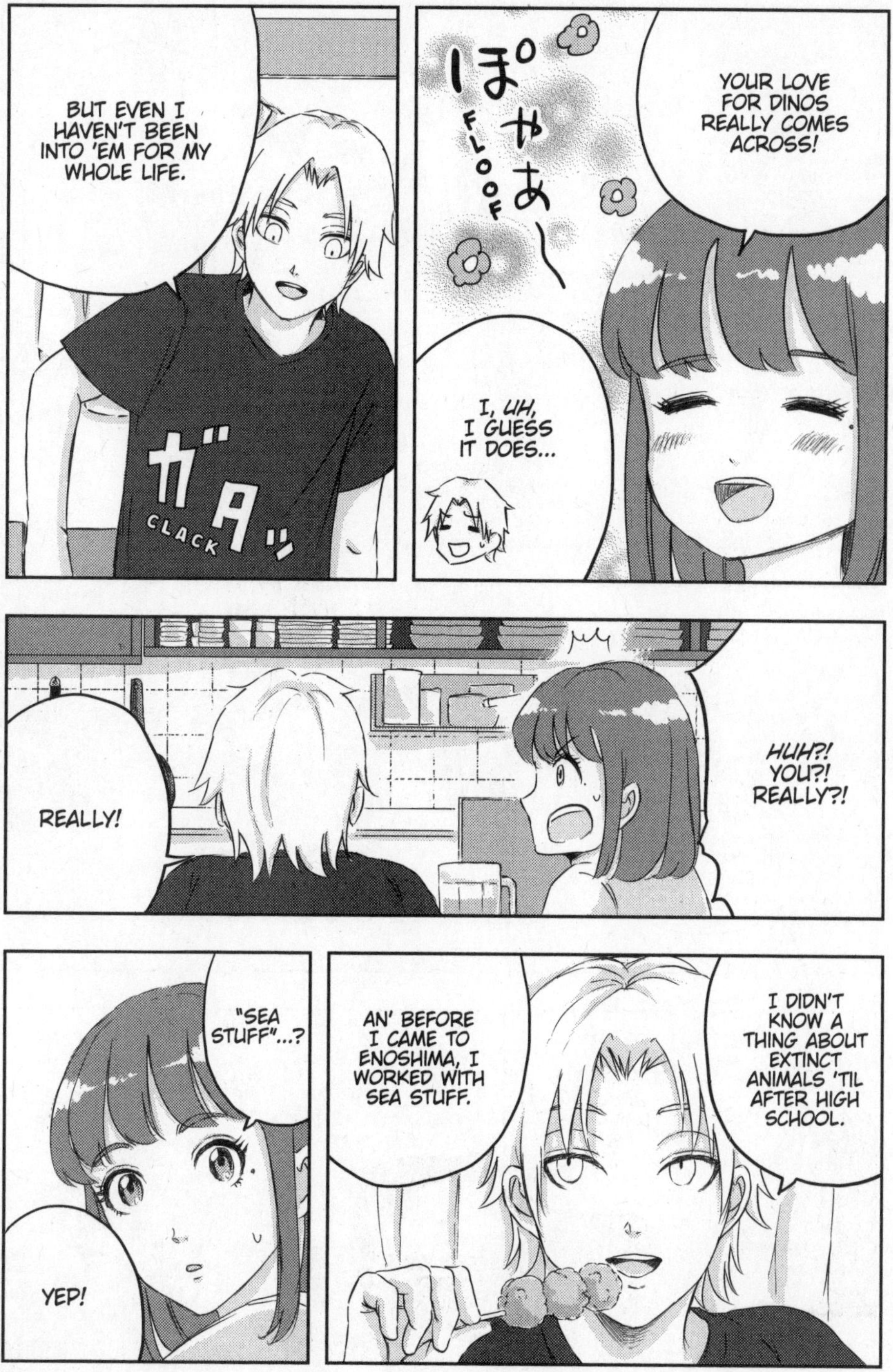
ぽやあ〜
FLOOF
YOUR LOVE FOR DINOS REALLY COMES ACROSS!
I, UH, I GUESS IT DOES...
BUT EVEN I HAVEN'T BEEN INTO 'EM FOR MY WHOLE LIFE.
ガタッ
CLACK
HUH?! YOU?! REALLY?!
REALLY!
I DIDN'T KNOW A THING ABOUT EXTINCT ANIMALS 'TIL AFTER HIGH SCHOOL.
AN' BEFORE I CAME TO ENOSHIMA, I WORKED WITH SEA STUFF.
"SEA STUFF"...?
YEP!

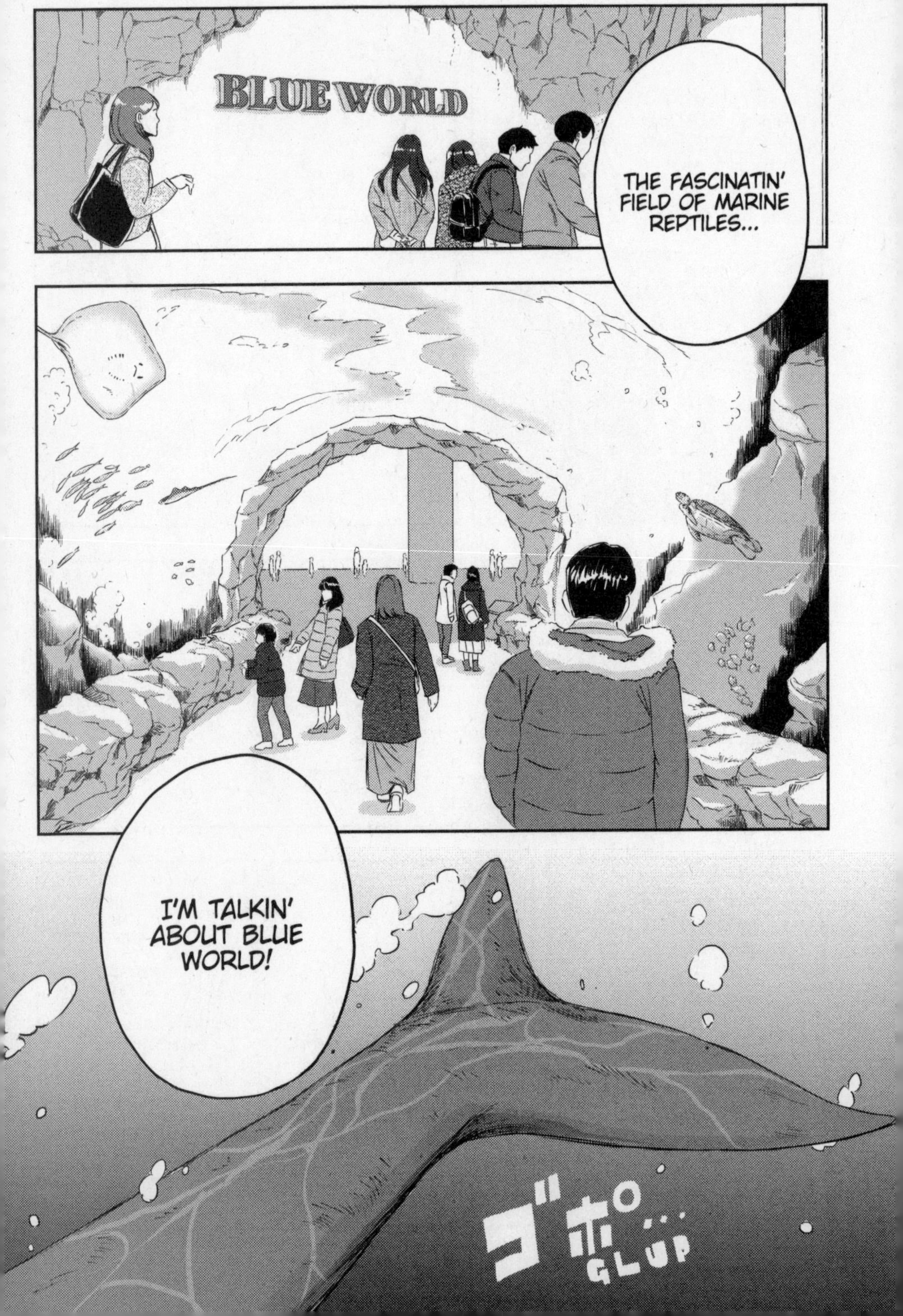
BLUE WORLD
THE FASCINATIN' FIELD OF MARINE REPTILES...
I'M TALKIN' ABOUT BLUE WORLD!
ゴボ…
GLUP

Dr. Dino's Lab Log

FILE. 16 A Cozy Heating System

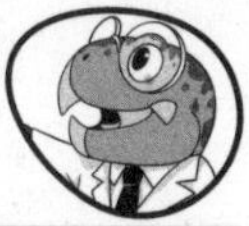

The cells in animals' bodies use oxygen to burn glucose from the food they eat, thus generating the energy they need to live. The "cinders" left behind from the burning are expelled as carbon dioxide. This process is called cellular respiration. As it flows through blood vessels, blood carries oxygen to cells throughout the body—and takes the leftover carbon dioxide away. Oxygen and carbon dioxide aren't the only things that blood moves around the body, however; it also plays a vital role by transmitting *heat*.

When you stand in sunlight or soak in a hot spring, the surface of your body gets warmer. In spots where there are a lot of blood vessels near that surface, a lot of your blood gets warmer, too. As that blood flows through your body, it spreads its warmth all over. It works kind of like floor heating in that regard. Conversely, if a lot of wind or water hits a part of your body through which several blood vessels flow, the blood there cools down—and, gradually, so does the rest of your body.

In human beings, several thick blood vessels are gathered together in our armpits, groin, and neck—so if you happen to be laid up in bed with a fever, it's a good idea to keep those areas cool. I've heard that cats, on the other hand, have a lot of blood vessels concentrated in their bellies. Elephants avoid overheating by keeping the blood vessels in their ears cool; dogs, the blood vessels in their tongues.

Modern-day lizards, crocodiles, birds, and turtles have body parts that are covered with a hard layer of keratin—scales, horns, beaks, what-have-you. Many scaled animals have osteoderms (bony deposits in the skin) directly under their scales, and these have networks of blood vessels running through them. So do the bones directly below birds' beaks. When photographed with a thermographic camera—which detects heat using infrared light—these keratin-covered parts show up in colors indicating that they're warmer than the other parts of the body. That means these parts play a major role in regulating heat for theses animals—both dissipating heat from their bodies and gathering heat from their surroundings. Meanwhile, feathers seal in heat like a Thermos, and thus feathery parts show up in cooler colors than beaks do.

The scientific name of *Stegosaurus* means "roof lizard"—a name which makes sense when you consider the large plates of osteoderms that cover its back. These osteoderms are called dermal plates. It's thought that, when *Stegosaurus* was alive, these plates were covered with a layer of keratin, too.

In 2010, the scientists James O. Farrow, Shoji Hayashi, and Glenn J. Tattersall demonstrated that the dermal plates of *Stegosaurus* contained a whole network of thick, branching blood vessels. A few pages back in this very manga, you saw Momiji the *Stegosaurus* basking by turning her big dermal plates to catch the sun. It's thought that these dermal plates, filled as they were with blood vessels, served as an extremely effective system for regulating their body temperature. I bet that if you were to take a thermographic picture of a *Stegosaurus,* the dermal plates would show up in a splendidly warm red!

(Incidentally, Hayashi-san and I happen to be only one school year apart. We've been quite well acquainted since our days as students!)

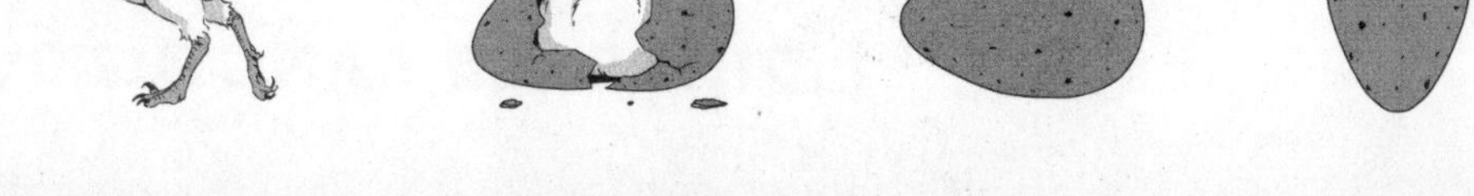

DINOSAUR SANCTUARY

EVER SINCE LIFE ON EARTH BEGAN 38 HUNDRED MILLION YEARS AGO...

MOST OF IT HAS LIVED IN THE OCEANS.

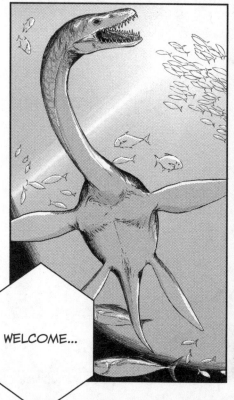

WELCOME...

DIVE WITH US...

INTO THAT DEEP BLUE DOMAIN.

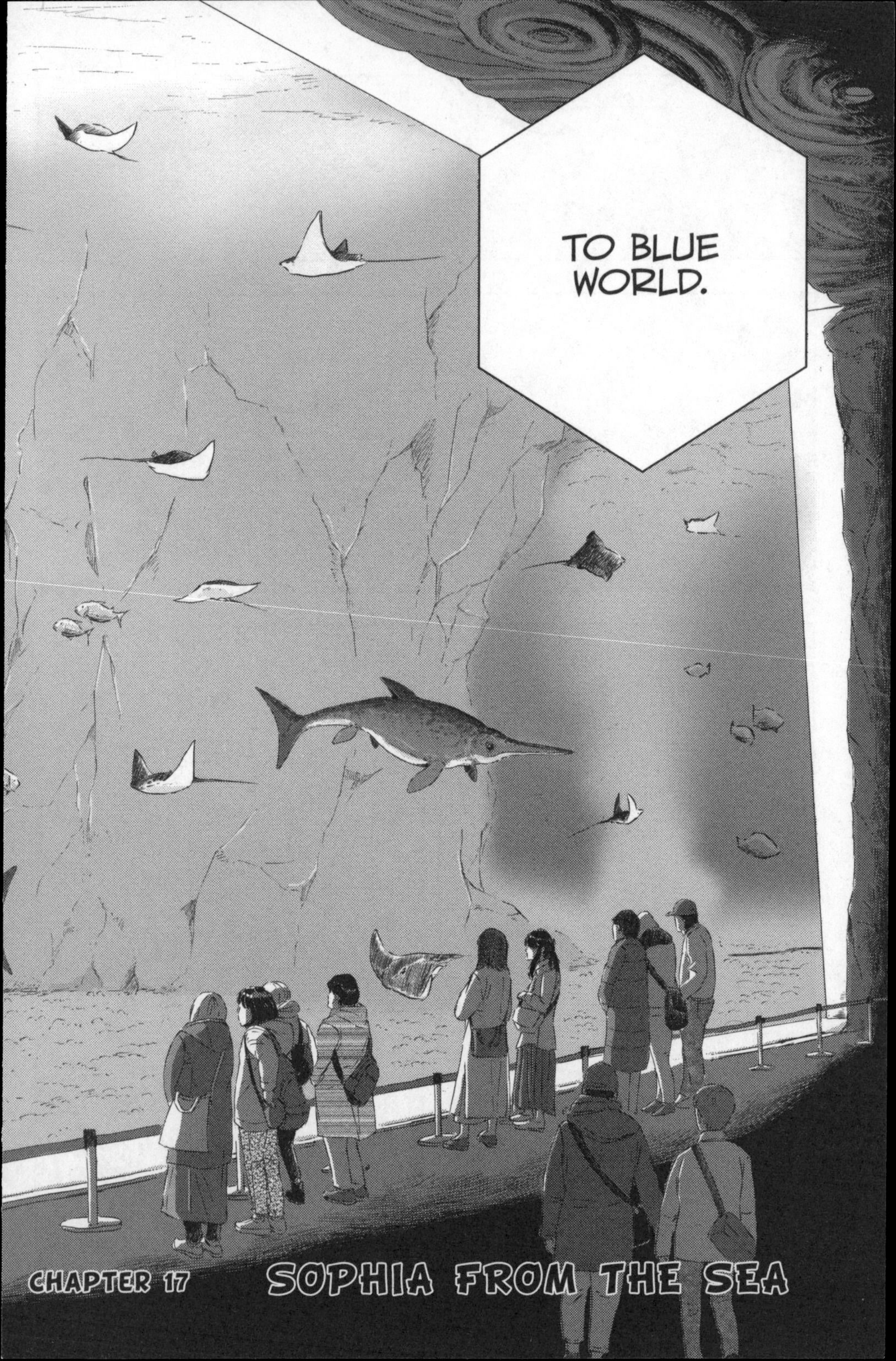
TO BLUE WORLD.
CHAPTER 17
SOPHIA FROM THE SEA

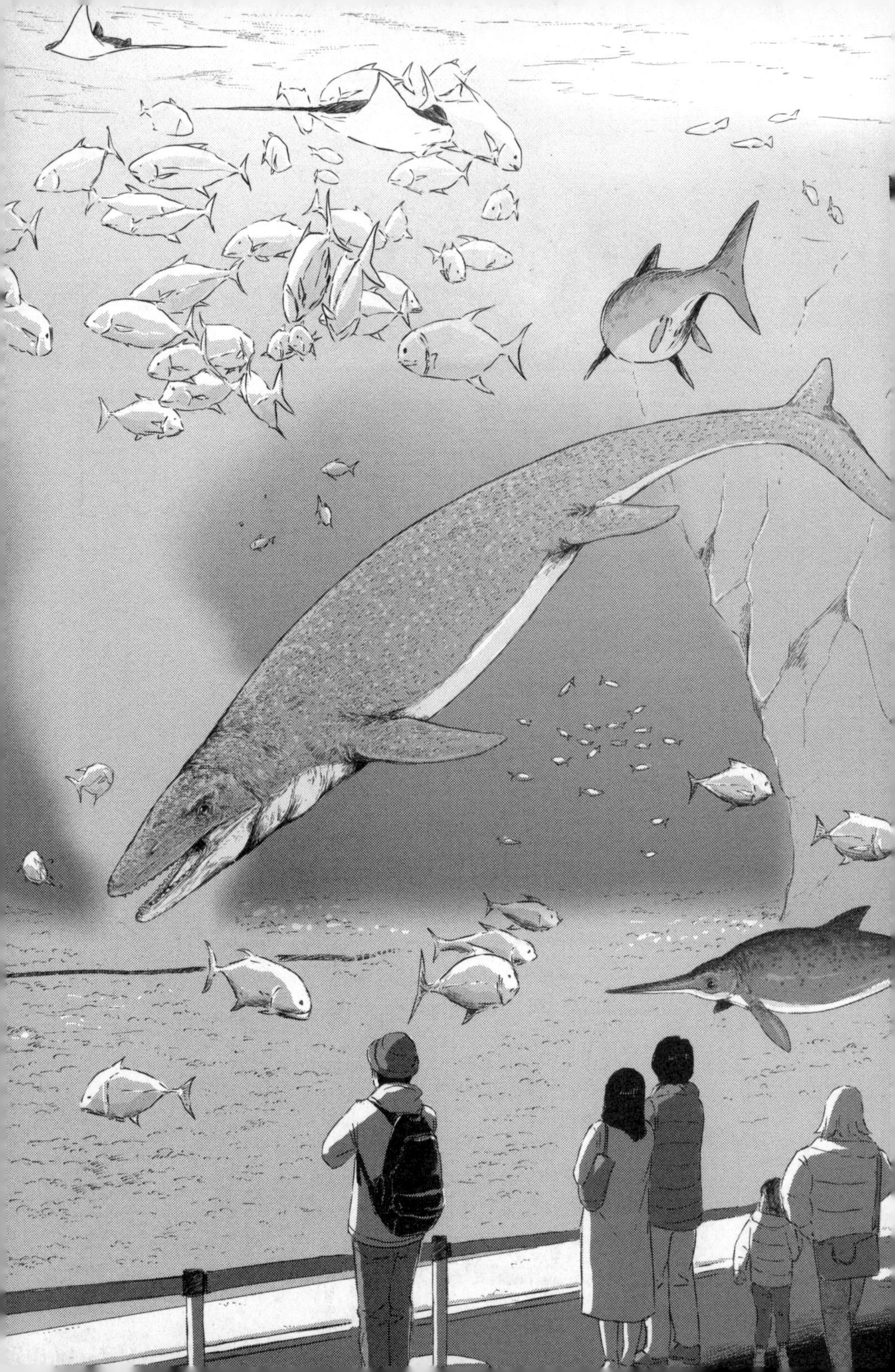

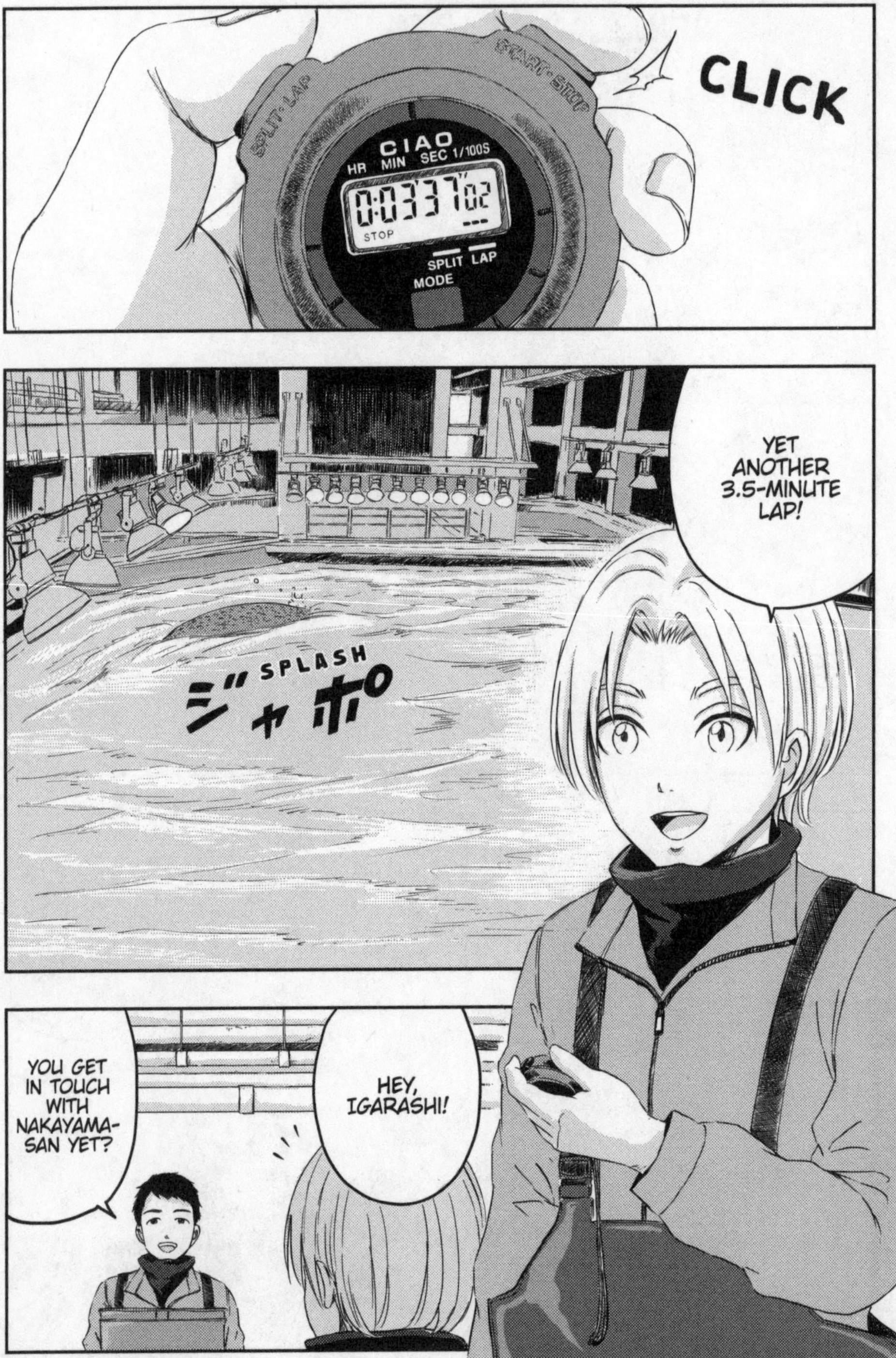
START·STOP
SPLIT·LAP
CIAO
HR MIN SEC 1/100S
STOP
SPLIT LAP
MODE
CLICK
YET ANOTHER 3.5-MINUTE LAP!
SPLASH
ジャポ
HEY, IGARASHI!
YOU GET IN TOUCH WITH NAKAYAMA-SAN YET?

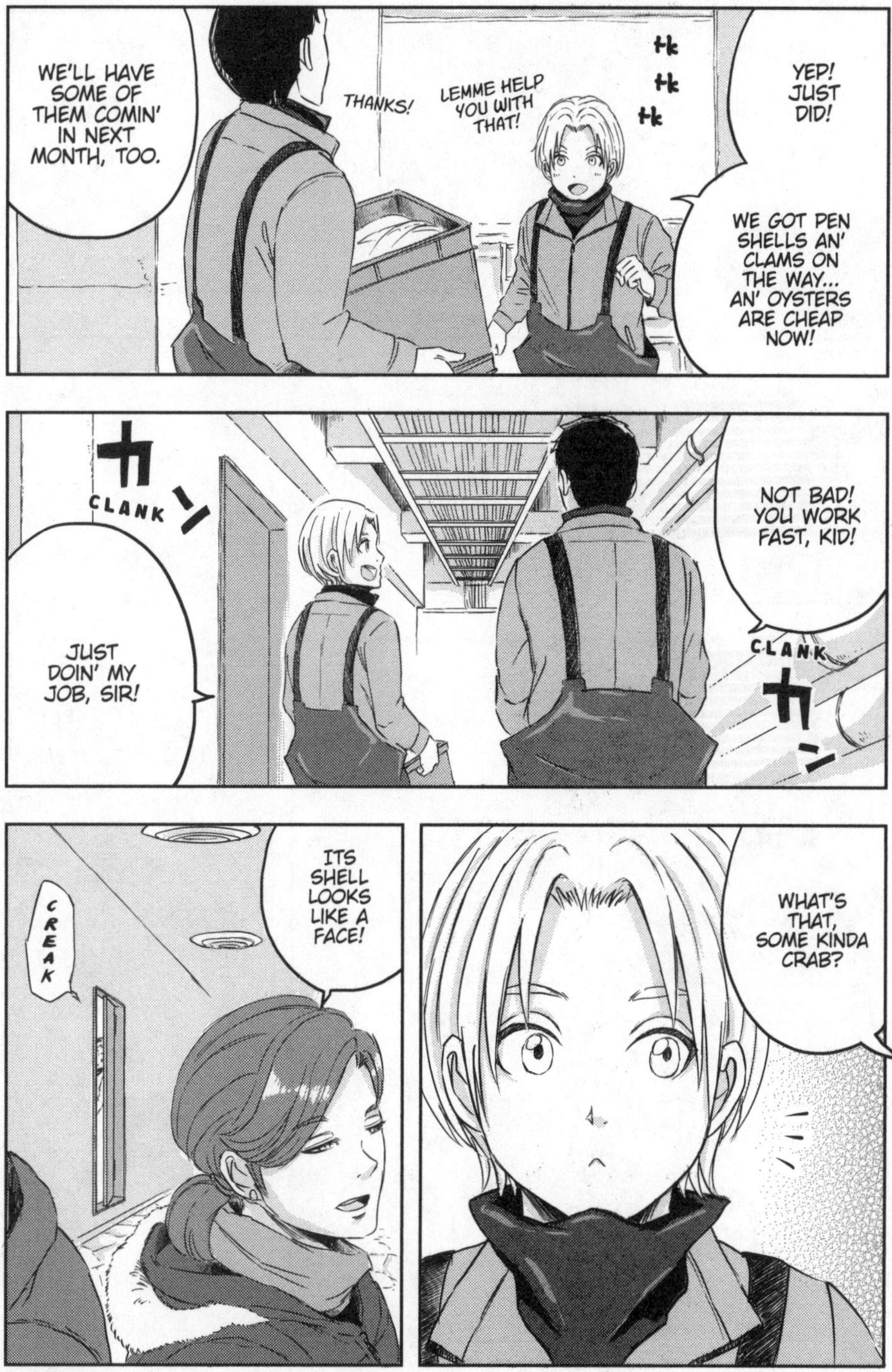
YEP! JUST DID!
WE GOT PEN SHELLS AN' CLAMS ON THE WAY... AN' OYSTERS ARE CHEAP NOW!
tk tk tk
LEMME HELP YOU WITH THAT!
THANKS!
WE'LL HAVE SOME OF THEM COMIN' IN NEXT MONTH, TOO.
NOT BAD! YOU WORK FAST, KID!
CLANK
カン
CLANK
カン
JUST DOIN' MY JOB, SIR!
WHAT'S THAT, SOME KINDA CRAB?
ITS SHELL LOOKS LIKE A FACE!
CREAK

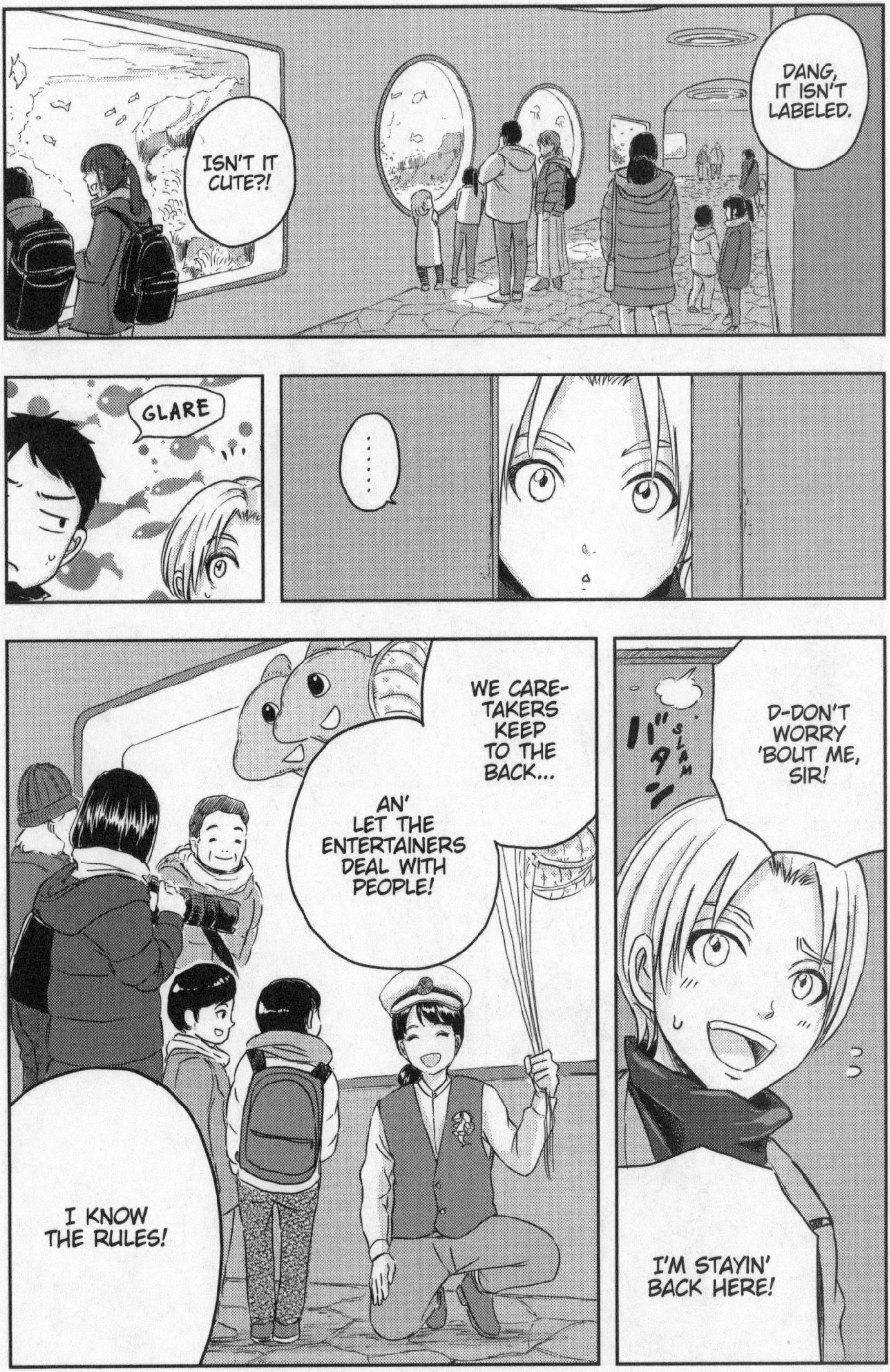
DANG, IT ISN'T LABELED.
ISN'T IT CUTE?!
......
GLARE
D-DON'T WORRY 'BOUT ME, SIR!
SLAM
I'M STAYIN' BACK HERE!
WE CARE-TAKERS KEEP TO THE BACK...
AN' LET THE ENTERTAINERS DEAL WITH PEOPLE!
I KNOW THE RULES!

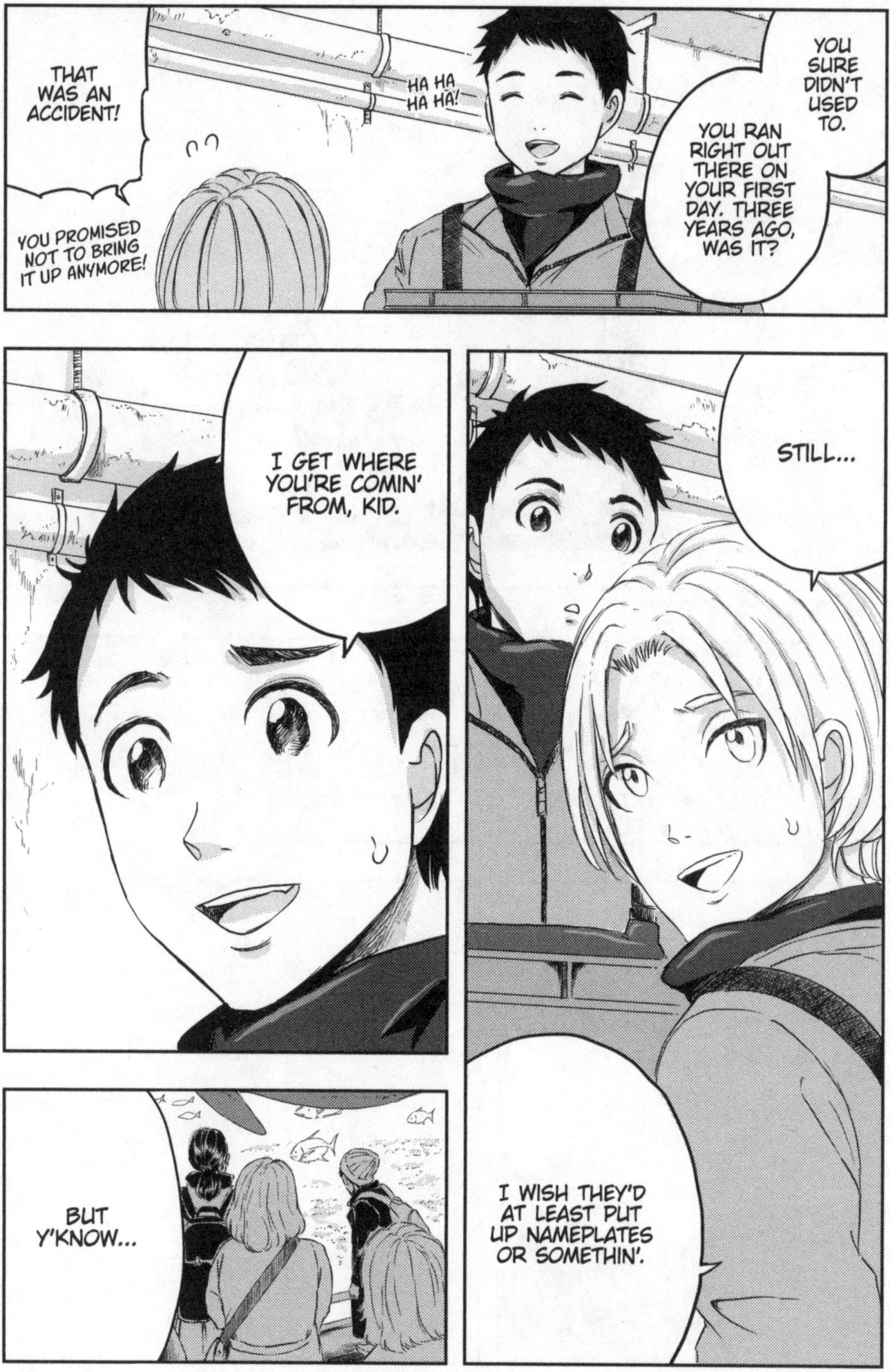
YOU SURE DIDN'T USED TO.
YOU RAN RIGHT OUT THERE ON YOUR FIRST DAY. THREE YEARS AGO, WAS IT?
HA HA HA HA!
THAT WAS AN ACCIDENT!
YOU PROMISED NOT TO BRING IT UP ANYMORE!
STILL...
I GET WHERE YOU'RE COMIN' FROM, KID.
BUT Y'KNOW...
I WISH THEY'D AT LEAST PUT UP NAMEPLATES OR SOMETHIN'.

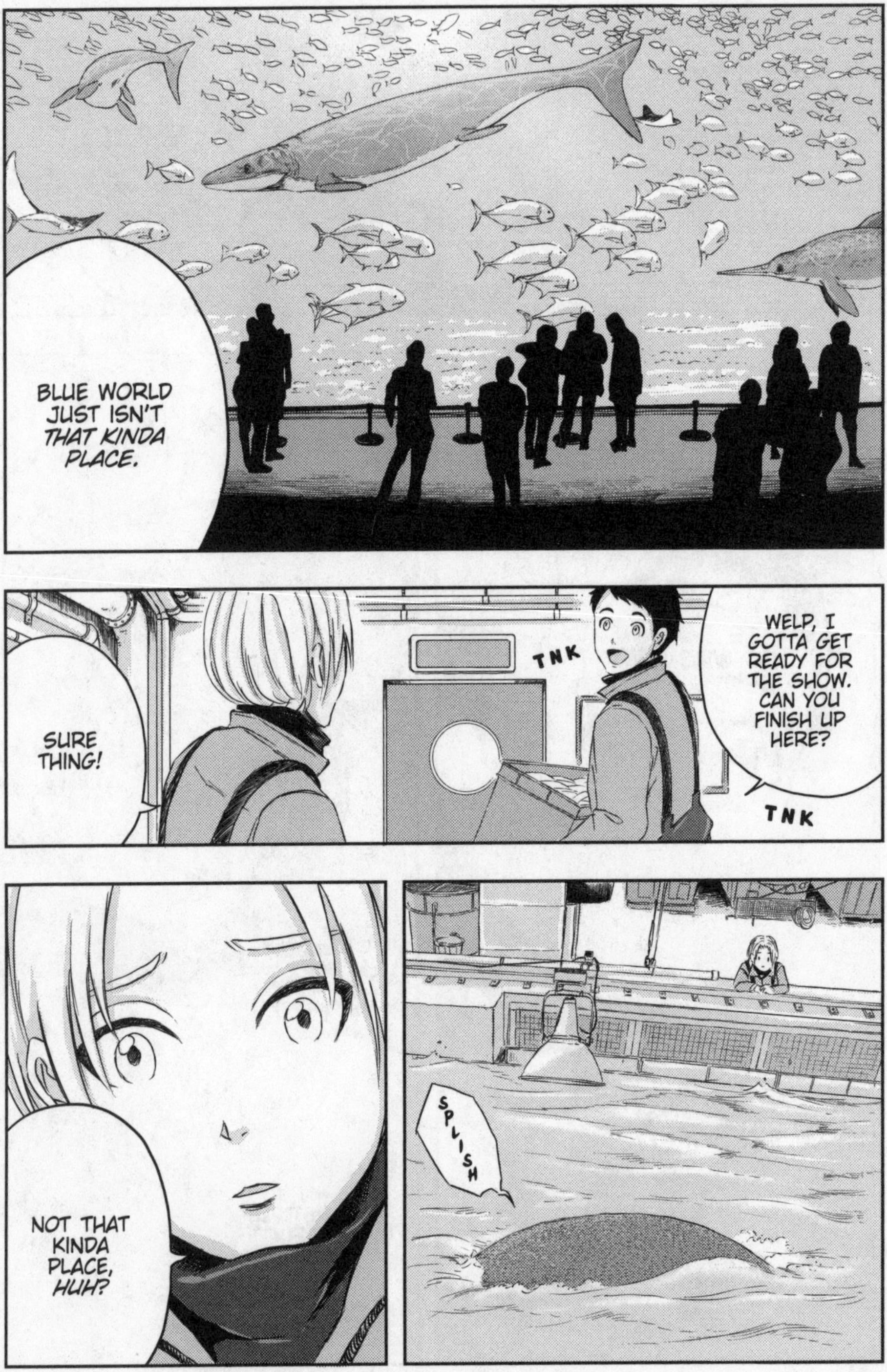
BLUE WORLD JUST ISN'T *THAT KINDA* PLACE.
TNK
WELP, I GOTTA GET READY FOR THE SHOW. CAN YOU FINISH UP HERE?
TNK
SURE THING!
SPLISH
NOT THAT KINDA PLACE, *HUH?*

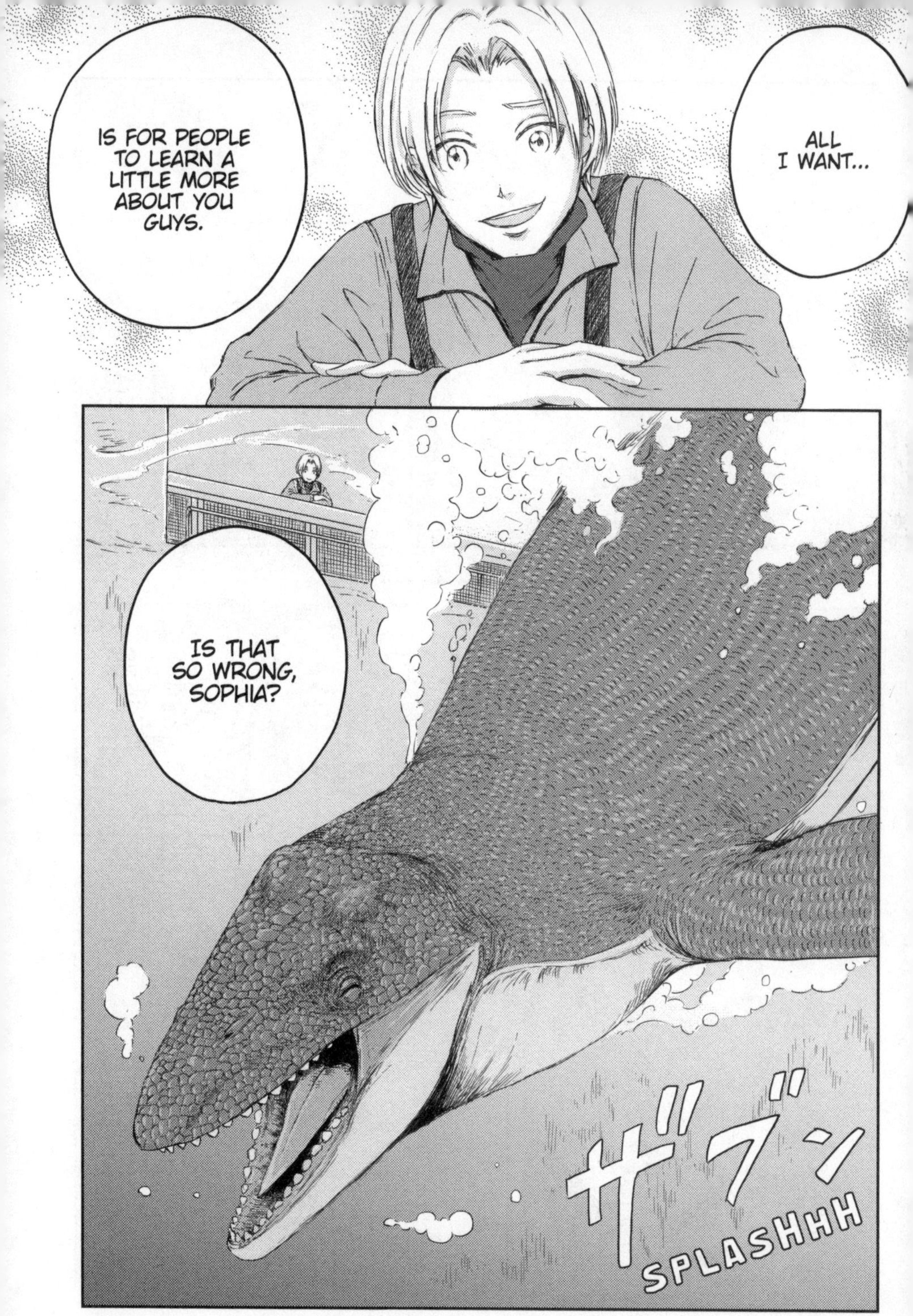
ALL I WANT...
IS FOR PEOPLE TO LEARN A LITTLE MORE ABOUT YOU GUYS.
IS THAT SO WRONG, SOPHIA?
ザブン
SPLASHHH

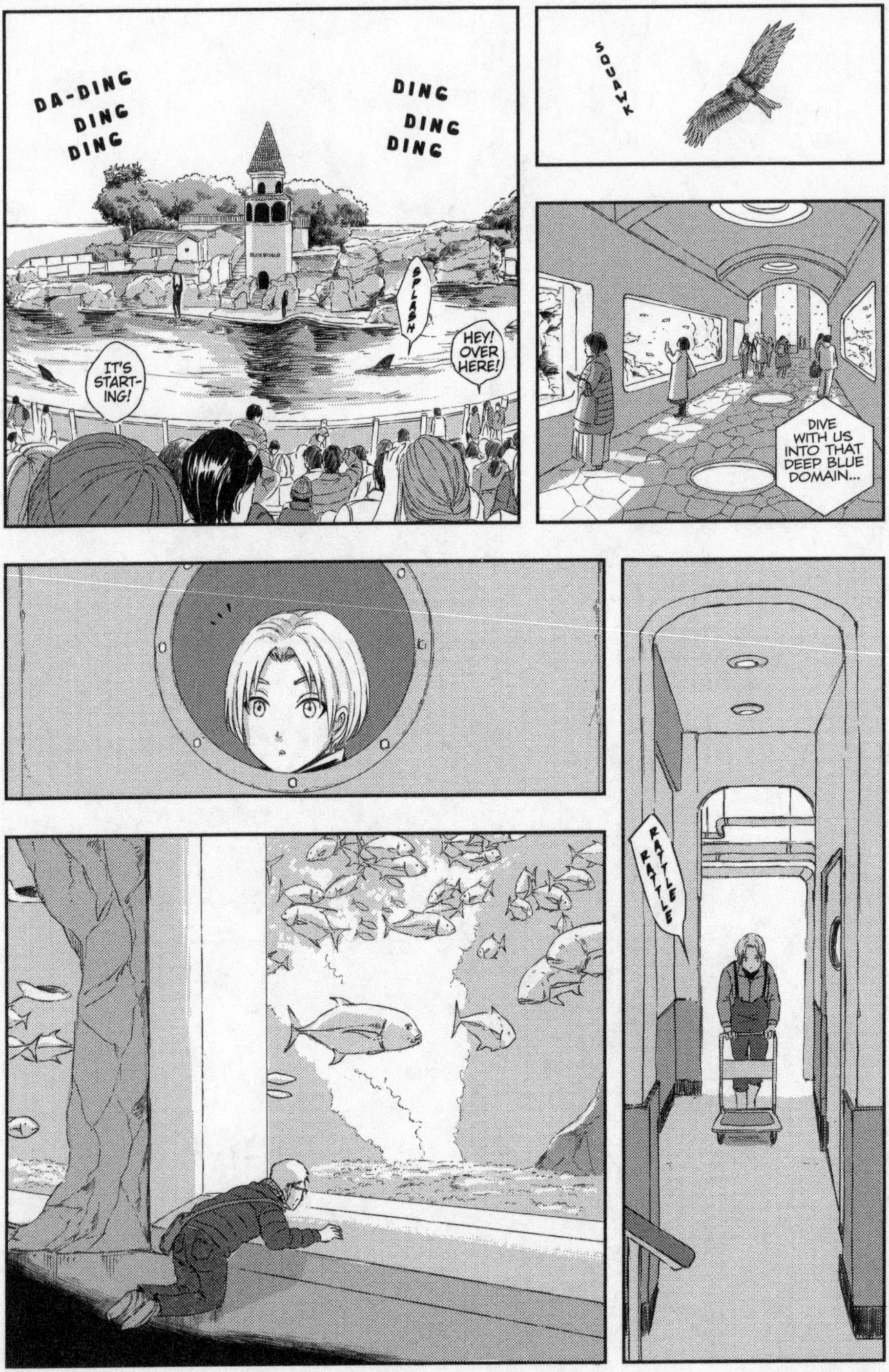
SQUAWK
DIVE WITH US INTO THAT DEEP BLUE DOMAIN...
DING DING DING
DA-DING DING DING
SPLASH
HEY! OVER HERE!
IT'S START-ING!
RATTLE RATTLE

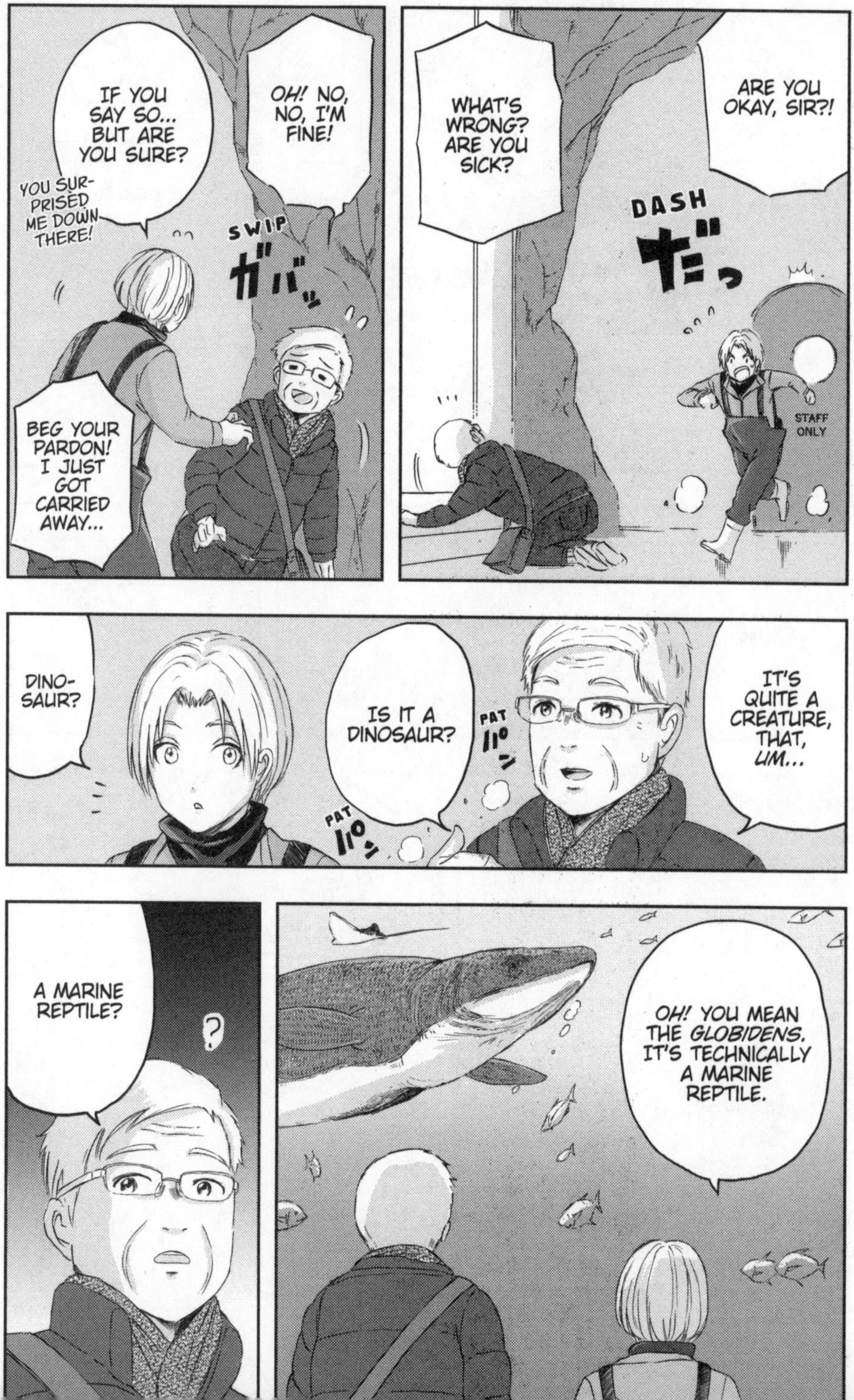
ARE YOU OKAY, SIR?!
WHAT'S WRONG? ARE YOU SICK?
DASH
だっ
STAFF ONLY
OH! NO, NO, I'M FINE!
SWIP
ガバッ
IF YOU SAY SO... BUT ARE YOU SURE?
YOU SURPRISED ME DOWN THERE!
BEG YOUR PARDON! I JUST GOT CARRIED AWAY...
IT'S QUITE A CREATURE, THAT, UM...
PAT
パッ
IS IT A DINOSAUR?
PAT
パッ
DINOSAUR?
OH! YOU MEAN THE *GLOBIDENS*. IT'S TECHNICALLY A MARINE REPTILE.
A MARINE REPTILE?
?

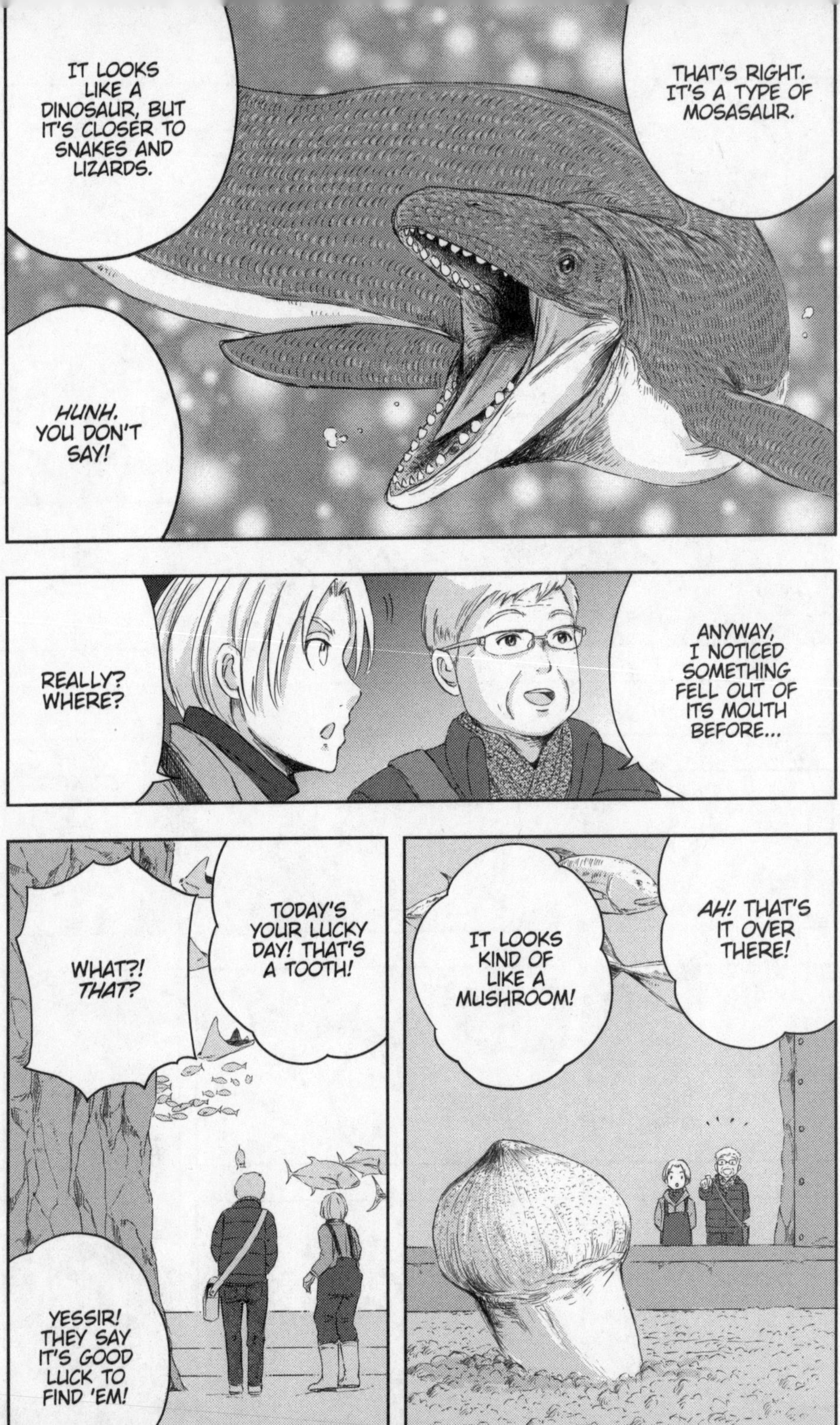
THAT'S RIGHT. IT'S A TYPE OF MOSASAUR.
IT LOOKS LIKE A DINOSAUR, BUT IT'S CLOSER TO SNAKES AND LIZARDS.
HUNH. YOU DON'T SAY!
ANYWAY, I NOTICED SOMETHING FELL OUT OF ITS MOUTH BEFORE...
REALLY? WHERE?
AH! THAT'S IT OVER THERE!
IT LOOKS KIND OF LIKE A MUSHROOM!
TODAY'S YOUR LUCKY DAY! THAT'S A TOOTH!
WHAT?! THAT?
YESSIR! THEY SAY IT'S GOOD LUCK TO FIND 'EM!

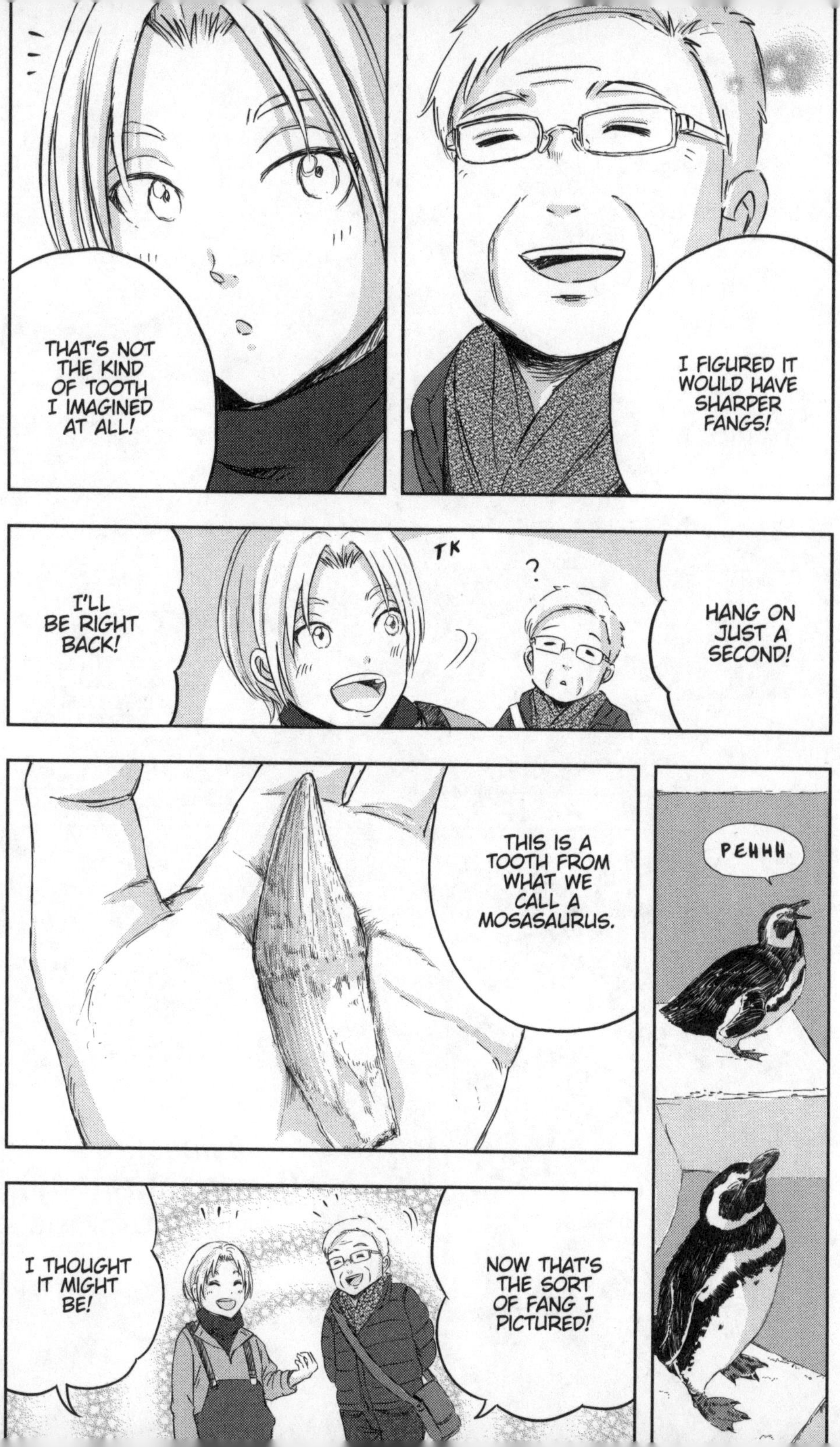
I FIGURED IT WOULD HAVE SHARPER FANGS!
THAT'S NOT THE KIND OF TOOTH I IMAGINED AT ALL!
HANG ON JUST A SECOND!
TK
I'LL BE RIGHT BACK!
PEHHH
THIS IS A TOOTH FROM WHAT WE CALL A MOSASAURUS.
NOW THAT'S THE SORT OF FANG I PICTURED!
I THOUGHT IT MIGHT BE!

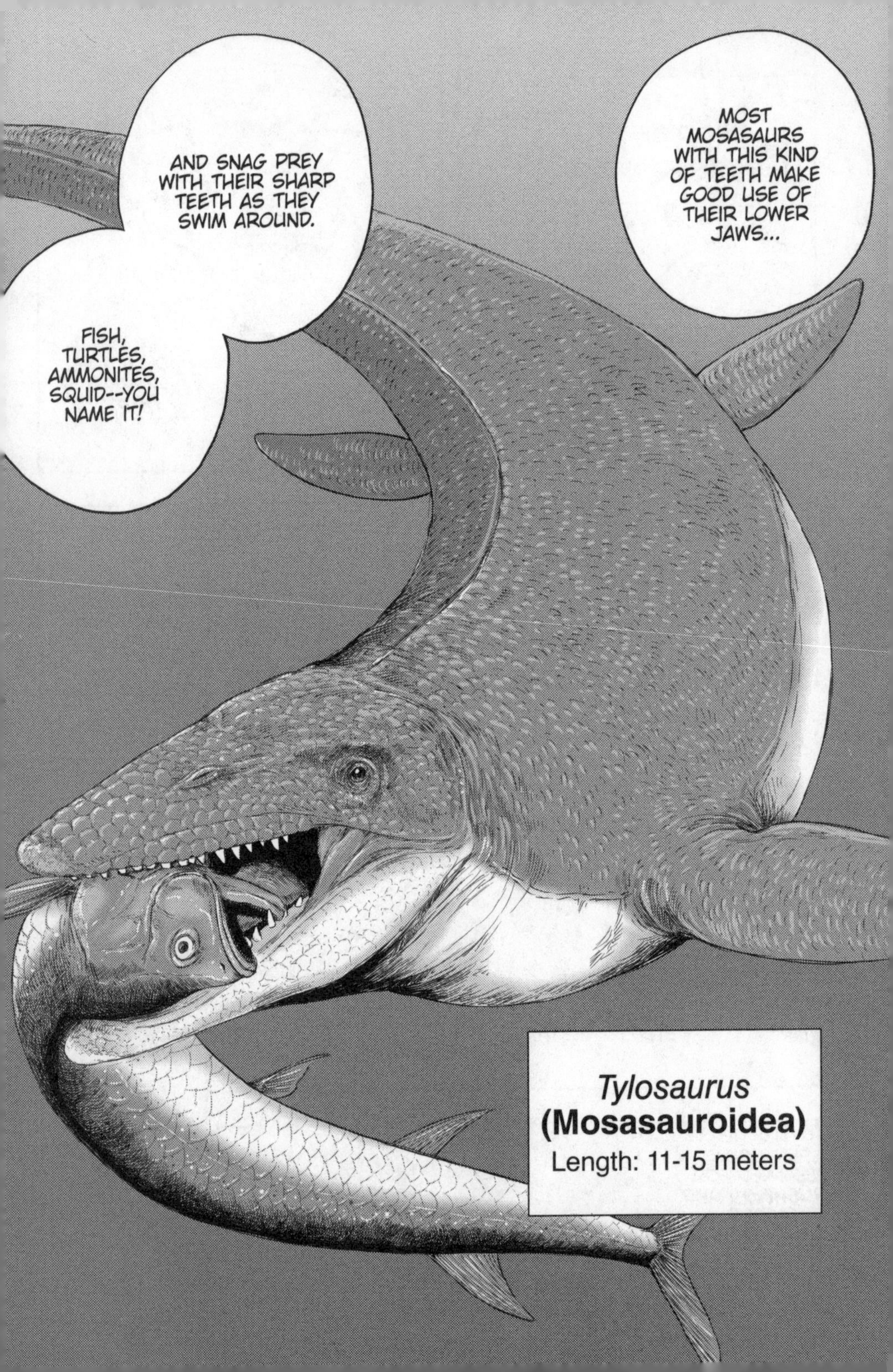
MOST MOSASAURS WITH THIS KIND OF TEETH MAKE GOOD USE OF THEIR LOWER JAWS...
AND SNAG PREY WITH THEIR SHARP TEETH AS THEY SWIM AROUND.
FISH, TURTLES, AMMONITES, SQUID--YOU NAME IT!
Tylosaurus
(Mosasauroidea)
Length: 11-15 meters

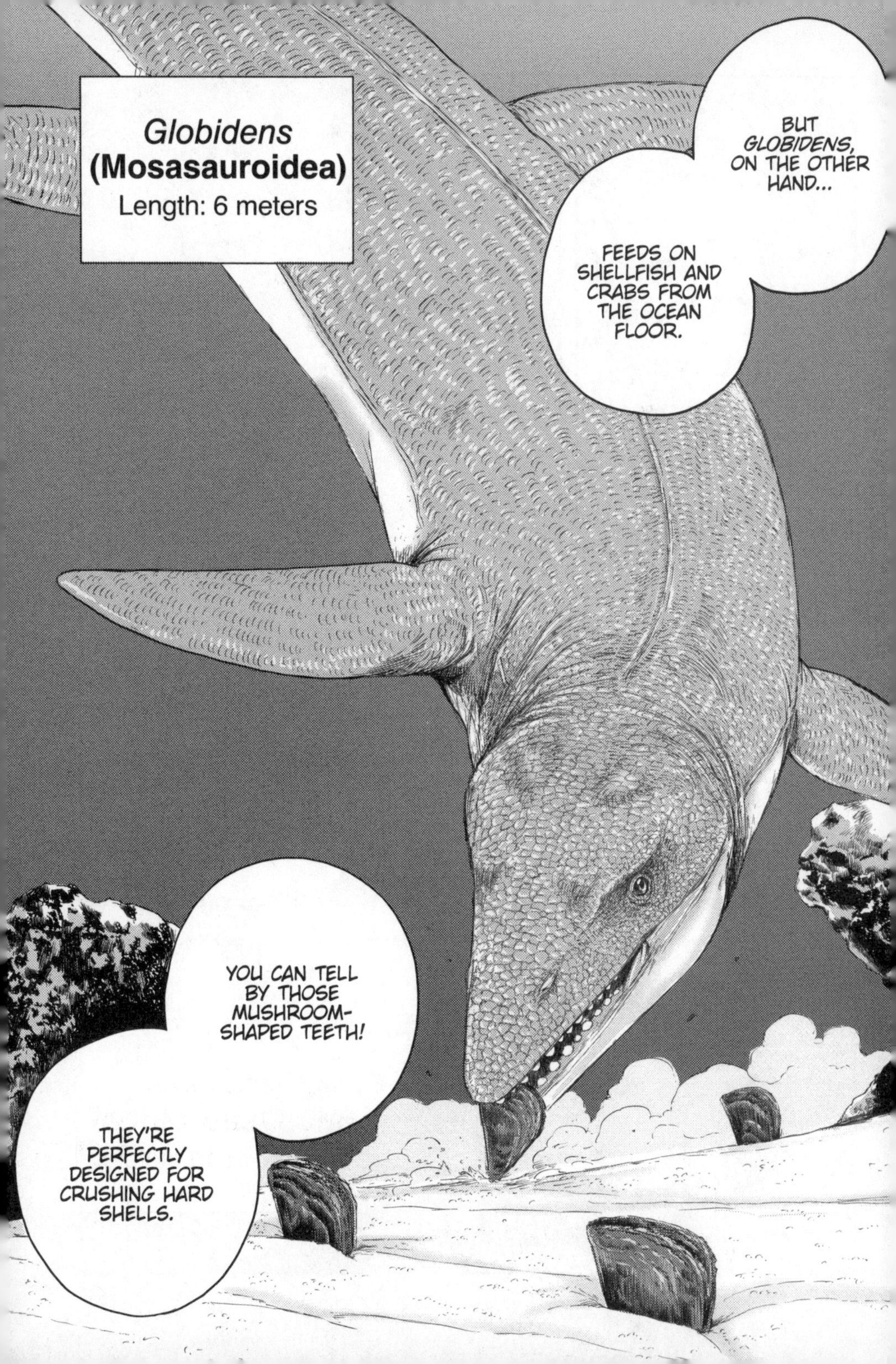
Globidens
(Mosasauroidea)
Length: 6 meters
BUT *GLOBIDENS*, ON THE OTHER HAND...
FEEDS ON SHELLFISH AND CRABS FROM THE OCEAN FLOOR.
YOU CAN TELL BY THOSE MUSHROOM-SHAPED TEETH!
THEY'RE PERFECTLY DESIGNED FOR CRUSHING HARD SHELLS.

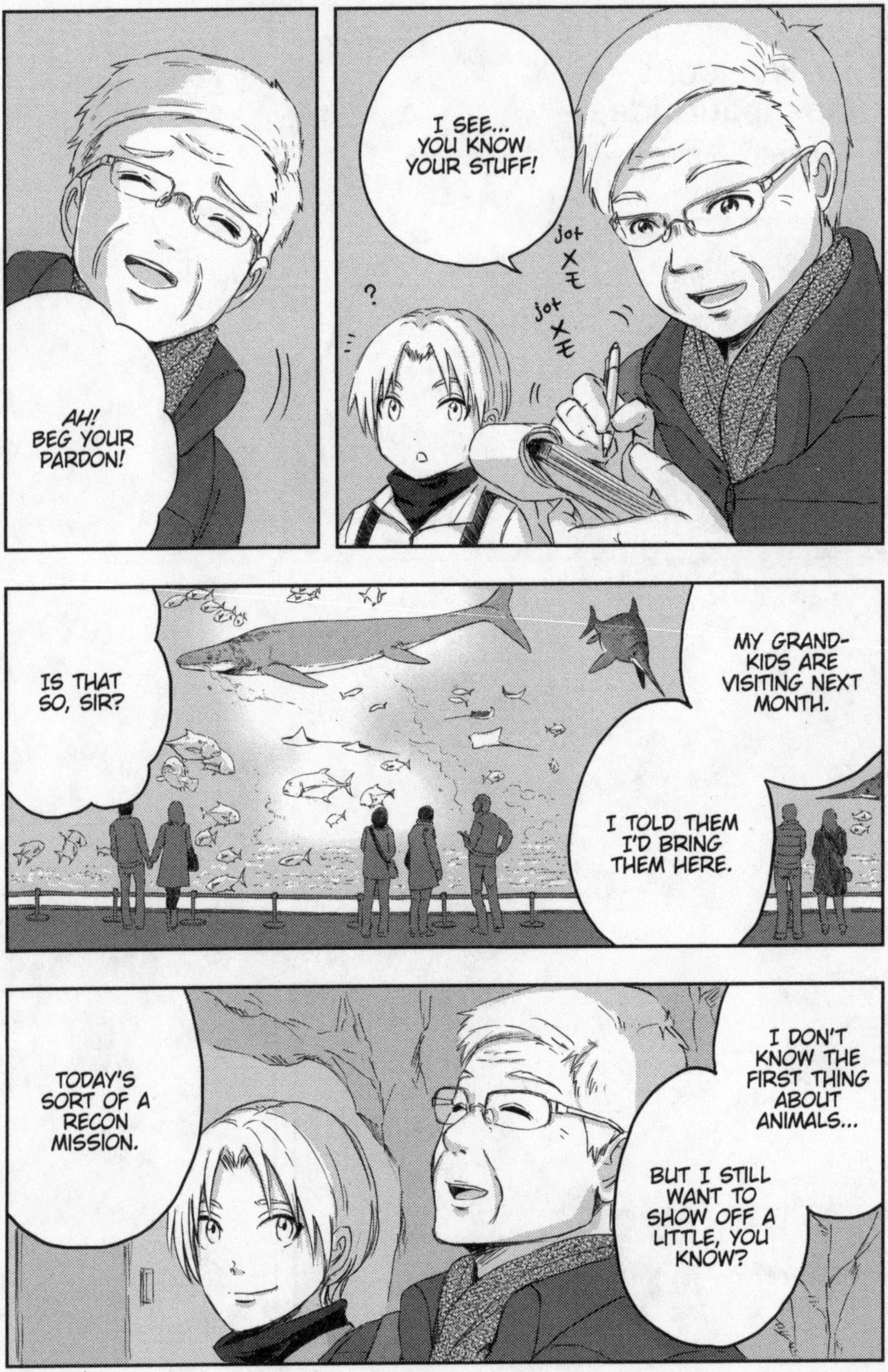
I SEE... YOU KNOW YOUR STUFF!
jot メモ
jot メモ
?
AH! BEG YOUR PARDON!
MY GRAND-KIDS ARE VISITING NEXT MONTH.
I TOLD THEM I'D BRING THEM HERE.
IS THAT SO, SIR?
I DON'T KNOW THE FIRST THING ABOUT ANIMALS...
BUT I STILL WANT TO SHOW OFF A LITTLE, YOU KNOW?
TODAY'S SORT OF A RECON MISSION.

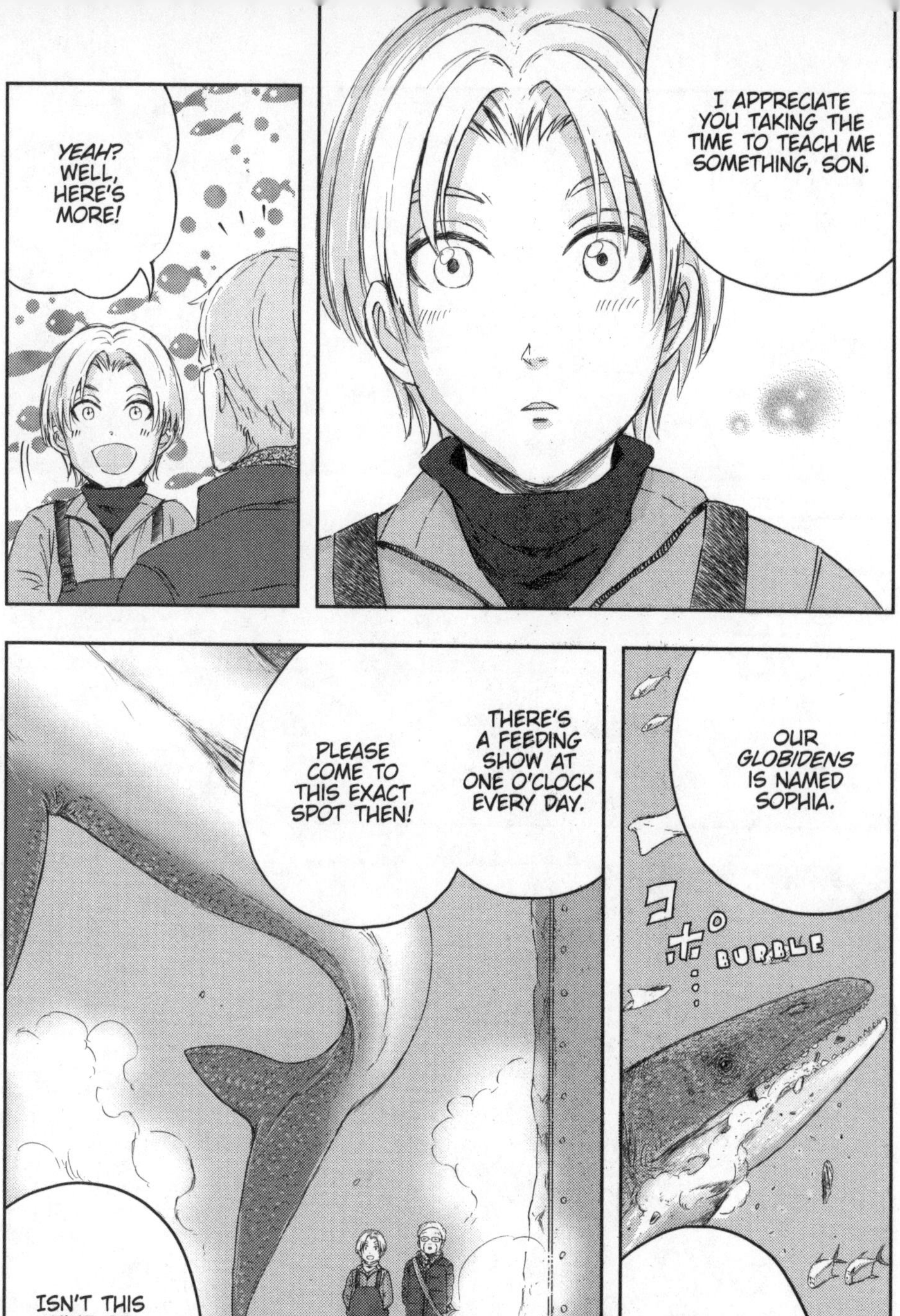
I APPRECIATE YOU TAKING THE TIME TO TEACH ME SOMETHING, SON.
YEAH? WELL, HERE'S MORE!
OUR *GLOBIDENS* IS NAMED SOPHIA.
BUBBLE
WHAT A PRECIOUS NAME!
THERE'S A FEEDING SHOW AT ONE O'CLOCK EVERY DAY.
PLEASE COME TO THIS EXACT SPOT THEN!
ISN'T THIS KIND OF OUT OF THE WAY?

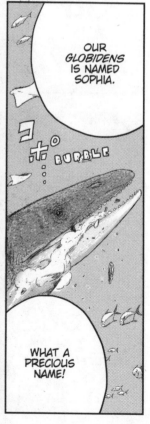

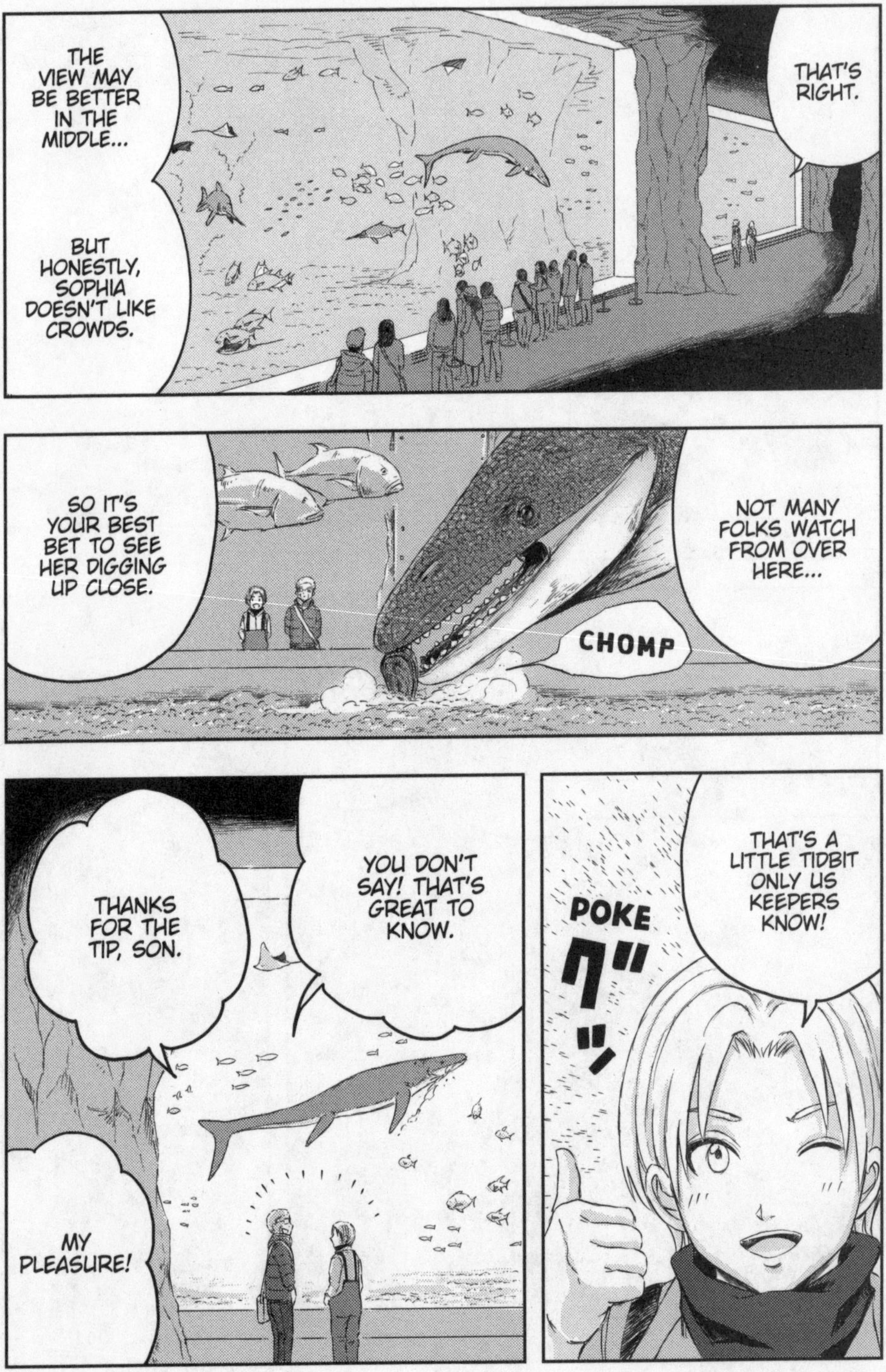
THAT'S RIGHT.
THE VIEW MAY BE BETTER IN THE MIDDLE...
BUT HONESTLY, SOPHIA DOESN'T LIKE CROWDS.
NOT MANY FOLKS WATCH FROM OVER HERE...
CHOMP
SO IT'S YOUR BEST BET TO SEE HER DIGGING UP CLOSE.
THAT'S A LITTLE TIDBIT ONLY US KEEPERS KNOW!
POKE
グッ
YOU DON'T SAY! THAT'S GREAT TO KNOW.
THANKS FOR THE TIP, SON.
MY PLEASURE!

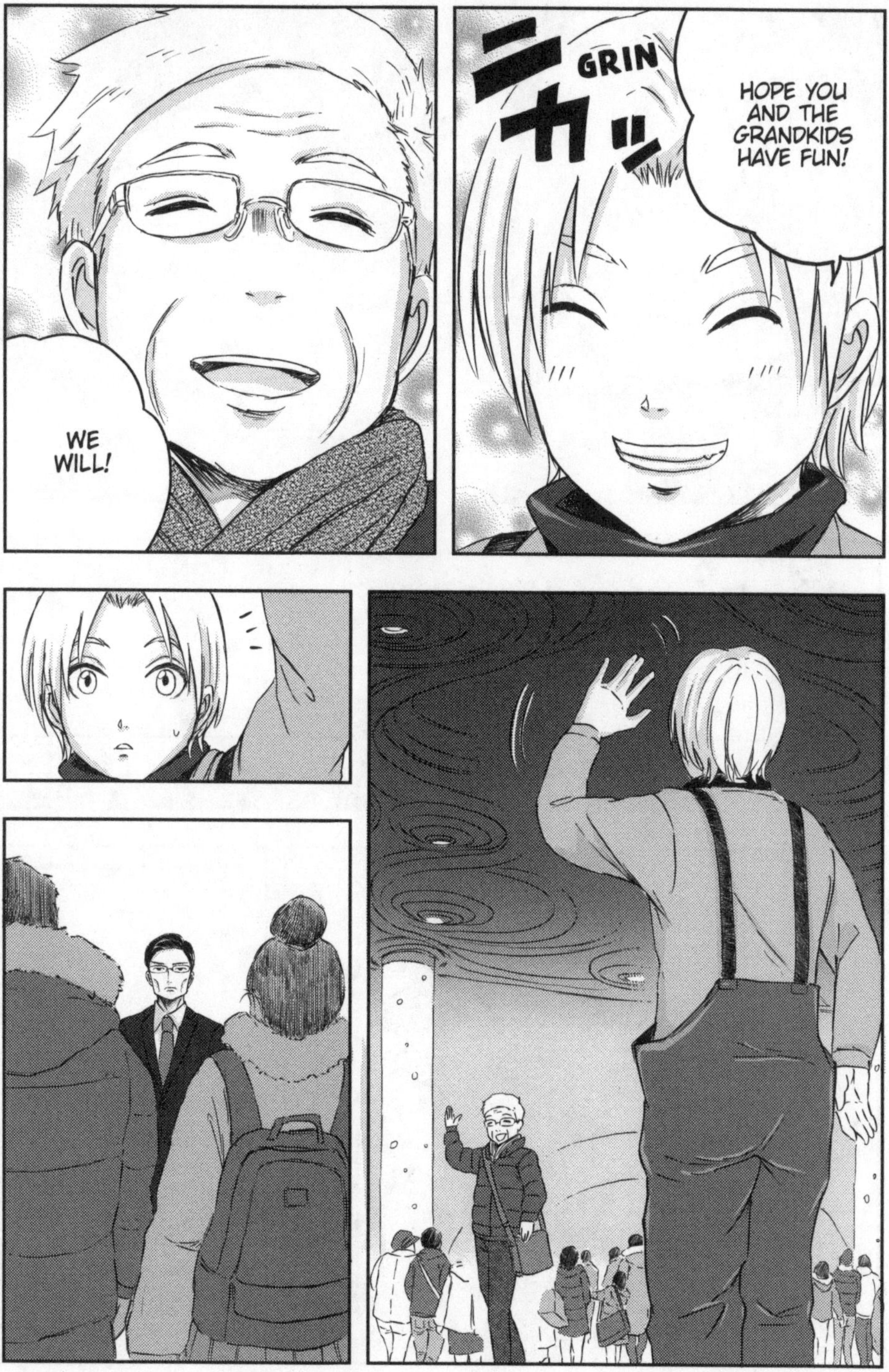
ニカッ
GRIN
HOPE YOU AND THE GRANDKIDS HAVE FUN!
WE WILL!

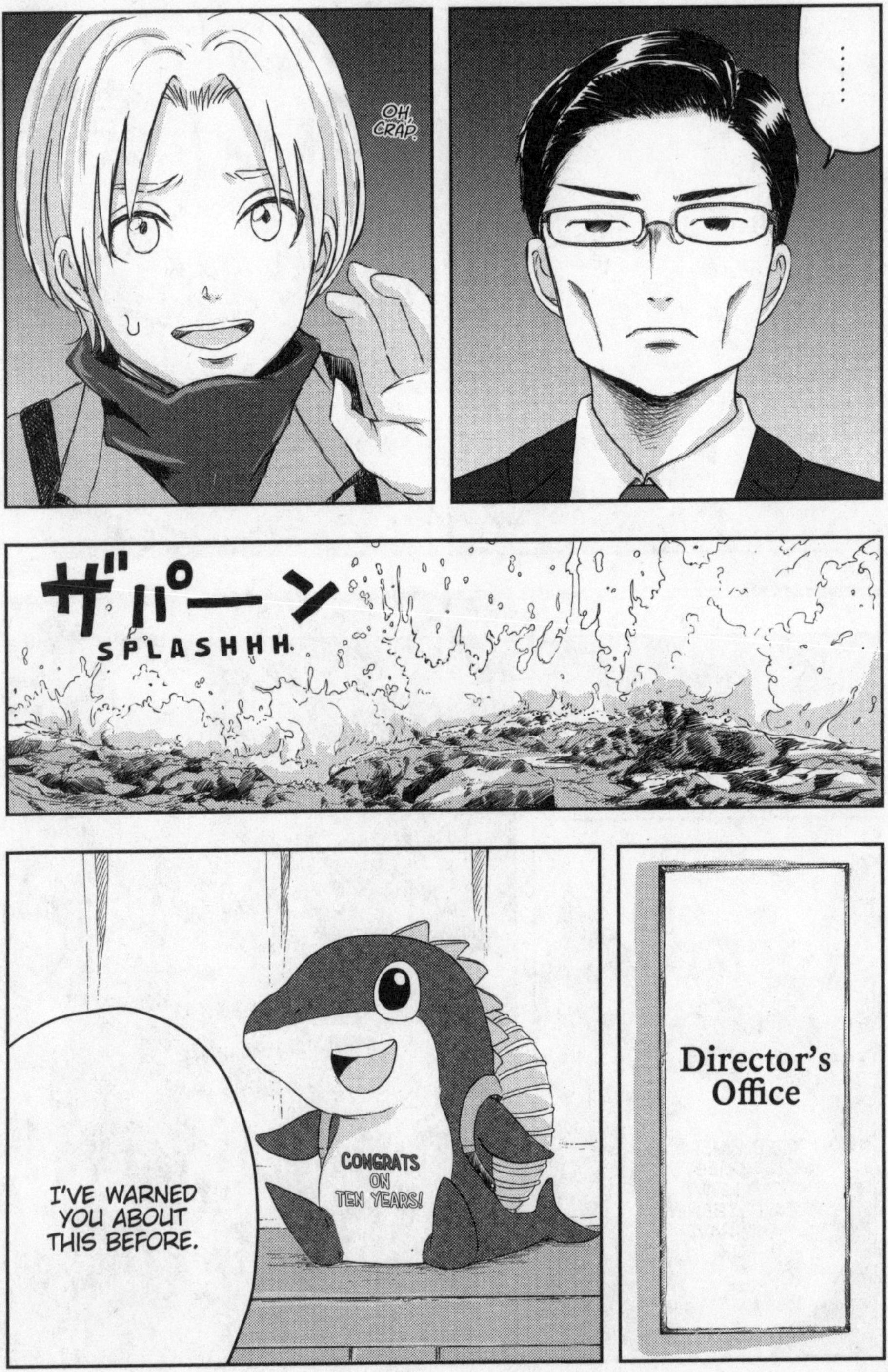
……
OH, CRAP.
ザパーン
SPLASHHH
Director's Office
CONGRATS ON TEN YEARS!
I'VE WARNED YOU ABOUT THIS BEFORE.

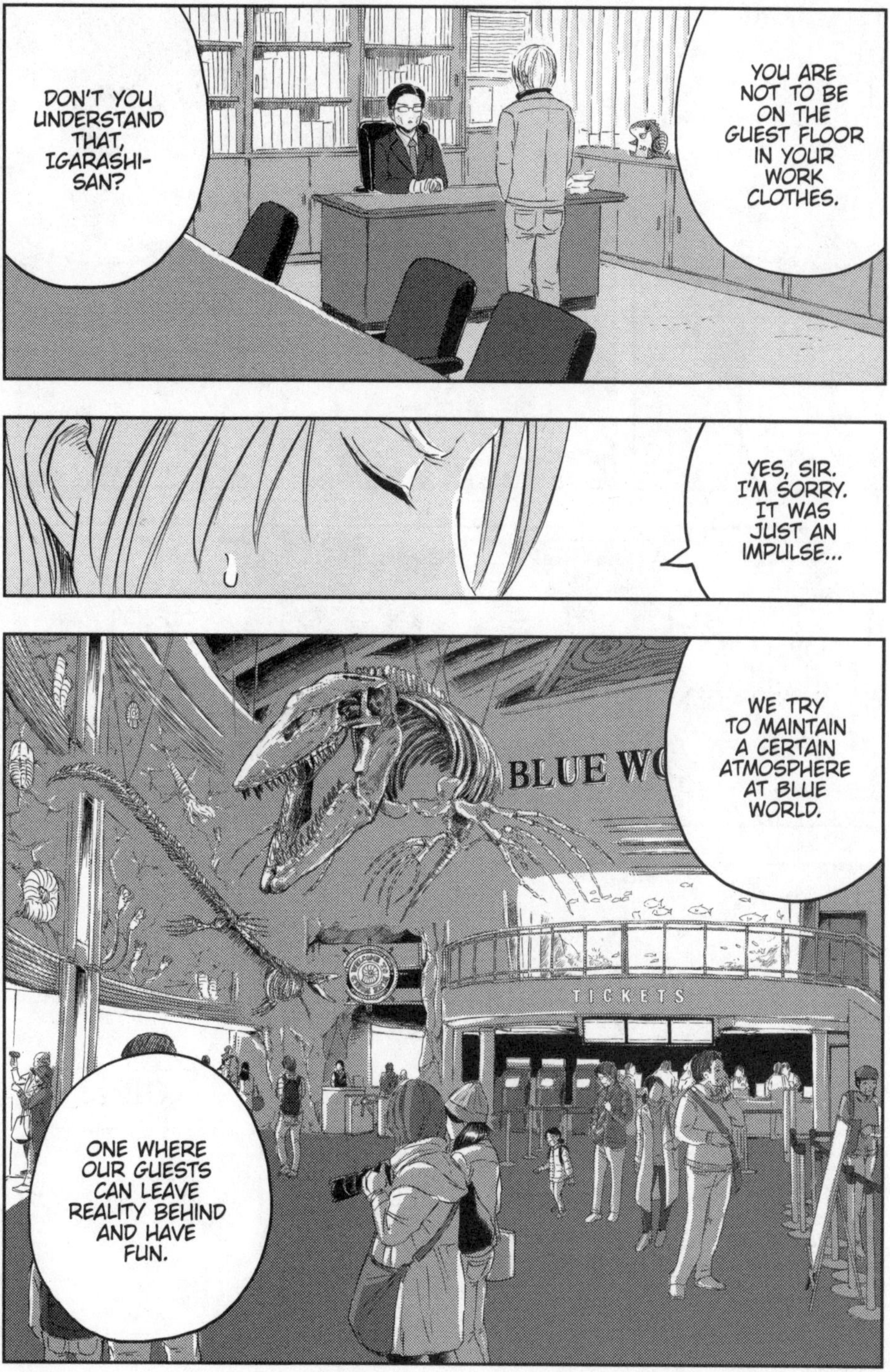
YOU ARE NOT TO BE ON THE GUEST FLOOR IN YOUR WORK CLOTHES.
DON'T YOU UNDERSTAND THAT, IGARASHI-SAN?
YES, SIR. I'M SORRY. IT WAS JUST AN IMPULSE...
WE TRY TO MAINTAIN A CERTAIN ATMOSPHERE AT BLUE WORLD.
TICKETS
ONE WHERE OUR GUESTS CAN LEAVE REALITY BEHIND AND HAVE FUN.

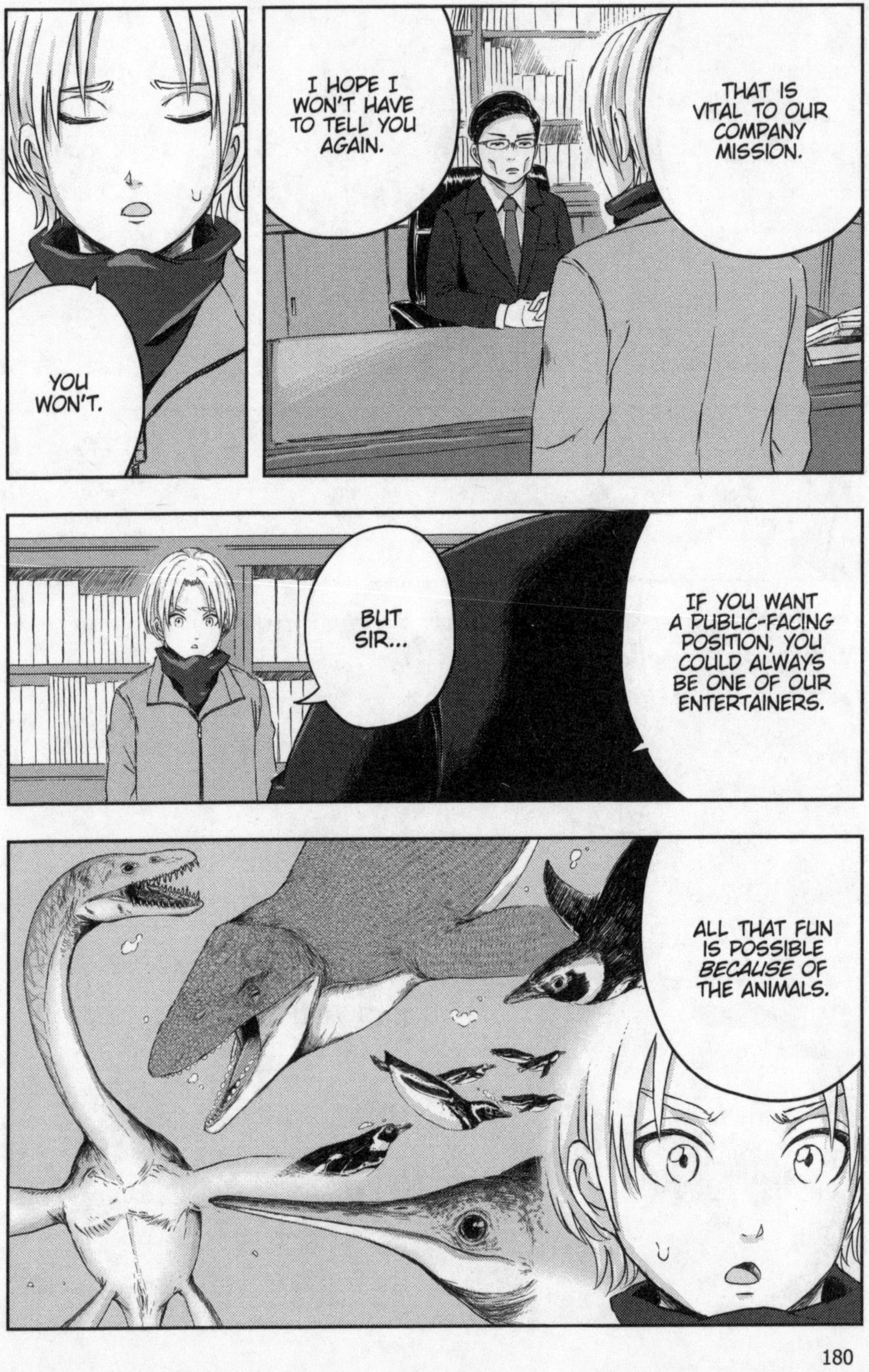
THAT IS VITAL TO OUR COMPANY MISSION.
I HOPE I WON'T HAVE TO TELL YOU AGAIN.
YOU WON'T.
IF YOU WANT A PUBLIC-FACING POSITION, YOU COULD ALWAYS BE ONE OF OUR ENTERTAINERS.
BUT SIR...
ALL THAT FUN IS POSSIBLE *BECAUSE* OF THE ANIMALS.

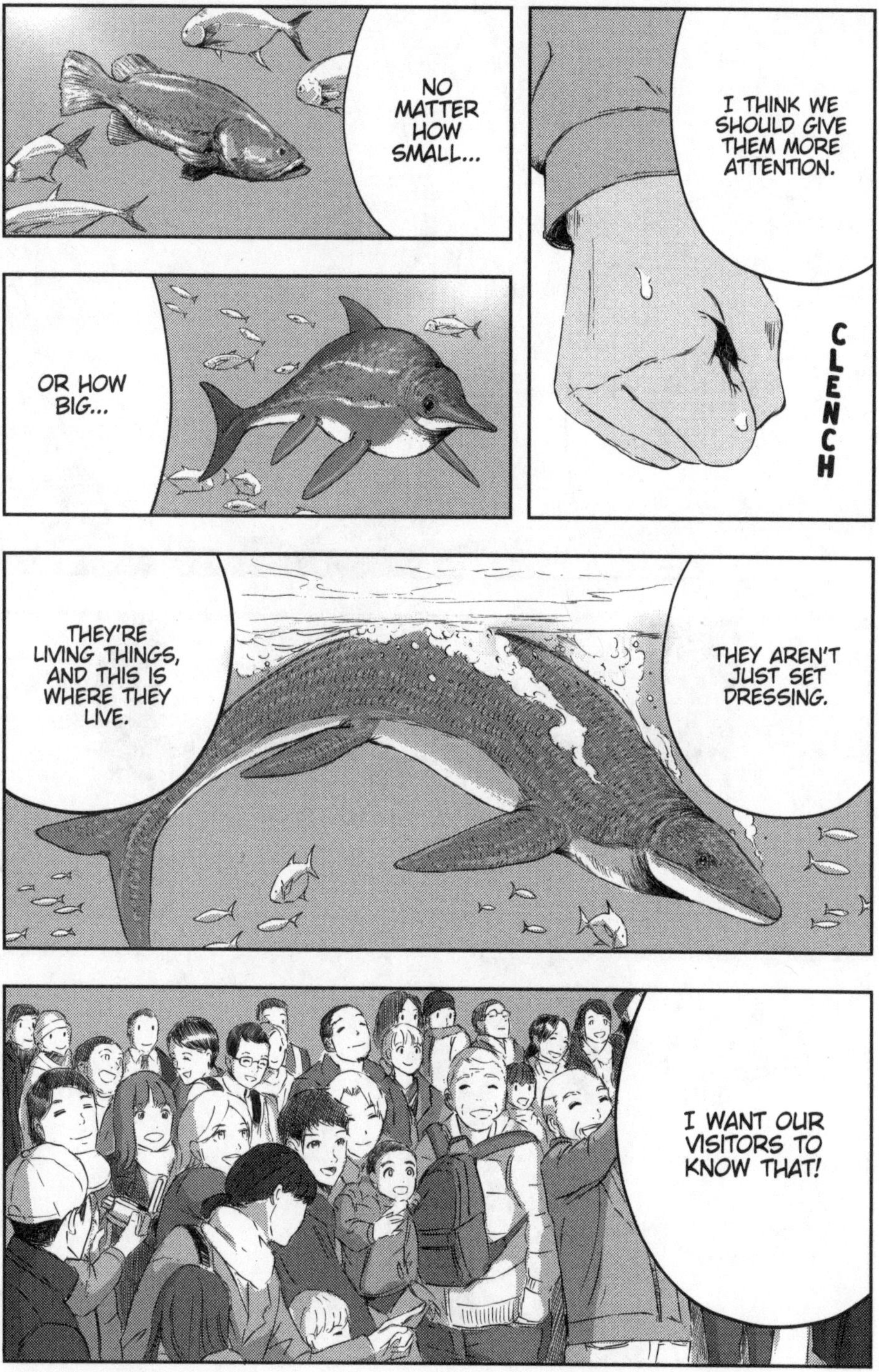
I THINK WE SHOULD GIVE THEM MORE ATTENTION.
CLENCH
NO MATTER HOW SMALL...
OR HOW BIG...
THEY AREN'T JUST SET DRESSING.
THEY'RE LIVING THINGS, AND THIS IS WHERE THEY LIVE.
I WANT OUR VISITORS TO KNOW THAT!

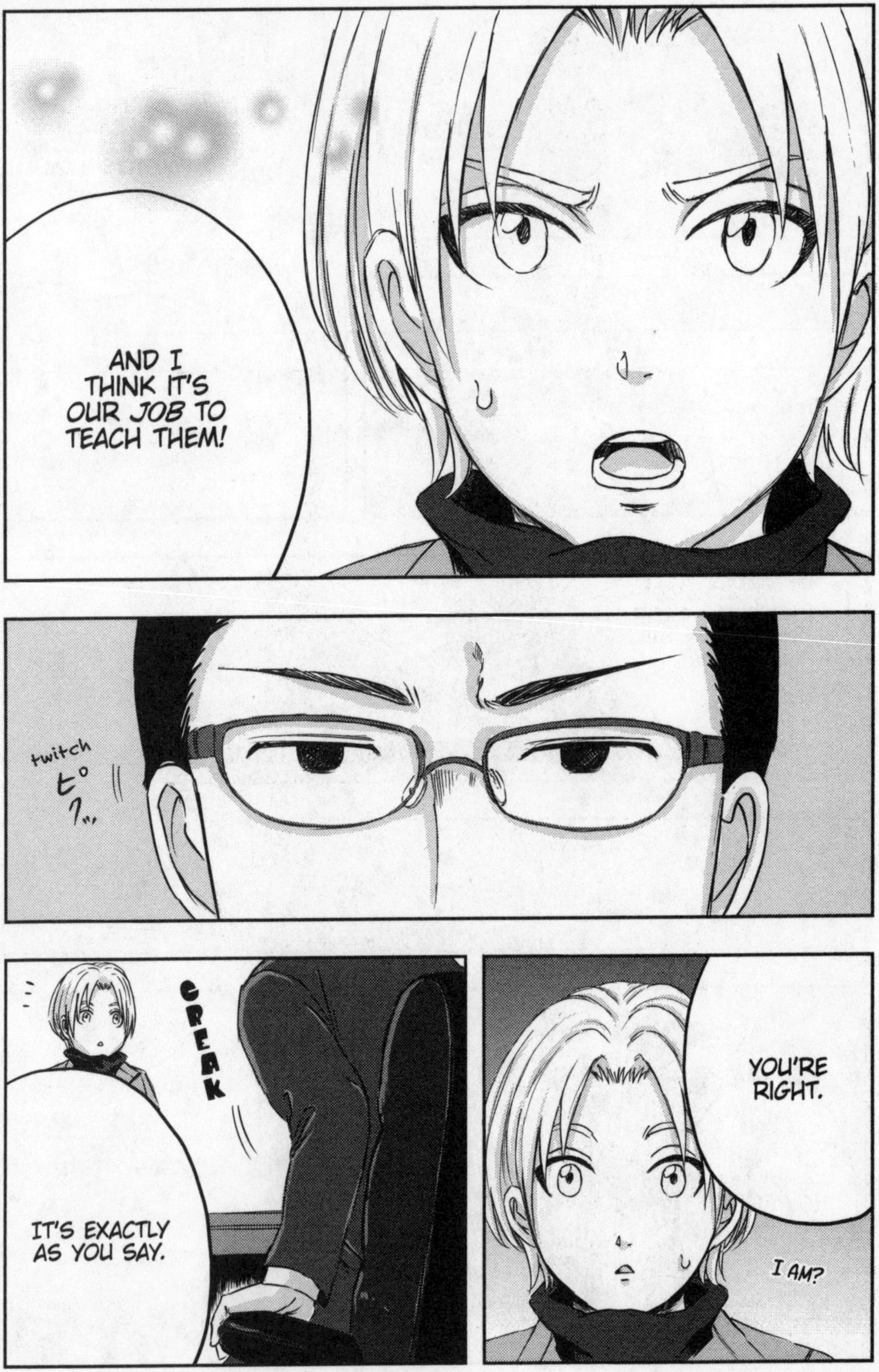
AND I THINK IT'S OUR *JOB* TO TEACH THEM!
twitch
ピクッ
YOU'RE RIGHT.
I AM?
CREAK
IT'S EXACTLY AS YOU SAY.

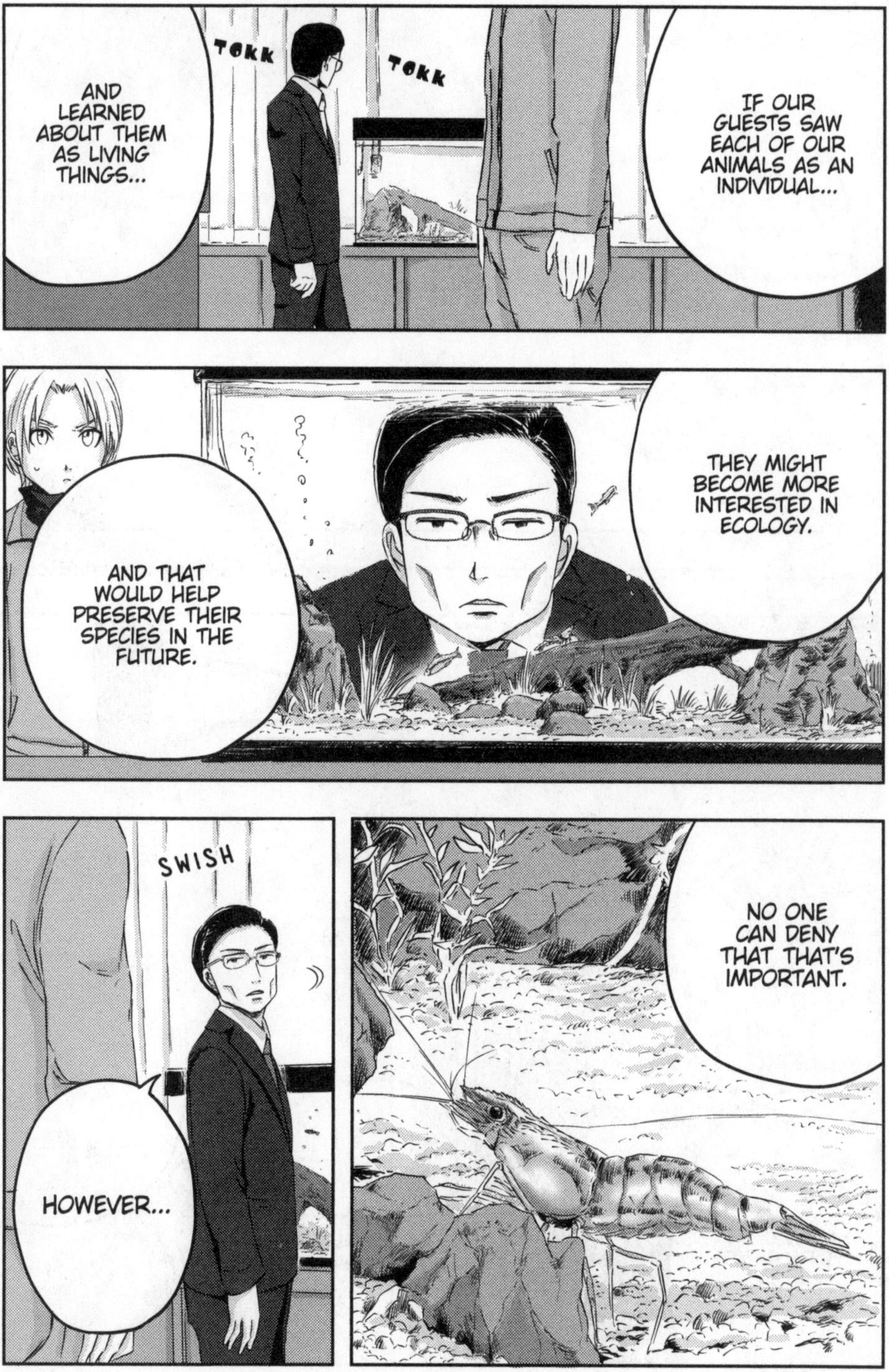
IF OUR GUESTS SAW EACH OF OUR ANIMALS AS AN INDIVIDUAL...
TOKK
TOKK
AND LEARNED ABOUT THEM AS LIVING THINGS...
THEY MIGHT BECOME MORE INTERESTED IN ECOLOGY.
AND THAT WOULD HELP PRESERVE THEIR SPECIES IN THE FUTURE.
NO ONE CAN DENY THAT THAT'S IMPORTANT.
SWISH
HOWEVER...

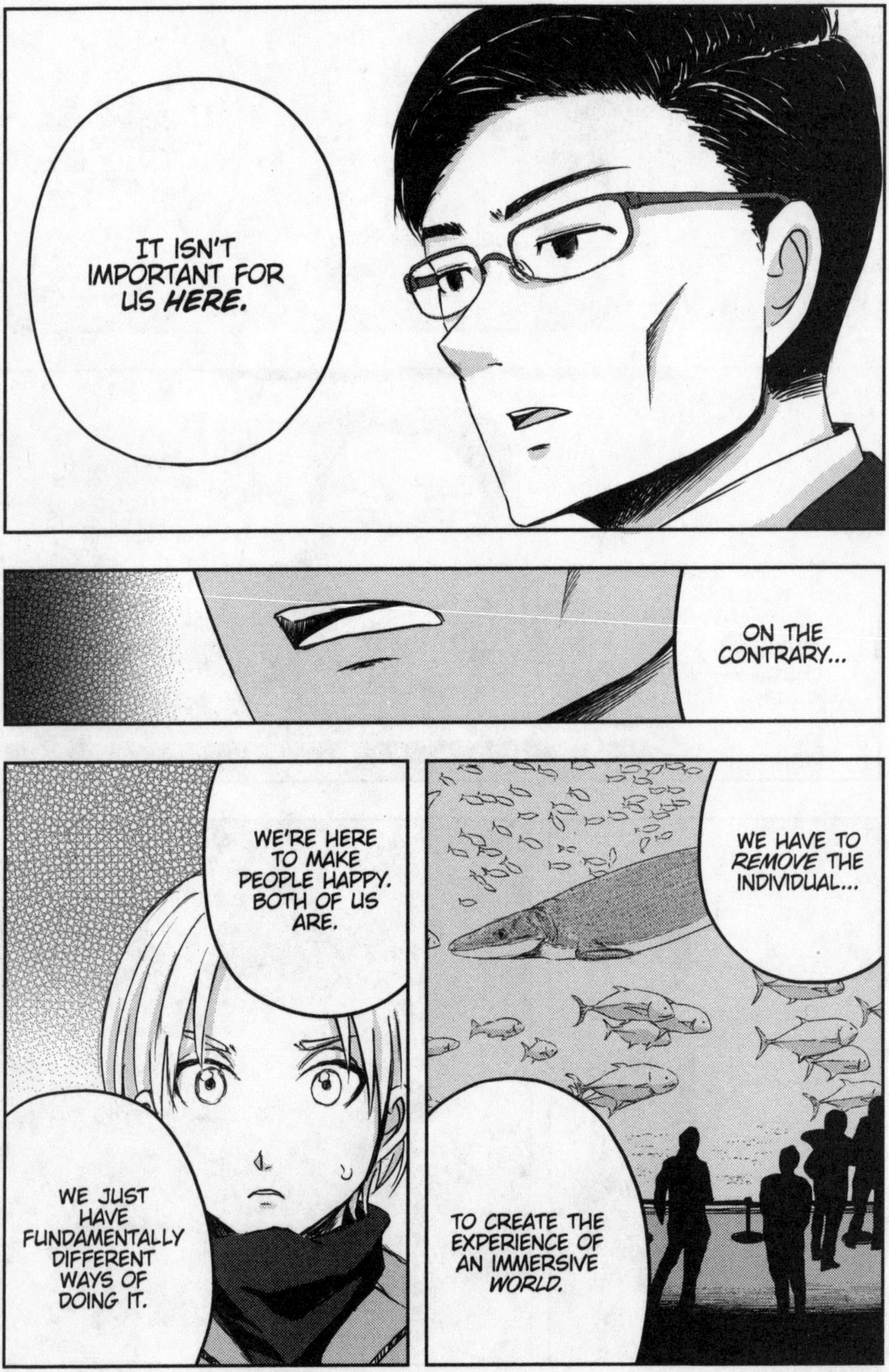
IT ISN'T IMPORTANT FOR US *HERE.*
ON THE CONTRARY...
WE HAVE TO *REMOVE* THE INDIVIDUAL...
TO CREATE THE EXPERIENCE OF AN IMMERSIVE *WORLD.*
WE'RE HERE TO MAKE PEOPLE HAPPY. BOTH OF US ARE.
WE JUST HAVE FUNDAMENTALLY DIFFERENT WAYS OF DOING IT.

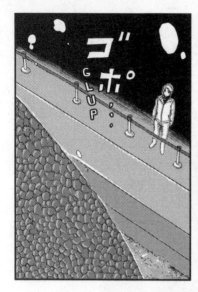

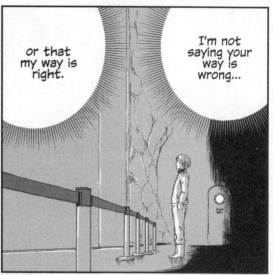

I'm not saying your way is wrong...
or that my way is right.
ゴポ
GLUP
But be that as it may...
ゴポポ
GLUPPP
If you can't get on board with the Blue World vision...

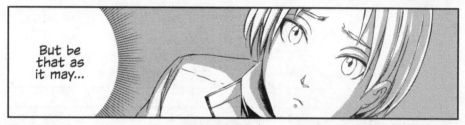

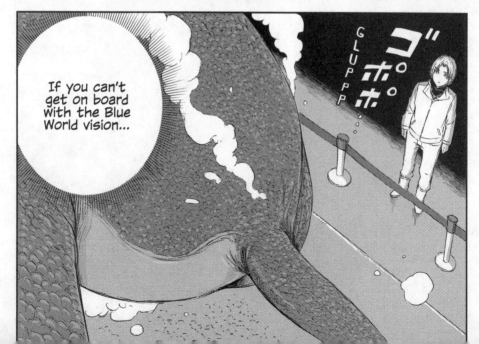

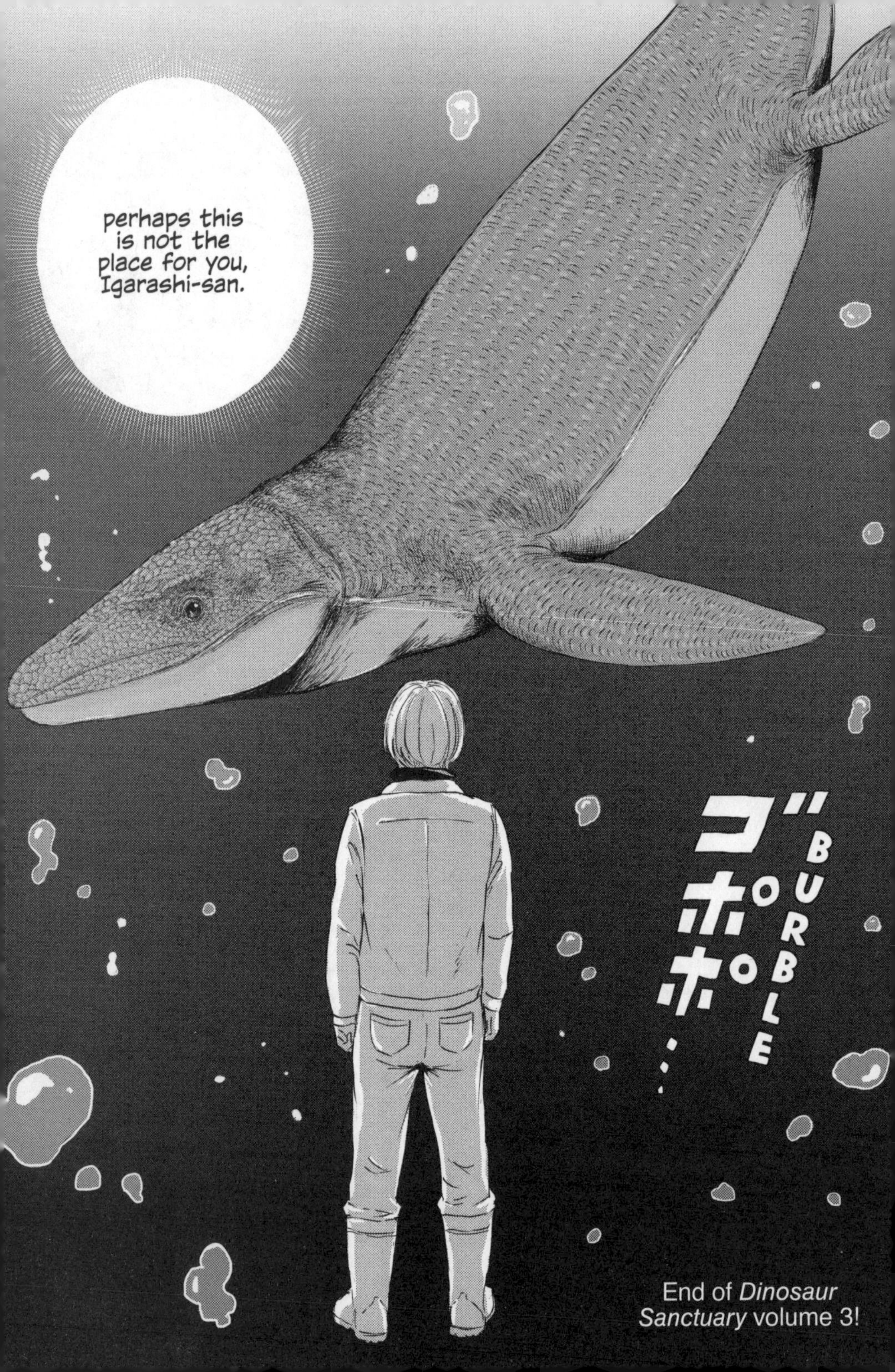
perhaps this is not the place for you, Igarashi-san.
ゴボボ…
BUBBLE BUBBLE

End of *Dinosaur Sanctuary* volume 3!

Dr. Dino's Lab Log

FILE. 17 Long Occipital Region? No Touching!

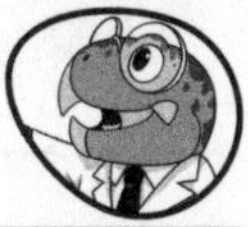

Some animals grow hard, armorlike shells to protect themselves from predators. Take, for instance, bivalve shellfish and crabs, deep in the ocean. Most other animals are incapable of eating prey wrapped in such hard armor. But the joke's on them—some other animals are *durophagous,* which means they're specifically adapted to crush through that armor to gobble up what's inside. To name-drop some famous durophages, there are alligators (the Chinese alligator in particular), snapping turtles, pufferfish, and stingrays like the ones you might have noticed swimming around in Blue World.

Mosasauroidea is a superfamily of marine-adapted relatives of lizards and snakes (Squamata). One genera of mosasaur is *Globidens,* which foraged for bivalves and other prey on the ocean floor. Just as you saw here, *Globidens* had rounded, mushroom-shaped teeth that it used to crush through the shells of its prey as it fed. Those teeth aren't the only hint we have about its feeding habits, either; remains of shattered shells have been found in places that suggest they were once in the stomach of a *Globidens*. It was quite the ocean floor gourmand!

One more thing: You really, *really* wouldn't want to be bitten by *Globidens.*

In fact, going by skull shapes, we can easily guess which animals do and do not present a real threat when they bite. If you come across an animal and its skull has a relatively long occipital region (the part behind the eye sockets) while the distance from its eyes to its snout is relatively short, I'd keep my hands away from its mouth if I were you—at least assuming you'd prefer to keep your fingers.

Why? Because behind the eyes, there are temples, and temples hold the muscles that close the jaw. If an animal has a long occipital region, then its jaw-closing muscles pass through a longer distance from the jaw joint. That means those jaw-closing muscles put out a lot of force and leverage for a powerful bite.

On top of that, if an animal's face is relatively short from the eyes to the snout, that means there's little distance between its jaw joint and the end of its mouth. Imagine trying to pry something open with a lever that's too short; that short lever is what unfortunate prey has to work with in order to escape a predator's jaws.

Now let's put them together. If a predator's occipital region is long, and its snout is short, that means it has an easier time exerting the torque it needs to bite down—while its prey has to put out more force than it can likely manage in order to escape. To give some modern-day examples, weasels and snapping turtles have relatively long occipital regions, and it's best to keep your fingers away from their mouths. All of this applies to plesiosaurs, the other group of extinct marine reptiles, too; you can tell from a look at their heads that you wouldn't want them to have a nibble. To top it all off, *Globidens* also has those back teeth built for smashing shells to smithereens. So, if you see one, keep your hands to yourself.

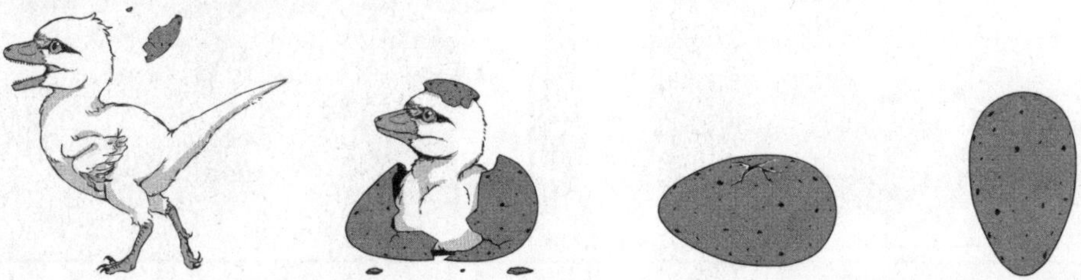

AFTERWORD

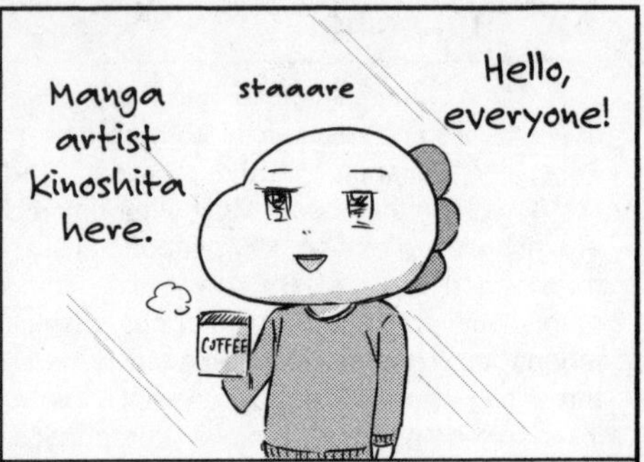
Hello, everyone!
staaare
Manga artist Kinoshita here.
COFFEE

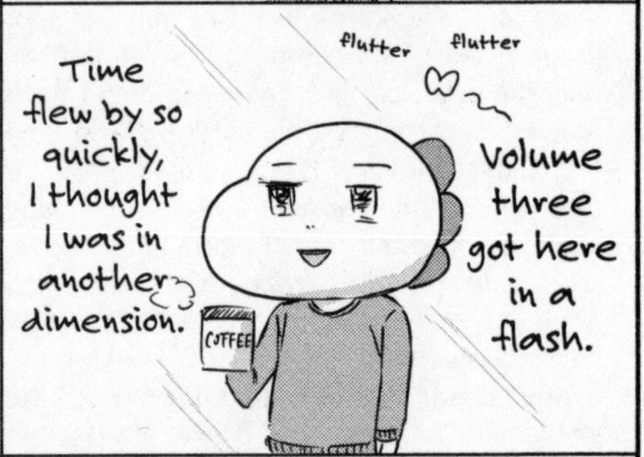
flutter flutter
Volume three got here in a flash.
Time flew by so quickly, I thought I was in another dimension.
COFFEE

Some of you may have noticed that we said this third volume would be out in winter, but I wanted to get it out quickly for a big, dino-mite summer! Thanks to the hard work of my editor and other folks, it hit shelves in September.

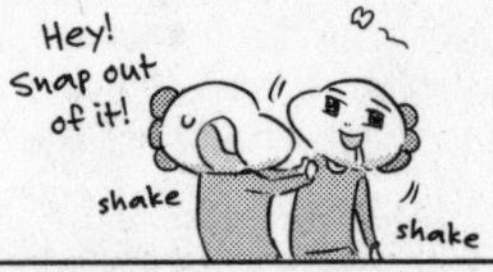
Hey! Snap out of it!
shake
shake

Thanks so much to all of you for sticking with *Dinosaur Sanctuary* beyond volume 2! I'm gonna keep working hard to show you more and more of the delightful world of dinosaurs, so please keep reading!

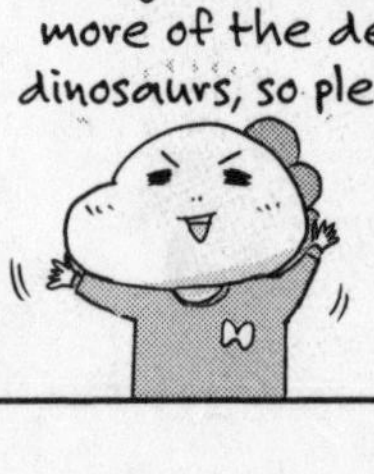

See you in the next volume!

SPECIAL THANKS

- My editor, TM
- Dr. Fujiwara
- Everyone at the *Comic Bunch* editorial board, business dept, and publicity dept
- The designer, Takeuchi-san
- Bookstores and everywhere else that deals with manga all across Japan
- My wife, family, and friends
- And everyone else who encouraged me throughout the writing and publishing of *Dinosaur Sanctuary*

The other day, I met with Kinoshita-san and his editor TM-san in person (not through a screen) for the very first time. We had a great time together! Since my involvement with *Dinosaur Sanctuary* began, I've had a lot more chances to really get to imagining a few dinosaurs I hadn't given a long, hard look before. It's been a pleasure--no, a blast!

If Enoshima Dinoland were real, I'm not sure whether I'd rather go as a visitor, or work there with the rest of the staff... *Hmm*... I think the urge to study would be too strong to pass up. But even on my days off, I'd bring my family along to walk around the park!

Shin-ichi Fujiwara

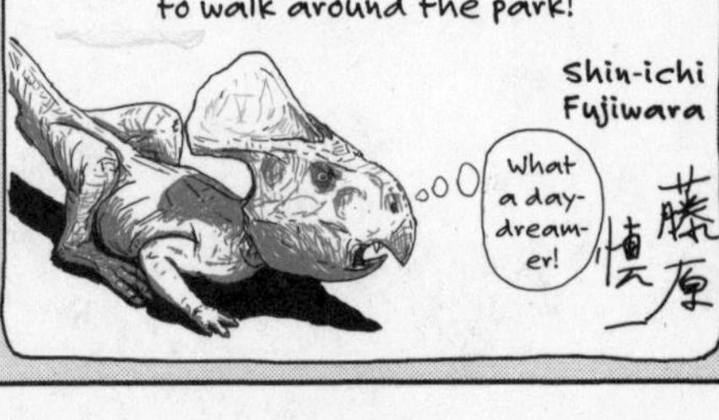
What a day-dreamer!
藤原 慎一

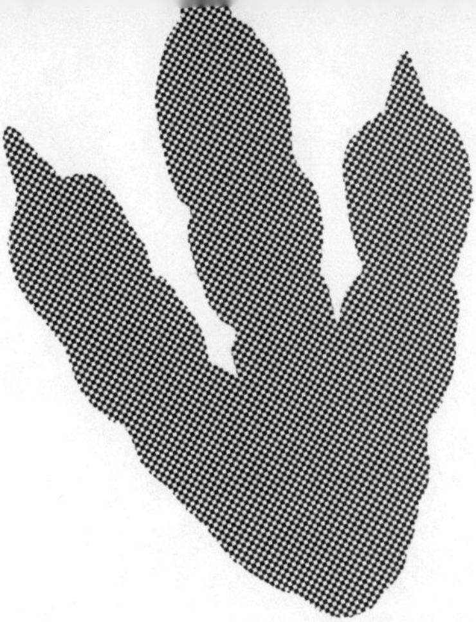

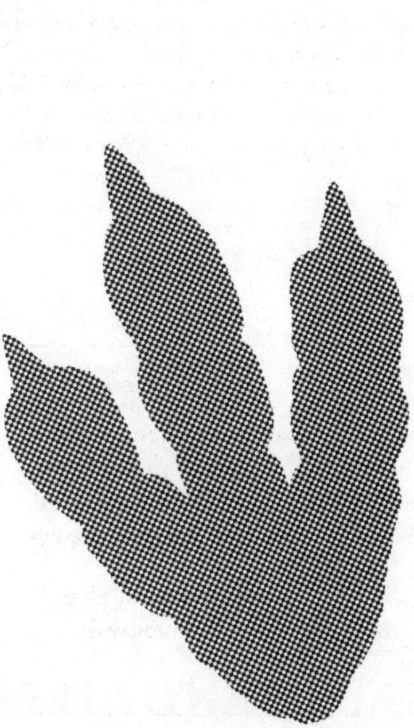

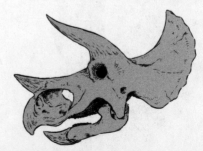

DINOSAUR SANCTUARY

BONUS MANGA: DAYS WITH DAISY

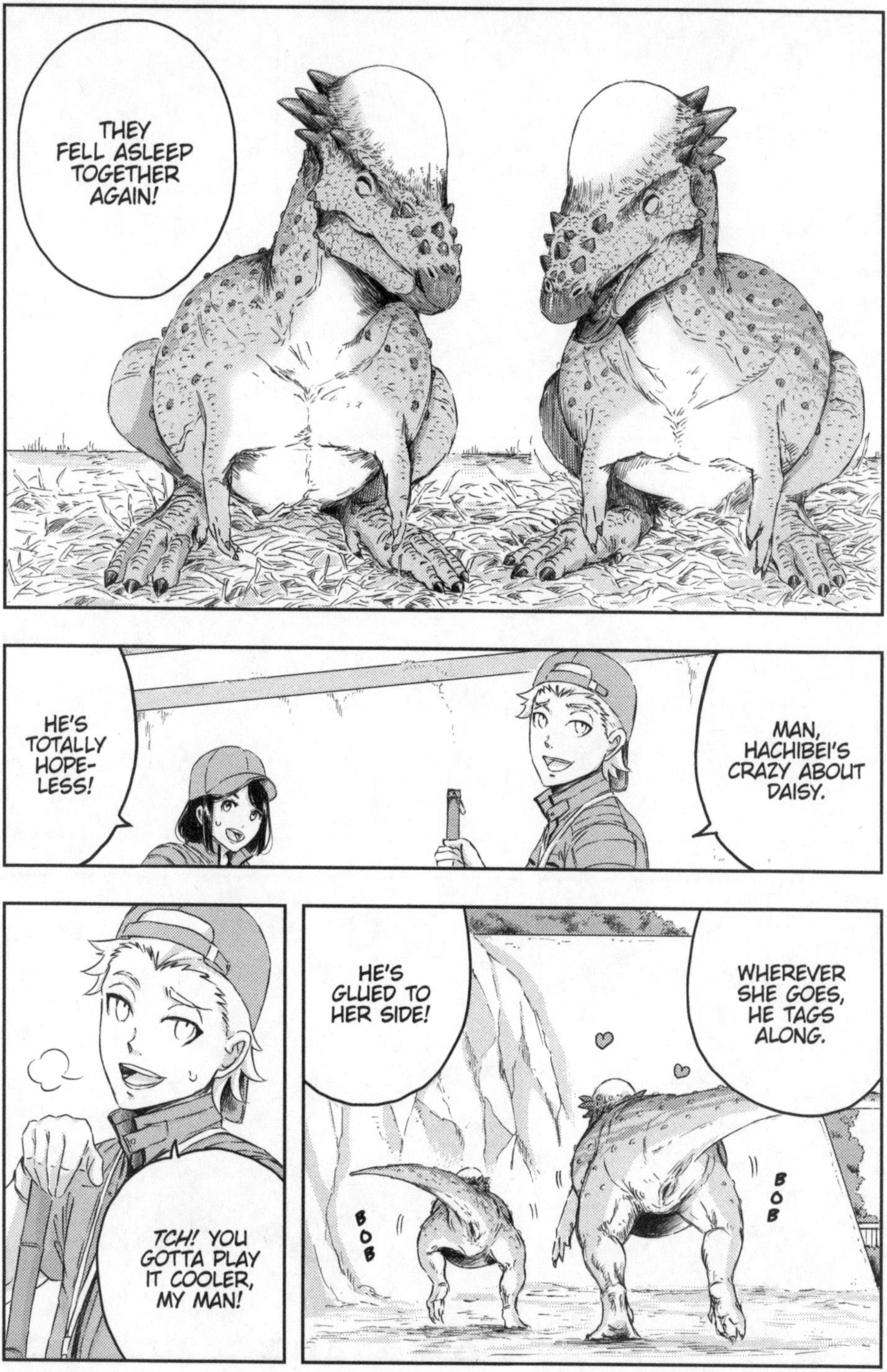
THEY FELL ASLEEP TOGETHER AGAIN!
MAN, HACHIBEI'S CRAZY ABOUT DAISY.
HE'S TOTALLY HOPE-LESS!
WHEREVER SHE GOES, HE TAGS ALONG.
HE'S GLUED TO HER SIDE!
BOB
BOB
TCH! YOU GOTTA PLAY IT COOLER, MY MAN!

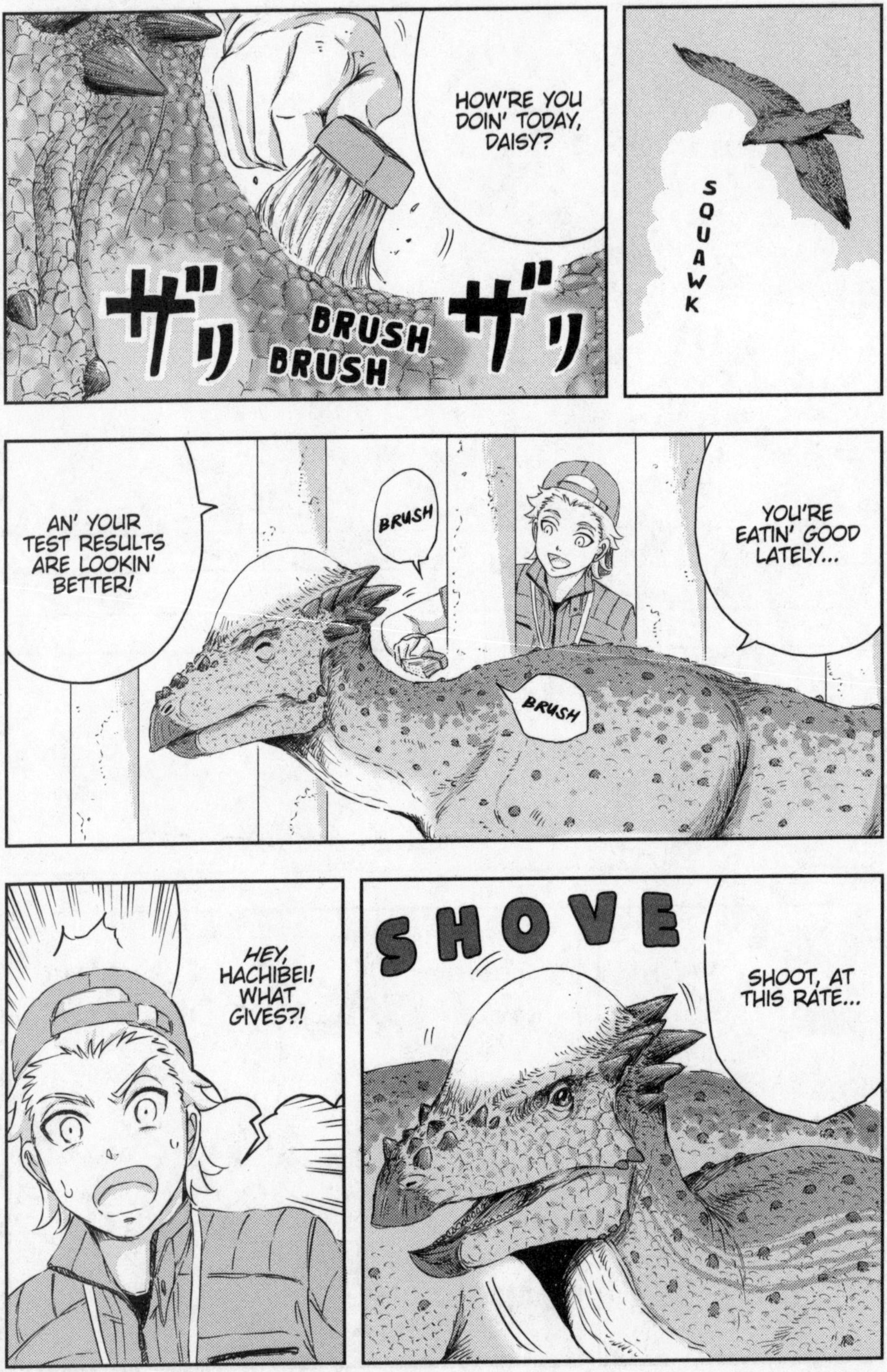
SQUAWK
HOW'RE YOU DOIN' TODAY, DAISY?
ザリ ザリ
BRUSH BRUSH
YOU'RE EATIN' GOOD LATELY...
BRUSH
BRUSH
AN' YOUR TEST RESULTS ARE LOOKIN' BETTER!
SHOOT, AT THIS RATE...
SHOVE
HEY, HACHIBEI! WHAT GIVES?!

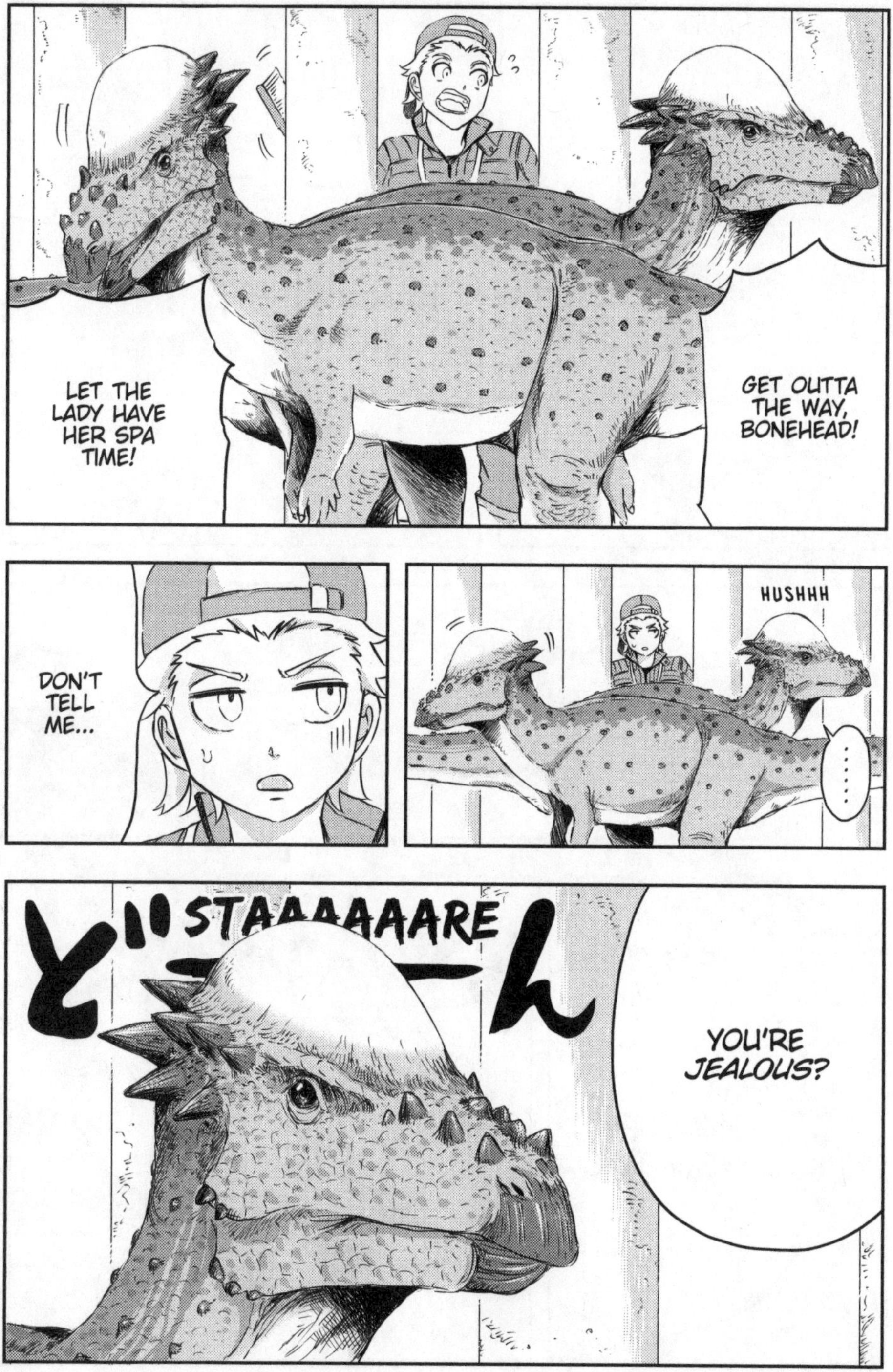
GET OUTTA THE WAY, BONEHEAD!
LET THE LADY HAVE HER SPA TIME!
HUSHHH
......
DON'T TELL ME...
STAAAAAARE
YOU'RE JEALOUS?

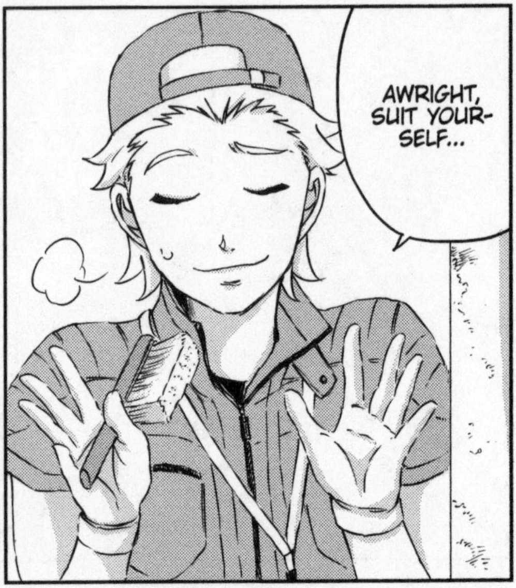
AWRIGHT, SUIT YOUR-SELF...

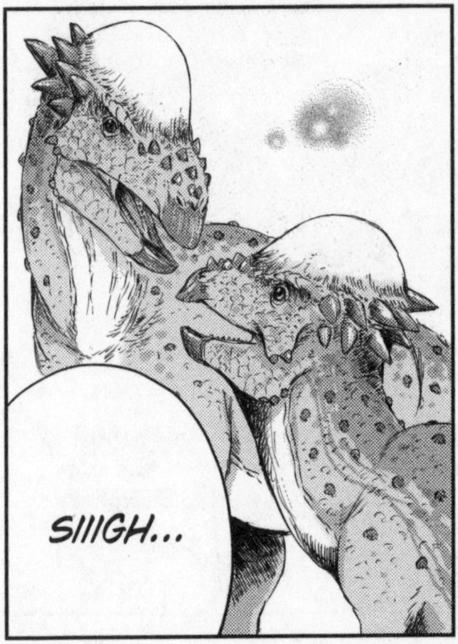
SIIIGH...

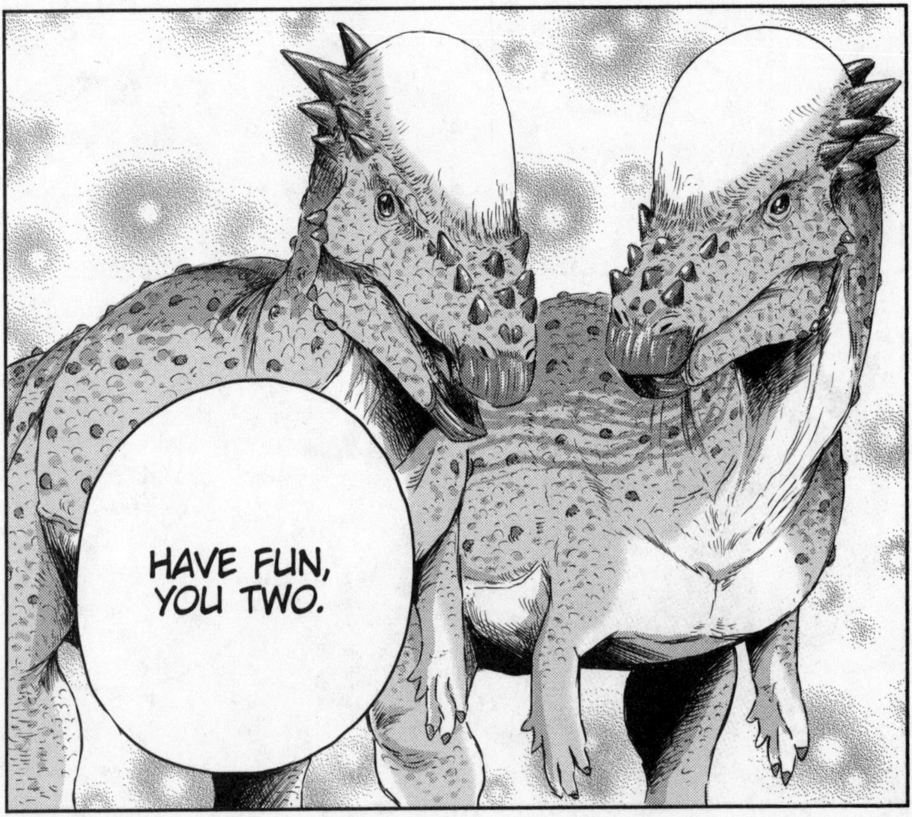
HAVE FUN, YOU TWO.

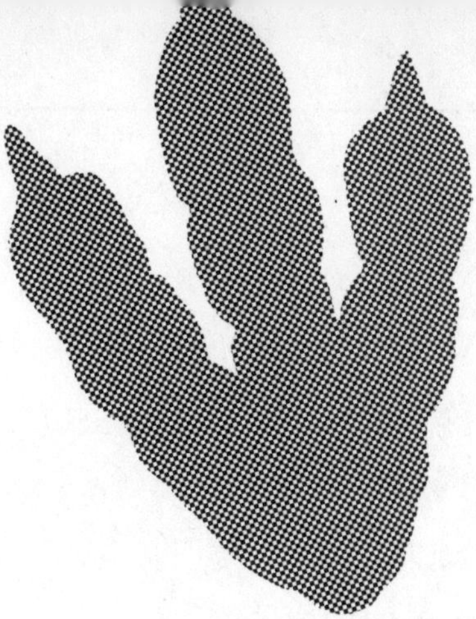
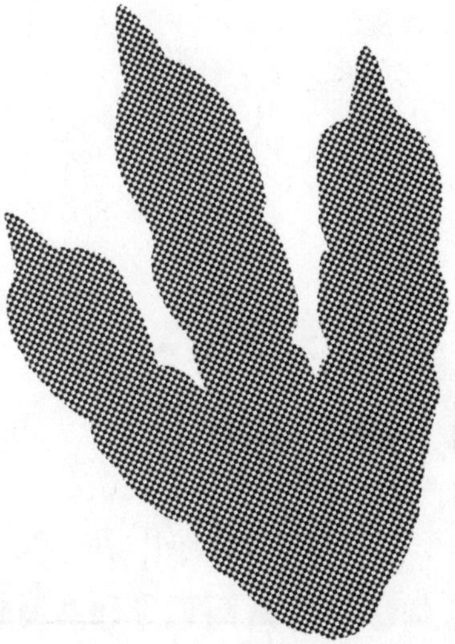

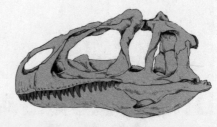

DINOSAUR SANCTUARY

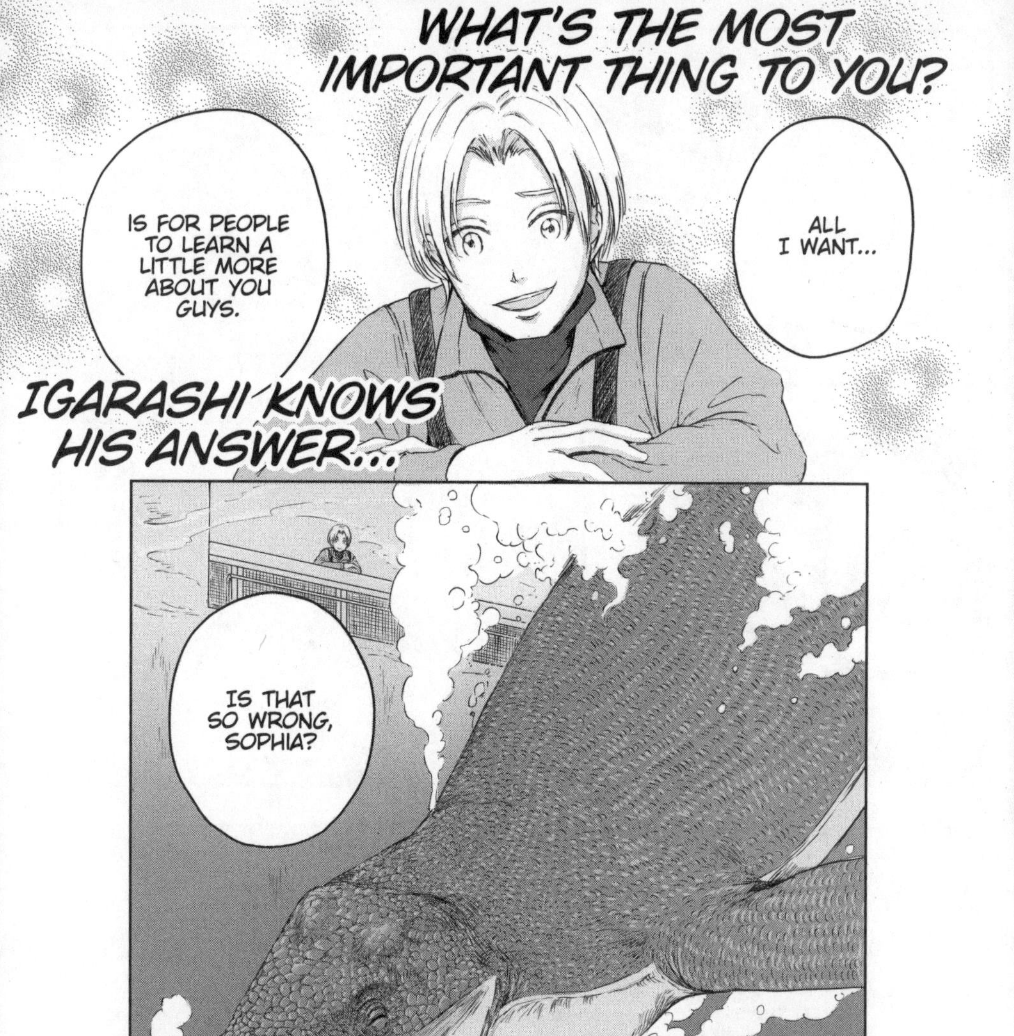
WHAT'S THE MOST IMPORTANT THING TO YOU?
ALL I WANT...
IS FOR PEOPLE TO LEARN A LITTLE MORE ABOUT YOU GUYS.
IGARASHI KNOWS HIS ANSWER...
IS THAT SO WRONG, SOPHIA?
ザブン
SPLASHHH

DINOSAUR SANCTUARY

VOLUME 4 COMING SOON!

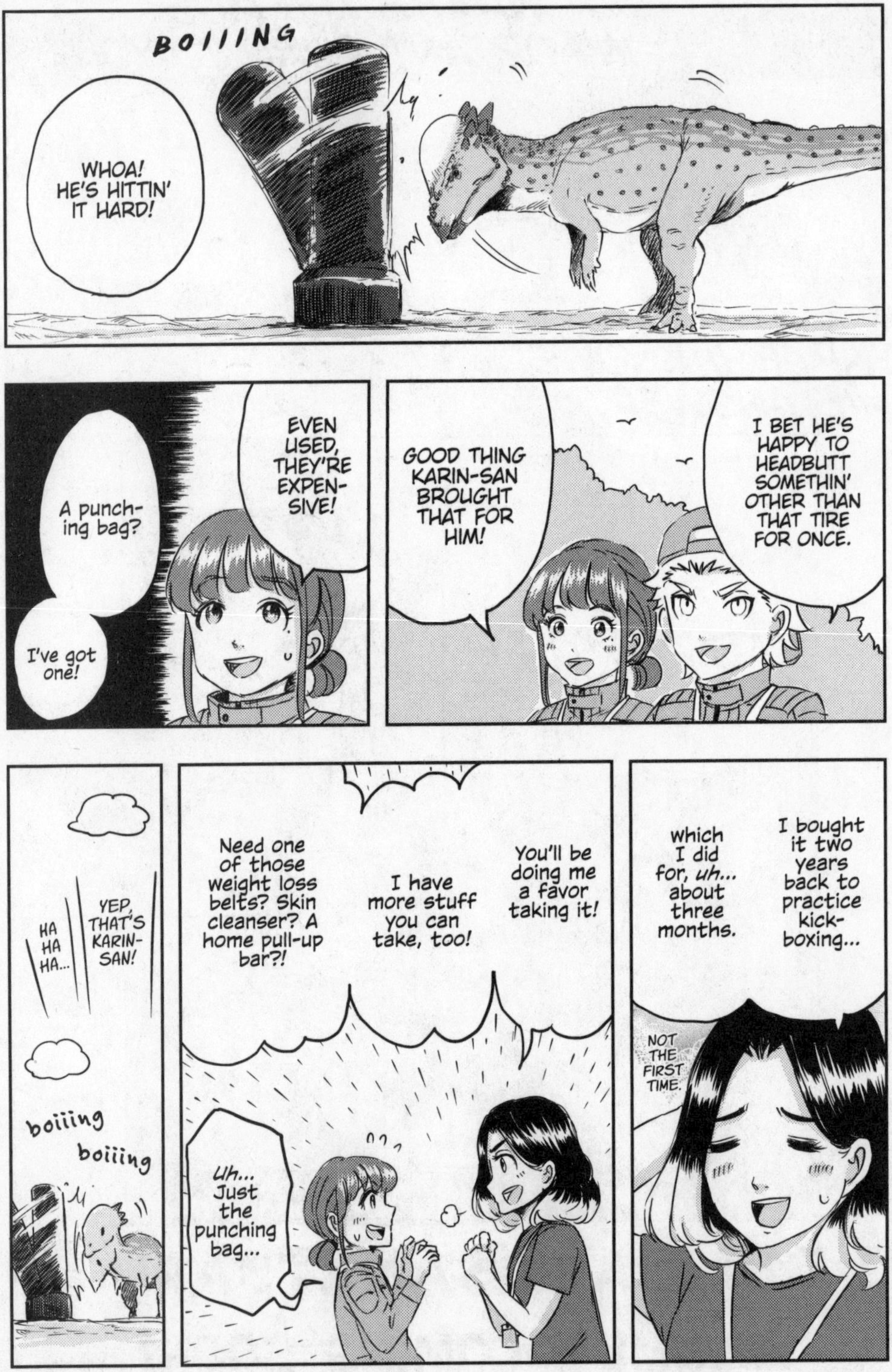
BOIIING
WHOA! HE'S HITTIN' IT HARD!
I BET HE'S HAPPY TO HEADBUTT SOMETHIN' OTHER THAN THAT TIRE FOR ONCE.
GOOD THING KARIN-SAN BROUGHT THAT FOR HIM!
EVEN USED, THEY'RE EXPEN-SIVE!
A punch-ing bag?
I've got one!
I bought it two years back to practice kick-boxing...
which I did for, *uh*... about three months.
NOT THE FIRST TIME.
You'll be doing me a favor taking it!
I have more stuff you can take, too!
Need one of those weight loss belts? Skin cleanser? A home pull-up bar?!
Uh... Just the punching bag...
YEP, THAT'S KARIN-SAN!
HA HA HA...
boiiing
boiiing

HOW LONG DO YOU WAIT FOR YOUR INSTANT NOODLES?

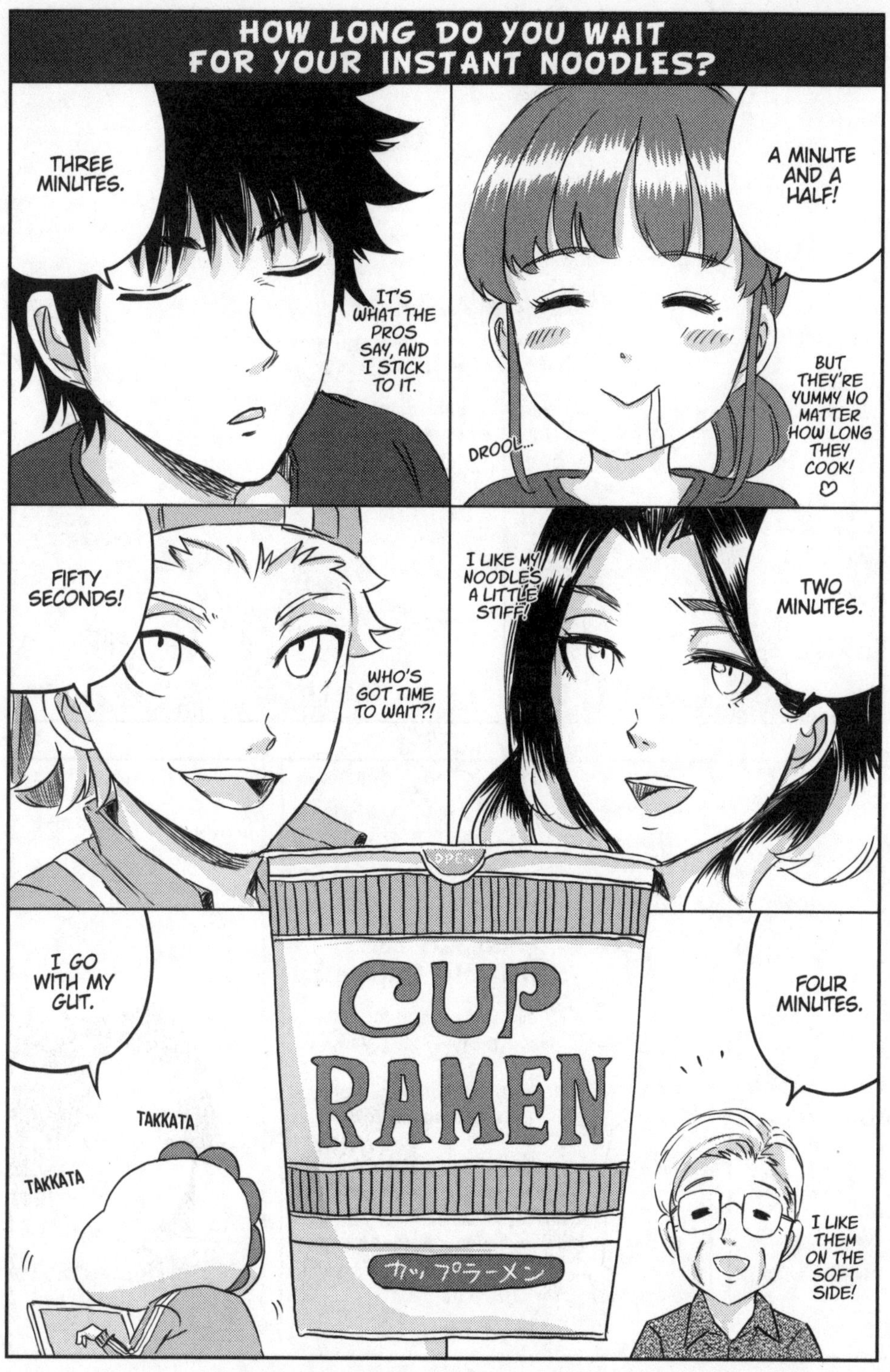
A MINUTE AND A HALF!
DROOL...
BUT THEY'RE YUMMY NO MATTER HOW LONG THEY COOK! ♡
THREE MINUTES.
IT'S WHAT THE PROS SAY, AND I STICK TO IT.
TWO MINUTES.
I LIKE MY NOODLES A LITTLE STIFF!
FIFTY SECONDS!
WHO'S GOT TIME TO WAIT?!
OPEN
CUP RAMEN
カップラーメン
FOUR MINUTES.
I LIKE THEM ON THE SOFT SIDE!
I GO WITH MY GUT.
TAKKATA
TAKKATA

Itaru Kinoshita

Kinoshita made his manga debut with
Gigant wo Ute for Kodansha.

His favorite dinosaur is *Giganotosaurus*.

Supervisor:
Shin-ichi Fujiwara

Fujiwara is a lecturer at the
Nagoya University Museum.

He has a doctorate from
the University of Tokyo.

His fields of specialization
are functional morphology and
vertebrate paleontology, and his
favorite dinosaur is *Psittacosaurus*.

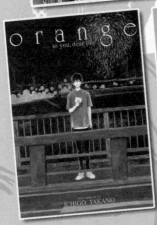

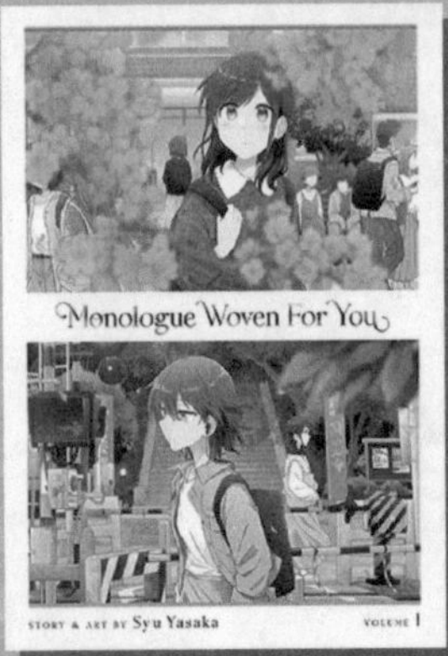
Monologue Woven For You
STORY & ART BY Syu Yasaka
VOLUME 1

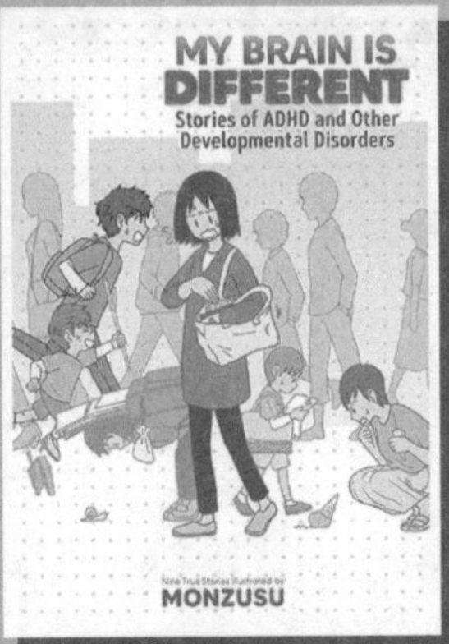
MY BRAIN IS
DIFFERENT
Stories of ADHD and Other Developmental Disorders
MONZUSU

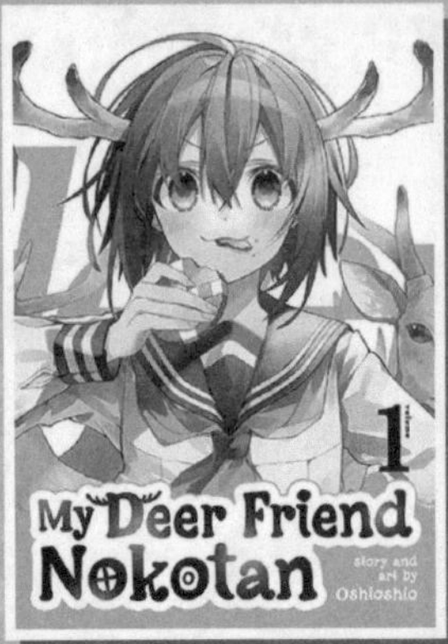
1
My Deer Friend
Nokotan
story and art by
Oshioshio

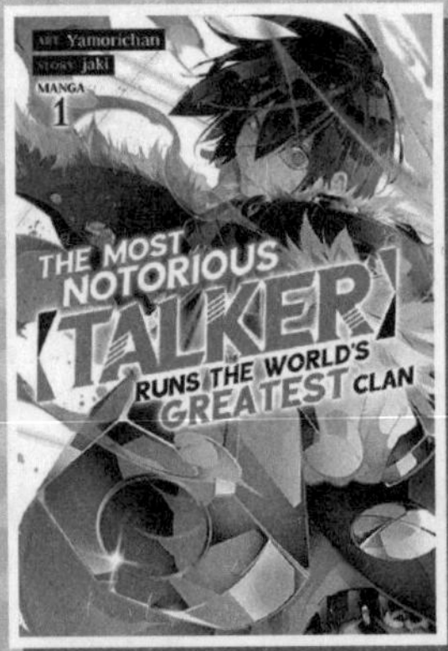
ART: Yamorichan
STORY: jaki
MANGA
1
THE MOST NOTORIOUS
TALKER
RUNS THE WORLD'S GREATEST CLAN

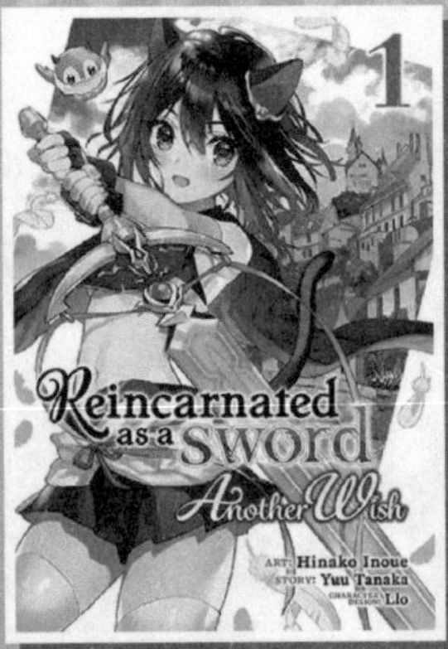
1
Reincarnated as a Sword
Another Wish
ART: Hinako Inoue
STORY: Yuu Tanaka
CHARACTER DESIGN: Llo

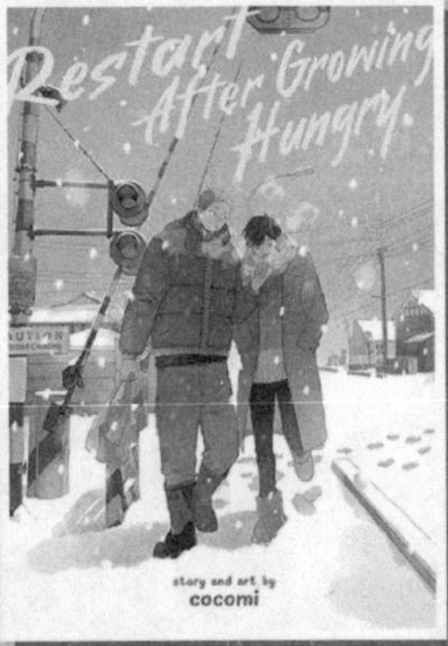
Restart After Growing Hungry
story and art by
cocomi

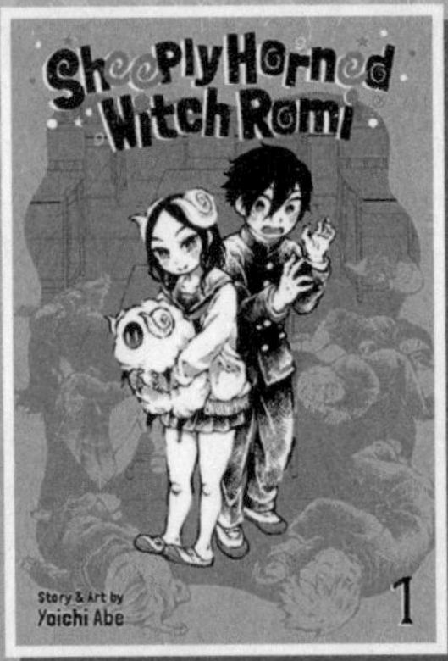
Sheeply Horned
Witch Romi
Story & Art by
Yaichi Abe
1

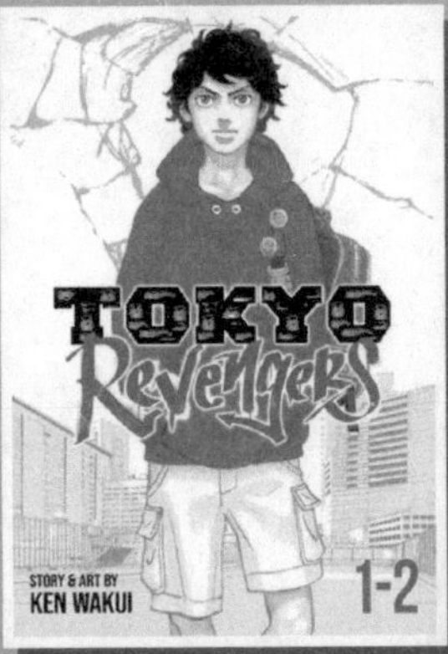
TOKYO
Revengers
STORY & ART BY
KEN WAKUI
1-2

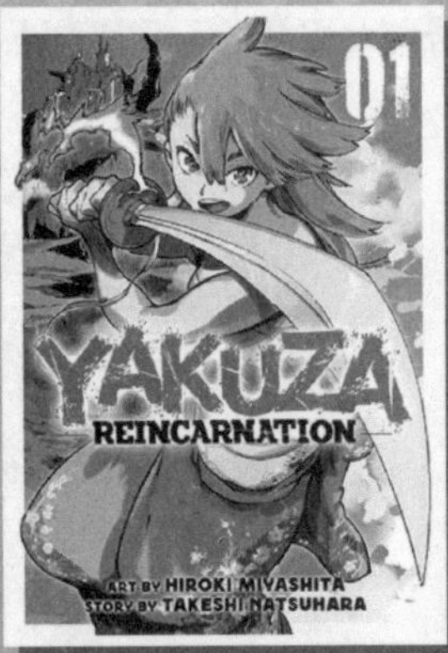
01
YAKUZA
REINCARNATION
ART BY HIROKI MIYASHITA
STORY BY TAKESHI NATSUHARA

SEVEN SEAS ENTERTAINMENT PRESENTS

DINOSAUR SANCTUARY

story and art: **ITARU KINOSHITA**   research consultant: **SHIN-ICHI FUJIWARA**   **VOLUME 3**

TRANSLATION
John Neal

LETTERING
JM Iitomi Crandall

COVER DESIGN
Hannah Carey

PROOFREADER
Danielle King

COPY EDITOR
Leighanna DeRouen

EDITOR
Linda Lombardi

PRODUCTION DESIGNER
Christina McKenzie

PRODUCTION MANAGER
John Ramirez

PREPRESS TECHNICIAN
Melanie Ujimori
Jules Valera

MANAGING EDITOR
J.P. Sullivan

EDITOR-IN-CHIEF
Julie Davis

ASSOCIATE PUBLISHER
Adam Arnold

PUBLISHER
Jason DeAngelis

ISBN: 979-8-88843-006-4
Printed in Canada
First Printing: September 2023
10 9 8 7 6 5 4 3 2 1

READING DIRECTIONS

This book reads from *right to left*,
Japanese style. If this is your first time
reading manga, you start reading from
the top right panel on each page and
take it from there. If you get lost, just
follow the numbered diagram here.
It may seem backwards at first,
but you'll get the hang of it! Have fun!!

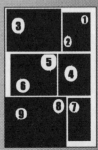

Follow us online: www.SevenSeasEntertainment.com